MILITARY POWER
LAND WARFARE IN THEORY AND PRACTICE

Edited by
Brian Holden Reid

FRANK CASS
LONDON • PORTLAND, OR

First published 1997 in Great Britain by
FRANK CASS & COMPANY LTD
Newbury House, 900 Eastern Avenue
London IG2 7HH

and in the United States of America by
FRANK CASS
c/o ISBS
5804 N.E. Hassalo Street, Portland, Oregon 97213-3644

Copyright © 1997 Frank Cass & Co. Ltd.

British Library Cataloguing in Publication Data

Military power : land warfare in theory and practice
1. Military art and science – United States 2. Military art and science – Great Britain
I. Reid, Brian Holden II. The journal of strategic studies
355

ISBN 0 7146 4768 3 (cloth)
ISBN 0 7146 4325 4 (paper)

Library of Congress Cataloging-in-Publication Data

Military power : land warfare in theory and practice / edited by Brian Holden Reid.
p. cm.
Includes bibliographical references (p.   ) and index
ISBN 0-7146-4768-3.– ISBN 0-7146-4325-4
1. Military history, Modern--20th century. 2. War.   I. Reid, Brian Holden.
D431.M55   1997
355.02--dc21   96-54594
                                                                                 CIP

This group of studies first appeared in a Special Issue on
'Military Power: Land Warfare in Theory and Practice' in *The Journal of Strategic Studies*,
Vol.19, No.4 (Dec. 1996)
published by Frank Cass & Co. Ltd.

All rights reserved. No part of this publication may be reproduced, stored in a retrieval system or transmitted in any form, or by any means, electronic, mechanical, photocopying, recording, or otherwise, without the prior permission of Frank Cass and Company Limited.

Printed by
Antony Rowe Ltd., Chippenham, Wilts.

Contents

List of Maps

Introduction   **Brian Holden Reid**   1

'Zealous for Annexation': Volunteer Soldiering, Military Government, and the Service of Colonel Alexander Doniphan in the Mexican–American War   **Joseph G. Dawson III**   10

The Spanish–American War: Land Battles in Cuba, 1895–1898   **Joseph Smith**   37

General Allenby and the Palestine Campaign, 1917–1918   **Matthew Hughes**   59

The British Expeditionary Force and the Difficult Transition to Peace, 1918–1919   **Ian M. Brown**   89

'Small Wars' and 'Imperial Policing': The British Army and the Theory and Practice of Colonial Warfare in the British Empire, 1919–1939   **T.R. Moreman**   105

Montgomery, Morale, Casualty Conservation and 'Colossal Cracks': 21st Army Group's Operational Technique in North West Europe, 1944–1945   **Stephen Hart**   132

'Tommy is No Soldier': The Morale of the Second British Army in Normandy, June–August 1944   **David French**   154

The British Army and Approaches to Warfare Since 1945   **John Kiszely**   179

Manoeuvre Theory in Operations Other than War   **J. J. A. Wallace**   207

The Buffalo Thorn: The Nature of the Future Battlefield   **Alistair Irwin**   227

About the Contributors   252

Index   255

Maps

1.	The US–Mexican War 1846–1848	14
2.	The Spanish–American War: Spanish Dispositions 20 June 1898	43
3.	Santiago Campaign: Initial Operations 22–24 June 1898	44
4.	Santiago Campaign: Situation About Noon 1 July 1898	48
5.	The Levant Theatre of War 1917–1918	61
6.	Gaza–Beersheba Front October 1917	65
7.	The Transjordan 'Raids' 1918	74

Introduction

BRIAN HOLDEN REID

Writing with uncharacteristic caution in 1925 on the impact of airpower on future warfare, Brigadier General William (Billy) Mitchell observed of future land warfare that 'the mission of land power and the army remain very much the same'.[1] Mitchell's conclusion was one of his more accurate, if less audacious, predictions. Military power remains the central, indispensable, means by which wars are won and the enemy's armed forces are overthrown. The study of land warfare has undergone an amazing renaissance over the last 30 years. For at least a quarter of a century after the end of the Second World War, it was taken as a truism that any future war, certainly any great war which might have broken out between the two competing alliances in central Europe, NATO and the Warsaw Pact, would within a matter of days or weeks have 'gone nuclear'. The nuclear balance transfixed politicians, military men and academic commentators alike. This kind of obsessive attention received a fillip in the 1980s due to the final round of rearmament in the last stage of the Cold War. Any book on defence matters invariably focused on the relative nuclear balance and the implications of new nuclear technologies or President Ronald Reagan's Strategic Defense Initiative, launched in 1983. In defence circles after the collapse of the Soviet Union in 1991, these issues, which were once discussed at great length, are now almost entirely forgotten.

Perhaps the most important result of these great changes has been a renewed confidence in the utility of military power, which had been written off during the nuclear age as impotent or even out-moded. Some writers still argue that this state of affairs has not changed and that highly advanced, conventional, technologically sophisticated armies (whose structure has not changed greatly since the Second World War) are now obsolescent; or at best do not give value for money in terms of military utility when set against the great cost which they incur.[2] Such commentators argue that the traditional large-scale set-piece confrontation between conventional armies is no longer cost-effective when increasingly wars are assuming an irregular character in which more nimble guerrilla forces can out-think and out-manoeuvre and often display greater resilience than regular armies. This issue is not neglected in the essays that follow, but such a view is essentially a minority position. The Gulf War of 1991 indicated that planners cannot neglect the possibility that a large-scale conventional war can suddenly erupt onto the world scene. Consequently, the renewed faith in the utility of military power has lead to a regeneration of tactical military thinking based on the texts of such writers as Baron Jomini, Carl von Clausewitz, J. F. C. Fuller and Sir Basil Liddell Hart. Such a revival has less to do with the specific predictions or military recommendations made by such writers (which may well be obsolescent or redundant) than with understanding and extending the conceptual basis on which these thinkers erected their ideas.

The most fruitful area for renewed thinking has been in developing the concept of the operational level of war. This is the area of military activity which lies between tactics and grand strategy and seeks to relate the tactical means to the strategic ends. Increased emphasis on this dimension of conflict – the stepping stones to victory – has led to a reappraisal of such themes as firepower, mobility, protection, logistics, command, and intelligence, and also military relationships with the media. Clearly, such a reappraisal is deeply rooted in a sophisticated knowledge of the military past, and one of the most interesting aspects of this increase in interest in the utility of military power has been a corresponding revival in the study of military history, especially in the United States and British Armies. There was, in short, a recognition that the gap between the military present and the military past was far less yawning that it was once supposed to be. Obviously, the scholarly study of military history was continued by historians regardless of the preoccupations of contemporary strategists and commentators; but there is no doubt that the study of military history has been given a great boost by the interest now evinced within the armed forces.[3]

Perhaps the most exciting aspect of this renaissance has been the increased contribution made by serving soldiers in writing about warfare on land. The great strength of this collection of studies is the combination of writing on military subjects, both by academics, and by serving officers who have experience of developing, teaching and implementing the subjects on which they write. Quite frequently an uncomprehending gap has developed between the academics writing within universities and serving officers studying within their staff colleges. Clearly, soldiers have their own jargon

INTRODUCTION 3

like other professions. But it is one of the great strengths of this book that academics and practitioners have been brought together, drawing from similar sources and working to the highest scholarly standards, but bringing their own perspectives to bear on complex military subjects.

In this collection the contributors consider the multifarious aspects of the Anglo-American approach to war. The structure, experience and social heritage of the British and United States Armies are fundamentally similar. Both developed as small, long-service forces which placed a premium on volunteer regulars and only resorted to conscription in times of national emergency. Both were essentially frontier constabularies, and failed to enjoy the same social prestige which benefited the French, German, and Russian armies. Indeed both had to contend with the glamour of an overwhelmingly Anglo-American naval tradition and were placed bottom of the list of budgetary priorities.[4]

Professor Dawson's account of Colonel Alexander W. Doniphan's service in the Mexican War (1846–48) explores the tradition of volunteer soldiering in the United States in the mid-nineteenth century. The contribution of volunteer officers to the 'small wars' of the United States was important. They were not just incompetent nuisances who hamstrung the war effort. Dawson shows that Doniphan's legal skills and experience were extremely important in drawing up the so-called Kearny Code which was the first formulation of American military government in an occupied territory in the nineteenth century. This document certainly provoked controversy. But it would not have been so useful to the American forces in Mexico if Doniphan had not drawn it up. The name of his senior commander, Brigadier General Stephen W. Kearny, was attached to the legal code, but Doniphan was the main author. The Kearny Code formed the basis of New Mexico's territorial laws throughout the rest of the nineteenth century until statehood was assumed in 1912. But Dawson also shows that volunteer officers could be effective leaders and commanders in battle even under hazardous circumstances. Basing his analysis on the work of his distinguished mentor, T. Harry Williams, Professor Dawson analyses Doniphan's military career with special reference to the Battle of Sacramento (28 February 1847). But the overall thrust of Dawson's contribution is to underline how in 'small wars' political and legal ramifications are just as important to commanders as strict military considerations. This is a recurring theme in such conflicts.

Between the Mexican War and the Spanish–American War of 1898, the second American small war under consideration here, the United States engaged itself in a massive Civil War, which is often dubbed by commentators 'the first modern war'. The many bloody and indecisive battles of the Civil War were a traumatic experience for the armies that engaged in them. But despite this experience, and the impact of new weapons technology on the battlefield, the Civil War left little mark on United States Army organisation. The US Army did not produce its first real tactical manuals until the Leavenworth series were published in 1891. Throughout the post-1865 period, the United States Army remained very small. A mere 28,562 officers and men were in 1883 scattered across 115 posts; its 'forts' in the West were essentially frontier villages. Secure from invasion by an enemy of the very first rank, large scale manoeuvres by the US Army were not only costly, but thus deemed by politicians to be unnecessary. Therefore senior officers remained untrained in the higher techniques of command and the US Army's fundamental principles were not developed or subject to even cursory scrutiny. The US Army also lacked a general staff free from the parochial concerns of individual units. There are some very clear parallels here with the British Army.[5] Thus when the United States undertook another 'small war' – against Spain in 1898 – and invaded Cuba, American commanders had to cope with a considerable degree of expansion to their tiny forces. Joseph Smith's essay on the land battles in Cuba during the Spanish–American War attempts a cautious defence of the overall American commander, General William A. Shafter, who is not one of the most highly regarded commanders in American military history. Dr Smith also emphasises how the campaign in Cuba should be set within a broader context of a bloody colonial war that had been waged by the Spanish against the Cubans since 1895. The United States made an effective intervention three years later which brought this conflict to an end. Dr Smith is not uncritical of Shafter's generalship and emphasises his inexperience in conducting military manoeuvres at the higher level throughout the campaign. Such inexperience was symptomatic of the lack of preparedness of the US Army at the end of the nineteenth century for extended operations of war. Commanders had to stretch their minds mentally to cope with an increased scale of conflict as well as to adjust to increased numbers of troops deployed in the field.

In the British experience, the most striking example of such a process is during the First World War. But the First World War, especially on the Western Front, has come to symbolise to the British the futility and horror of war in a way that the Second World War has never done. We can hardly escape the all-pervading gloom and doom that surrounds so much writing about 1914–18. The composition of much historical writing has been influenced by powerful literary and artistic images which expressed revulsion at the folly of war. The Western Front with its barbed wire, trenches, mud, artillery and machine-guns has thus come to assume a symbolic significance which transcends the humdrum conclusions of historians. General Sir Edmund Allenby's campaign in Palestine has often

INTRODUCTION

been held up as an exception to the attritional grind in France and Flanders. Unlike the Western Front which was gripped by a trench deadlock, cavalry was used extensively in Palestine. Matthew Hughes in his essay has sought critically to analyse the assumptions made about the differences between the Palestine campaign and operations on the Western Front. He examines three battles fought by Allenby: the Third Battle of Gaza, October–December 1917; the Trans–Jordan 'Raids', March–May 1918; and the Battle of Megiddo, September–October 1918. He argues that the effectiveness of cavalry in Palestine needs to be understood in relation to the use of the other arms, notably the infantry and artillery. He also explores the role of the commander in the Palestine Campaign. The impact of Allenby as a forceful individual on the course of operations is underlined. Dr Hughes also shows that Allenby was an effective leader as well as an impressive commander.

The other contribution on the British experience of the First World War reverses the usual stereotype. Dr Brown's analysis details the administrative excellence of Field-Marshal Sir Douglas Haig's five armies deployed in France rather than any supposed incompetence. He argues that this strength in administration and logistics formed the basis of the increased flexibility of these armies and their ability to launch the operational thrusts which brought the Germans to the brink of utter defeat by the late autumn of 1918. Dr Brown points out, however, that by June 1919 these administrative structures had been allowed to wither so quickly, that if the Germans had failed to accept the Treaty of Versailles and hostilities resumed, the British Army would have lacked the logistic capability to support the offensive operations necessary to enforce its provisions.

The British Army soon reverted to the 'real soldiering' of small wars and imperial policing between 1919 and 1939. T. R. Moreman examines the theory and practice of colonial warfare in the British Empire in the inter-war years. While the origins of British counter-insurgency have recently been covered in some detail by British and American historians, a considerable amount of work still remains to be done on the approach taken by both the British and Indian armies in carrying out their duties as an imperial police force. Dr Moreman's contribution deals with how both imperial armies addressed the conflicting requirements of operations carried out in deserts, mountains, jungles, and open plains, primarily in terms of doctrine. He also touches on how such operations affected military organisation and equipment. Underlying Dr Moreman's analysis is the view that British military history has become rather too Eurocentric, and has, comparatively speaking, ignored the insistent military demands of Empire which form the dominant experience of the majority of officers. Clearly, this experience influenced heavily the organisation and equipment of the British Army at home and in India. He brings out the true extent of the influence of Major-

Generals Charles Callwell and Charles Gwynn, and General Sir Andrew Skeen. These are theorists whose writing has been perhaps unjustly neglected by historians who concentrate on the more famous theorists, such as Fuller and Liddell Hart, whose primary interests lay in armoured, continental-style warfare.

Two essays analyse the Normandy Campaign of 1944 from different perspectives. The British Army's contribution to Operation 'Overlord' was in many ways the turning point in its evolution in the middle of the twentieth century. Adapting a viable structure and doctrine for continental warfare from the small wars experience of 1919–39 was a protracted and complicated process. By 1944 Montgomery had developed such a style focusing around 'colossal cracks'. This relied upon overwhelming firepower and set-piece advances as a means of preserving morale. Montgomery also sought to reconcile the need to defeat the German Army in the field with keeping casualties down. Dr Hart analyses in some detail Montgomery's motivation for choosing this style of warfare. Montgomery's style, based on a continental model, dominated the British Army's outlook until at least the early 1980s. It was based on a 'master plan' which examined every feasible aspect of the operation about to be undertaken and relied heavily on a highly structured form of warfare involving detailed orders and deliberate preparation. Throughout Dr Hart is concerned with presenting the historical context in which Montgomery developed his technique.

As a gloomy assumption about the fragile morale of the British Army in the last two years of the Second World War is central to Montgomery's style of warfare, David French explores this complicated issue with reference to the morale of the Second British Army in the summer of 1944. He stresses the complexity of dealing with the subject of 'morale' and he argues that much of the evidence on which previous generalisations have rested is frequently misleading. He contends that the pessimistic picture which has sometimes been painted about the state of Second Army's fragile morale requires modification. He stresses that there is no single measurement for morale. Morale was a dynamic, constantly changing factor, which evolved, rose and fell over very short periods of time. Indeed Professor French infers occasionally that the psychiatrists attached to Second Army were themselves part of the problem because of the crudity of the concepts with which they were working, certainly by comparison with psychiatry in the late twentieth century. They were prone to assume that they had access to the oracle but Professor French shows that this was far from being the case.

Although the performance of the British Army in the Second World War has been analysed exhaustively it is surprising how little work has been completed on the post-war British Army, as opposed to study of the Royal

INTRODUCTION

Air Force or the Royal Navy, or the general issues raised by post-war British defence policy. Whereas the Navy and the Royal Air Force have received more attention, doubtless stimulated by the nuclear deterrents deployed by both services since the 1950s, the Army has been completely neglected.[6] Major-General John Kiszely attempts to redress some of this neglect in his essay on the British approaches to warfare since 1945. His essay is not primarily historical in its thrust but he does have much of interest to say for historians on the reasons why the British Army chose its particular approach to battle. He emphasises the immense post-war influence of Field-Marshal Montgomery and his imitators. He underlines how the attritional approach to warfare was not seriously challenged in Britain for many years. Some discussion of the overlapping issues occurred in the *Journal of the Royal United Services Institute*. Yet this discussion was limited to a small group of commentators. And much of the debate focused around, not so much the validity of the attrition concept itself, as on historical reassessments of the two World Wars. Another central issue was the validity of the claims made by Sir Basil Liddell Hart for the universal application of his strategy of the indirect approach. On many occasions this seemed to be the prime object of the discussion rather than reaching an informed consensus on the comparative merits of the concepts advanced in the debate. Not the least of the interesting arguments made by General Kiszely is that these claims and counter-claims made either for or against Liddell Hart often tended to take arguments to an extreme, and implied that either attrition or manoeuvre on their own could win a war. Liddell Hart certainly implied that the indirect approach to strategy had completely undercut any requirements for attrition in war.

General Kiszely examines the reasons behind the evolution of a less attritional war-fighting style in the British Army, stressing the importance of related thinking in the US Army after the Vietnam imbroglio and the resultant evolution of a putative concept of manoeuvre warfare. He gives full attention to the importance of the emerging understanding of the concept of the operational level of war in this process. He surveys the writing of Edward N. Luttwak, Richard Simpkin, William Lind and the younger generation of authors, Richard D. Hooker Jr and Robert Leonhard. He also stresses the crucial role in the British Army of Field-Marshal Sir Nigel Bagnall during the 1980s in developing the concepts of the operational level of war and manoeuvre warfare, and creating structures that could implement a form of war which, unlike Montgomery's style, stresses the initiative enjoyed by subordinates and eschews detailed orders.

Colonel Wallace, in his stimulating essay on manoeuvre theory and operations other than war, combines the approaches taken by General Kiszely and the earlier essays on small wars by attempting to show how the concept of manoeuvre warfare can be applied to the small wars of the 1990s. He stresses how in many low intensity operations a sense of urgency in the execution was either overlooked in the plan or lost in the execution of it. The undertow of Colonel Wallace's essay is that the theory of manoeuvre warfare is just as applicable to levels of conflict less ambitious than armoured, continental-style wars. Earlier work on manoeuvre warfare was based on a NATO–Warsaw Pact confrontation in Central Europe that would soon develop into the 'Third World War'. His essay therefore binds together and draws out common themes from the initial essays on small wars with those which deal with the experience of continental warfare. He stresses that it is the unique politico-military nature of low intensity conflict that demands a warfighting doctrine based on manoeuvre theory. It follows, therefore, that the important political component which emerged in the nineteenth-century conduct of small wars is no less relevant as we move towards the dawn of the second millennium.

The final essay in this volume is Brigadier Irwin's challenging discussion of the battlefield of the twenty-first century. His main theme is the enduring nature of the principles of war, the prominence of manoeuvre warfare, and the relevance of the strategy of the indirect approach as interpreted with the requirements of twenty-first century technology in mind. He explores the nature of the future battlefield, touching upon the influence of new weapons, especially on the armoured battlefield; but he does not ignore peace-support operations, the role of the terrorist, and the growing influence of the 'invisible' battlefield (especially biological, chemical and electronic warfare). He explores the factors affecting the future conduct of war, including demography, technology, ecology, the news media, public opinion, and financial constraints. With this as his background, he explores how future operations are likely to be conducted and the doctrinal demands that will be made on preparations for such operations. He also examines the likely structures of armies in the future. He argues that formations will become smaller, and command and control systems will be highly dependent upon information technology (IT). Brigadier Irwin's entire analysis is based upon an assumption of the fundamental continuity of military thought and practice.

Reviewing the ten studies which form this book, I am reminded of a passage in Leo Tolstoy's novel *War and Peace* in which he observes how, 'the first proceeding of the historian is taking an arbitrary series of continuous events to examine it apart from others, while in reality there is not, and cannot be, a beginning to any event, but one event flows without any break in continuity from another'.[7] Taken together these essays illustrate the fundamental axiom of Baron Jomini that the principles of war – its essential structure and conduct – remain constant, even though the

INTRODUCTION 9

means of seeking victory, namely weapons technology, continually changes. In war everything changes, yet nothing changes. The scholarly studies of the ten authors represented here present a vehicle – a model – whereby our understanding of land warfare can be further enhanced. They also testify to the central importance of an understanding of the historical context in which decisions are taken, often under the most arduous circumstances. History might not offer clear-cut 'lessons' to decision makers, but experience shows how unwise it is to base opinions on operations and strategy if you misunderstand their historical setting.

NOTES

1. William Mitchell, *Winged Defense* (NY: Putnam's 1925) p.215.
2. See Evan Luard, *The Blunted Sword: The Erosion of Military Power in Modern World Politics* (London: I.B. Tauris 1988), and Martin van Creveld, *The Transformation of War* (NY: Free Press 1991).
3. Brian Holden Reid, 'Introduction', in idem, *The Science of War* (London: Routledge 1993) pp.1–11.
4. See Brian Holden Reid, 'Tensions in the Supreme Command: Anti-Americanism in the British Army, 1939–1945', in idem and John White (eds.) *American Studies: Essays in Honour of Marcus Cunliffe* (London: Macmillan 1991) pp.272–3, and idem, 'United States', in André Corvisier and John Childs (eds.) *A Dictionary of Military History* (Oxford: Blackwell 1994) pp.829–35.
5. Perry D. Jamieson, *Crossing the Deadly Ground: United States Army Tactics, 1865–1899* (Tuscaloosa and London: U. of Alabama Press 1994).
6. See, for example, Eric Grove, *From Vanguard to Trident* (London: Bodley Head 1987), and Humphrey Wynn, *The RAF Strategic Nuclear Forces: Their Origins, Role and Deployment 1946–1969* (London: HMSO 1994).
7. Leo Tolstoy, *War and Peace* [1869] (Harmondsworth: Penguin 1972) p.888.

'Zealous for Annexation': Volunteer Soldiering, Military Government, and the Service of Colonel Alexander Doniphan in the Mexican–American War

JOSEPH G. DAWSON III

During the 1840s, Alexander William Doniphan (1808–87) and thousands of other US citizens believed that their nation would expand by acquiring more land between the Mississippi River and the Pacific Ocean. In the mid-nineteenth century, critics of US territorial expansion branded men such as Doniphan 'annexationists'.[1] Doniphan's military actions during the Mexican-American War represent a significant personal expression of American expansionism, delineated so strongly in the popular term 'Manifest Destiny'.[2] Moreover, as a volunteer army officer, Doniphan fulfilled in a spectacular way another popular American expectation: that the nation would rely mostly on citizen-soldiers in wartime.[3] Remarkably, his service also included actions that contributed to US strategic goals in the war and provided the initial instance of American military government in captured enemy territory.

Doniphan endorsed the expansionist outlook that was in vogue across America in the 1840s, except that he was a maverick member of the Whig Party. By favoring war with Mexico and annexing Mexican lands, Doniphan stood apart from several prominent members of his party, among them Abraham Lincoln, Henry Clay, and Alexander H. Stephens. As early as September 1845 Doniphan was one of many Americans writing to Secretary of War William L. Marcy and offering to raise a regiment when war broke out. In his letter Doniphan emphasized that 'the American people ... have been warm friends of Texas and zealous for her annexation [into the US]'. He assured Secretary Marcy that Missourians were well prepared to 'be efficient soldiers in repelling the predatory and guerrilla excursions by which Mexico will doubtless harass the frontier of the State of Texas'.[4]

Aged 38 in 1846, Doniphan was an imposing figure, standing six feet four inches tall and weighing more than 200 pounds. His high, broad forehead gave him what many in the nineteenth century assumed was evidence of intellectuality. An exceptional ability as a public speaker in courtrooms and political campaigns made him a recognized orator. An adopted Missourian, Doniphan was a native of Kentucky and graduate of Augusta College, a frontier academy in Augusta, Kentucky. He had moved to Missouri in 1830, passed into the bar, and established a successful law practice in Liberty, near Kansas City. In 1836 he was elected to the Missouri legislature. By then he had built his reputation in several court cases as an energetic advocate on behalf of the Mormons. To gain military experience, Doniphan held a political appointment as brigadier general in the Missouri state militia. In the so-called Mormon War of 1838 he rejected orders from the major general of militia to attack a group of Mormons, thus averting bloodshed between members of the controversial sect and other Missourians. Neither his legal defense of the Mormons nor his actions during the Mormon War dimmed his popularity in the state; he was re-elected to the legislature in 1840.[5]

In the spring of 1846 Doniphan and many other Americans responded to the calls of President James K. Polk and state governors to raise state volunteer regiments after the start of the Mexican–American War. In contrast to 1845, Doniphan not only recommended guarding the frontier of Texas. Taking a more strategic view, he also urged Secretary of War Marcy to send 'a [military] force to the provinces of New Mexico & Chihuahua'. Such an expedition would 'afford ample protection to our own [commercial] traders now in that country…', as well as seize the opportunity for the United States to conquer and annex lands in the region. On 10 June, Doniphan officially mustered in as a private for a one year enlistment and, drawing upon his reputation as an experienced lawyer and state legislator, promptly put himself forward for election as colonel of the new outfit, styled the 1st Regiment of Missouri Mounted Volunteers. On 18 June the soldiers elected Doniphan colonel by a wide margin over John Price, a veteran of the Seminole War.[6]

Recruitment and Training for Kearny's Expedition

Enlisting from several western Missouri counties, and including attached mounted and artillery units from St Louis, the 1st Missouri Regiment numbered around 1,200 men. It assembled for rudimentary training at Fort Leavenworth, Kansas. Regular army officers of the 1st Dragoons, commanded by Colonel Stephen Watts Kearny, conducted the tactical drills. Some volunteers also had army experience. As Doniphan recalled: 'like most other volunteer commands we had some officers who had graduated [from West Point], and some who had been [t]here for several years [as cadets]. To the training received from these sources I attribute much of the efficiency of the column.' Among others, Doniphan alluded to two of his key officers. Charles Ruff, lieutenant colonel of 1st Missouri, had graduated from the Military Academy in 1838 and served with the dragoons from 1838 to 1842. Another volunteer, Major William Gilpin, enrolled as a cadet at West Point from 1834 to 1835, and then served as a lieutenant in the dragoons from 1836 to 1838.[7]

The period of training lasted about three weeks for Doniphan's volunteers but it is doubtful how much army routine they learned. One enlistee recalled a demanding schedule of mounted tactical drills twice a day, probably accompanied by admonitions from the regulars about the prospects for combat against the Mexicans. Lieutenant Richard Elliott, an officer serving with the Leclede Rangers, a St Louis volunteer cavalry outfit, claimed that his men promptly learned the 'School of the Trooper', as taught by a dragoon officer, but implied that Doniphan's soldiers lagged behind the Rangers in proficiency. Under such circumstances, three weeks is a short time to turn civilians into soldiers.[8]

Having only a few days to train his unit before beginning a campaign would be a serious drawback for any commander, but Doniphan was twice fortunate. A rigorous overland march from Fort Leavenworth to Santa Fe provided a sort of field training prelude before encountering the enemy; and Colonel Kearny, soon promoted to brigadier general, commanded the expedition. Doniphan found that serving under Kearny, one of the best senior officers in the US Army, was a form of education in itself. In public, Kearny set a high standard of soldierly qualities and provided practical advice to Doniphan, but always delivered it with courtesy.[9] In private, the two probably discussed the war in general, prospects for the campaign, and unit organization. For his part, Kearny was favorably impressed with Doniphan. Their relationship was an exceptional example of good co-operation in a war replete with many instances of friction, hostility, and distrust between regulars and volunteers.[10]

Secretary Marcy and President Polk selected Kearny to command the 'Army of the West' and gave it ambitious multiple objectives. His civilian superiors wanted Kearny 'to take earliest possession of Upper California' as well as to gain control of Santa Fe, the region's most important commercial trading center. Marcy anticipated that 'what relates to the civil government will be a difficult and unpleasant part of your duty', but that once Santa Fe fell to US forces, Kearny would decide how 'to provide for retaining safe possession' of all of New Mexico. Marcy also discussed several other topics, including routes to California and relations with Indian tribes. Finally, the Secretary of War directed: 'Should you conquer and take possession of New Mexico and Upper California, ... you will establish temporary civil governments therein ... and *continue in their employment all such of the existing [civil] officials as are known to be friendly to the United States, and will take the oath of allegiance to them* [emphasis added]'. Marcy concluded: 'it is the wish and design of the United States to provide for them [the people of New Mexico and California] a free government ... similar to that which exists in our [US] territories. They will then be called on to exercise the rights of freemen in electing their own representatives to the *territorial legislature* [emphasis added].' Kearny reasonably interpreted his orders to mean that the campaign would be the first step toward bringing these territories – California and New Mexico – under the permanent control of the United States. In addition to Doniphan's regiment, Kearny would lead 300 regulars from the US 1st Dragoons, associated units, such as the Leclede Rangers, and a sizable number of civilian supply wagons. Kearny's expedition totaled about 1,600 soldiers, not equal to two full-strength regiments, and stretching the term to call it an 'Army'.[11]

The 850-mile journey on the Santa Fe Trail took six grueling weeks. Horses and mules collapsed, water and food were scarce, and Kearny had to order the men to subsist on half rations. After stopping to take on supplies at Bent's Fort, the Americans expected that enemy soldiers might offer battle as they approached Santa Fe, but those expectations were not realized. New Mexico's governor failed either to recruit soldiers or establish defensive positions. The march assumed heroic stature in the memories of veterans, but it turned out to be more high adventure than desperate military gamble. William Waldo, a soldier in 1st Missouri, wrote home with an understated conclusion after arriving in Santa Fe: 'We encountered the usual hardships in crossing the plains, ... but upon the whole it was a fair trip.' On 18 August 1846, only three months after the declaration of war, Kearny and Doniphan led their troops into the capital of New Mexico without firing a shot.[12]

Marching in a campaign to capture Santa Fe, Doniphan contributed to US strategic goals in the war – military conquest of Mexican land to be annexed under the banner of 'Manifest Destiny'. Before that annexation could be official, and before Doniphan could resume his campaign deeper into Mexico, other steps were needed. Doniphan's military service soon included legal tasks associated with military government, unexpected duties for a volunteer officer that could be held up as examples to US military officers during a second age of American expansionism in the 1890s.[13]

Before the War with Mexico US Army officers had been drawn into civil affairs in several ways, usually involving the operation of territorial governments. Territorial constabulary experiences had included protecting

14 MILITARY POWER: LAND WARFARE IN THEORY AND PRACTICE

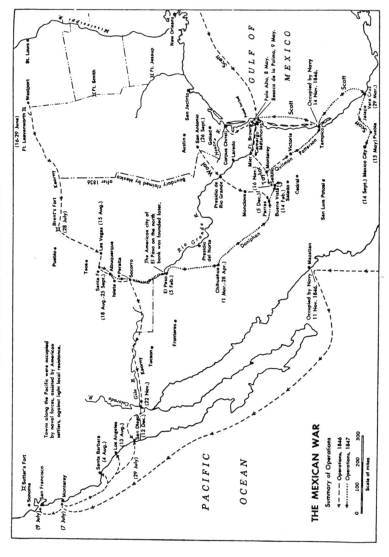

MAP 1
The US–Mexican War 1846–1848

governors, patrolling public lands, negotiating with Indian tribes, collecting customs duties, and arresting persons charged with crimes. In carrying out such duties, army officers assisted civil officials without superseding them. The few significant instances of martial law included Andrew Jackson's supervision of New Orleans in 1814–15 and his one-year post as military governor of Spanish Florida in 1821.[14]

In the 1840s Americans were going to have to distinguish between martial law and military government. A modern scholar, Theodore Grivas, explains that martial law is a *temporary* circumstance imposed after an enemy invasion or a natural disaster. The military can act in support of existing civil government, which, due to a crisis, cannot carry out its routine obligations. Under such conditions, the military expects that civil government will be restored in a few weeks, or perhaps a few months. Army or navy officers need to work closely with elected officials, assisting them in their duties, protecting them if civil police forces are inadequate, and appointing temporary officeholders until elections could be held. In contrast, military government is designed to override civil government and is usually used in temporarily-occupied enemy territory or conquered enemy lands that are expected to be annexed into the conquering nation. Grivas concludes: 'Martial law supports civil government; military government supplants it.' Prior to the War of 1846–48 the United States had no acquaintance with military government.[15]

During and after the Mexican–American War, the US Army operated its first military governments, and Doniphan's was the earliest of them. American military officers became administrators of occupied cities, such as Matamoros, Vera Cruz, and Mexico City, and military governors of captured territories, such as California and New Mexico. In some instances, regular officers assigned the duties of military government to a volunteer officer rather than to another regular. Two important examples are Major General Winfield Scott's choice of John A. Quitman, a volunteer general from Mississippi, to be 'military governor' of Mexico City, and Brigadier General Stephen Kearny's pick of Colonel Doniphan for the initial responsibilities in the military government of New Mexico.[16]

Military Government in New Mexico

Doniphan, of course, took his lead in civil affairs from the example set by Brigadier General Kearny. On 19 August 1846, basing his authority on his orders from Secretary of War Marcy, Kearny took the first steps toward US control of New Mexico. As Doniphan stood nearby, Kearny made a formal proclamation on the plaza in Santa Fe: 'You are no longer Mexican subjects; you are now become American citizens, subject only to the laws of the

United States. A change of government has taken place in New Mexico and you no longer owe allegiance to the Mexican government.' Kearny expressed his 'intention ... to continue in office those by whom you have been governed, except the governor, and such other persons as I shall appoint to office by virtue of the authority vested in me'. To curry favor with local leaders, Kearny designated a long-time New Mexico resident, an Anglo settler named Charles Bent, as acting civil governor.[17] Hoping to gain some support for the new regime, Kearny also designated several Mexicans as officeholders, notably Donaciano Vigil as secretary to the provisional governor, a position virtually equal to the post of lieutenant governor. To solidify American control, however, the American commander picked other Anglos to hold such basic positions as US attorney, territorial auditor, and territorial treasurer. Then Kearny turned his attention to the details of his march to California and on 31 August he shifted the burden for military supervision to Colonel Doniphan.[18]

Given Doniphan's legal and legislative experience, the Missourian was the natural choice for his new assignment. Doniphan faced three demanding tasks in Santa Fe. First, he, not civil Governor Charles Bent, would have the primary responsibility for writing a territorial constitution and a set of laws for the captured province. Second, Doniphan (again, not Governor Bent) had to negotiate a treaty with the Navajo Indians. The Mexicans had engaged in sporadic campaigns against the tribe, which was the strongest in the territory. Now it would be up to US authorities to stop Navajo raids, but tribal leaders already realised the weakness of American military forces in New Mexico, and Doniphan found it difficult to negotiate with them. Finally, alongside his responsibilities in military government, Doniphan's third duty was to prepare his regiment for its next campaign, south along the Rio Grande in an effort intended to capture and annex more Mexican lands.[19]

In only three weeks time Doniphan and a select coterie wrote interim laws for New Mexico Territory. Assisting the colonel were other members of his regiment, Private Willard P. Hall and Captain David Waldo. Originally from Virginia, Hall had graduated from Yale College, moved to Missouri in 1840, and made his mark as an attorney. Waldo, a graduate of Transylvania College in Kentucky, was a practising physician fluent in Spanish. Also contributing to the projects were the civil governor, Charles Bent, and Francis P. ('Frank') Blair, Jr. The prestigious Blair family included members active in politics in both Missouri and Maryland. Frank Blair had graduated from Princeton College and joined his brother Montgomery in a law practice for two years in St Louis before moving to New Mexico prior to the outbreak of the war.[20]

The colonel related that 'In addition to other duties, Willard P. Hall and myself are arranging the Government, &c, trying to get the machine in operation. It is a very arduous matter – the laws are all in Spanish, and everything is done through an interpreter, and there is much in the laws conflicting with our [US] Constitution to be altered.' Their labors yielded a 100-page booklet, printed in parallel columns of English and Spanish, containing a comprehensive treatment of government. Doniphan's booklet included a territorial constitution with a bill of rights, provisions for trial by jury and habeas corpus, and notification that all free adult men would be allowed to register to vote. Furthermore, the document promulgated dozens of laws and regulations as well as defining the responsibilities of civil officeholders. Doniphan and his associates said later that they depended upon the US Constitution, the state constitutions of Missouri and Louisiana, as well as the laws of Texas and Kentucky to write what came to be called the 'Kearny Code'.[21]

Preparing his regulars for the California expedition, Kearny gave the lengthy document cursory attention before signing it on 22 September 1846. Writing to the US Army's adjutant general in Washington, Kearny awarded appropriate credit to the code's primary authors: 'I take great pleasure in stating that I am *entirely indebted* for these laws to Col. A.W. Doniphan ... who received much assistance from private Willard P. Hall...'. Only three days later, Kearny and a few hundred regulars set out for California, leaving Doniphan in charge of supervising the American occupation of the territory.[22]

The 'Kearny Code' drawn up by Doniphan and his associates became the first major document of American military government in conquered territory, and naturally engendered some controversy. Kearny had made a wise decision to use citizen-soldiers experienced in legal practice to write such laws: their presence as military personnel carried weight to their lawmaking that drafts written primarily by civilians, even Anglo residents of New Mexico, would not have had. A more accurate label for the laws would have been the 'Kearny-Doniphan Code' or even the 'Doniphan-Hall Code'. As the senior officer, however, Kearny bore the responsibility and he got the credit for approving the document, which formed the foundation of New Mexico's territorial laws throughout the rest of the nineteenth century and on to statehood in 1912.[23]

In 1846 and throughout most of the rest of the nineteenth century Doniphan's accomplishments in military government went largely unappreciated. The US Army had not yet developed a sophisticated understanding of the need for planning the tasks of military government in occupied enemy territory. The Army had no reference book to guide its officers assigned to such duties. At the turn of the century, however, America's acquisition of Spain's former island colonies in the Spanish–

American War of 1898 produced the need to prepare better its officers for assignments in military government. Charles Magoon, a civilian attorney working on the staff of the US Bureau of Insular Affairs, complied *The Reports of the Law of Government in Territory Subject to Military Occupation by the Military Forces of the United States*, known by contemporaries as *Magoon's Reports*. In this 700-page book, Magoon pointed out that the new 'military governments under consideration [in Cuba, Puerto Rico, Philippines, and Guam] were established to deal with conditions resulting from successful invasion' of enemy territory during wartime – duplicating the need for special wartime governments in Santa Fe and California in 1846. Thus Magoon's treatise emphasized that the US Army had carried out similar duties more than 50 years before the War with Spain.[24]

Meanwhile, in the politically charged atmosphere of wartime Washington in the 1840s, some Whig members of Congress criticized Doniphan's lawmaking. Bending under some of this pressure, members of the Polk administration and the President himself announced that they had some qualifications about the comprehensive manner in which Kearny announced the takeover of New Mexico Territory. These political issues were settled when the United States officially acquired New Mexico and other lands by the terms of the peace Treaty of Guadalupe Hidalgo (1848).[25]

Treaty with the Navajo Indians and the Taos Revolt

Back in Santa Fe, keeping one eye on potentially rebellious Mexicans, Colonel Doniphan sent out officers carrying messages to the region's Indian leaders. Bands of Apaches, Utahs, and Zunis roamed the countryside, but it was the Navajos who were the dominant tribe, and General Kearny had ordered that they must sign a treaty with US authorities. John Hughes, who became the unofficial historian of the Doniphan expedition, contended that 'the Indians are much more troublesome than the New Mexicans'. The Navajos had attacked Mexican travellers and ranchos almost with impunity before the Americans arrived, and Doniphan made it clear that the tribe must end such attacks. Rather than concluding a treaty in a matter of days, as Doniphan and Kearny had hoped, negotiations dragged out for weeks. Eventually most of the Navajo chiefs signed a treaty on 22 November 1846, promising to end their depredations and acknowledging that the United States had replaced the Mexican administration.[26]

The weak US military presence in New Mexico permitted the Navajos to begin new raids in a matter of weeks after signing the treaty. Governor Charles Bent alertly reported to US Secretary of State James Buchanan that he had 'but little ground to hope that it [the Navajo treaty] will be permanent'. Bent urged Buchanan to arrange for more US soldiers to be sent to Santa Fe, judging that a single regiment was inadequate to the task of consolidating American control of the territory. Bent had struck the key to the United States' takeover of New Mexico. Despite its belligerence and successful offensive actions thus far in the war, the United States did not have the military power to allocate strong forces to accomplish all that President Polk wanted: garrison New Mexico, patrol the Navajo country, invade California, occupy northern Mexico, and embark an expedition down the Rio Grande and into Chihuahua. The US forces would be vulnerable at one or more places. The companies of Doniphan's regiment began leaving the Santa Fe area in late November. Only Colonel Sterling Price's 2nd Missouri Volunteer Regiment remained on occupation duty.[27]

In the Taos Revolt of 19 January 1847, Mexicans killed Governor Charles Bent and tried unsuccessfully to reassert Mexican control over New Mexico. The leaders of the rebellion raised 1,500 Mexicans to oppose the US occupation of their province. The Mexicans had several reasons, including opposition to the new laws of Doniphan's code, to strike back at American occupying forces. However displeased the Mexicans were with the new laws, the fact was that Kearny and Doniphan had left behind a fragile civil administration supported only by a modest contingent of soldiers. The inability of the United States to deploy more than Price's regiment in New Mexico was the key to precipitating the Taos Revolt.[28]

Putting aside matters of territorial constitutions and Indian negotiations, Doniphan turned his attention to the prospects of leading his regiment in combat. He had already contributed to the American war effort by helping to capture Santa Fe and laying claim to all of New Mexico. Now he had set out to take El Paso del Norte (modern Ciudad Juárez) and Chihuahua. Capturing these cities would help to fulfill the military designs of President Polk and Secretary of War Marcy, but also were among the strategic objectives Doniphan himself had specified at the start of the war.

Doniphan and Regimental Command

In order to assist the volunteers on their campaign, Kearny had assigned three regular army officers to accompany Doniphan's column. These were Captain Philip Thompson, Lieutenant Charles Wooster, and Lieutenant Bezaleel Armstrong. Evidently, Kearny did not precisely define the roles of these regular officers, but they offered guidance and technical expertise to the volunteers. How useful they would be depended on how diplomatically they presented their advice and how willing the volunteers were to take it. Captain Thompson, of 1st Dragoons, joined the Army of the West on 26 October 1846, so he had less than two months to work with Doniphan before a battle was fought. The colonel and the captain soon enjoyed friendly relations. On the other hand, Lieutenant Wooster, an artillery officer, was assigned to Doniphan's regiment on 25 September and their relationship is less clear, perhaps closer to correct than cordial. Lieutenant Armstrong, of 2nd Dragoons, appears to have played a minor part in the coming campaign.[29] Most sources, with the exception of Wooster, indicate that Doniphan exercised the responsibility for making decisions on the expedition: if the Americans won, Doniphan would get the credit; if they were defeated, he would get the blame. He was the colonel.

What made a good regimental commander? One of the best analyses is by T. Harry Williams, who studied a Civil War volunteer colonel, Rutherford B. Hayes. Williams contends that the colonel's personality and how seriously he took his job had much to do with shaping his regiment.[30] A good citizen colonel had to be both fair but also solicitous of his men. The best volunteer commanders knew when to be familiar with their soldiers and when to be formal. Doniphan was known personally or by reputation to most of his men at the time the regiment mustered in. His unpretentiousness heightened his popularity. One soldier remarked: 'his great charm lies in his easy and kind manner. On the march he could not be distinguished from the other soldiers, either by dress, or from his conversation.' Another elaborated: Doniphan was the kind of 'man who can familiarize himself with the poorest private, by some kind word, or ride among the troops, and make us forget that we were hungry or thirsty, by some pleasant converse, in our long and and toilsome march; [moreover, he was] the [kind of] man who can forget his own personal safety in the hour of danger...'.[31]

Williams also points out that successful Civil War colonels possessed certain traits often associated with good military leadership in any age: among these were courage; using language to inspire soldiers; competence to evaluate terrain and enemy forces; some degree of technical military proficiency; and finally, sound health or even above average stamina. Doniphan met all these stipulations except the last one. For a large, impressive looking man, Doniphan had only satisfactory health. He suffered from recurring bouts of bronchitis and eventually became worn down after many weeks on the march.[32]

Doniphan fought two battles as an independent regimental commander, one along the Rio Grande near El Paso in December 1846 and the other along the Sacramento River near Chihuahua City in February 1847. Doniphan's approach to the Rio Grande was one of several US invasions of Mexico. Doniphan's offensive followed Major General Zachary Taylor's invasion of northern Mexico in the summer, Brigadier General John E. Wool's operations around Monclova and Parras in the fall, and the incursions of US forces into California. Furthermore, a large US expeditionary force was being assembled to attack Vera Cruz in March

1847. The Americans were carrying out a cordon offensive, multiple attacks stretching Mexico's defenses and resources to the breaking point.

The Battle of Brazito

Doniphan's first battle occurred on 25 December 1846, near an 'arm' of the Rio Grande – hence the name Brazito.[33] Under Colonel Antonio Ponce de Leon, Mexican forces numbering between 1,100 and 1,300 took the initiative, approaching the 1st Missouri Regiment in an open area.[34] In order not to deplete water, wood and forage, Doniphan had dispersed his regiment in a long line of march. Mexican lookouts claimed that the Americans moved with a lack of security, 'Which permitted Ponce to reconnoiter them to his satisfaction and unobserved.' However, Missouri scouts rode ahead of the American column and one of Doniphan's soldiers recollected that the colonel and other officers had conducted a thorough inspection of the entire regiment on 24 December, in case they should encounter Mexican troops sent out to defend El Paso. Doniphan called a halt at around 2.00 pm. It was Christmas Day, the spot had good water, and it afforded a likely place to consolidate the regiment. While the soldiers searched for firewood and began enjoying the holiday afternoon, their commander sat down to a game of cards. He posted no sentinels.[35]

As the Mexican forces moved toward the Missourians' camp, they created a considerable dust cloud. A volunteer officer drew Doniphan's attention to the dust, and they decided that it must be the enemy. Jumping up, the colonel told his card-playing chums that they would have to resume the game later. Doniphan began shouting a series of orders to prepare for his first battle. Only about half of his regiment (around 500 men) was present, with none of its supporting artillery, and his camp was disorderly – indeed, it almost seemed chaotic. Although he could have tried to pull back in order to consolidate his regiment, Doniphan gave no indication of considering retreat.[36] His decision to give battle against an enemy of undetermined strength and without his full regiment present is revealing. Doniphan and his men possessed unbounded self-confidence.[37] They had received numerous reports of local Mexican militias preparing to fight at defenses in the vicinity of Santa Fe, but enemy resistance there had failed to materialize. Aggressiveness combined with curiosity about their enemy made the Missourians eager to take the measure of the approaching Mexican force, whose composition, weapons, and leadership they did not know.

As the Mexicans marched closer, the Americans noticed their impressive array. One Missouri soldier said that the Mexicans 'drew up in good order.... [T]heir cavalry [was] in bright scarlet coats with ... snow white belts, carrying polished sabres and carbines and long lances, with red and green pennons...'. Another Missourian took note of the 'long, bold, beautiful front of the enemy', a sight that made his 'blood flow chill'. Dazzled, he watched 'as they came abreast. Their beautiful steeds ... prancing and tossing their heads to the sound of the bugles, the riders erect and firm in the seats, their red coats, high brazen helmets plumed with bear skin, and each armed with a carbine, lance, holsters, and sabre, were indeed worthy of admiration.' A third volunteer was impressed by the enemy's 'gallant and imposing appearance'. As the Mexican battle line approached, a lieutenant said 'their charge was a handsome one'. Such anecdotes indicate that the US soldiers were aware of their enemy's apparent quality, use of tactical drill, and belligerent intent.[38]

Before the combat came a kind of action deemed by some dramatic and by others comic-opera. The Mexican commander sent out a staff officer carrying a black flag to demand that Doniphan discuss surrender – or face battle with no quarter asked or given. Several veterans of 1st Missouri Regiment left recollections of the 'black flag incident'. Each account varies slightly, but there is a basic agreement on the tenor of the episode: the intimidating gesture of waving a black flag emblazoned with skull and bones was not lost on the Missourians. Thomas Caldwell, a volunteer fluent in Spanish and acting on behalf of Doniphan, met the Mexican officer about 100 yards from the American line. Caldwell rejected the cavalryman's demand that Doniphan present himself for parley or surrender.

> 'We shall break your ranks and take him...', shouted the Mexican officer.
> 'Come and take him', Caldwell shouted back, undaunted.
> 'A curse upon you; prepare for a charge. We give no quarter and ask none', yelled the Mexican officer as he waved the black flag for emphasis. 'Damned be he who first cries hold, enough.'

Caldwell galloped back to the assembled American volunteers and 'went up and down the line explaining to the men what was meant by a Black or Pirates [sic] Flag and screaming at the top of his voice, hurra [sic] for the American Stars and Stripes...'.[39] This display of Mexican bravado and the verbal exchange between the two officers gave the Americans valuable time to prepare for the fight. The regulars, especially Captain Thompson and Lieutenant Wooster, assisted Doniphan by forming the volunteers in line of battle.[40]

Doniphan surveyed the enemy's approach and decided to try a *ruse de guerre* on his right wing. After the first Mexican volley, Doniphan ordered some of his men to lie down or kneel in the tall grass. After another enemy volley, more Americans appeared to go down. Delivering volley fire demonstrated that the Mexican units had undergone some formal training and drill. They fired three volleys, coming at around 400, 300, and 200 yards, respectively. Then the Mexicans cheered and surged forward, thinking that their musket shots had made casualties of many of the Americans.[41]

Doniphan wanted his men to fire back when the enemy came inside a range of 100 yards. One of the Missourians, Marcellus Edwards, recalled how hard it was for them to withhold their fire. Showing surprising discipline, the volunteers understood the plan and obeyed orders, even as some agreed that they had shot small game at a greater distance than the enemy line moving toward them. Drawing upon his oratorical skills, the colonel walked among his soldiers, asking them to 'Remember Okeechobee' – the 1837 embarrassment to Missouri in the Second Seminole War when the state's soldiers had broken and run from the battlefield: he wanted his men to remove that stain from their state's military record. At the right moment Doniphan yelled for them to stand and shoot. The heavy American volley inflicted serious casualties on the attacking Mexicans and repulsed the enemy assault on Doniphan's right.[42]

Meanwhile, a second Mexican attack, against the American left flank, also failed, and, after receiving a deadly volley from the Americans, the Mexicans sheared off to their right and sought out what appeared to be the vulnerable American supply wagons. The Missourians kept up a sharp fire into the Mexicans, who then met 'a very warm reception' from the trader's wagons. Repulsed in three assaults against the Missourians, and losing heavily among their regular units, the Mexican line of battle fragmented. The Americans rushed forward and captured a cannon and Captain John Reid, responding to Doniphan's order, sortied with an ad hoc group of 20 horsemen, maintaining a pursuit for four miles. The battle had lasted only about an hour.[43]

Estimates of Mexican losses at Brazito vary from 30 to 63 killed, and between 150 to 172 wounded. These losses range somewhere between 15 and 20 per cent of the total force available, but would be higher if calculated as a percentage of the Mexican forces engaged, probably about 800 soldiers. American losses were seven wounded. Not only did the Mexicans suffer high casualties, they also lost quantities of valuable supplies. These included a cannon, dozens of muskets with powder and shot, along with perhaps 300 horses, stock which the Americans used as remounts for the next stage of their campaign. Furthermore, the Missourians promptly drank up casks of captured wine, ate quantities of bread and other food the enemy had prepared, and smoked tobacco and cigarillos they had left behind. The Americans also picked up pieces of Mexican uniforms and discarded equipment.[44]

In his book *The War with Mexico* (1849), Major Roswell S. Ripley criticized both Doniphan's leadership and the performance of his volunteers. The major asserted that the Missourians had been taken by surprise at Brazito and had assembled in 'uncouth formations'. According to Ripley, the Missouri regiment only overcame with bravery what 'want of method' – tactical drill as practiced by the regulars – should have provided. Ripley dismissed or declined to weigh the evidence that the Missourians displayed discipline in holding their fire until Doniphan's order, and that they stood their ground against a Mexican force outnumbering them at least two to one.[45]

Beyond Ripley's carping, and more importantly for the broader picture, the Battle of Brazito was obviously a lost opportunity for Mexico. First, in a conflict that had so few bright spots for Mexican arms, a victory would have provided a needed boost in morale – both in northern Mexico and for Mexicans nationally. Second, if the Mexicans had won at Brazito they would have likely forced Doniphan back to Santa Fe. News of a defeat of Doniphan's regiment in December might have inspired greater popular support in January 1847 for the Taos Revolt in which Governor Bent was killed. The prospect of a victorious Mexican army marching on Santa Fe could have had a galvanizing effect on Mexicans and perhaps a demoralizing effect on the US forces occupying the city.[46]

Doniphan's victory at Brazito made another contribution to the overall American war effort and boosted the colonel's status. The battle helped to affirm the US hold on New Mexico, drove the Mexican forces south of the Rio Grande, thus supporting the US annexation of Texas, and posed a threat to Chihuahua. Doniphan's victory so badly damaged the Mexican force that it made no effort to defend El Paso del Norte. The Mexicans retreated south to Ciudad Chihuahua, opening the way for Doniphan to continue his campaign. Thus Brazito lent momentum to the latest US invasion of Mexico. The battle also gave Doniphan important practical experience as a regimental leader in combat. Finally, the victory of the US volunteers at Brazito raised the morale of the Missourians and strengthened Doniphan's self-confidence.

Doniphan and his regiment moved across the Rio Grande to El Paso del Norte and camped there for several weeks (from 27 December 1846, to 8 February 1847), leaving the colonel time to make several decisions. It would avail him little to stay near El Paso. He could either go as ordered to Chihuahua, though he had no recent communications confirming those orders, or he could pull back to Santa Fe, where he might comfortably pass the remaining five months of his enlistment. Proceeding to Chihuahua would mean that the regiment must have artillery support. Doniphan concluded that he would continue his campaign and, accordingly, he sent a request to Santa Fe for Major Meriwether L. Clark's artillery battery. Clark and his six cannon reached El Paso by 2 February. Strengthened by these reinforcements, Doniphan and his regiment sought to add to their laurels as well as maintain the offensive and prepared to march on Chihuahua City.[47]

Just before the regiment was ready to march, a messenger handed Doniphan the news of the Taos Revolt, raising the possibility that Mexicans would reassert control over Santa Fe. The Missourians could return to New Mexico and help Colonel Sterling Price suppress the revolt, or push on to Chihuahua as planned. Doniphan decided that Price had enough troops on hand in New Mexico to regain US control of the territory and that 1st Missouri Regiment would keep on the offensive. A less determined and less aggressive commander would have fallen back to Santa Fe.[48]

The march south to Chihuahua took 20 days. The Americans traversed nearly waterless terrain inhospitable to an invading force depending on horses and mules for transportation. Until the Missourians were within a few miles of the city, it was unclear what sort of defenses the Mexicans would be preparing near Chihuahua.

To defend Chihuahua,[49] General José A. Heredia assembled an army estimated at 3,000, including both regulars and militia, more than twice Doniphan's total of about 1,300.[50] According to a Mexican source, most of their regular soldiers had been in service less than 100 days; they were supplemented by a force of militia or National Guardsmen. Heredia's subordinate, General Pedro García Condé, was the former minister of war for the Republic of Mexico. Conde planned to make the best use of the inexperienced men by putting them in field fortifications. Rumors that circulated before the Missourians had arrived at Santa Fe had foretold of non-existent Mexican regiments and cannon emplacements. Outside Chihuahua the defenses were genuine and the Mexican forces numerous.[51]

General Condé designed and supervised the construction of the field works, including eight redoubts holding cannon and a series of supporting emplacements near the juncture of the Sacramento River and the Chihuahua road, about 15 miles north of the city. One of the Mexican gun emplacements crowned a hill that overlooked the river crossing and the entire battlefield. Each redoubt was adequately designed and, though hastily built, the defenses commanded the approaches to the river and took advantage of the imposing natural scarp of the plateau rising above the Arroyo Seco. But the Mexican commanders made an error common enough among nineteenth-century army leaders: they wanted and expected the enemy army to attack the strongest part of their defenses. Believing that the terrain on their left flank was impassable because of a deep gulch, the Mexican officers did not foresee that the Americans could use that approach. Thus the expectations of the Mexican commanders was one of the crucial factors in the coming battle.[52]

The Battle of Sacramento

Prior to the battle, fought on 28 February 1847, Doniphan made a remark intended to inspire his soldiers. He declared: 'Well, boys, I have issued an order this morning that we are to camp in the enemies [sic] entrenchments tonight.' Although the statement may now appear to be shop-worn, such an announcement from their colonel boosted the spirits of the Missouri volunteers. They expected him to proclaim his plans in bold terms, and he did not disappoint them.[53]

Other than offering inspiring words to his soldiers, more critical factors included Doniphan's decisions to order a thorough reconnaissance of the Mexican fortifications and not to rush into battle. At least two officers of 1st Missouri Regiment reconnoitered the Mexican defensive lines. Major Clark, the artillery commander, scouted the Mexican artillery emplacements, and Lieutenant Colonel David Mitchell, attached to Doniphan from Price's 2nd Missouri Regiment, led the other reconnaissance. Doniphan and his officers were thus apprised of the enemy's defenses. At a spot about one and a half miles from the Mexican army Doniphan held a conference and his officers passed around a telescope, discussing the terrain and dispositions in light of the reconnaissance reports. It is not clear who proposed to outflank the heart of the Mexican position by crossing the gulch, but that choice was the key tactical decision of the battle. Leaving the road and forming his supply wagons and traders' wagons into a sort of moving defensive box, Doniphan ordered hundreds of his men forward with shovels and, to the amazement of the Mexicans, they piled up dirt for a ramp, allowing the regiment to pass through the gulch and advance.[54]

Responding to the threat, 300 Mexican lancers rode out to disrupt the American formation, but Doniphan sent forward Captain Richard Weightman with two cannon. Fire from these guns devastated the lancers, who retreated, 'unmasking a body of twelve hundred cavalry and the battery [of three guns] which opened upon ... [the Missourians] a continuous blaze...'. Most of the Mexican cannon shots flew high, but several of the American's horses were killed. Doniphan was heard to exclaim: 'Well, they're giving us ... [hell] now, boys!' Closing within 300 yards of one of the largest redoubts, the Americans then formed into a battle line, with Major William Gilpin leading the attack by dismounted volunteers in the center. Mexican artillery continued to fire, but with little effect.[55] At about this time Doniphan wanted a general advance, but his messenger, aide-de-camp Lieutenant James De Courcy, galloped down the line babbling incoherently and garbling the colonel's instructions. Here and there individual horsemen dashed toward the redoubt and then others followed, including Captain Reid supported by Weightman's cannon. Meanwhile, some American companies held fast as others surged forward on foot, but Major Clark brought his artillery to bear with decisive results.[56]

Doniphan was worried that these piecemeal attacks would fail. One of his volunteers, Frank Edwards, heard the colonel exclaim: 'My God! they're gone! The boys will all be killed!' Doniphan shouted for the soldiers standing nearby to attack and, determined to lead by example, he spurred forward and joined the mêlée. The resulting enthusiastic multiple rushes produced a pincers attack on the main redoubt and broke the will of the inexperienced Mexican infantry. Some other gun emplacements held out longer than others, but when the Missourians reached most of the Mexican positions they found dead and wounded Mexicans, abandoned equipment, and a demoralized enemy in full retreat, despite the efforts of individual Mexican officers to rally their soldiers. One well-placed Mexican cannon directed its fire at the Americans from across the Rio Sacramento. While the attackers put the remaining defenders to rout on the north side of the river bed, Major Clark directed his guns to knock out the last Mexican redoubt.[57]

The battle lasted more than three hours. Four Americans were killed and eight wounded, but the Mexican losses were very heavy. The Americans claimed to count 169 Mexican soldiers killed, made 79 prisoner, and an undetermined number, perhaps 300 or more, were wounded. If these casualty totals were accurate, the Mexican forces suffered losses of about 20 per cent. In addition, the Americans captured hundreds of horses and mules, 20 wagons, several hundred sheep, ten cannon, quantities of ammunition, plus boxes of copper and silver coins.[58]

Several factors combined to produce the American victory at Sacramento. First, the US artillery played a crucial role outside Chihuahua, as it had in other battles in the war. Second, Doniphan generously acknowledged his debt for sound advice from Captain Thompson, the attached officer from 1st Dragoons. The colonel offered favorable mention of the parts played by other subordinates, including Major Clark, Captain Weightman, Major Gilpin, and Lieutenant Colonel Mitchell. In a battle with multiple attacks, Doniphan had not displayed tight control over each element of his command, but he had provided the important element of inspirational leadership, a crucial factor at the regimental level. Lieutenant Charles Wooster overstated the case by asserting that Doniphan 'was rather at a loss what to do during the action, and readily assented to any advice given by myself or Captain Thompson.... In fact, ... the movements generally during the engagement were made at my [Wooster's] suggestion.' In sharp contrast to Wooster, one of the Missourians, William Richardson, concluded that the American 'success is to be attributed entirely to the superior skill of our commander [Doniphan]'. The colonel drew upon the advice of the regular officers, but he was not completely reliant on them.

Doniphan was the inspirational leader at the battle and of the expedition.[59]

The Battle of Sacramento obviously did not equal in size or complexity Zachary Taylor's triumph on 22–23 February at Buena Vista/La Angostura, but Sacramento did have notable consequences for both sides. The defeat in detail of the Mexican army at Sacramento put to rest any Mexican hopes of retaking Santa Fe.[60] Moreover, the fall of the provincial capital of Ciudad Chihuahua on 2 March 1847, lowered Mexican national morale. Yet another defeat highlighted the deficiencies of the Mexican Army. It had been unable to mount sturdy defenses or turn back any of the United States invasions into Mexico's northern provinces. In addition, the American victory also prevented the Mexican military from obtaining a large quantity of guns, ammunition, trade goods and other supplies carried by Missouri merchants who accompanied Doniphan's column.[61] Doniphan's win over an entrenched army also deprived the Mexicans of the intangible yet potentially significant uplift that a victory over any American force would have given Mexican arms. Thus Sacramento reinforced both the image and the reality of US military prowess and Mexican ineptitude.[62]

Doniphan's victory at Sacramento helped boost American morale and received remarkably good coverage in newspapers across the United States, even as it occurred near the time of Taylor's battle at Buena Vista/La Angostura and Winfield Scott's landing at Vera Cruz (9 March). For example, the Washington *National Era*, a Whig paper otherwise critical of the Polk administration's handling of the war, struck a strategic note from the US point of view by pointing out that the victory helped guard 'the safety of New Mexico'. The New Orleans *Daily Picayune* gushed that 'the battle of Sacramento and the capture of Chihuahua are among the most glorious events of the whole war'. Trumping the *Picayune*, the Natchez *Free Trader* postulated that 'This battle, considering the disparity of forces engaged, is one of the most brilliant achievements of American arms during the existing war....' Missouri newspapers had to work to match such accolades, but the Columbia *Statesman* called Sacramento a 'splendid victory', and the papers of several towns proudly printed official dispatches and letters describing the actions of the state's most famous regiment. Other southern newspapers chimed in. The Charleston *Courier* and Tallahassee *Floridian* both hailed the battle as a 'brilliant action', the Savannah *Republican* termed it 'a very brilliant achievement', and the Richmond *Whig and Advertiser* (no friend of the war) styled it a 'brilliant exploit'. Other accolades came from the North. For instance, the Indianapolis *Indiana State Sentinel* saluted the 'Missouri sharp shooters' on their victory and the Cleveland *Plain Dealer* and the Cincinnati *Enquirer* exclaimed the 'Glorious News!!' of Sacramento as 'Another American Victory !!!' The Newark, New Jersey, *Advertiser* could not pass up the opportunity to trumpet that 'Wherever the American arms encounter the Mexicans they triumph, whatever may be the odds.'[63]

Conclusion

The El Paso–Chihuahua campaign added strength to the tradition of the American volunteer army officer. Basically a novice in military matters in 1846, Doniphan appeared to many of his contemporaries to be a natural military leader who personified the America's faith that such capable commanders would step forward when the nation needed them. Certainly, his regiment accomplished remarkable things and he was one of the best volunteer regimental commanders of the war. The long marches of 1st Missouri Regiment became the stuff of legend and prompted numerous contemporary writers and speechmakers to liken Doniphan to Xenophon, a respected Greek military commander of ancient times.[64] The New Orleans *Delta* accurately characterized Doniphan as a 'citizen commander of citizen soldiers', but the Washington *Daily Union* went so far as to rank Doniphan among Taylor, Scott, Kearny, and John C. Frémont as the top officers of the war.[65]

The national high command was gratified at the outcome of Doniphan's campaign. Before hearing the news about the battle of Sacramento, Secretary of War Marcy expressed his concern to Missouri's governor that Doniphan had been swallowed up by the Mexican desert, or worse, defeated by a Mexican army. When he learned the outcome of Doniphan's march, Marcy praised the colonel's 'gallant action and ... glorious victory at Sacramento' in a letter to General Kearny. President Polk allowed his hyperbole free reign when he exclaimed that 'The battle of Sacramento ... [was] one of the most decisive and brilliant achievements of the War.' The commander in chief paid the volunteer colonel a high compliment, especially considering that Polk was a Democrat and Doniphan a Whig.[66] In recognition of Doniphan's victories and personal leadership, the War Department invited him (along with other dignitaries) to serve as a member of the Board of Visitors at the US Military Academy and to give a commencement address to the cadets in 1848.[67]

Doniphan contributed both administratively and strategically to the US war effort against Mexico. He took personal gratification that his successful expedition had resulted in expanding the territory of the United States. General Stephen Kearny led the 'Army of the West' to Santa Fe, but Doniphan supervised the initial US occupation forces in New Mexico. There Doniphan's role in military government helped to establish guideposts included years later in a comprehensive survey by Charles Magoon. *Magoon's Reports* described Doniphan's New Mexico territorial constitution – the first American experience with military government. Although modest, Doniphan's example indicated that the American military previously had carried out such responsibilities and that officers of the early twentieth century involved with military government in US overseas colonies had American precedents to follow. Unlike their fellow regular officers of the 1840s, by the 1940s American military planners recognized that the United States would be called upon to provide both occupying troops and administrators who would supervise defeated nations and conquered territory.

Doniphan's battlefield victories as a regimental commander won him acclaim in his own time and his regiment took actions that strategically affected the war. The tactical victory in the battle at Brazito, near El Paso, consolidated the US hold on the province of New Mexico as well as reasserted the US claim to the Rio Grande as the international boundary between the United States and Mexico. Doniphan's overwhelming victory at Sacramento meant it was unlikely that Mexico could mount an expedition to recapture Santa Fe. This Missouri volunteer colonel was a striking personal example of an American annexationist.

NOTES

1. Richard L. Bartlett, *Dictionary of Americanisms* (Boston: Little, Brown 1859) p.9.
2. Among the many works dealing with 'Manifest Destiny' two are David M. Pletcher, *The Diplomacy of Annexation: Texas, Oregon and the Mexican War* (Columbia: U. of Missouri Press 1973) and Gene M. Brack, *Mexico Views Manifest Destiny, 1821–1846* (Albuquerque: U. of New Mexico Press 1975).
3. In *Year of Decision: 1846* (Boston: Little, Brown 1943), Bernard DeVoto gives one of the best secondary works on Doniphan's expedition from Kansas through New Mexico and Texas to Chihuahua. Several of the one volume histories of the war also cover the expedition. See e.g. K. Jack Bauer, *The Mexican War* (NY: Macmillan 1974), Otis A. Singletary, *The Mexican War* (U. of Chicago Press 1960) and John E. Weems, *To Conquer a Peace* (NY: Doubleday 1974). The best of the contemporary accounts is John T. Hughes, *Doniphan's Expedition* (Cincinnati: UP James 1848).
4. Alexander W. Doniphan to Sec. of War William L. Marcy, 5 Sept. 1845, filed with Sec. of War Applications File, 1846–48, Box 9, Records of the US Sec. of War, Record Group (RG) 107, National Archives (NA), Washington DC.
5. Heman C. Smith, 'The Hero of Sacramento, Alexander W. Doniphan', *Jnl of History* 4 (1911) pp.344–9; Kenneth H. Winn, *Exiles in a Land of Liberty: Mormons in America, 1830-1846* (Chapel Hill, NC: UNC Press 1989) pp.103, 105, 139, 142–3; Andre P. Duchateau, 'Missouri Colossus: Alexander Doniphan, 1808–1887' (Ed.D. diss. Oklahoma State U. 1973) pp.49–67, 69–94; Roger D. Launius, 'Alexander Doniphan: Missouri's Forgotten Hero', in F.M. McKiernan and R.D. Launius (eds.) *Missouri Folk Heroes of the 19th Century* (Independence, MO: Independence Press 1989) pp.69–70.
6. In a letter, Doniphan and Henry L. Routt to Sec. of War Marcy, 16 May 1846, filed with Secretary of War Applications File, Box 9, RG 107, NA, Doniphan and fellow Missourians 'again tender[ed] their Services to the Government'; Doniphan Military Pension Record, RG 75, NA; Doniphan's election is confirmed in Army of the West Order No.1, 19 June 1846, Orders of Brig. Gens. S.W. Kearny and Sterling Price, Records of the US Army Adjt Gen's

Office, Microcopy T-1115, roll 1, RG 94, NA. According to M.B. Edwards, of Capt. John Reid's company, Doniphan openly 'declared himself a candidate for colonel', indicating his desire for command. See M.B. Edwards, *Marching with the Army of the West* (Ralph P. Bieber ed.) (Glendale, CA: Arthur H. Clark 1936) pp.110, 115.
7. Doniphan, Graduation Address to Army Cadets, 16 June 1848, *Addresses Delivered in the Chapel at West Point*.... (NY: Burroughs 1848), copy in the US Military Academy (hereafter US MA) Archives, West Point, NY. On the regiment's major, see Thomas L. Karnes, *William Gilpin, Western Nationalist* (Austin, TX: U. of Texas Press 1970) pp.19–21, 29–45. See also Francis B. Heitman, *Historical Register and Dictionary of the United States Army*, 2 vols. (Washington DC: GPO 1903) Vol.1 pp.458, 850. Others on the expedition with West Point training included artillery officers in attached units: Meriwether L. Clark (Class of 1830) had resigned from the army in 1833, and Richard H. Weightman attended the Academy 1835–37, but did not graduate. Ibid. Vol.1, pp.305, 1014.
8. John T. Hughes (note 3) repr. in William E. Connelley, *Doniphan's Expedition* (Topeka KS: pub. by author 1907) p.132; Richard Elliott, *Notes Taken in Sixty Years* (St Louis: R.P. Studley 1883) p.222. M.B. Edwards recalled two hours of mounted drills before breakfast, but he did not specify the rest of the training schedule for 1st Missouri. M.B. Edwards (note 6) p.112. Writing under the nom de plume 'John Brown', Richard Elliott specified drills from 5.00 to 7.00am and 4.00 to 6.00pm daily for the Leclede Rangers (Brown to editors, 20 June 1846, in *St Louis Weekly Reveille*, 29 June 1846), and indicated that the 300-acre 'drill ground ... had become a plain of dust and sand, having been walked, trotted and galloped over for ten days past by from five to seven hundred horses' of the several companies of Missouri volunteers (Brown to editors, 23 June 1846, ibid. 6 July 1846). Elliott is identified as 'Brown', ibid. 7 Jan. 1847.
9. Doniphan to D.C. Allen, 19 Sept. 1883, Alexander W. Doniphan Papers, Missouri Historical Society, St Louis. Kearny entered the army as a Lt in 1812 and served with infantry units through the 1820s. He was promoted Lt Col of dragoons in 1833 and to Col of 1st Dragoons 1836. He received notice of his promotion to brig. gen. on the march to Santa Fe. The full biography is Dwight Clarke, *Stephen Watts Kearny: Soldier of the West* (Norman, OK: U. of Oklahoma Press 1961).
10. A standard treatment of the tension between volunteers and regulars is found in Singletary (note 3) pp.128–9, 143–7. Another study is Richard Bruce Winders, 'Mr Polk's Army: Politics, Patronage, and the American Military in the Mexican War' (PhD diss., Texas Christian U. 1994) pp.180–7.
11. Marcy to Kearny, 3 June 1846, in House Exec. Doc. No.19, 29th Congress, 2nd Session, pp.5–7. See also Clarke (note 9) pp.394–7. At close to full strength, a standard US Army regiment in the nineteenth century enrolled around 1,000 soldiers.
12. A good summary is William Y. Chalfant, *Dangerous Passage: The Santa Fe Trail and the Mexican War* (Norman: U. of Oklahoma Press 1994) pp.6–18. Waldo Johnson to William Waldo, 24 Aug. 1846, Waldo Johnson Letters, Western Historical MSS Collection, U. of Missouri Library, Columbia.
13. Charles E. Magoon, *Reports on the Law of Civil Government in Territory Subject to Military Occupation by the Military Forces of the United States* (Washington DC: GPO 1903) pp.12, 16–17, 20, 22, 96–100, 166, 218–19, 273, 277, 501–2, 689–730.
14. An outstanding treatment of the development of the US Army's officer corps in the early nineteenth century is William B. Skelton, *An American Profession of Arms: The Army Officer Corps, 1784–1861* (Lawrence, KS: UP of Kansas 1992) pp.68–86, 300–1. See also Robert V. Remini, *Andrew Jackson and the Course of American Empire* (NY: Harper & Row 1977) pp.308–15; Theodore Grivas, *Military Governments in California, 1846–1850* (Glendale, CA: Arthur H. Clark 1963) pp.30–1.
15. Grivas (note 14) pp.13–16, quote on p.16.
16. For Quitman in Mexico City, see Robert E. May, *John A. Quitman, Old South Crusader* (Baton Rouge, LA: Louisiana State UP 1985) pp.194–8; regarding American occupation and use of the port city of Matamoros, see Joseph E. Chance (ed.) *Mexico Under Fire: Being the Diary of Samuel Ryan Curtis, 3rd Ohio Volunteer Regiment during the American Occupation of Northern Mexico, 1846–1847* (Fort Worth, TX: Texas Christian UP 1994). See also Neal

Harlow, *California Conquered: War and Peace on the Pacific, 1846–1850* (Berkeley, CA: U. of California Press 1982).
17. Bent had been involved in the western fur trade since the 1820s. In 1832 he purchased a residence in Taos and married a Mexican woman. See Harold H. Dunham, 'Charles Bent', in LeRoy Hafen (ed.) *Mountain Men and the Fur Trade of the Far West: Biographical Sketches of the Participants*, 10 vols. (Glendale, CA: Arthur Clark 1965–72) Vol.2 pp.27–48.
18. Original Kearny Proclamation, with the same announcement in both English and Spanish, 22 Aug. 1846, in Benjamin Read Collection, New Mexico State Records Center, Santa Fe, also quoted in Ralph E. Twitchell, *The History of the Military Occupation of the Territory of New Mexico from 1846 to 1851* (Denver, CO: Smith-Brooks 1909) p.74; Army of the West, Orders No.13, 17 Aug. 1846, in NA Microcopy T-1115, roll 1; Kearny to Marcy, 22 Sept. 1846, in Letters Received by the Office of the Adjt Gen., Main Series, 1822–60, Microcopy M-567, roll 319, RG 94, NA; see also Clarke (note 9) pp.146, 148. The sometimes confusing duality of a civilian governor (in this case Charles Bent) functioning alongside an influential – even dominating – military officer in a military government setting would be duplicated during the 1860s in the Federal Army's 'Reconstruction' duties in the southern states and also in the island possessions of America's 'new empire' of the 1890s. See James E. Sefton, *The United States Army and Reconstruction, 1865–1877* (Baton Rouge, LA: Louisiana State UP 1967), and John M. Gates, *Schoolbooks and Krags: The United States Army in the Philippines, 1898–1902* (Westport CT: Greenwood Press 1973).
19. Twitchell (note 18) p.95; Johnson to Waldo, 24 Aug. 1846, Johnson Letters, U. of Missouri, Columbia. Johnson indicated that Doniphan believed that he might have to leave Santa Fe for El Paso 'in a few days'.
20. On Hall and Waldo, see Connelley (note 8) pp.238–9 n.51, and 133–4, n.18. On Blair's background, see Ezra J. Warner, *Generals in Blue* (Baton Rouge: Louisiana State UP 1964) pp.35–6.
21. Doniphan to Ed., *Liberty Wkly Tribune*, 10 Oct. 1846; Alexander Doniphan and Willard Hall, Laws of the Territory of New Mexico (Santa Fe, NM: 1846; repr. Santa Fe: Historical Society of NM 1970); Twitchell (note 18) p.84; Clarke (note 9) pp.149–50; Doniphan interview in *Santa Fe Era Southwestern*, 7 Aug. 1880; Grivas (note 14) pp.35–6; Army of the West Order No.20, 30 Aug. 1846, NA Microcopy T-1115, roll 1; Duchateau (note 5) pp.142–4; David Y. Thomas, *History of Military Government in Newly Acquired Territory of the United States* (NY: Columbia UP 1904) p.105; William E. Daugherty and Marshall Andrews, *A Review of US Historical Experience with Civil Affairs, 1776–1954* (Bethesda, MD: Operations Research Office of Johns Hopkins U. 1961) p.56; Connelley (note 8) pp.238–43.
22. Kearny to US Army Adj Gen, Washington DC, 22 Sept. 1846, (emphasis added), quoted in James Cutts, *The Conquest of California and New Mexico* (Philadelphia, PA: Carey & Hart 1847; repr. Albuquerque, NM: Horn & Wallace 1965) p.64.
23. In the main, historians have treated the code favorably. For instance, Theodore Grivas called the code a 'notable and lasting achievement' (Grivas [note 14] pp.35–6), and Dwight Clarke compliments 'Kearny's Code' for its practical utility and longevity (Clarke [note 9] pp.149–50). See also Duchateau (note 5) p.151. For a more detailed treatment of Doniphan's experiences with civil affairs see Joseph G. Dawson III, 'American Civil-Military Relations and Military Government: The Service of Colonel Alexander Doniphan in the Mexican War', *Armed Forces & Society* 23 (Summer 1996) pp.555–72.
24. Magoon (note 13) quote on p.16; refer also to pp.20, 22, 96–100, 218–19, 273, 277, 501–7, 689–730. A modern summary also refers to Doniphan's and Kearny's actions: see Daugherty and Andrews (note 21) pp.54–9.
25. Marcy to Kearny, 11 Jan. 1847, William L. Marcy Papers, Library of Congress, Washington DC; Polk to Congress, 22 Dec. 1846, in James D. Richardson (comp.), *Messages and Papers of the Presidents, 1789–1897*, 10 vols. (Washington DC: GPO 1897) Vol.4 pp.506–7; Sister Mary Loyola [Carnes], 'The American Occupation of New Mexico, 1821–1851', *New Mexico Historical Review* 14 (April 1939) p.166; Justin H. Smith, *The War with Mexico*, 2 vols. (NY: Macmillan 1919) Vol.2 pp.216–17; Thomas (note 21) pp.106, 115–16, 156, 158.
26. Kearny to Doniphan, Army of the West, Order No.32, 2 Oct. 1846, NA Microfilm T-1115, roll 1; Twitchell (note 18) pp.96, 98, 100; Duchateau (note 5) pp.157–64; John T. Hughes to

Ed., 25 Sept. 1846, printed in *Liberty Wkly Tribune*, 14 Nov. 1846; Hughes to Ed., 20 Oct. 1846, ibid. 5 Dec. 1846; Roswell S. Ripley, *The War with Mexico*, 2 vols. (NY: Harper 1849) Vol.2 p.467, compliments Doniphan's Navajo treaty.
27. Charles Bent to James Buchanan, 26 Dec. 1846, House Exec. Doc. No.70, 30th Congress, 1st Session, p.17; Francis Paul Prucha concludes that 'American military force in New Mexico was not enough to guarantee the peace that Kearny had so sanguinely promised'. Prucha, *The Great Father: The United States Government and the American Indians*, 2 vols. (Lincoln, NE: U. of Nebraska Press 1984) Vol.1 p.367. See also Frank McNitt, *Navajo Wars: Military Campaigns, Slave Raids, and Reprisals* (Albuquerque, NM: U. of NM Press 1972) pp.112–13.
28. Warren A. Beck, *New Mexico: A History of Four Centuries* (Norman, OK: U. of Oklahoma Press 1962) pp.134–7; John S. D. Eisenhower, *So Far from God: The US War with Mexico, 1846–1848* (NY: Doubleday 1989) pp.233–7.
29. Thompson, from Georgia, graduated from the USMA 36th of 56 cadets in 1835, but had been delayed one year for academic deficiencies. He went into the dragoons and made captain 11 years after graduation. Wooster, from New York, graduated from West Point 31st of 50 members of the Class of 1837. He served with artillery units and was promoted 1st Lt 1842. Armstrong, from Georgia, graduated 22nd in the Academy Class of 1845, so he had been commissioned only a few months when the war began. George W. Cullum, *Biographical Register ... of the US Military Academy*, 2 vols. (3rd ed. Boston: Houghton, Mifflin 1891) Vol.1 pp.616, 687; Heitman (note 7) Vol.1 pp.169, 1060.
30. T. Harry Williams, *Hayes of the Twenty-Third: The Civil War Volunteer Officer* (NY: Knopf 1965) pp.18–38. See chapter entitled 'The Good Colonels'. Hayes became the 19th US president.
31. The first soldier quotation is from Frank S. Edwards, *A Campaign in New Mexico with Colonel Doniphan* (Philadelphia: Carey & Hart 1847) p.76; the second is from William B. McGroarty (ed.) 'William H. Richardson's Journal of Doniphan's Expedition' (hereafter 'Richardson Journal'), *Missouri Historical Review* 22 (July 1928) p.535.
32. By the summer of 1847 Doniphan was exhausted and his poor health was probably the major reason that he did not sign on to fight for the duration of the war.
33. The difficulty of locating the Brazito battlefield is covered in George Ruhlen, 'Brazito – The Only Battle in the Southwest between American and Foreign Troops', *Password: The Qtly Jnl of the El Paso County Hist. Soc.* 2 (Feb. 1957) pp.4–13; Ruhlen, 'The Battle of Brazito: Where Was It Fought?' ibid. 2 (May 1957) pp.53–60; Andrew Armstrong, 'The Brazito Battlefield', *New Mexico Historical Review* 35 (Jan. 1960) pp.63–74.
34. Putting the Mexican force at about 1,200 were Jacob S. Robinson in Carl L. Cannon (ed.) *A Journal of the Santa Fe Expedition under Colonel Doniphan* (Princeton UP 1932) p.67, Frank S. Edwards (note 31) p.87, and Mr Murray to Editor, *Liberty Wkly Tribune*, 13 March 1847. Lt Christian Kribben estimated 1,100 (Lt Kribben to Maj. M.L. Clark, 26 Dec. 1846, in Meriwether L. Clark Letterbook, Beinecke Library, Yale U. New Haven, CT, quoted in Gibson, *Soldier under Kearny and Doniphan*, Bieber (ed.) p.303. Gibson himself put the number somewhat lower than the others, between 800 and 1,000 (ibid. p.308). Doniphan recalled a figure of about 1,300 (Doniphan interview, *Santa Fe Era Southwestern*, 5 Aug. 1880), an estimate supported by John Hughes (Connelley [note 8] p.371). Most of those giving estimates split the Mexican force between regulars (500–600) and militia or National Guard (the remainder).
35. Ramón Alcaraz *et al. The Other Side: or, Notes for the History of the War Between Mexico and the United States*, Albert C. Ramsey (trans.) (1850; repr. NY: Burt Franklin 1970) p.169; Gibson (note 34) p.299. Gibson also observed that although 'all things have been made ready for a fight', the return to a loose line of march meant the Missourians were 'not expected to meet the enemy' (ibid. pp.299, 300). Therefore, security appeared to be lax.
36. Frank S. Edwards (note 31) pp.82–3; Gibson (note 34) p.300.
37. M.B. Edwards (note 6) p.231.
38. Frank S. Edwards (note 31) p.83; M.B. Edwards (note 6) pp.230–2; Connelley (note 8) pp.370–1; Lt Kribben, quoted in *Liberty Wkly Tribune*, 27 Feb. 1847; Hughes to Ed. ibid. 4 Jan. 1847.

34   MILITARY POWER: LAND WARFARE IN THEORY AND PRACTICE

39. Frank S. Edwards (note 31) p.84; M.B. Edwards (note 6) p.230; Gibson (note 34) p.304; Connelley (note 8) p.373; Lt Kribben to Maj Clark, 26 Dec. 1846, Clark Letterbook, Yale U.; Mr Murray to Editor, *Liberty Wkly Tribune*, 13 March 1847.
40. Indeed, in his report, Doniphan acknowledged that Capt. Thompson 'acted as my aid and advisor, and was of the most essential service in forming the line during the engagement'. Doniphan to US Army Adjt Gen. Roger Jones, 4 March 1847, quoted in Connelley (note 8) p.378n. Gibson was more emphatic: 'Thompson was consulted upon all occasions, and his opinion followed throughout.' Gibson (note 34) p.307.
41. As Col. Antonio Ponce de Leon described the scene, 'four [soldiers] in the enemy's second line were seen to fall, besides various others among the enemy, who died in the hail of fire so well sustained by the [Mexican] infantry and sections of the cavalry...'. See F.M. Gallaher (trans.) 'Official Report of the Battle at Temascalitos (Brazito)', *New Mexico Historical Review* 3 (Oct. 1928) p.387.
42. The battle from the American point of view is drawn from Doniphan to Adjt Gen Jones, 4 March 1847, in Connelley (note 8) p.377n; Gibson (note 34) pp.300, 305; Frank S. Edwards (note 31) pp.84–5; Mr Murray to Ed. (note 39); Doniphan interview, *Santa Fe Era Southwestern*, 5 Aug. 1880; M.B. Edwards (note 6) p.231; 'Richardson Journal' (note 31) p.347; William B. Franklin to Editor, 27 Jan. 1847, *Liberty Wkly Tribune*, 19 April 1847.
43. M.B. Edwards (note 6) p.234. See also Lt Kribben to Maj Clark, quoted in Gibson (note 34) p.303; Doniphan to Adjt Gen. Jones (note 42); and Maj William Gilpin's description in *St Louis Wkly Reveille*, 10 May 1847.
44. Various casualty reports and captured goods are given in Gibson (note 34) pp.308–9; Frank S. Edwards (note 31) pp.87–8; M.B. Edwards (note 6) pp.234–6. Doniphan's estimate of the Mexican casualties: 43k and 150w. Doniphan to Adjt Gen. Jones, 4 March 1847, quoted in Connelley (note 8) p.378.
45. Ripley (note 26) Vol.1 p.457.
46. Lewis Garrard, an American trader in the Southwest, recalled on 11 Feb. 1847 that, 'We ... felt badly indeed – Doniphan's regiment was in [the state of] Chihuahua, with no force to support it, and its certain defeat would give the Santa Feans [Mexican rebels] additional courage.' Lewis H. Garrard, *Wah-to-Yah and the Taos Trail* (1850; repr. Glendale, CA: Arthur H. Clark 1938, ed. Ralph P. Bieber) p.201. Hughes concluded that for the Americans, 'Defeat [at Brazito] would have been ruinous.' Connelley (note 8) p.375.
47. Col. Sterling Price, commanding 2nd Missouri Regt of Volunteers, did not want to release Clark's artillery due to the prospect of unrest in New Mexico, discussed in Capt. W.M.D. McKissack, Santa Fe, to Quartermaster Gen. Thomas Jesup, Washington DC, 9 Jan. 1847, Office of the QMG Consolidated Correspondence File, Box 262, RG 92, NA; Daniel Hastings Diary, Jan. 1847, in Justin H. Smith Papers, Benson Latin American Collection, U. of Texas, Austin; and Maj. M.L. Clark to Doniphan, 31 Dec. 1846, Clark Letterbook, Yale U. See also John P. Bloom, 'Johnny Gringo at the Pass of the North', *Password: Qtly Jnl of the El Paso County Hist. Soc.* 4 (Oct. 1959) pp.134–40.
48. M.B. Edwards (note 6) p.246. With Doniphan were dozens of merchants driving more than 300 heavily laden wagons. The traders wanted to sell their goods at Chihuahua, not to return to Santa Fe. There was the prospect that the offensive might lead to another bloodless victory like Kearny's at Santa Fe, or that Mexican forces would prepare positions near Chihuahua and defend the city against the American invasion. Rumors abounded in El Paso del Norte.
49. In hindsight, Alcaraz (note 35) pp.171–2 saw Doniphan's drive southward as a part of a concerted US strategy in 1847. That strategy included Taylor holding a threatening position on Mexican soil at Buena Vista (battle on 22–23 Feb.), Doniphan moving to Chihuahua (battle on 28 Feb.), and US naval and military forces off the Mexican Gulf coast (landing near Vera Cruz on 9 March). In 1847 authorities in Washington DC were not able to fine-tune such movements, but had positioned the forces in such a way to try to bring about the war's conclusion in ways favorable to the US. Obviously, the forces under Taylor (5,000) and Scott (12,000) were more important than Doniphan's reinforced regiment, but Mexican leaders still had to deal with three potential US threats. Santa Anna consolidated most of his forces to aim at Taylor, while other Mexican units defended Vera Cruz and Chihuahua. Regarding Santa Anna's decision to hold one unit with his army that might have gone to Chihuahua, see Santa Anna to Minister of War,

12 Oct. 1846: 'I have ordered [Gen.] Isidro Reyes not to march to Chihuahua', in Justin H. Smith (ed.), 'Letters of General Antonio Lopez de Santa Anna Relating to the War Between the United States and Mexico, 1846–1848', *American Historical Association Report for 1917*, 2 vols. (Washington DC: GPO 1920) Vol.2, p.370.
50. Doniphan's total included 714 men of 1st Missouri; 93 men under Lt Col David Mitchell attached from 2nd Missouri; 117 artillerymen under Maj. Clark; and about 350 traders and teamsters with supply wagons and commercial wagons. American estimates of Mexican forces ranged from 3,000 (Clark to Doniphan, 2 March 1847, quoted in Frank S. Edwards [note 31] p.173), to 4,000 (M.B. Edwards [note 6] p.268; Gibson [note 34] p.349). Doniphan himself estimated 4,100 (Doniphan to Adjt Gen. Jones, 4 March 1847, in Connelley [note 8] p.434). A Mexican recollection almost 50 years after the battle put the Mexican troops at around 3,100. See Rómulo Juarrieta, 'Batalla de Sacramento, 28 de Febrero de 1847', *Boletín Sociedad Chihuahuaense de Estudios Históricos* 7 (No.4, 1950) pp.415–16.
51. Condé had, among other assignments, served with the military engineers, and his varied experience made him one of the best officers in the Mexican Army in 1847. See Alberto M. Carreño, *Jefes del Ejército Mexicano en 1847: Biografías de Generales de División y de Brigada...* (México: Secretaria de Fomento 1914) pp.160–1.
52. Alcaraz (note 35) p.175; Hastings Diary, 28 Feb. 1847, Smith Papers, Benson Collection, U. of Texas, Austin.
53. Doniphan's prediction is quoted in Hastings Diary, 28 Feb. 1847, Smith Papers, Benson Coll., U. of Texas, Austin. The Mexican officers offered their own form of inspiration to their soldiers. Anticipating victory, the Mexicans had gathered handcuffs and cut ropes for use in restraining US prisoners.
54. Isaac George, *Heroes and Incidents of the Mexican War, Containing Doniphan's Expedition* (NY: Review Publishing Co. 1903) p.92; Clark to Doniphan, 2 March 1847, in Frank S. Edwards (note 31) p.172; Hastings Diary, 28 Feb. 1847, Smith Papers, Benson Collection, U. of Texas; description of Mitchell's reconnaissance in *St Louis Wkly Reveille*, 24 May 1847. Cadmus M. Wilcox related that one of the regulars, Capt. Philip Thompson, also scouted the Mexican positions. Wilcox, *History of the Mexican War* (Washington DC: Church News Publishing 1892) p.157.
55. Capt. Weightman had attended West Point for two years (1835–37) but had not graduated. Heitman (note 7) Vol.1 p.1,014. Hastings Diary, 28 Feb. 1847, Smith Papers, Benson Collection, U. of Texas (first quotation); Frank S. Edwards (note 31) p.112 (second quotation); Robinson (note 34) p.74.
56. Notes of recollection by an American artillerist are William C. Kennerly to Justin H. Smith, c.1900, in William C. Kennerly Papers, Missouri Historical Society, St Louis. For the fluidity of the battle see M.B. Edwards (note 6) pp.263–4; Frank S. Edwards (note 31) pp.113–14; Doniphan to Adjt Gen. Jones, 4 March 1847, in Connelley (note 8) pp.429–31. On the value of the artillery units to the US offensives see Eisenhower (note 28) pp.379–80.
57. Frank S. Edwards (note 31) p.120; Alcaraz (note 35) p.177; Robinson (note 34) pp.75–6.
58. M.B. Edwards (note 6) p.267, gives some specifics on Mexican losses. Other sources give varying estimates ranging up to a combined total of 1,000k, w and PoWs: *The Anglo Saxon* (occupation newspaper of American forces in Chihuahua), 19 March 1847, copy at Barker History Center, U. of Texas, Austin; Robinson (note 34) p.76; Frank S. Edwards (note 31) p.118; Gibson (note 34) pp.350–1. The Mexican gunpowder was found to be defective and this was one reason their artillery was ineffectual.
59. Jerome Kearful, 'Doniphan's Artillery', *Field Artillery Jnl* 40 (Jan.–Feb. 1950) p.71; Doniphan to Adjt Gen. Jones, 4 March 1847, quoted in Connelley (note 8) pp.433–4; Wooster to idem, 7 March 1847, quoted in Gibson (note 34) p.346n. 'Richardson Journal' (note 31) p.512.
60. The Mexicans had discussed such an intention prior to the battle. See Alcaraz (note 35) p.174.
61. Gibson (note 34) p.344. The problems of merchants travelling with Doniphan's column are mentioned by several diarists. One merchant in particular (Manuel X. Harmony) was required to make his goods and wagons available for use by the volunteers. The disagreement between Doniphan and his subordinate Lt Col Mitchell, on the one hand, and Harmony on the other, over damage to Harmony's property later resulted in a legal dispute that reached the US Supreme Court: Mitchell v. Harmony 13 Howard 115 [1852] pp.75–90. The best

36 MILITARY POWER: LAND WARFARE IN THEORY AND PRACTICE

analysis of the case is William E. Birkhimer, *Military Government and Martial Law* (Washington DC: Chapman 1892) pp.252–61.
62. As George L. Rives put the matter, 'Doniphan's spectacular success served also to confirm the Mexican hopelessness.' George L. Rives, *The United States and Mexico, 1821–1848*, 2 vols. (NY: Scribner's 1913) Vol.2, p.376.
63. The New Orleans newspapers presented the most thorough coverage, and other papers across the nation provided varying editorial comments. See New Orleans *Daily Picayune*, 10 April, 5 May (quotation), 15 May 1847, and *Daily Delta*, 5 and 12 May 1847; Washington *National Era*, 22 April (quote), 20 May 1847; Natchez *Mississippi Free Trader*, 5 May 1847 (quote), also 14 and 21 April, 12 and 19 May 1847; Columbia *Missouri Statesman*, 23 April 1847. Doniphan's hometown newspaper, the *Liberty Weekly Tribune*, gave many columns to the battle on 24 April, 22 and 29 May 1847; the St Louis *Daily Missouri Republican* had extensive coverage on 19 and 28 April, and 13 and 19 May 1847. The Fayette, Missouri, *Boon's Lick Times* wrote up the story on 24 April 1847, as did the Springfield, Missouri, *Advertiser*, on 4 May 1847. The St Louis *Wkly Reveille* devoted coverage on 3 and 24 May 1847. The Columbia *Statesman* added lengthy columns on 4 June 1847. Comments from other papers: Charleston, SC, *Courier*, 8 May 1847; Tallahassee *Floridian*, 24 April and 15 May 1847 (quote); Savannah, GA, *Daily Republican*, 10 May 1847; Richmond, VA, *Whig and Advertiser*, 7 May 1847; Indianapolis *Indiana State Sentinel*, 9 and 19 May 1847 (quote); Cleveland, Ohio, *Plain Dealer*, 5 May 1847; Cincinnati *Daily Enquirer*, 15 April and 2 May 1847; Newark, NJ, *Daily Advertiser*, 19 April 1847. Many other papers reported the battle; see, for instance, Baltimore *Niles National Register*, 1 and 15 May 1847; NY *Weekly Evening Post*, 22 April 1847; Hartford, CT, *Weekly Times*, 15 and 20 May 1847; Philadelphia, PA, *North American*, 17 and 19 April 1847; Little Rock *Arkansas State Gazette*, 24 April and 22 May 1847; NY *Tribune*, 19 April 1847; NY *Herald*, 19 April and 5 May 1847; Richmond, VA, *Enquirer*, 7 May 1847; Cincinnati, OH, *Daily Commercial*, 21 April and 4 May 1847; Baltimore, Maryland, *Sun*, 8 and 17 April 1847; Baltimore *Daily Republican and Argus*, 5 May 1847; Frankfort *Kentucky Yeoman*, 20 May 1847; Milwaukee, WI, *Daily Sentinel and Gazette*, 8 May 1847; Augusta, GA, *Constitutionalist*, 9 May 1847; Houston *Democratic Telegraph and Texas Register*, 31 May 1847.
64. Nineteenth century contemporaries and twentieth century writers have favored the comparison between Doniphan and Xenophon. Perhaps the most important such reference came in the tribute by William Cullen Bryant, editor of the NY *Evening Post*, in the *Post's* issue of 25 June 1847, but the New Orleans *Daily Delta* (7 and 14 May 1847) may have led the way with the first Xenophon reference. The Baltimore *Daily Republican and Argus*, 15 May 1847, repr. the *Delta's* 7 May article, and that was followed by *Niles National Register*, 12 June 1847 (quoting the St Louis *New Era*). Comparisons of Doniphan to Xenophon are also found in John S. Jenkins, *History of the War between the United States and Mexico* (Philadelphia: J.E. Potter c.1850) p.320; Santa Fe *Era Southwestern*, 5 Aug. 1880; George (note 54) pp.31, 149; Connelley (note 8) pp.438–40n.; E. Alexander Powell, *The Road to Glory* (NY: Scribner's 1915) p.237; Bernard DeVoto, 'Anabasis in Buckskin', *Harper's Magazine* 180 (March 1940) pp.400–10.
65. New Orleans *Daily Delta*, 14 May 1847; Washington *Daily Union*, 19 April 1847.
66. Marcy to Missouri Gov. John Edwards, 25 March 1847, Letters Sent by the Sec. of War Relating to Military Affairs, 1800–89, Microcopy M-6, roll 27, RG 107, NA; Marcy to Kearny, 10 May 1847, Marcy Papers, Library of Congress; *Diary of James K. Polk*, Milo M. Quaife (ed.), 4 vols. (Chicago: McClurg 1910) entry for 4 May 1847, Vol.3, p.10. An introduction to the politics of Polk's dealings with army officers is Singletary (note 3), pp.102–27.
67. Doniphan interview, Santa Fe *Era Southwestern*, 5 Aug. 1880; Marcy to Maj Samuel McKee (St. Louis), 23 May 1848, Secretary of War Letters Sent, Microcopy M-6, roll 28, RG 107, NA; Doniphan, Commencement Address, 16 June 1848, *Addresses Delivered in the Chapel at West Point* (note 7). Coverage of Doniphan's trip to West Point is in NY *Herald*, 18 June 1848; ibid., 24 June 1848. In the twentieth century, the army accorded Doniphan another honor. He was the only volunteer officer, with no experience in the regulars, out of 66 generals and two colonels selected to be in the 'Hall of Fame' for officers who have served at Ft Leavenworth, KS, during the history of the post.

The Spanish–American War: Land Battles in Cuba, 1895–1898

JOSEPH SMITH

The Spanish–American War between Spain and the United States began in late April 1898 and ended in mid-August 1898. The fighting in Cuba consisted of only one land battle of note and has attracted little attention from historians and military experts. 'There are few, if any, lessons for the British Army to learn from the conduct of this campaign', concluded a British military attaché who accompanied the American invasion in 1898.[1] More interest is shown in the conduct of senior army generals, most of whom emerged from the conflict with damaged rather than enhanced reputations. The most controversial figure is the American commander, Major General William R. Shafter, who is often portrayed as incompetent and old-fashioned.[2] Critics unkindly attribute his 'successes' to the fact that his Spanish opponents were even more prone to committing tactical blunders.[3] Sympathetic writers stress, however, the considerable organizational difficulties faced by Shafter in conducting a military campaign in the tropics.[4] Similarly, the negative attitude of the Spanish commanders in Cuba was not limited merely to the fighting during the summer of 1898, but should be understood in the context of a longer war which had started in 1895 as the 'Spanish–Cuban War' and involved the Spanish army in three years of unsuccessful counter-insurgency against a determined and resilient enemy seeking national liberation.[5]

The Spanish–Cuban War

At the beginning of 1895 the mood of the Spanish army in Cuba was positive rather than negative. On his arrival at Havana in March 1895, General Arsenio Martínez Campos expressed confidence that his troops could quickly overwhelm the insurrection which had recently broken out in the eastern province of Oriente. He publicly described his task as first, the containment of the activities of a few bandits and then, their isolation and systematic destruction. In private Martínez Campos spoke wistfully of returning home victoriously to Spain by November. But the expected military success was not forthcoming. In January 1896 Martínez Campos was replaced by General Valeriano Weyler who promised to 'fight war with war' and predicted that the conflict would be brought to an end in less than two years.[6] At first, Weyler sent out a succession of 'flying [cavalry] columns' to exert constant pressure on the various insurgent units. When the dry season began in November 1896, he mobilized a large army of 12,000 men which marched from Havana to search and destroy the enemy forces in Oriente.

The offensive operations of both Martínez Campos and Weyler were fully supported by the government in Madrid which met repeated requests for additional military resources by dispatching more than 200,000 troops – virtually one half of the Spanish Army – to the island during the period from 1895 to 1898. Consequently, Martínez Campos and Weyler could formulate their strategy with the knowledge that the forces under their command were vastly superior to the insurgents in terms of men and military equipment. But these advantages proved of little material value when the Spanish army moved from the western plains to the mountainous terrain of central and especially eastern Cuba, where the insurgents were mostly located. In addition, sustained campaigning in these particular regions was essentially restricted to the dry winter months because the rainy season, which lasted from May until September, frequently made roads impassable and transformed streams into rivers.

Cuban Guerrilla Tactics

Moreover, the Spanish generals had to contend with skilful and determined adversaries. The insurgent leaders, Máximo Gómez and Antonio Maceo, were veterans of the earlier Ten Years' War, a guerrilla conflict which had lasted from 1868 to 1878. In particular, Máximo Gómez proved to be an effective commander whose ability to elude capture and avoid defeat attracted favourable comparisons with George Washington in the American press. Instead of being contained and isolated by Martínez Campos, Máximo Gómez defiantly claimed in the summer of 1895 that he was in command of a 'Liberating Army' which had grown to more than 20,000 men. The 'army' never actually came together as a collective unit,[7] but was divided into small mobile bands of between 20 and 100 men usually operating as cavalry in their own local region where they were able to live off the land and find means of escape and shelter when necessary. Their orders were to avoid pitched battles and to concentrate on hit and run raids against vulnerable targets such as railway and telegraph lines and remote sugar plantations. An American observer stressed the inconclusive nature of the fighting:

> A well-planned, long-sustained battle is unknown in Cuba. The Cubans if taken by surprise, scatter immediately. The Spaniards have been ambushed so often that they are very loath to follow. Unless in greatly superior numbers, they avoid trying issues with detachments they may chance to meet. In the uplands and mountains the Cuban bands are fairly secure from assault. They dash into the open country, pounce upon a column, kill a few soldiers, and get away with small loss. The Spaniards fear to pursue, lest they be led into a narrow pass and [are] shot to pieces – a fate which many a valorous column has met.[8]

Replying to Spanish criticism that 'Cuban generals don't put up a fight', Máximo Gómez, astutely remarked: 'This means they don't put up a fight on the Spanish-chosen territory. They put up a fight when they want to, and they refuse to enter a combat which would favour the enemy.'[9]

The successful guerrilla tactics of the insurgents meant that, instead of being deployed on offensive operations, the majority of Spanish troops in Cuba had to be assigned to defensive duty protecting forts, towns, property and lines of communication. In particular regions, where the loyalty of the civilian population was regarded as uncertain, Weyler implemented what became known as the policy of 'reconcentration'. In effect he empowered his commanders to empty the countryside of people, crops and livestock. The displaced Cubans would be 'reconcentrated' in fortified camps close to towns and cities with large Spanish garrisons. Without supplies and aid from the rural population, Weyler reckoned that the insurgents would disintegrate as a fighting force. But few military gains were forthcoming. Although the insurgents were weakened, the ruthless strategy of 'fighting war with war' merely increased economic devastation and contributed to the further alienation of the civilian population from Spanish rule.[10]

The failure to secure tangible military successes against the insurgents steadily reduced the morale of the Spanish army. In fact, service in Cuba was very unpopular, so that most of the reinforcements from Spain were not regular soldiers but young conscripts who were hurriedly despatched overseas with minimal training and preparation. Moreover, their motivation and physical condition were soon severely tested by the grim conditions of service in the tropics. Not only were they fighting a fierce and elusive enemy in an unfamiliar country, but they also ran the risk of contracting one of the many tropical diseases endemic during the Cuban rainy season.

Indeed, the Spanish forces were permanently weakened by sickness. For every single Spanish soldier killed in combat, it was estimated that ten died from disease. Once when Máximo Gómez was asked who were his best generals, he replied, 'June, July, and August'.[11]

Despite their proclaimed intention to move aggressively against the enemy, both Martínez Campos and Weyler were eventually compelled to halt their offensive operations and concentrate on defence. Although Spanish control remained secure in the loyal western provinces, it was very different in Oriente where the insurgents gained in strength and vigorously contested control of the countryside, so that Spanish troops became increasingly reluctant to venture outside their protected forts and garrisons. The collapse of Spanish optimism was symbolically underlined in November 1897 when Weyler was replaced by General Ramón Blanco. Instead of 'fighting war with war', Blanco stressed a policy of reconciliation and quietly cancelled Weyler's plan for a major winter offensive against the insurgents. It was an admission that, after almost three years of warfare, the Spanish army no longer believed it could defeat the insurgents by military means.[12]

The US Declares War

The formal outbreak of hostilities between Spain and the United States on 25 April 1898 did not immediately alter what had become a state of virtual military standstill in Cuba. The fact that the rainy season was imminent led the Spanish government to assume that any major invasion by American forces was not likely to occur before October at the earliest. In the meantime, the island was more than adequately defended by an army of 150,000 Spanish soldiers including a substantial force of 40,000 in or close to the city of Havana, which was regarded as the probable first point of attack by the Americans. It was also expected that the Americans would prefer to use their powerful navy and mount a naval blockade of the island rather than risk an armed invasion. Consequently, Spanish hopes of ultimate military success rested not on the outcome of land battles but on the performance of their navy and its ability to break the American blockade and gain command of the seas.

In the United States the popular slogan of 'on to Havana' implied that American troops would soon be landed in Cuba to seize the capital city. Such optimism, however, was quite unfounded because the American army initially lacked the means and the manpower to launch a successful attack against entrenched defensive forces. In fact, senior army officers regarded a major invasion as unnecessary because the decisive battles were expected to occur at sea. They anticipated therefore that the army's role in the actual fighting would be restricted to the landing of small mobile units to supply and assist the Cuban insurgents. The strategy of emphasizing the combat role of the insurgents also had the advantage of limiting the exposure of unacclimatized American troops to the deadly tropical diseases which were known to be endemic in Cuba during the rainy season.

President William McKinley recognized the crucial importance of the war at sea, but he was mindful of the considerable political and public pressure for an early and substantial operation by the army against the Spaniards in Cuba. Accordingly, orders were issued to assemble an invasion force at Tampa, Florida. The troops consisted mainly of regular units of the Fifth [Army] Corps under the command of Major General William Rufus Shafter. Shafter was a Civil War veteran who had spent much of his subsequent military career serving in the West. Although he had no experience of leading large numbers of troops in battle, his appointment to command Fifth Corps was explained by a combination of seniority, his friendship with the Adjutant General, Henry Corbin, and the fact that he hailed from Michigan, the home state of Secretary of War, Russell Alger. More than 60 years old and weighing over 330 pounds, Shafter would find service in the tropics physically trying and debilitating.

Soon after assuming command Shafter was informed that his mission would be to organize a major assault on Havana (see Map 2). In early May President McKinley approved a plan that envisaged an amphibious landing to secure a beachhead at Mariel, about 25 miles west of Havana. This would then be followed by an advance on the capital. The operation proved impracticable, however, so long as the reputedly powerful Spanish squadron of armoured warships under Admiral Pascual Cervera remained at large. Until the enemy ships were located and destroyed, the commander of the North Atlantic Squadron, Rear Admiral William T. Sampson, could not release any warships to provide protective cover for the transportation of American troops from Tampa to Cuba. On 29 May, however, it was learned that Cervera's squadron had taken refuge at the southeastern end of the island, in Santiago de Cuba. Sampson immediately proceeded to Santiago de Cuba and mounted a naval blockade of the harbour.

Cervera's action suddenly transformed a remote region into the focal point of American strategic concern. Sampson wished to strike at the Spanish ships as quickly as possible, but he judged that the powerful artillery batteries mounted in forts on either side of the entrance to the harbour made a direct naval attack too risky. He needed the support of ground troops and recommended a joint assault by the army and navy. Consequently, President McKinley postponed the projected operation against Havana and instructed Shafter to mobilize the Fifth Corps for naval convoy to Santiago de Cuba, make a landing at a suitable point and 'cooperate most earnestly' with the navy to destroy the Spanish fleet in the harbour.[13] The convoy containing almost 17,000 troops left Tampa on 14 June and joined the American squadron in the waters off Santiago de Cuba on 20 June.

The US Landing

The first matter for Shafter to decide was where to disembark his army. A landing close to Santiago de Cuba was ruled out by the high cliffs and bluffs that extended for several miles to the east and west of the harbour. Guantánamo Bay offered the best facilities for disembarking a large army, but it was more than 40 miles distant from Santiago de Cuba. Moreover, Shafter had no intention of repeating what all the military manuals regarded as a disastrous decision made by the British in 1741, when a British army of 5,000 men was decimated by fever and disease in attempting to march from Guantánamo to Santiago de Cuba. By default, the best sites were the small coastal villages of Siboney and Daiquirí which were less than 20 miles from the city (see Map 3). After discussion with Sampson and the local insurgent leader, Calixto García, Shafter chose Daiquirí.

The operation was approached with apprehension because it was feared that the Spanish garrison at Daiquirí would entrench themselves in strong defensive positions on the cliffs overlooking the beach. But there was no resistance to the disembarkation which commenced at Daiquirí on 22 June.[14] By evening 6,000 men had landed and the beachhead was successfully established. The disembarkation of the troops, their equipment and supplies continued for several days.[15] On land the Fifth Corps was organized into three main divisions. There were two infantry divisions each numbering 5,000 troops, the large majority of whom were regular soldiers. Brigadier General J. Ford Kent commanded 1st Infantry Division. Brigadier General Henry W. Lawton headed 2nd Infantry Division. In command of the Cavalry Division of 2,700 men was Major General Joseph Wheeler. With the exception of a few senior officers, cavalrymen were without horses and fought as infantry or 'dismounted cavalry' throughout the whole campaign. In addition, an Independent Brigade of about 1,100 regular infantry under Brigadier General John C. Bates acted as a reserve unit. The arrival on 27 June of a transport ship containing 2,500 Michigan Volunteers led to the creation of a brigade of volunteer infantry commanded by Brigadier General Henry Duffield. There were also separate units of engineers, signal corps, medical personnel and a battalion of light artillery with the capacity to deploy 16 3.2in field guns and four Gatling machine-guns.

As the beachhead was being established at Daiquirí, Shafter ordered Lawton to take two regiments of 2nd Infantry Division and advance to the

THE SPANISH–AMERICAN WAR: LAND BATTLES 43

MAP 2
The Spanish–American War: Spanish Dispositions, 20 June 1898

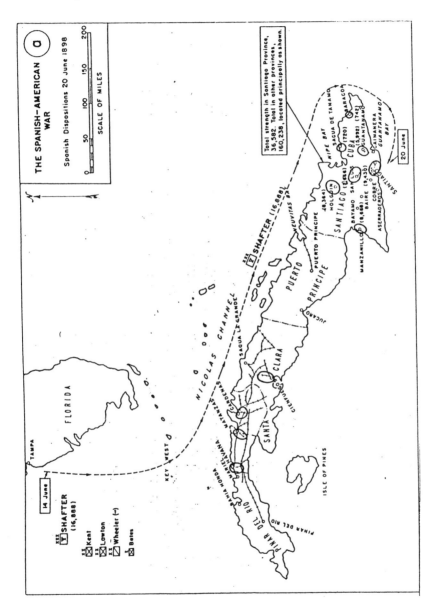

Source: The West Point Atlas of American Wars I (1689–1900)

MAP 3
Santiago Campaign: Initial Operations 22–24 June 1898

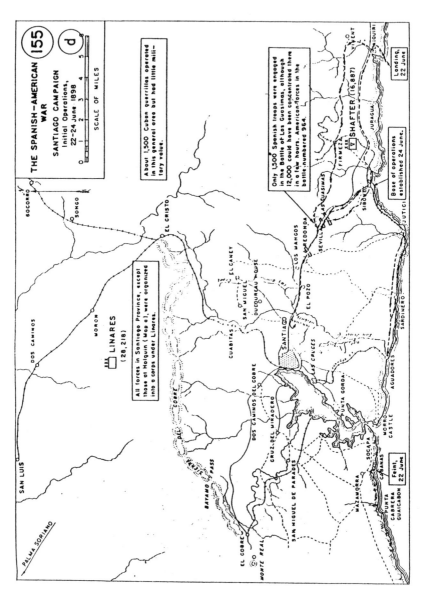

Source: *The West Point Atlas of American Wars I (1689–1900)*

larger village of Siboney, which was seven miles distant. Lawton made slow progress along the Camino Real [Royal Highway], an unpaved single-track 'road' with dense tropical undergrowth on each side, but reached Siboney without mishap on the following morning. The Spanish garrison had evidently repeated the example of their colleagues at Daiquirí and had withdrawn as the Americans approached. On learning this, Shafter subsequently sent instructions to his generals at Daiquirí to move their units also to the vicinity of Siboney. Fearing a possible counter-attack from the large Spanish army in Santiago de Cuba estimated to be in excess of 10,000 men, Shafter's intention was evidently to build up a strong defensive position at Siboney until the disembarkation was successfully accomplished.

Skirmish at Las Guásimas

Shafter's cautious approach clashed with the eagerness of his officers and men to spring into combat with the enemy. The combative spirit was exemplified in 'Fighting Joe' Wheeler, an ex-Confederate cavalry general with a bellicose reputation gained from the Civil War. While proceeding with his dismounted cavalry regiments towards Siboney on 23 June, Wheeler learned that about 1,500 Spanish soldiers from the local garrisons and forts were regrouping at Las Guásimas, a stopping-place on the Camino Real, close to the hamlet of Sevilla about three miles to the northwest. Confident of an easy victory, he gave orders for a 'reconnaissance in force' against the enemy.[16] Almost 1,000 cavalrymen, including the regiment of 1st Volunteer Cavalry popularly known as the 'Rough Riders', resumed their march at daybreak on 24 June. Previously the Spaniards had avoided combat with the Americans, but, on this occasion, they positioned themselves behind stone fortifications on the top of a ridge. Colonel Theodore Roosevelt, the most celebrated member of the 'Rough Riders', was initially delighted by his first sight of the tropical forest in all its splendour, but he was soon disconcerted by the particular dangers of jungle warfare:

> The air seemed full of the rustling sound of the Mauser bullets, for the Spaniards knew the trails by which we were advancing, and opened heavily on our position. Moreover, as we advanced we were, of course, exposed, and they could see us and fire. But they themselves were entirely invisible.[17]

Fierce fighting began at 8 a.m. when the Americans charged forward and sparked off a battle that raged for more than two hours. The experience was a rude awakening to reality for American troops who had become accustomed to believe that the Spaniards lacked the will to fight. Wheeler was taken aback by the sheer amount of rifle fire and reckoned that it was more intense than any he had experienced during the Civil War. The explanation was simple. The Spaniards were using rifles equipped with magazines which enabled them to fire much more rapidly than the rifled muskets of 33 years previously. Just after 10 a.m., however, the firing decreased as the Spanish troops began to pull back towards Santiago de Cuba. Wheeler was jubilant and, with his thoughts set on another time and place, reportedly cried out: 'We've got the damn Yankees on the run.'[18] Although the American press proclaimed a notable victory for the United States cavalry, a more accurate description was that a skirmish had taken place in which the Spaniards had made a tactical withdrawal. As regards casualties, 16 Americans died and 52 were wounded while Spanish losses were 10 killed and 25 wounded.

Even though Wheeler had flouted the intent of his orders, Shafter was pleased that the enemy had been dislodged from a strategic position guarding the road to Santiago de Cuba. 'Your news is excellent', he wrote personally to Wheeler.[19] Instructions were given for the speedy despatch of reinforcements of men and artillery so that the American military front was decisively shifted inland to Sevilla. This development was unwelcome to Sampson who firmly believed that the priority of any land operation should be the prompt destruction of the artillery batteries at the entrance to the harbour. The American navy would then be able to enter the bay and destroy the Spanish squadron. Shafter, however, favoured an inland advance on the city which lay five miles north of the harbour entrance. In doing so he was not only unilaterally rejecting Sampson's scheme but also adopting a strategy to capture Santiago de Cuba which emphasized the combat role of the Army while significantly diminishing the contribution of the Navy.[20]

Spanish Dispositions

The American military build-up at Sevilla was greatly facilitated by the curious unwillingness of the Spaniards to move aggressively against the invading forces. Part of the explanation was that the Spanish commander at Santiago de Cuba, General Arsenio Linares Pomba, had never seriously expected the city to become the target of an American land invasion.[21] Blockaded from the sea and conscious of large insurgent forces operating in the countryside, Linares clung to the siege mentality so characteristic of Spanish military strategy. He showed no inclination to reinforce and deploy the local garrisons at Siboney, Daiquirí and Guantánamo to confront the Americans as they landed and attempted to establish their beachhead. Instead, he chose to concentrate on organizing the defence of Santiago de Cuba. The largest number of troops supported by heavy artillery were placed around the harbour entrance, because it was considered the most likely point of attack by the Americans. The threat of insurgent raids meant that the outskirts of the city were already lined with rows of trenches and rifle-pits protected by barbed wire. On the eastern side about half a mile away on the hilly ground of the San Juan Heights (see Map 4), were several strategically located blockhouses that overlooked the Camino Real and the various trails which approached the city from the north and east. Fewer than 500 Spanish soldiers manned the fortified positions on San Juan Hill and Kettle Hill, the two prominent ridges on the San Juan Heights, while a similar number were assigned to defend the hamlet of El Caney five miles to the northeast. The numbers were relatively low because Linares regarded these garrisons as advance fortified positions rather than vital defensive strongholds.

The strategy of static defence pursued by Linares effectively handed the military initiative to Shafter. It was a heavy responsibility for a general who had no previous experience of conducting a major military campaign. Believing that Linares possessed ample resources to launch a surprise attack or out-flanking manoeuvre, Shafter initially concentrated on completing the disembarkation and establishing a viable system of command and supply on land. Following on from the decision to build a forward base at Sevilla, Shafter formulated a plan to attack El Caney to the northeast of the city rather than the forts at the harbour entrance, where the main Spanish forces were known to be located. The intention was simply to overwhelm the Spanish defensive line at what was considered to be its weakest point. The general's cautious attitude was underlined in a dispatch to the Secretary of War, Alger, on 28 June, explaining that any forward advance would be delayed until the maximum number of troops were available. 'There is no necessity for haste', Shafter argued, 'as we are growing stronger and they weaker each day.'[22]

Shafter's careful preparations were disrupted, however, by a report that a Spanish relief column from Manzanillo had been sighted to the northwest and was only a few days march away. The Spaniards were estimated to number at least 8,000 men with plentiful supplies of weapons, ammunition and provisions. Their arrival would significantly transform the military balance in favour of Linares. Appreciating the need for urgent action, Shafter scheduled his attack for Friday 1 July. However, a combination of inexperience and haste resulted in orders being communicated verbally rather than in written form. Although the exact objective was never specified, senior officers understood that they were to move forward and be prepared to fight to gain control of the San Juan Heights. Shafter's plans also retained a preliminary attack upon El Caney because he feared the hamlet might be used by the Spaniards as a base to outflank the American troops engaged in attacking the San Juan Heights.

MAP 4
Santiago Campaign: Situation about noon 1 July 1898

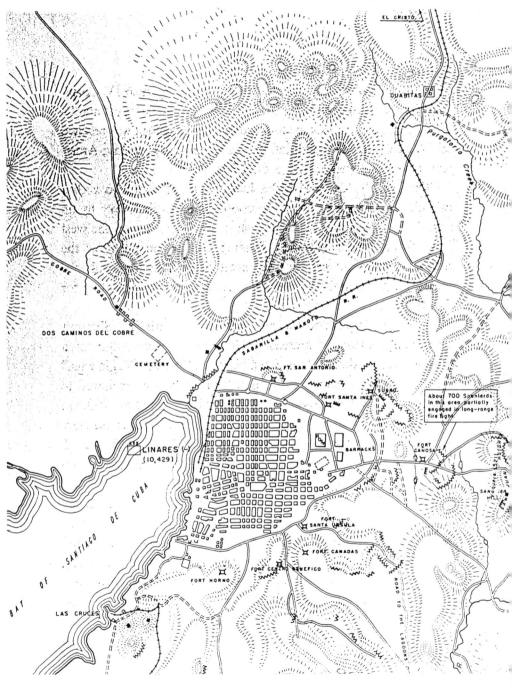

Source: The West Point Atlas of American Wars I (1689–1900)

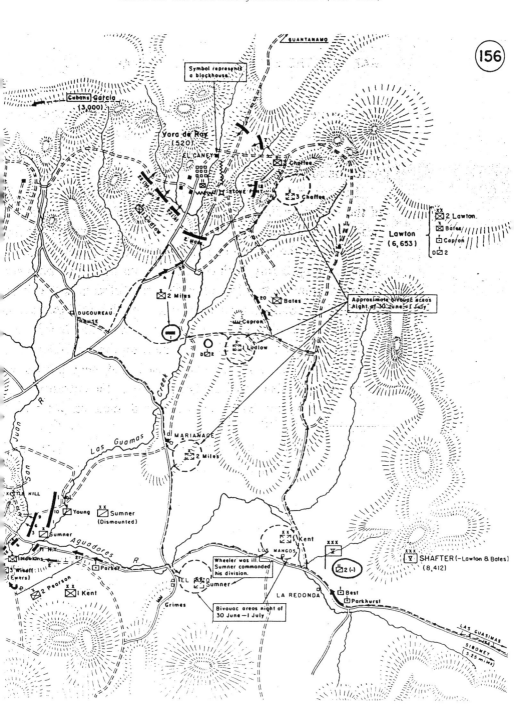

The task of capturing El Caney was assigned to Lawton's 2nd Infantry Division with support from a light artillery battery commanded by Captain Allyn Capron. Influenced by the recent example of Las Guásimas, in which 1,500 Spaniards had been forced into retreat by less than 1,000 American cavalrymen, Lawton confidently predicted that the garrison of 500 at El Caney would surrender in two hours. He would then swing south to join Kent's 1st Infantry Division and Wheeler's Cavalry Division, both of which would have already positioned themselves for the final advance on the San Juan Heights. Shafter's straightforward plan of battle also included a diversionary raid by Duffield's Michigan Volunteers against Fort Aguadores at the harbour entrance. The intention was to divert attention away from the San Juan Heights by leading Linares to believe that a major attack was about to take place at the harbour entrance.

The US Capture of El Caney

The feint along the coast proceeded exactly according to plan. At daybreak on 1 July, the Michigan Volunteers under General Duffield marched from Siboney towards Fort Aguadores. Ahead of their advance Admiral Sampson ordered a brief bombardment of the fort.[23] In the afternoon Duffield duly returned to Siboney without having directly engaged the enemy. Meanwhile, more dramatic events were occurring further to the north. Overnight Lawton had approached El Caney with 5,000 men of 2nd Infantry Division. Shortly after 6.30 a.m. on 1 July Capron's artillery battery opened fire. At 7 a.m. the infantry brigades began their advance across the open ground in front of the Spanish positions. They were halted in their tracks by continuous volleys of rifle fire and forced to withdraw. A fierce battle ensued which lasted for several hours and prevented Lawton from supporting the attack on the San Juan Heights as planned. At 2 p.m. Shafter ordered Lawton to break away from El Caney and join the main assault against the San Juan Heights. 'I would not bother with little block-houses; they cannot harm us', he remarked.[24] After committing one third of his army to its capture, Shafter's sudden dismissal of El Caney as strategically insignificant appeared puzzling and implied that he had made a tactical mistake in dividing his attacking forces. In effect, the new orders were redundant because Lawton's troops were so actively engaged in combat that it was not feasible to pull them back. The fighting therefore continued until the Americans eventually won control of El Caney at 4.15 p.m..

Of the original Spanish garrison of 520 men, 235 had been killed or wounded and 120 taken prisoner. American casualties were listed at 81 dead and 360 wounded. The American commanders were at a loss to explain how 520 Spaniards could resist 5,000 Americans for more than nine hours. They could only believe that the Spaniards fought so bravely out of the conviction that they would be slaughtered without mercy if they surrendered. In reality, the Americans showed that they were tactically naive and lacked experience of combat. They had approached the battle without fully appreciating the difficulties of mounting a frontal assault across open and difficult terrain against a well-entrenched and resolute enemy. But El Caney was not a unique experience. A similar infantry battle was taking place just a few miles to the south at the San Juan Heights.

Early in the morning of 1 July, 8,000 American troops were assembled at El Pozo, a hill to the west of Sevilla. The sound of guns firing to the north indicated that the assault at El Caney had begun on schedule. At 7 a.m. Brigadier General Samuel S. Sumner's[25] Cavalry Division set off on foot. Their instructions were to continue along the Camino Real for about two miles at which time the San Juan Heights would come into view and they would then move towards the right in order to mount an attack upon Kettle Hill. Kent's 1st Infantry Division followed behind the cavalrymen. They would seek to branch to the left and aim for San Juan Hill, which was the larger ridge located about 200 yards to the west of Kettle Hill. All available units were included in the advance. Evidently, Shafter was confident that the San Juan Heights were lightly defended and that his 8,000 men would overwhelm the enemy. The fact that there was no mention of an attack on the city of Santiago de Cuba indicates that Shafter's purpose was a forward advance to gain a position of strategic advantage rather than to fight a pitched battle.

Progress was painfully slow as thousands of fully-equipped soldiers groped their way along the congested 'road', the dismounted cavalry to the right and the infantry to the left. As planned, the advance received artillery support. Just after 8 a.m. Captain George Grimes' battery of four 3.2in guns near El Pozo began firing on the Spanish positions. After a lull of some minutes the Spanish artillery replied with shrapnel shells that fell close to Grimes' battery and inflicted numbers of casualties. The deadly accuracy of the Spanish gunners was greatly assisted by their ability to pinpoint the position of their opponents from the smoke of the black powder ammunition used by the American guns.[26] By contrast Grimes could not locate the Spanish guns because the latter used smokeless powder. Consequently, Grimes' battery was able to contribute little to assist the American advance.

The US Storming of San Juan Hill

Except for shots from Spanish snipers concealed in the brush, American troops did not come under sustained fire as they struggled along the Camino Real. The Spaniards on the San Juan Heights patiently held their fire until 10 a.m. when the advance detachments of Americans emerged from the jungle and came into open view as they forded the San Juan River about 400 yards away. The 71st New York Volunteers were the first of the American units to experience the full impact of Spanish crossfire from rifles and artillery. The volunteers panicked and were only prevented from rushing into headlong retreat by the fact that it was impossible to fall back against the mass of men moving forward. In retrospect, this proved fortunate because Shafter had prepared no contingency plans for a retreat, whether tactical or enforced. The American journalist, Richard Harding Davis, graphically described the infantrymen as having entered a 'chute of death'. He explained:

> The situation was desperate. Our troops could not retreat, as the trail for two miles behind them was wedged with men. They could not remain where they were for they were being shot to pieces. There was only one thing they could do – go forward and take the San Juan hills by assault.[27]

Americans in the rear of the forward movement were startled by the transformation of the front line into a virtual 'killing zone'. Confusion increased as casualties mounted and units became separated and entangled in the brush and jungle adjoining the Camino Real. Shafter's aide at the front line, Lieutenant John D. Miley, used couriers to communicate with senior officers in an effort to reform their units and coordinate a forward advance. At 1 p.m. a direct attack was launched on the Heights. As the men of 1st Infantry Division surged forward they were supported by four Gatling machine-guns which a detachment commanded by Lieutenant John Parker had managed to drag to the front. The Gatling guns effectively demonstrated their value as an offensive weapon. Each gun sprayed 900 rounds per minute at the Spaniards on San Juan Hill. There was only enough ammunition for eight minutes, but that proved long enough to unnerve the majority of the defenders who abandoned their positions and fled towards Santiago de Cuba. San Juan Hill was in American hands at 1.30 p.m. The achievement was vividly evoked in the eye-witness report by Richard Harding Davis:

> It was a miracle of self-sacrifice, a triumph of bull-dog courage, which one watched breathless with wonder. The fire of the Spanish riflemen, who still stuck bravely to their posts, doubled and trebled in fierceness, the crests of the hills crackled and burst in amazed roars, and rippled with waves of tiny flame. But the blue line crept steadily up and on, and then, near the top, the broken fragments gathered together with a sudden burst of speed, the Spaniards appeared for a moment outlined against the sky and poised for instant flight, fired a last volley and fled before the swift moving wave that leaped and sprang up after them.[28]

The charge up the hill was undoubtedly a brave and heroic action, although Davis omitted to point out the considerable numerical superiority of the Americans. He also exaggerated the degree of resistance offered by the Spaniards. The Spanish trenches and rifle-pits were dug into the crest of the ridge so that rifle fire could be directed into the distance at troops in the valley below. It was, however, much more difficult to fire upon an enemy advancing up the hill. This factor plus the shock given to the Spaniards of suddenly receiving a hail of bullets from the Gatling guns allowed the American troops to rush the Spanish positions without suffering heavy casualties.

As Kent's infantry were storming San Juan Hill, Sumner's cavalrymen similarly charged up Kettle Hill, as the surviving Spaniards chose to fall back to Santiago de Cuba rather than defend their positions to the death. Having captured the San Juan Heights, however, the American attack came to a stop. An advance on Santiago de Cuba was tempting, but was hardly feasible for men who had experienced several hours of continuous marching and fighting. American officers were more concerned about the possibility of an enemy counter-attack and instructed their troops to dig trenches and establish fortified positions on the hill. Another necessary task was to remove the dead and tend to the wounded. Shafter initially believed that American losses were limited to 400 and was shocked to learn later that they were more than three times the first estimate. Altogether 205 Americans were killed and 1,180 wounded. At El Caney 81 were killed and 360 wounded. Kent's Infantry Division listed 89 killed and 489 wounded in the attack on San Juan Hill, while Sumner's Cavalry Division recorded 35 killed and 328 wounded at Kettle Hill. Spanish casualties were 591 consisting of 215 killed and 376 wounded.

In fact, the capture of the Heights was initially assessed as only a partial American success because a large and yet to be defeated Spanish army still remained behind the formidable defences of Santiago de Cuba. Despite receiving reliable information that the Spaniards were desperately short of food and supplies, Shafter could not eliminate the possibility that they would launch either a counter-attack against the vulnerable American position on the San Juan Heights or an out-flanking movement against the extremely thin American defensive line which now stretched all the way from the coast to El Caney. The chances of a vigorous Spanish response would also be increased by the imminent arrival of the relief column from Manzanillo. On 2 July Shafter informed the War Department that he was seriously considering falling back to a more easily defensible position. After receiving this telegram, Secretary of War Alger gloomily noted: 'Sunday, the 3d of July was the darkest day of the war.'[29]

The course of events, however, was dramatically affected by a battle taking place at sea rather than on land. Shafter's strategy proved successful to the extent that the loss of the San Juan Heights resulted in Cervera and his fleet attempting to escape from the harbour on 3 July. The Spanish warships were completely destroyed in less than four hours. Ironically, by removing the original purpose for sending the Fifth Corps to Santiago de Cuba, Cervera's disastrous sortie actually strengthened the case for a tactical American withdrawal from the San Juan Heights. But such action was unnecessary because the Spaniards were thoroughly demoralized and disheartened. Despite its impressive listed strength, the garrison at Santiago de Cuba was no different to the rest of the army in Cuba in being badly affected by constant privation and sickness. On 1 July the Spaniards had suffered not only defeat at El Caney and the San Juan Heights but also the loss of General Linares, who had been seriously wounded and evacuated to hospital in Santiago de Cuba. Although the new Spanish commander, General Jose Toral, accepted the inevitability of military defeat, he did not possess the authority to surrender the city. This decision rested with the Captain General in Havana and the Spanish government in Madrid. A state of virtual truce ensued for several days between the American and Spanish forces while Toral waited for definite instructions from his superiors.

Spanish Surrender

Suffering from ill-health and still dismayed by the scale of casualties incurred on 1 July, Shafter welcomed the military standstill which served his purposes very well because it afforded time to reinforce and strengthen the army's defensive line. To his further relief, there was no need to launch an assault on the city.[30] In Madrid, the Spanish government accepted that the war must be brought to an end. On 15 July Toral received the necessary authority to surrender and next day signed the articles of capitulation. On 17 July Shafter and the Fifth Corps formally marched into Santiago de Cuba and took possession of the city. The total of Spanish troops surrendered eventually came to 22,700, of whom 13,558 came from the city of Santiago de Cuba, and the rest from the other neighbouring garrisons in Oriente.

Cervera's surprise decision to dock in Santiago de Cuba had proved advantageous to the American army in that the major land battle of the war did not take place, as had generally been expected, in the centre of Spanish military power around Havana. Consequently, the large majority of Spanish troops in Cuba never entered into combat against the Americans. Ironically, this allowed the Spanish army to claim that it had never actually been defeated in a pitched battle in Cuba. Nevertheless, senior army officers were condemned for pursuing a misguided strategy of concentrating large numbers of troops in defensive positions where they simply waited for the

THE SPANISH-AMERICAN WAR: LAND BATTLES 55

enemy to appear. Such tactics failed to defeat the insurgents and had little chance of succeeding against the superior military resources of the Americans. Indeed, with the exception of the resolute defence of El Caney and the San Juan Heights, the Spanish Army derived precious little military glory from three years of warfare which claimed the lives of more than 50,000 soldiers and sailors, bankrupted the country, and brought about the effective dissolution of the Spanish empire.

Shafter's Generalship

For Americans the conflict between their country and Spain was summed up in the celebrated phrase 'splendid little war'.[31] Success was attributed to superior American military skill and strength of character, as exemplified by the likes of Colonel Roosevelt and the naval hero of Manila Bay, Commodore George Dewey, both of whom were spoken of as future American presidential material. General Shafter also enjoyed praise from contemporaries, but his military reputation soon came under criticism. His overall strategy was regarded as being overly cautious. Naval officers such as French Ensor Chadwick were particularly aggrieved that Shafter did not follow Sampson's recommendation to launch an early assault on the forts at the harbour entrance. Whether this would have resulted in quicker military success and fewer casualties than at El Caney and the San Juan Heights cannot be conclusively demonstrated. Certainly, the harbour entrance was strongly defended so that Shafter had good reason to prefer advancing by an interior route. On the other hand, the resulting personal tension between Shafter and Sampson definitely impaired co-operation between the army and navy.[32]

A similar debate has concerned the wisdom of Shafter's insistence on attacking El Caney. Critics have argued that dividing the attacking army meant that 5,000 American soldiers were not available for the purpose of concentrating maximum force in the assault on the San Juan Heights or as reserves to exploit the victory and advance into Santiago de Cuba. In Shafter's defence, Lawton had confidently predicted that El Caney would be captured in two hours. Moreover, the absence of Lawton's troops in the attack on the San Juan Heights did not make the difference between victory and defeat because the 8,000 men actually committed to the assault proved sufficient to overrun the Spanish positions.[33] No doubt, Linares can be faulted for not rushing substantial reinforcements to the battle, but this should not detract from the fact that Shafter had actually perceived and taken advantage of a weak point in the Spanish defensive line.

The most telling criticism of Shafter's generalship is that he failed to exercise effective command and control on 1 July. His inexperience in conducting complicated military manoeuvres showed in the lack of thorough reconnaissance of the battlefield and the compression of 8,000 men into one long marching column. Officers were confused by the absence of written orders and their commander's reluctance to state the exact objective of the advance. Nor was this rectified by personal leadership in the field. Suffering from gout and heat exhaustion, Shafter remained at his headquarters to the east of El Pozo where he attempted to maintain contact with the front line by telephone and the use of mounted couriers. It was not the most efficient means of communications, but the general's aides at El Pozo and the front line ensured that the advance continued until the San Juan Heights were captured.

The outcome was a military victory which significantly contributed to a rapid end of the war. It might be argued that Shafter was fortunate in facing an enemy that was already crippled and demoralized by three years of colonial warfare. But Spaniards could fight tenaciously in defence as was demonstrated at Las Guásimas, El Caney and the San Juan Heights. Whatever the criticism of the strategy and tactics, Shafter could claim an impressive record of achievement. In less than four weeks he had commanded an army which had landed on enemy territory and defeated the enemy in a small but decisive battle that had resulted in the capture of Cuba's second largest city and the surrender of more than 20,000 prisoners. In a fitting tribute to Shafter and the Fifth Corps, Secretary of War Alger remarked that 'the expedition was successful beyond the most sanguine expectation'.[34]

NOTES

1. The comments of Capt. Arthur H. Lee, cited in Edward Ranson, 'British Military and Naval Observers in the Spanish–American War', *Jnl of American Studies* 3 (1969) p.51. American troops were also despatched to Puerto Rico and the Philippines, where the opposition was weaker than in Cuba. The fighting came to an abrupt end in mid-Aug. 1898, although the American army became subsequently entangled in a colonial war against the Filipino insurgents which dragged on until July 1902. The most detailed accounts of military events are French Ensor Chadwick, *The Relations of the United States and Spain: The Spanish–American War* (London: Chapman & Hall, 3 vols. 1911) and Herbert H. Sargent, *The Campaign of Santiago de Cuba* (Chicago, IL: McClurg, 3 vols., 1907). A concise modern study is Joseph Smith, *The Spanish-American War: Conflict in the Caribbean and the Pacific, 1895–1902* (London: Longman 1994).

2. The negative image owes much to the widely-quoted remarks of Theodore Roosevelt that: 'Not since the campaign of Crassus against the Parthians has there been so criminally incompetent a General as Shafter.' See Roosevelt to Lodge, 5 July 1898, cited in Elting E. Morison (ed.) *The Letters of Theodore Roosevelt* (Cambridge: Harvard UP, 8 vols. 1951) Vol.ii, p.849. Similar comments have described Shafter's conduct of operations as 'worthy of the best military thinking of the early Middle Ages' and 'suggestive of the inarticulate, unimaginative generalship of the First World War'. See Newton F. Tolman, *The Search For General Miles* (NY: Putnam 1968) p.198 and Jack Cameron Dierks, *A Leap To Arms: The*

THE SPANISH-AMERICAN WAR: LAND BATTLES 57

 Cuban Campaign of 1898 (Philadelphia: Lippincott 1970) p.185.
3. E.g. see Dierks (note 2) pp.182–3.
4. See the balanced appraisal in Sargent (note 1) Vol.i, pp.150–66.
5. For the significance of events predating American intervention in 1898 see Louis A. Pérez Jr, *Cuba Between Empires, 1878–1902* (Pittsburgh UP 1983) and Philip S. Foner, *The Spanish-Cuban-American War and the Birth of American Imperialism, 1895–1902* (NY: Monthly Review Press, 2 vols. 1972).
6. Valeriano Weyler, *Mi Mando en Cuba* (Madrid: Felipe González Rojas, 5 vols. 1910–11) Vol.iv, p.398.
7. Insurgent groups might sometimes join together to outnumber local Spanish forces or carry out a major operation. The most notable example of the latter was in Nov. 1895 when Máximo Gómez and Maceo mobilized an 'Invading Army' of more than 3,000 men to cross the length of Cuba from Oriente to Pinar del Río. Martinez Campos was compelled to declare a state of siege in the provinces of Havana and Pinar del Río.
8. Thomas G. Alvord Jr., 'Why Spain has failed in Cuba', *The Forum* 23 (1897) p.567.
9. Cited in Foner (note 5) Vol.i, p.30.
10. The policy of 'reconcentration' was also damaging politically because it provoked controversy and outrage in the US.
11. Cited in Foner (note 5) Vol.i, p.20.
12. The view that an insurgent victory was only a matter of time has led historians to question whether American military intervention was necessary to defeat the Spaniards. In particular, Marxist historians such as Foner have argued that the US deliberately intervened to prevent the emergence of an anti-capitalist state in Cuba. For a guide to Cuban historical works on this subject, see Duvon C. Cubitt, 'Cuban Revisionist Interpretation of Cuba's Struggle for Independence', *Hispanic American Historical Review* 43 (1963) pp.395–404.
13. Corbin to Shafter, 31 May 1898, cited in Russell A. Alger, *The Spanish-American War* (NY: Harper & Bros 1901) pp.64–5.
14. The lack of Spanish resistance was also explained by the activities of local insurgent forces who provided what amounted to a protective cordon for the landing Americans. See Foner (note 5) Vol.ii, pp.354–5.
15. From 23 June onwards most of the landing vessels were diverted to the calmer waters off Siboney.
16. See Alger (note 13) p.103.
17. Theodore Roosevelt, *The Rough Riders* (NY: Scribner's 1902) p.89.
18. Cited in Walter Millis, *The Martial Spirit: A Study of Our War with Spain* (Boston: Houghton Mifflin 1931) p.274.
19. Shafter to Wheeler, 25 June 1898, cited in Alger (note 13) p.117.
20. The aftermath of Las Guásimas not only highlighted strained relations between Shafter and Sampson, but also revealed a growing friction between Fifth Corps and the insurgents. Despite the assistance of the insurgents in the disembarkation, American soldiers soon developed an attitude of contempt for their nominal allies. See Joseph Smith, 'The American Image of the Cuban Insurgents in 1898', *Zeitschrift für Anglistik und Amerikanistik* 40 (1992) pp.319–29.
21. The possibility of a smaller attack on Santiago de Cuba involving the US Navy and insurgent land forces had been considered by Spanish military authorities. See David F. Trask, *The War With Spain in 1898* (NY: Macmillan 1981) p.197.
22. Shafter to Alger, 28 June 1898, cited in ibid. p.227. Shafter also realised that delay was dangerous because it greatly increased the risk of his troops succumbing to tropical disease.
23. Sampson was complying with a written request from Shafter. This was the only direct military contribution of the US Navy to the battle on 1 July.
24. Shafter to Lawton, 1 July 1898, cited in Alger (note 13) p.143.
25. Brig. Gen. Samuel S. Sumner assumed command of the Cavalry Div. because Wheeler was incapacitated by fever.
26. The use of the outdated .45in calibre Springfield rifle caused a similar problem for the American volunteer soldiers. The regulars were equipped with the superior .30in calibre Krag-Jorgensen rifle.
27. Richard Harding Davis, *The Cuban and Porto Rican Campaigns* (London: Heinemann 1899)

pp.198, 201. It could be argued that the forward advance demonstrated the ability of American officers and soldiers to show initiative in battle and to conduct operations in small combat units. See Perry D. Jamieson, *Crossing the Deadly Ground: United States Army Tactics, 1865–1899* (Tuscaloosa, AL: U. of Alabama Press 1994) pp.136–8.
28. Davis (note 27) p.206.
29. Alger (note 13) p.172.
30. A breakdown in negotiations provoked a brief resumption of active hostilities on 10–11 July involving an exchange of rifle and artillery fire at the San Juan Heights and naval bombardment of the city.
31. Hay to Roosevelt, 27 July 1898, cited in Millis (note 18) p.340.
32. This is not to suggest that Shafter was to blame or that rivalries only occurred between the army and the navy. Sampson had already clashed over tactics with his naval colleague, Commodore Winfield S. Schley.
33. For criticism of Shafter's strategy see Mathew F. Steele, *American Campaigns* (Washington, DC: Combat Forces Press 1951) p.303. Shafter is defended in Graham H. Cosmas, 'San Juan Hill and El Caney, 1–2 July 1898', in Charles E. Heller and William A. Stofft (eds.) *America's First Battles, 1776–1865* (Lawrence, KS: UP of Kansas 1986) p.145.
34. Alger (note 13) p.296.

General Allenby and the Palestine Campaign, 1917–18

MATTHEW HUGHES

At the start of the First World War Britain's concern in Egypt was protection of the Suez Canal to allow safe transit of Indian and Anzac troops sailing for France. By 1916 the British-led force in Egypt, the Egyptian Expeditionary Force (EEF), had moved onto the offensive, and by October 1918, when the Ottoman Empire sued for peace, the EEF had advanced to Aleppo in northern Syria.[1] The bulk of this 800-kilometre advance, from the town of Gaza to Syria, was attained in two short battles in the last year of the war. The terrain was arid and inhospitable; there were inadequate perennial sources of potable water beyond what could be drawn manually from village wells. While the British constructed a pipeline across the Sinai Peninsula to provide water for the EEF, strict rationing was required as demand constantly outstripped supply, and providing sufficient water for the horses of the mounted divisions was a particular problem. Moreover, communications in the Middle East were awful, there were few metalled roads, and a limited railway network that ran on three different gauges. The success in Palestine is the more remarkable when compared to the typically static conflict in France. The battles on the Western Front were marked by heavy casualties for both attacker and defender, and assumed the proportions of attritional mini-campaigns of several months' duration.[2] In Palestine casualties were relatively light, engagements were both bold and rapid, and there were none of the disasters like Kut-al-Amara or Gallipoli, that blighted the other British campaigns waged against the Ottoman Empire. These factors suggest that the Palestine campaign was extraordinary.

The trenches of France were an infantryman's war, characterised by 'pushes' of a few kilometres into the enemy lines. These attacks were supported by increasingly intense, devastating and accurate artillery fire that came to dominate the battlefield. It was not until the closing months of the war that the Germans' defensive network was seriously breached, and effective German rearguards kept their retreat from becoming a rout. The much sought-after breakthrough on the Western Front was something of a will-o'-the-wisp.[3] In Palestine the expeditionary force achieved the elusive breakthrough following which cavalry could exploit the gap in the enemy's defences, and the deployment of cavalry enabled the EEF to penetrate deep behind the Turks' lines. *Entente* morale was boosted by the capture of Gaza, Jerusalem, Damascus, Beirut and Aleppo. The use of cavalry in Palestine can be compared to the uselessness of this arm of war in France, where horses were best employed in a logistical role supplying the infantry and artillery in the front line.

In June 1917, when General Sir Edmund Allenby took charge of the EEF, it had two infantry corps (XX and XXI), totalling seven divisions, and a cavalry corps of three divisions (the Desert Mounted Corps – DMC). With re-organisation in 1918, following the Ludendorff offensives, the cavalry corps was increased to four divisions.[4] These mounted troops were used in a fighting role. That the Marquess of Anglesey devoted a whole volume to operations in Palestine in his recent study on the history of cavalry is indicative of the importance of mounted troops in this theatre of operations.[5] Palestine was a 'side-show' for its impact on the outcome of the First World War, and it is the seemingly successful use of cavalry which militarily marks out the campaign. The war of 1914–18 emphasised significant advances in military technology and in the nature of warfare. The industrial revolution of the nineteenth-century, coupled with societal changes associated with nationalism, radically changed the 'face of battle'.[6] The effect was to render cavalry obsolete in the face of entrenched mass conscript armies supported by rapid-fire weaponry. The development of the tank in the inter-war years revived mobility, and the armoured Blitzkrieg of the Second World War was a product of the challenge posed by the failure of cavalry in the Great War. The use of cavalry in Palestine thus seems an exception to the view that only infantry and artillery could engage the enemy; in Palestine it seemed as though time had stood still and a war quite different to the one in France could be fought.

In three major sets of engagements Allenby took the EEF first from Gaza to Jerusalem by December 1917, then to Amman in Transjordan in the spring of 1918, and at the Battle of Megiddo in September 1918 Allenby's Anzac, Indian and British cavalry swept forward to capture Muslimie Junction beyond Aleppo. The final push after Megiddo of some 600 kilometres was no mean feat for a war where advances were measured in tens of kilometres. It is also worth considering that Allenby's cavalry

MAP 5
The Levant Theatre of War 1917–1918

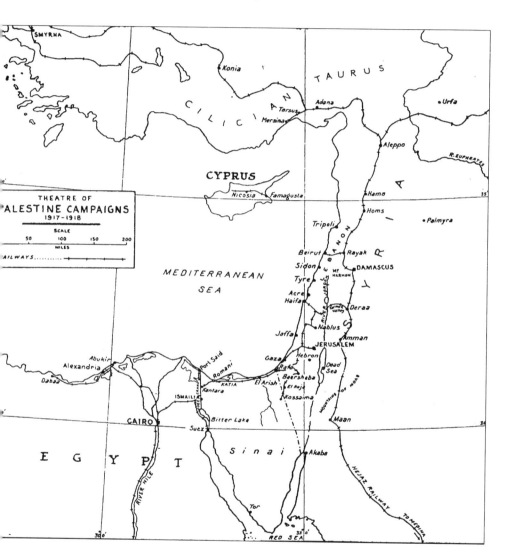

Source: Archibald Wavell, *Allenby: A Study in Greatness* (NY: Oxford UP 1940)

reached Cilicia in the space of about four weeks. Sir Basil Liddell Hart's description of this final battle as the 'Annihilation of the Turkish Armies' is fitting.[7]

The successes in Palestine are more striking considering the demoralised condition of the EEF when Allenby took over from Lt-General Sir Archibald Murray, the previous commander.[8] In March and April 1917 the EEF suffered two reverses at Gaza because of hopeless command and control by Murray and his staff. The beneficial result of these defeats at Gaza was the replacement of Murray with a vigorous new general, Allenby. Murray's defeats left Allenby with an army that was both 'psychologically fragile', and in desperate need of a victory.[9] Murray's listless tenure until 1917, coupled with the failures in early 1917, made Allenby's task more difficult, and his victories more impressive.[10]

Under Allenby the EEF fought three major battles: the Third Battle of Gaza, October–December 1917; the Transjordan Raids, March–May 1918; the Battle of Megiddo, September–October 1918. Allenby's cavalry played a major part in these actions, and were not left, as was usual in France, as a reserve to await the anticipated success of the infantry. However, there were limitations to what the cavalry could do, and a complete analysis of cavalry effectiveness in Palestine needs to look at the interaction with infantry and artillery. The romantic appeal of the EEF cavalcade through lands with profound historical and religious attachments has done little to encourage objective study. Following Jerusalem's fall *Punch* had a drawing of King Richard I looking on Jerusalem with the caption: 'The Last Crusade, Coeur-de-Lion (looking down on the Holy City). "My Dream Comes True".'[11] Allenby was portrayed as a crusader reversing Saladin's victory of 1187, local papers such as north London's *Islington Daily Gazette* reported how: 'By the capture of Jerusalem, General Allenby has made his Palestine campaign historic. More than military significance attaches to the surrender into British hands of a city held in reverence by all Christendom.'[12] Momentous events such as the taking of Jerusalem have overshadowed the humdrum staff work upon which victory relied. They have also led, not unnaturally, to an acceptance that victory was the result of the dash and mobility of cavalry. This was not always the case. Cyril Falls, author of the official history volumes on Palestine, described how Megiddo gave cavalry 'a magnificent opportunity to wind up its career in success and glory'.[13] Falls' comment ignores the fighting of the Russian Civil War, 1917–22, and mounted forces such as Semyon Budenny's Soviet First Cavalry Army.[14] It would be more accurate to say that Palestine was almost the swan-song for cavalry.

This study, while acknowledging the role played by cavalry in Palestine, will show that more analysis is needed of how the mounted forces co-

ALLENBY AND THE PALESTINE CAMPAIGN 63

operated in an all-arms endeavour to defeat the Turks. Exploits such as the Australian Light Horse (ALH) charge that took Beersheba at the Third Battle of Gaza, or the capture of Damascus by British-led cavalry on 1 October 1918 (and, of course, the controversy over whether the EEF or the Arabs were the first into Damascus) have attracted the most attention.[15] These cavalry actions were, however, the product of combined efforts with infantry and artillery support, and whether victory could have been achieved without this assistance is a question of some importance. The mobile operations of Prince Feisal's Northern Arab Army (NAA), and the part played by T. E. Lawrence ('of Arabia'), on Allenby's eastern desert flank have also served to divert attention from the essential components making up Allenby's actions west of the River Jordan.

It is also necessary to touch upon the role of command in the Palestine campaign. Allenby had a forceful personality that could turn to fury when confronted by slovenly work by subordinates. While Allenby's temper, on occasion, got the better of him, he was not driven by a sense of malice, but by professionalism, and the energy that Allenby brought with him to the Middle East had an impact on the campaign. Major-General George Barrow, commander of Allenby's 4th Cavalry Division, remembered how

> Haig could not bear contradiction and was intolerant of any opinion – certainly of any opinion on military matters – contrary to his own. Allenby was always glad to listen to other opinions and advice, provided this was backed by knowledge and common sense. What angered him was stupidity, negligence and, most of all, disregard of orders.[16]

Allenby certainly stands out when compared to Murray under whom the high command in Palestine 'had completely lost the confidence of subordinate commanders'; a situation which fed down the line 'until the private soldier mistrusted his lance-corporal'.[17] Allenby's arrival marked a new and more active period for the EEF. It may be that Allenby was not a 'moral giant', but he was a big improvement over Murray, and attempts to revise Murray's reputation upwards, and Allenby's downwards, stumble on the fact that having Allenby in charge made a considerable difference.[18] This was the view of those in Palestine on the sharp end doing the fighting. Searching for a hagiography around Allenby seems rather pointless.

The Third Battle of Gaza, October–December 1917

The Third Battle of Gaza was two separate engagements fought 50 kilometres apart and on different days. On 27 October 1917 Lt-General Sir Edward Bulfin's XXI Infantry Corps opened the preparatory bombardment of the Turkish trenches in front of Gaza, and the town was taken on 1–2 November. Meanwhile, Lt-General Sir Philip Chetwode's XX Infantry Corps, and two cavalry divisions of Lt-General Sir Henry Chauvel's DMC, attacked, and captured, Beersheba on the eastern desert flank on 31 October. The plan was that Chauvel's cavalry would then move west and north, and turn the Turks' defences, that ran in a ragged line from Gaza to Beersheba. The distance between the two EEF forces was screened by the Yeomanry Mounted Division. The weight of Allenby's mobile force, namely two of his three cavalry divisions, was deployed against Beersheba. Whether this was the most efficacious course of action has been the cause of some debate, with a 'Gaza School' arguing that Allenby should have concentrated his cavalry opposite Gaza, and not dissipated them in an attack in the desert.[19]

Four relevant points emerge from the Third Battle of Gaza and the decision to divide the EEF for battle: first, the absence of water in the desert was the crucial factor limiting the range of the cavalry as they attempted to roll up the Turkish lines from the east; second, Turkish defences at Gaza and Beersheba – indeed, along the whole of their front – were in such an inadequate state of readiness that comparisons with the Western Front are invalid; third, because of the Turks' predicament Allenby's artillery destroyed their defences at Gaza in a way unimaginable in France; finally, Allenby made little or no contribution to the plan to concentrate the cavalry against Beersheba.

Beersheba and Water Supply

The Australian cavalry assault on Beersheba as dusk fell on 31 October was a dramatic affair, and quite how charging horses overcame the machine-guns and infantry defending Beersheba is discussed in Ian Jones' 1983 article (with the apt title 'The Light Horse Charge and the Making of Myths').[20] When Beersheba was captured, the seven wells of biblical times had increased to some 17 in number. The speed of the light horse charge into Beersheba helped minimise destruction, and only two wells were demolished by the Turco-German force defending the town. The German officer charged with the wells' destruction seems to have been away on leave, and considering the Germans' skill at demolition and setting booby-traps this was good luck for the EEF.[21] The EEF was also fortunate that the Turks left behind 90,000 gallons of water in reservoirs at Beersheba.[22] The whole operation hinged on Beersheba's wells, as Brigadier-General William Bartholomew (Chetwode's Brigadier General-General Staff – BGGS) pointed out in June 1917: 'there is apparently no water fit for the troops to drink on any part of the enemy's present line between Gaza and Beersheba, except at those places'.[23]

Even with Beersheba's intact and enhanced water supply, the cavalry

MAP 6

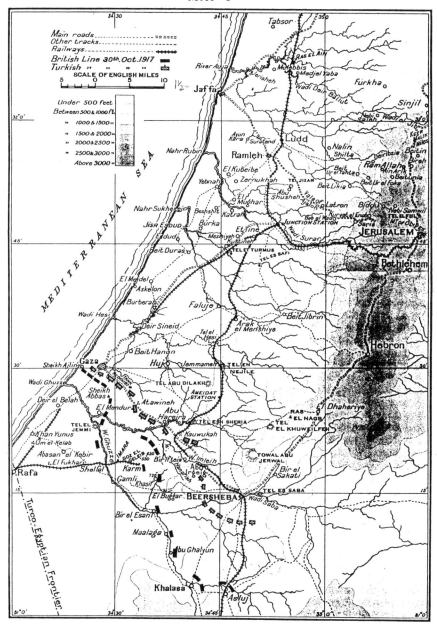

Source: Col. A. P. Wavell, *The Palestine Campaigns*, 3rd ed. (London: Constable 1932), Map VIII.

advancing from Beersheba ran into real difficulty, with troopers and their horses suffering so badly from lack of water that operations were brought to a standstill. Like the tanks of the Second World War, Chauvel's cavalry discovered that fuel, in this case water rather than petrol, was essential to maintain momentum. Barrow remembered how some horses went 84 hours without water, and Brigadier-General Granville Ryrie of the ALH wrote to his wife about the difficult position regarding water.[24] Soldiers from 60th (London) Infantry Division in XX Corps dropped out from thirst, while Allenby wrote in 1929 that horses went 72 hours without water.[25] The war diaries for the cavalry units outline the increasingly serious nature of the water shortage as squadrons attempted to advance, but were unable to pursue the retreating Turks without water.[26] Sir Henry Gullett, Australia's official historian, noted how the depth of the few wells found meant that troops had to be sent back to the pipeline head at Karm for watering as it was physically impossible to draw enough water when confronted with a bucket and a deep well.[27] This state of affairs defeated the whole purpose of the flanking operation.

The cavalry attempting to turn the Turkish flank were caught in the dry and largely uninhabited country between Gaza and Beersheba. This allowed the Turks to retire in order to fight another day, as R. M. P. Preston pointed out in his account of the campaign: 'Once free from the harassing menace of the mounted troops, the Turks, who could always outmarch our infantry, would have experienced little difficulty in retiring rapidly to the north.'[28] Chetwode after the war admitted that there was several days' delay due to water difficulties, and this hiatus meant that it 'was now clear that the attempt to cut off the enemy forces had failed'.[29] Had the Turks been more efficient in their demolition work, the cavalry might have had to evacuate Beersheba, and retire to the water pipeline terminal near Gaza. Colonel Kress von Kressenstein, German commander of the Turkish Eighth Army at the Third Battle of Gaza, remembered how 'he gave the strictest orders' to have the wells at Beersheba 'destroyed'.[30] The arguments expounded by the 'Gaza School' are ones to be taken seriously, in view of the evidence outlined above.

The dependence on water was a limitation on the effectiveness of cavalry in Palestine. This criticism is qualified when one realises how devastating the cavalry would have been had they been available at Gaza, where their presence would have turned the Turkish retreat into a rout. In Palestine Allenby's cavalry had much potential but they had to be used thoughtfully, and in conjunction with Allenby's not inconsiderable infantry and artillery. Had the mounted attack gone through Gaza, the EEF would have had their own railhead directly behind them. The coastal plain was less arid, and contained more villages from which water could be extracted. The

Royal Navy could also assist with supply from the sea as the railway was being pushed forward. Supply from the sea was not straight-forward, as there were no good harbours before Jaffa, but the navy were able to land supplies on the Mediterranean beaches, and did so using Rarotongan islanders from the Pacific as boatmen.[31]

The Turks had laid standard gauge track on their railway from Istanbul to Palestine only as far as Rayak in Lebanon. South of Rayak the Turks relied on a narrow-gauge 1,050 metre line that extended to Gaza, Beersheba and Medina. (With incomplete tunnels through the Taurus and Amanus Mountains north of Alexandretta, Turkish matériel for the Palestine front had to be loaded on and off railway wagons five times.) It was possible for the British to use the retreating Turks' railway. The British ultimately laid a completely new track up to the Jaffa–Jerusalem line, but by temporarily using the Turkish narrow-gauge railway the British by the beginning of 1918 'possessed a complete 1.050m gauge railway system in southern Palestine'; by 20 November 1917 the Turkish line was 'working up to Junction Station, the invaluable but rather worn-out captured locomotives being used'.[32] This extemporisation allowed the British to distribute supplies from Egypt brought to Gaza and Beersheba by standard-gauge rail, and to Jaffa by sea. Logistics in Palestine were never easy, but difficulties were less pronounced when operating on the coastal plain.

The decision to attack Beersheba was influenced by the 'general repugnance in many minds for another assault after the two earlier repulses' at Gaza in the spring of 1917.[33] Murray's defeats linked in with a desire to use the cavalry in an aggressive fashion, and with an awareness that infantry and artillery had failed in France to break the enemy lines. The result was the impressive capture by cavalry of Beersheba, but co-ordination with the main body of EEF infantry and artillery at Gaza was practically non-existent. It was as though there were two third battles of Gaza.

Ottoman Overstretch

Following the Russian Revolution, the Ottoman high command opted for an expansionist drive in the Trans-Caucasus, and Baku was captured by a Turkish-led 'Army of Islam' in September 1918 (a pyrrhic victory considering that all the effort expended by the Turks came to nothing).[34] The result of Turkish ambitions in the Caucasus was that their Palestine front became a neglected and subsidiary theatre which received little in the way of men and matériel.[35] Some nine fully-equipped Turkish divisions were raised for use in the Caucasus, and while this was a threat which Britain had to counter, using these troops in Palestine and Mesopotamia would have tied down more British forces.[36] The Germans tried unsuccessfully to stop Turkey denuding her other fronts. Turkish troops employed in the Caucasus were promised increased pay and promotion with the effect that, the 'consequent drain on the Palestinian units became enormous, for only the sick and mortally exhausted could resist the lure of money and fame.'[37]

The result of Turkey's irredentist pretensions was that Turkish troops opposing the British in Palestine were in a frightful condition: 'Facing the numerically superior and well equipped forces of General Allenby with generally undernourished and ill-clad troops', Marshal Liman von Sanders, the German commander from March 1918, 'was particularly outraged by the fact that the Turks were frittering away both soldiers and supplies in their Transcaucasian adventures'.[38] Australians taken prisoner by the Turks all remembered how the first thing that their captors did was to strip them, and take their clothes, giving the prisoners-of-war in return the Turkish rags that passed for uniforms.[39] Writing to Djemal Pasha, one of the triumvirate ruling the Ottoman Empire, in September 1917, von Kressenstein complained that he was losing 4,000 men each month, largely through disease.[40] For von Kressenstein there was little he could do, except wait for Allenby to make his attack: 'Dans ces conditions, l'offensive anglaise était attendue avec une vive anxiété.'[41] The morale of the Turkish troops was low, and they lacked most of the comforts enjoyed by the men of the EEF. Some of the Turks had received no mail from home in years, and they awaited the British assault in 'fragile tents' with 'nothing to cheer their spirits'.[42] British estimations were distorted by a Turco-German force codenamed Yilderim sent to Palestine in late 1917, but the force was, in reality, not the threat it seemed.[43] Had the British been better informed of the plight of the Turks in Palestine they might have realised that they were dealing with a situation different to the one in France: one where artillery was to prove most effective in effecting the breakthrough.

On 12 July 1917 Allenby sent his first dispatch back to London detailing his requirements.[44] In his report Allenby reviewed the Turkish defences thus:

> The position at present occupied by the Turks on the Gaza Beersheba line are of considerable natural strength.... He [the Turk] has made Gaza into a strong modern fortress heavily wired and entrenched. Its centre is a mass of houses, gardens and Cactus hedges offering every facility for protracted defence.[45]

In assessing Gaza's defences to be formidable, Allenby was adopting Chetwode's view.[46] Chetwode was not alone in thinking Gaza well defended, and best taken by threatening its flank, but was Chetwode's appreciation the correct one?[47] Von Kressenstein recollected that the 'wire entanglements were poor owing to lack of material', while Franz von Papen, the future German Chancellor, who served in Palestine as a staff officer with the Turkish Fourth Army, remembered in his memoirs that the whole of his 'long front was very thinly held, but with the exception of one or two modest reserve units, every available man was in the front line. There was no defence in depth.' Von Papen went on to observe that while the defences might have been adequate by 1914 standards, they would never have stood up to a typical Western Front bombardment.[48]

The flexible defence in depth that the Germans employed to such deadly effect in France could not be developed in Palestine. It was felt that the average Turkish soldier was unable to cope with mobile warfare; the lack of soldiers, building materials and equipment prevented the Germans from constructing a series of defensive layers with the front line held lightly. The Germans expected a heavy artillery barrage from Allenby, but they could do little to counter this threat.[49] It is misleading to extrapolate from the perceived failure of artillery in France, and conclude that it would therefore have failed in Palestine. Allenby's superiority in artillery was helped by Turkish intransigence. Talking to General Refet Pasha, XXII Corps' commander at Gaza, von Papen pointed out the desirability of keeping two (of three) divisions in reserve, while manning the forward positions as lightly as possible. The future Turkish War Minister 'gave me a charming smile and replied, "J'ai bien compris, mon cher Commandant, mais j'y suis, j'y reste".'[50]

Closer analysis of the respective orders of battle shows that Britain had an overwhelming advantage, and this situation has been overlooked in accounts of the Palestine campaign. Archibald Wavell gives the Turkish forces at the Third Battle of Gaza as 40,000 to 45,000 rifles, 1,500 sabres and 300 guns.[51] The *Official History* lowers this to 33,000 rifles, and as the EEF could field some 60,000 to 75,000 rifles and 12,000 to 17,000 sabres, odds of two-to-one are created.[52] This gives the impression of rather even odds given the inherent advantage of defence over offence. Looking at the other side of the hill it soon becomes apparent that the Turks were in a weak position. Von Kressenstein gave his rifle strength as 23,000, with divisions such as the 54th down to 1,500 effectives. Many regiments – a Turkish division was nominally composed of nine battalions in three regiments – were down to under 500 rifles, and with a running sick rate of 3,000 to 4,000, 25 per cent of the total force was usually in hospital.[53] The medical services seem to have lacked most of the basics required for rehabilitating soldiers, including shortages of anaesthetics.[54] Colonel Hussein Husni Amir Bey estimated the Turks' average divisional rifle strengths in Palestine as 3,000: 'that is to say about 21,000 along the whole front'.[55] Focusing on the Turkish XXII Corps defending Gaza the figures come down further as one looks at its three divisions. The *Official History* written by Falls gives respective rifle strengths for 53rd, 3rd and 7th Divisions of 3,100, 3,698 and

2,886. Falls, it seems, took these figures from appendix 14 of Hussein Husni's unpublished book 'Yilderim'. What is omitted is that 53rd Division holding the line next to the sea was only 66.5 per cent Turkish, and the Arabs who made up the balance were seen as most unreliable. While 3rd Division was 84 per cent Turkish, 7th Division, which seems to have been something of a reserve, had a rifle strength of under 3,000.[56] Also, the Turkish 54th Division of XX Corps, positioned some five miles east of Gaza, which was the next unit in the line after 3rd Division, was under strength at 2,738 (or only 1,500 according to von Kressenstein's account).[57] Gullett's notes indicate that Allenby on 28 November 1917 believed the Turkish force to have been 41,000.[58] This seems to be a highly inflated figure, and one wonders what would have happened if the cavalry, and, indeed, Chetwode's XX Infantry Corps, had been available to back up XXI Corps at Gaza. Colonel Clive Garsia, one of the first exponents of the 'Gaza School', spoke to von Kressenstein after the war, and wrote to Major-General Stewart Hare of 54th (East Anglian) Infantry Division of how he 'could not quite get' von Kressenstein to 'admit that with one more division we would have walked straight through his Gaza front; but you and I know that this would have been the case'.[59]

Allenby's Artillery

Analysing Allenby's artillery pool shows how effective this arm of war could be when faced with weak defences, and when supplied with an adequate number of guns. Allenby assessed his needs as being some 116 heavy pieces, besides a full complement of divisional 18-pounders and 4.5in howitzers. That is, the infantry divisions would have 48 guns in three brigades of three batteries with 36 18-pounders and 12 4.5in howitzers; the cavalry would have 12 13-pounders. in three Royal Horse Artillery batteries in one brigade.[60] The EEF received, in toto, between 82 and 90 of the heavy guns, and all the divisional artillery with the exception of two six-gun batteries.[61] Allenby also seems to have made his heavy gun requirements based on eight infantry divisions, so his reduced number of 82–90 guns was for seven divisions only. The *Official History* concluded that Allenby's 'demands for heavy artillery were ... cut down, but not seriously. Generally speaking he had not been stinted.'[62] This sentiment was echoed by the Chief of the Imperial General Staff (CIGS), General Sir William Robertson, who felt that Allenby 'would have received nearly all the artillery he had asked for'.[63]

General Allenby's July report 'included a request to be supplied with heavy artillery on the same scale as the Western Front'.[64] For Bulfin's 'softening up' of Gaza he was able to employ the 48 guns of each of his three infantry divisions, 68 heavy corps guns, and eight mountain guns in a composite force. The *Official History* records that the bombardment 'was the heaviest carried out in the course of the war outside the European theatres'. The official account is also good in bringing out the comparative aspect:

> It is interesting to note that 68 heavy guns to 4,000 yards [main attack frontage], or one to every 60 yards, is exactly the proportion employed by the British on the first day of the Battle of the Somme ... when we take into account the naval artillery and the enormous weight of its projectiles ... this bombardment must be reckoned a very heavy one by any standard.[65]

Franz von Papen, on the receiving end, remembered a 'tremendous bombardment', while one of the ratings offshore in the destroyer HMS *Comet* was equally struck by the power of the naval shelling.[66] The Battle of the Somme is not the best example for the successful use of artillery, but the mined dugouts and all-round military efficiency of the Germans stood in marked contrast to the Ottoman Empire, and its relatively effete armed forces. Anthony Clayton's description of the really quite formidable 'Hindenburg Line' in France, when compared to, say, Commandant Larcher's analysis of the Turks' deficiencies in Palestine, shows that the defensive systems were so different that comparison is difficult.[67] Considering the desperate odds it says something for the bravery and hardiness of the Anatolian recruits serving far from home that they carried on fighting with such determination.[68]

Visitors after the battle were struck by the quantity of ordnance used, and the resulting devastation. In December 1917 Colonel Ronald Storrs, who became the military governor of Jerusalem, visited Gaza and wrote in his diary how he 'passed shell craters, many from 8in guns, on all sides as we clambered up to Ali Muntar, which commands the whole district.... The hill itself had been almost shelled away, and must have been untenable long before we could occupy it.'[69] Writing to his wife on 2 November, Brigadier General Guy Dawnay, Allenby's BGGS, described the ease with which the Turks at Gaza collapsed, adding, 'though we didn't get many prisoners ... as our bombardment had more or less blasted the ... enemy's front line system before we went in'. Dawnay's comment on Turkish counter-attacks, 'three of which were blown to pieces by our artillery fire before they could develop', conveys the dominance that the British had in this arm.[70] Hare, commander of 54th Division at Gaza, echoed Dawnay's observations in a letter to his father on 9 November. Hare not only remarked on the pounding that the Turks had received for six days, but also that their wire had been well cut, and the enemy positions fell 'without difficulty'.[71]

In the Australian archives at Canberra a report by a Major Pardoe supports the view that Gaza's defences were so weak that Allenby should have concentrated his cavalry by the coast.[72] Examining the defences straight after the battle, Pardoe commented on the rough nature of the defences and that these defences were only evident in the front line. Thus, any breakthrough would not have come up against the formidable reserve trenches typical of the Western Front, or any substantial reserve force. Pardoe felt that the Turks had neglected the basic principles that made the machine-gun, the paragon of automatic warfare, so efficient; Turkish redoubts had no proper cover, and Pardoe was struck by the accuracy and destructive power of the EEF bombardment on these rough emplacements (a major problem was the lack of wood to build strongpoints).[73] The Turks were also without proper gas masks, and while the official history asserts that none was used at Third Gaza by the EEF, Gullett notes otherwise and concludes that it was most effective.[74]

If the plan to attack Beersheba was flawed, it is worth asking who exactly drew it up. While several senior officers worked out this new plan the one notable absentee was Allenby. This is not necessarily a criticism, as Allenby would naturally listen to the senior officers with local expertise: indeed the EEF had a staff system precisely to inform and advise its commander. The records show that Chetwode and Dawnay were the major planners behind the idea to concentrate the cavalry against Beersheba, and not Gaza.[75] The idea to assault Beersheba came at the time of the first two battles of Gaza, and both Major-General S. F. Mott, commander of 53rd (Welch) Infantry Division, and Lt-General Sir Charles Dobell, Eastern Force commander before Chetwode, also seem to have had a hand in the plan to attack the Turkish flank.[76] This is not to say that Allenby thoughtlessly adopted the wrong plan. Writing to Garsia after the war, Chetwode remarked how Allenby 'very generously included' Chetwode's appreciation 'in his official papers, but I can assure you that he did not accept the plan until he had gone most closely into all possible alternatives'.[77]

General Allenby arrived too late in Palestine to contribute to the plan for the Third Gaza. This was a result of confused British war policy which allowed Murray to stay on as commander, and thus delay the Third Battle of Gaza. Murray should have been replaced sooner, and Allenby correspondingly ordered to Palestine earlier in 1917. Allenby was under considerable pressure to give the British Prime Minister, David Lloyd George, 'Jerusalem before Christmas', and so could do little but follow the advice of his staff, inherited as they were from Murray.[78]

The EEF won the Third Battle of Gaza and made an impressive, if methodical, advance to Jerusalem, but it was not a decisive victory, and the capture of Jerusalem took over five weeks, with much shifting of troops, as Allenby's exhausted yeomanry had to be withdrawn from the hills around Jerusalem. The 60th Division that replaced the yeomanry, and finally took the city on 8–9 December, had originally been deployed with Chetwode's XX Corps at Beersheba.[79] Once XXI Corps and the Yeomanry Mounted Division advanced through Gaza in pursuit of the Turks, XX Corps and the DMC were left idle in the desert. Hussein Husni remarked on the timid nature of the British pursuit in his account of the campaign, and rightly concluded that: 'Once again, the British wasted four or five weeks. Instead of capturing JERUSALEM in the first week of November the town fell on 8th December.'[80]

The cavalry divisions had only 12 13-pounders per division, and this lack of inherent firepower was compounded by the need to leave men behind in battle to look after tethered horses. They also needed large amounts of water, and had trouble fighting in hilly terrain such as around Jerusalem. Allenby's mounted troops were, however, a means in the First World War of making warfare more fluid and dramatic. This they did not do at the Third Battle of Gaza (excepting the bold, but pointless, capture of Beersheba). The cavalry would have been more threatening had they been deployed behind Gaza. The Turkish defences at Beersheba seem to have been so weak that the Australians were able to charge in and take the town. The Turkish defences at Gaza were of sufficient strength to prevent this, and artillery was required to punch a hole in the Turkish lines. It is the neglected artillery which emerges as the unsung hero of Third Gaza. The breakthrough was created but the cavalry were not there to follow through and exploit this success.

The Transjordan 'Raids', March–May 1918

The two Transjordan raids towards Amman were comprehensive defeats, and weakened Britain's standing in the Middle East. The failure to secure the Amman area 'contributed to shake the confidence of the Bedouin tribes in our strength and power. Only a signal victory over the Turco-Germans on the Palestine front can restore our prestige among the Arabs.'[81] Quite why Allenby embarked on these 'raids', the official battle nomenclature for two multi-divisional attacks, is not readily apparent. It seems that they were the result of a mix of political and military factors, including pressure from London to attack; by a need to help Feisal's NAA, and to secure the EEF's eastern flank before an advance along the coast. Chauvel's comment after the war that Allenby 'always appeared to have a hankering after this flank' across the Jordan is a partial explanation, but considering the confusion surrounding the raids the conclusion of Chauvel's biographer, Alec Hill, seems more appropriate: 'As Allenby left no memoirs and the war diaries reveal little apart from the orders themselves, it is difficult to explain such disjointed strategy.'[82] Both raids exhibit a peculiar combination of confusion tinged with hopefulness, making elucidation difficult.

74 MILITARY POWER: LAND WARFARE IN THEORY AND PRACTICE

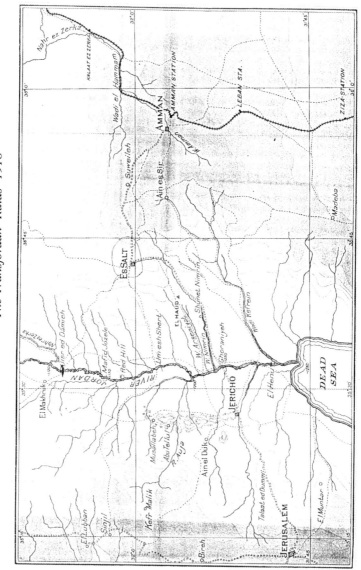

MAP 7
The Transjordan 'Raids' 1918

Source: Col. A. P. Wavell, *The Palestine Campaigns*, 3rd ed. (London: Constable 1932), Map XVI.

The deployment of cavalry in these attacks develops themes introduced in the previous section on Third Gaza: first, the importance of heavy artillery at critical moments during mobile operations, and the concomitant lack of firepower within a cavalry division; second, the consequences this had when mounted troops came up against entrenched and reasonably determined resistance; third, the detrimental effect rough terrain and inclement weather had on cavalry mobility, and on logistics in general. Allenby's role, as in the autumn of 1917, was circumscribed as he was again forced into operations which, given more time to plan, he might have conducted differently, or avoided altogether. Allenby's position was complicated by the need to send the bulk of his trained troops to France following the Ludendorff offensives.

The 'front' on the River Jordan where the Turkish Fourth Army, based at Es Salt, faced the EEF was, in fact, an exiguous series of observation posts. This is evident in the ease with which the cavalry advanced in the Transjordan raids around the Turkish positions and pushed east towards Amman. The lack of a contiguous defensive system was not typical for the First World War, even on the expanses of the Eastern Front, and was one of the peculiar features of the Palestine campaign. This situation obviated the need for artillery to create a breakthrough, but once the cavalry had pushed the 50 kilometres to Amman they encountered serious difficulties. In a rapid and decisive operation, comparable to the taking of Beersheba, the cavalry reached Amman, but they were then handicapped by the weather, by poor roads stretching back to Jerusalem which hampered logistics, and, above all, by the lack of artillery with which to take Amman.

The heavy rains that turned the two just passable routes to Amman into muddy tracks during the Transjordan raids were not unusual, and are even mentioned in the Bible, which Allenby was familiar with.[83] The dreadful weather is described vividly in the New Zealand Official History where the exploits of the New Zealand Mounted Rifle Brigade (NZMRB) are recorded.[84] The tracks to Amman could only take artillery and wagons under favourable weather conditions and this did not augur well for the advancing troops. The road from Shunet Nimrin to Es Salt had 'been cut out of the sides of the hills, having a very high cliff on one side and a deep gorge on the other.... It was thus impossible to get off the road.'[85] Artillery, of as large a calibre as possible, was essential as the Turks were willing to concede Es Salt, but Amman, on the railway to Medina, was a different proposition, and they were determined to hold this strategic town.

The First Raid

Once Es Salt had been taken on 25 March the two divisions involved in the raid, the 60th Infantry and Anzac Mounted, plus the Imperial Camel Corps (a brigade), moved on Amman by way of Suweileh and Ain es Sir. In Wavell's account of the campaign he points out that 'it was found impossible to take wheels' up onto the Moab plateau.[86] The road on to Amman was little better, with the commander of 2nd ALH Brigade writing to his wife how he had to turn his 'guns back as the road which had been reported good ... was an almost impassable goat track.... I thought sometimes that we would never get through.'[87] The war diary of the Camel Corps recorded how the unit was 'heavily handicapped in not having artillery support [it] being impossible to get them up'.[88] For four days the cavalry fought to capture Amman with only 'four small pack mountain guns' for support: 'we had to make one big attack at 2 o'clock in the morning in blinding rain and cold as ice. We had a good many casualties.'[89] The guns of 60th Infantry Division might have sufficed to break the Turks but it was impossible to bring these guns, or the infantry, to bear. The number of men lost is evidence of the difficulty of the operation, with a 'prisoner-of-war and missing' total for Palestine from March to May 1918 of 543.[90]

The war diary of Ryrie's 2nd ALH Brigade detailed the assault thus: 'Attack against AMMAN launched but owing to the difficulties met with in the way of weather and ground conditions, the enemy's great natural facilities for defence, their superiority of machine-gun fire, with the additional assistance of field guns – which we lacked – little progress was made.'[91] This skilful use of automatic fire was also commented upon in the war diary of 7th ALH Regiment, which mentions 'sangars bristling with machine guns from which an incessant and deadly fire was poured in on us as we stood up or lay down in the barley'.[92] The main Turkish position just south of Amman was on a hill 3,039 feet high, and to assault this dominating feature the NZMRB had just one pack 12-pounder to provide fire support.[93] The photograph in Arslan Bakig's picture volume on Amman of Hill 3039, taken from the Citadel to the north, illustrates the dominance of this feature.[94] Amman's natural position within a ring of hills made the task of the exhausted and cold men of the EEF a daunting one. To add to an already fraught situation, while the railway line north and south of Amman was cut by raiding parties, none of the major tunnels or viaducts were damaged, thus 'the enemy kept bringing up fresh reinforcements from Damascus [so] we had to pull out'.[95] Those unlucky enough to become casualties had to make the journey back to the River Jordan strapped to horses, or in *cacolet* stretchers attached to camels; balanced against a wounded man on the other side of the camel, the hapless casualty would be bounced against the side of the camel: many seriously wounded preferred to walk the muddy distance back to the field hospitals.[96]

The Turkish defenders of Amman fought on while temporarily isolated

ALLENBY AND THE PALESTINE CAMPAIGN

by the cutting of their railway line. While they held out the Ottoman high command had the line fixed and railed in reinforcements. The force attacking Amman was not strong enough to penetrate the Turkish lines. Certainly, a bombardment of the intensity of that at the Third Battle of Gaza would have broken the Turks' will to resist. The cavalry fought as hard as they could but without proper all-arms co-ordination Amman was not going to fall. Poor weather and harsh terrain made almost impossible the establishment of the logistical train needed for the combined effort which was essential to take, and hold, Amman. The first Ludendorff offensive had broken on 21 March against Third and Fifth Armies in France and the result was to denude Allenby of most of his trained troops, who were rushed to France. These were replaced with untrained Indian troops, and thus re-organisation and training were required. Wider war strategy impinged upon any long-term British commitment to stay in Amman, and shows the importance of successful operations being conducted within a well thought-out plan at all levels of war.

The Second Raid

The events of the second raid confirm that when unsupported cavalry came up against infantry willing to fight they would lose. The objective of the second raid at the end of April was the same as the first, to secure Amman, but this time the mounted troops advanced only as far as Es Salt. Meanwhile, the substantial cavalry flank guard by 'Red Hill', on the eastern bank of the River Jordan, was attacked by Turkish troops who had crossed the river from the west on a secret pontoon bridge at Mafid Jozele. As Chauvel pointed out the 'existence of this pontoon bridge was not known until later though the pontoons must have been close [and] handy. They had never been seen by our aeroplanes and, so far as we knew, there was no available crossing short of the bridge at [Jisr ed] Damieh.'[97] Security appears to have been poor. An Australian Sergeant of 12th ALH Regiment, taken prisoner on 1 May, remembered that the 'Turkish authorities state to have known our weakness'.[98] Gullett supports the view that there was an intelligence error, recording that

> The first principles of surprise attack were neglected. Everyone in Palestine and as far back as Cairo, knew of these operations which depended absolutely upon secrecy, two or three weeks before they were carried out. The second venture East of Jordan was more jealously guarded, but even then the coming attack was fairly common knowledge.[99]

The Turks' preparation of pontoons does support Gullett's assessment, and as von Sanders remembered, the attack using this secret bridge 'was a complete surprise for the enemy' as the Um esh Shert crossing was protected by EEF troops on the west bank, and the Jisr ed Damieh bridge was considered to be the only other crossing point.[100]

The Turks assembled for their attack on 'Red Hill' 3rd Cavalry Division, 24th Infantry Division, and the German Infantry Regiment Nr. 146.[101] Turkish troops marched through the night using the track down from Nablus and Beisan and attacked on 1 May 'immediately on arrival'.[102] Considering that the effectives of an average Turkish infantry division by 1918 numbered a few thousand at best, and that the German Regiment 146 was a battalion, it did not take much to defeat the cavalry. The accounts of the desperate efforts made in defence obscure the humiliation inflicted by the Turks. The cavalry pushed into the hills to the east by the Turkish assault eventually lost two of their 13-pounder batteries: the only nine guns lost to the enemy in the whole of the Palestine campaign.

The force of the Turkish attack would have been easier to absorb if the Turkish Shunet Nimrin position to the south had fallen. However, 60th Division was unable to take this position and thus widen the frontage of attack. The division was too weak and lacked the necessary artillery, the more so as the removal of troops to France was now in full swing. Gullett's notes on the Shunet Nimrin assault read very much like accounts of the Second Battle of Gaza: 'Shunet Nimrin 60th Division attacked about 400 to the battalion, very heavy losses. Division stale when show started and practically finished at end. Had 40 per cent to 50 per cent casualties. Turks had high ground.'[103] The rough terrain again hampered operations; it being impossible, for instance, for the cavalry at Es Salt to move south on the track to Shunet Nimrin and overwhelm the Turkish fixed defences from the rear. The EEF should have been aware of these problems, if only from the fact that they had crossed the same terrain in the first raid. The position of the troops in Es Salt was made untenable by the Turkish advance from Mafid Jozele as the one route back to the Jordan north of the Turks holding out at Shunet Nimrin, via tracks near Wadi Arseniyat, was in danger of being cut. The EEF was unable to defeat the Turks and 'the crowning folly was the undignified windy scuffle out of Es Salt' for a second time on 3 May 1918.[104]

In correspondence with Wavell after the war Major-General John Shea, commander of 60th Division, and himself heavily involved in the Transjordan raids, remembered how shocked Allenby was by the withdrawals from east of the River Jordan: 'He was curiously quiet ... I never saw him like that before or since.'[105] General Allenby was complacent in assuming that the Turkish Fourth Army could be so easily defeated. Allenby's typically tight grip on events weakened during the Transjordan raids. One major shortcoming was Allenby's failure to allot adequate forces for the raids, especially the second attack at the end of April. Shea was the commander for the first raid, and Chauvel for the second, and whether they, or Allenby as supreme commander, were at fault is not clear. Chauvel's BGGS in 1918, Howard-Vyse, was 'in Allenby's opinion outstanding', and this indicates that at the second raid the fault was with Allenby's staff.[106] This should be measured against the poor intelligence and planning for both raids and which were Shea's and Chauvel's responsibilities.

Before criticising Allenby it is worth considering the wider context of the Transjordan raids. On 1 February 1918 the Supreme War Council accepted Joint Note 12, which proposed that 'the Allies should undertake a decisive offensive against Turkey with a view to the annihilation of the Turkish Armies and the collapse of Turkish resistance'.[107] Joint Note 12 formed part of the long-running dispute between Lloyd George and Robertson over the value of the Palestine campaign. Robertson saw little or no military benefit to be had from the campaign, while Lloyd George's wider view, taking in non-military factors, was that victory in Palestine would be a great asset. Robertson was ultimately forced to relinquish his post as CIGS, or as A. J. P. Taylor put it: 'On 18 February Robertson read in the morning papers that he had resigned. He was given the command in eastern England – a good joke at the expense of an uncompromising "westerner".'[108]

General Allenby was caught up in this squabbling and it did little to help him in his task. Lloyd George sent General Jan Smuts on a mission to Egypt from 12 to 22 February to determine how best to implement the conclusion of Joint Note 12.[109] Allenby was under pressure to do something, and the capture of Amman was a means of placating Lloyd George. Allenby's scheme was to advance along the coastal plain, a plan that the Ludendorff offensives ruined as most of the EEF troops had to go to France. This was a determining factor in the inadequate force organised for the second raid. For Allenby the Transjordan raids were preparation for the major advance along the line Jaffa–Jerusalem, and the capture of Amman was useful, but not vital. Allenby had his own plan of attack, and before it could be developed the Ludendorff offensives concentrated attention elsewhere. The training and re-organisation required for the raw Indian troops delayed the coastal advance until September 1918, when, at the Battle of Megiddo, the three Turkish armies facing Allenby were shattered irrevocably. It may be, as von Papen observes in his *Memoirs*, that the Turks 'managed to hold down Allenby's armies in Palestine until September 1918, when the outcome of the war was being decided not in the Middle East but on the Western Front'.[110] But Allenby was never given a chance to show what he could do, as he was the victim of military events and political disputes beyond his control.

The gravity of the German offensives in France was such that the EEF had to supply France with infantry units to an extent that the EEF was left with only one trained 'all-white' infantry division (54th) with 12 British battalions. The replacement Indian divisions had nine Indian and three British battalions. This is a point worth emphasising in any analysis of war strategy. Allenby had to absorb some 216 partially-trained Indian infantry companies (54 battalions), as well as 13 Indian cavalry squadrons, so as to bring his force back up to strength. Allenby wrote to General Sir Henry Wilson, Robertson's replacement as CIGS, that 'the new arrivals are short of training', and added that some Pathans had deserted to the Turks.[111] The Ottoman Sultan was the spiritual leader for Sunni Muslims, and as some 29 per cent of Allenby's newly arrived infantry were Muslims, this made Allenby's re-organisation particularly problematic. In July 1918 Allenby cabled the War Office about his concern over unrest within his Indian drafts, and of the worrying presence of seditious documents written in 'Indian vernacular'.[112] If Allenby had developed his attacks in the spring of 1918 he would have had to do so with 54th Division: the only infantry division left to him intact (Allenby's Anzac mounted troops were also left as complete units).

The Transjordan Raids, like the Third Battle of Gaza, seem somehow unfulfilled. The military historian is left with the feeling that cavalry still had potential, but it was not realised for a variety of reasons, not least that the mounted troops seemed to operate without proper co-ordination with the available infantry and artillery. The thesis that aggressively handled cavalry could somehow take on infantry in Palestine is very difficult to sustain considering the events up to the spring of 1918. Cavalry were effective when the Turks' front was either weak or non-existent. The actions of Feisal's Arabs operating east and south of the Dead Sea only confirm this view as the largely mounted NAA could not defeat the entrenched Ottoman units along the Medina railway. With the dubious exception of the Battle of Tafilah in January 1918, the Hashemite forces were completely unable to fight the Turks in set-piece battles.[113] The Arabs were reliant, militarily, on the strength of the EEF, and this might was represented by infantry, and especially artillery, which in the spring of 1918 were sent to France.

The Battle of Megiddo, September–October 1918

The cavalry sweep following the opening of the Battle of Megiddo on 19 September was impressive. Allenby's Australian, 4th Indian and 5th Indian Cavalry Divisions pushed deep into Syria and captured Damascus early in the morning of 1 October.[114] Meanwhile, the Anzac Mounted Division took Amman, and then advanced down the Medina railway to join with Arab forces coming up from the south. The 5th Indian Cavalry Division went on to take Aleppo to the north on 26 October, and was accompanied in this operation by elements of the NAA. The Turkish forces in the Levant effectively ceased to exist after late September 1918. The undoubted success following Megiddo was a result of the Turkish line in Palestine being so fragile that the infantry and artillery assault on 19 September had the effect of knocking in a very rotten door. There were no Turkish reserve forces to stop the advancing cavalry and the Turkish retreat rapidly turned into a *sauve qui peut*. By late 1918 the EEF were facing an enemy weakened by the long summer, and the drain of the Caucasian offensive towards Baku. Turkish morale was appreciably worse in late 1918 than in 1917. The one body of troops whose morale held fast was the small German force in Palestine. Lawrence's account of how disciplined German rearguards held up the advance outside Damascus shows how motivated infantry, with machine-guns, could still dominate the battlefield.[115]

The problems with water and poor terrain at the two earlier actions analysed were not so apparent following Megiddo. However, endemic malaria behind the Turkish lines was to prove more effective than the enemy in impeding movement. The malaria-carrying anopheline mosquito was rife following the rainy season, and as the EEF pushed deep into Syria the lack of prophylactic measures behind the Turkish lines meant that malaria struck hard.[116] Many British Empire soldiers who had survived four years' fighting died from malaria, while many took the disease back home and succumbed at a later date. The 5th Cavalry Division was the only formation able to make the long march north from Damascus to Aleppo. The other three cavalry divisions were too debilitated by malaria.[117] The presence of residual Turkish troops in Cilicia was enough to prevent any further advance by this one weakened division. Had the Turks not been about to surrender 5th Division would have been in a perilous position. Supply and medical services could not keep up with an advance over devastated and malarial terrain.

While cavalry were decisive at the Battle of Megiddo the infantry could move relatively rapidly when there was no opposition. The 7th (Indian) Infantry Division reached Beirut on 8 October a week after the cavalry took Damascus. The early use of aeroplanes to strafe the retreating Turks portended developments in twentieth-century warfare. The British by late 1917 had achieved total air superiority, and at Megiddo the defiles through which the Turks were trying to escape north and east were turned into impassable shambles. Captured Turkish documents after Megiddo revealed how the EEF had 'enormous superiority.... Things have got so far that no further air reconnaissance is done by the 7th and 8th [Turkish] Armies.'[118] Aeroplanes were able to range over the battlefield in a way impossible for land-based troops. Palestine was one of the final campaigns for an arm of war which was to become redundant, and the beginnings of the use of air power which was to dominate future battlefields.[119] Again, the early use of armoured cars for reconnaissance and pursuit was to presage future mobile warfare.[120] The speed of the cavalry kept them close on the heels of the Turks and this allowed them to destroy what remained of the Turkish army. The cavalry prevented the Turks from re-grouping to fight another day. However, by late 1918 the weakness of the Turks was more profound. The First World War, and the decision to join the Central alliance, marked the end of the demise of the once great Ottoman Empire. The demoralised condition of the Turks in Palestine puts the victory at the Battle of Megiddo into context.

Conclusion

At Megiddo Allenby was finally able to show his mettle with a crushing defeat of the enemy. He was himself an impressive figure whose personality and physical presence were essential for motivating the EEF. Allenby was, however, a victim of circumstances beyond his control, and the Palestine campaign highlights the importance of measuring the personality of a commander against wider war strategy decided by politicians and their military advisers. Differences of opinion over how to conduct a war invariably confuse the objectives of a campaign, and contribute to a lowering of morale. Political decisions could be decisive in determining the success or failure of a campaign. There was never a consensus in London on the Palestine campaign. The military were never behind it, and were lacklustre in their response to all the 'eastern' schemes proposed by Lloyd George. Lloyd George was himself a military amateur with no training in the art of war, and to overcome the opposition of those like Robertson he had to dismiss them.[121] There was not the agreement necessary for a united war effort with the 'frocks' and the 'brasshats' pulling together.[122] The capabilities and intentions of the enemy were also determining factors, and, too often, Turkish war strategy is ignored.[123] Had the Turks diverted the troops released by Russia's collapse to Palestine the EEF would have been facing a more formidable foe.

Brian Holden Reid's remark on Lawrence shows how operations in peripheral war zones would be juxtaposed to the generally static conflict in France: 'a glamorous figure thrown up by the last years of the Great War. His glamour shone all the more brightly because of the brutal and indecisive character of the First World War which shattered the romantic illusions cherished by so many in 1914.'[124] Like Lawrence, the Palestine campaign has had a romantic attraction, in part because of the use of cavalry, and this has tended to soften criticism of operations. In Palestine the efforts of the cavalry have been overstated in virtually all accounts of the campaign. Correspondingly, the artillery and infantry deployed are taken for granted, and their contribution overlooked. The three actions analysed show that, on the whole, combined operations in Palestine were not what they should, or could, have been, given more time to plan. The Palestine campaign marked the end of the age of cavalry; the age of machine-based warfare had arrived.

NOTES

I would like to thank the Trustees of the Liddell Hart Centre for Military Archives (LHCMA) for permission to quote from material for which they hold the copyright.

1. The terms Palestine, Trans-Jordan, Lebanon and Syria are used in this article, but did not come into existence, as states, until after the war. These were, however, widely used geographic terms of reference, and refer to the Ottoman *vilayets* of Syria and Aleppo (Syria and Trans-Jordan), and the *vilayet* of Beirut and the *sanjaks* of Jerusalem and Lebanon (Palestine and Lebanon). See the map in George Antonius, *The Arab Awakening* (London: Hamish Hamilton 1945) facing p.176.
2. For the historiography surrounding the First World War see the essays in Brian Bond (ed.) *The First World War and British Military History* (Oxford: Clarendon Press 1991)
3. Discounting the German Ludendorff offensives of early 1918 where the *Entente* lines were breached and the *Entente* 'Hundred Days' counter-offensives of late 1918 that continued until the Armistice.
4. Allenby's cavalry corps ultimately had four divisions of which two were cavalry and two mounted divisions. In this article the two terms will be used interchangeably but readers will be aware of some imprecision considering that the mounted troops had long bayonets instead of swords or lances. Allenby also had a camel brigade (the Imperial Camel Corps).
5. Anglesey, *A History of the British Cavalry 1816–1919, Volume 5, Egypt, Palestine and Syria, 1914–1919* (London: Leo Cooper 1994).
6. To borrow the title from John Keegan's ground-breaking book of that name.
7. Basil Liddell Hart, *History of the First World War* (London: Pan 1972) p.432.
8. For an analysis of the poor state of the EEF when Allenby took charge and how he lifted the spirits of the force see Matthew Hughes, 'General Allenby and the campaign of the Egyptian Expeditionary Force, June 1917–November 1919' (PhD Thesis: U. of London 1995) pp.9-25.
9. Expression used by J.D. Grainger, 'Subtlety, Misdirection, and Deceit: Allenby's Grand Tactics at Third Gaza', *RUSI Jnl* 140/2 (April 1995) p.59.
10. The oral history recordings at the Imperial War Museum, London (hereafter IWM), outline the harsh living conditions in the desert and how low was morale under Murray's command. For instance L. Pollock, IWM, 4200/B/A; Lord Harding, IWM, 8736/50, typescript of oral recording, p.57. See also Antony Bluett, *With Our Army in Palestine* (London: Andrew Melrose 1919) pp.182–3.
11. *Punch*, 19 Dec. 1917.
12. *The Islington Daily Gazette & North London Tribune*, 12 Dec. 1917, Islington Central Library, Holloway Road, London.
13. Quote from Cyril Falls, *Armageddon 1918* (London: Weidenfeld 1964) p.34. C. Falls and G. Macmunn, *Military Operations Egypt and Palestine* (London: HMSO 1928 and 1930) 2 vols. (hereafter *Official History* I or II). Macmunn was not up to the task of writing the official history and so Falls did the work with Macmunn's name appearing as a sop on Vol.I: see CAB16/52/Paper 20, pp.7–8, Public Record Office, London (hereafter PRO).

14. Isaac Babel's recently published 1920 *Diary* (ed. Carol Avins [Yale UP 1995]) of his time with Budenny's Cossacks gives some idea of the extensive mounted operations in Russia after the Great War.
15. For Beersheba see note 20 below. For Damascus see Elie Kedourie, *England and the Middle East: The Destruction of the Ottoman Empire 1914–21* (London: Mansell 1987) Ch.5; Kedourie, 'The Capture of Damascus, 1 October 1918' in *The Chatham House Version and other Middle-Eastern Studies* (Hanover and London: UP of New England 1984).
16. George de S. Barrow, *The Fire of Life* (London: Hutchinson 1942) p.46.
17. Russell to Wavell, 6 Aug.1937, p.2, Allenby Papers, 6/VIII/74, Liddell Hart Centre for Military Archives, King's College, London (hereafter LHCMA).
18. Jonathan Newell, 'Allenby and the Palestine Campaign', in Bond (note 2) p.225. See also J. Newell, 'British Military Policy in Egypt and Palestine August 1914 to June 1917' (PhD Thesis: U. of London 1990) and J. Newell, 'Learning the Hard Way: Allenby in Egypt and Palestine 1917–1919', *Jnl of Strategic Studies* 14/3 (Sept. 1991) pp.363–87.
19. First outlined in Clive Garsia, *A Key to Victory: A Study in War Planning* (London: Eyre & Spottiswoode 1940) although the 'Gaza School' is mentioned in *Official History* II, pp.32–3. See Garsia to CID, 10 Oct. 1928, CAB45/78, authors A–D, PRO. Garsia made the same point to Liddell Hart, 28 April 1934, Liddell Hart Papers, 1/306/1, LHCMA. Guy Dawnay (Allenby's BGGS) and Falls disagreed with Garsia: see Dawnay Papers, letters March–April 1937, 69/21/3, IWM and Falls to Liddell Hart, 14 May 1934, Liddell Hart Papers, 1/276/7, LHCMA.
20. Ian Jones, 'Beersheba: The Light Horse Charge and the Making of Myths', *Jnl of the Australian War Memorial* 3 (Oct. 1983) pp.26–37.
21. P.H. Dalbiac, *History of the 60th Division* (London: George Allen 1927) p.123. The Australian popular film *The Lighthorsemen* (1987) has an ALH trooper dramatically (and presumably erroneously) saving the wells.
22. H.S. Gullett, *Official History of Australia in the War, Volume VII, The Australian Imperial Force in Sinai and Palestine* (St Lucia: U. of Queensland Press 1984 reprint of 1923 ed.) pp.435–6. Hereafter *Australian Official History*.
23. Report to GOC, 17 June 1917, p.3, Bartholomew Papers, 1/1, LHCMA. The Turks could supposedly drink brackish water: see Henry Gullett Papers, 'Turks', AWM40/75, Australian War Memorial, Canberra (hereafter AWM).
24. Barrow to Archibald Wavell, 6 Jan. 1939, Allenby Papers, 6/VIII/19, LHCMA; Ryrie letter to wife, 5 Nov. 1917, Ryrie Papers, National Library of Australia, Canberra (hereafter NLA).
25. See Rowlands Coldicott, *London Men in Palestine and How They Marched to Jerusalem* (London: Edward Arnold 1919). Allenby to Edmonds, 22 July 1929, Edmonds Papers, II/2/197, LHCMA (see Hodgson to Barnard, 8 Feb. 1918, Hodgson Papers, 66/145/1, IWM for similar remarks).
26. For Australian war diaries see AWM4[10/9], app. to 4th ALH Regt, 28 Oct.–28 Nov. 1917, sheet 2 (AWM); also WO95/4550, GS Aust Mtd Div, Nov. 1917, war diary entries 3–10 Nov. 1917, PRO.
27. 'Beersheba', Gullett Papers, AWM40/59, AWM.
28. R.M.P. Preston, *The Desert Mounted Corps: An Account of the Cavalry Operation in Palestine and Syria, 1917–1918* (London: Constable 1921) p.50.
29. Chetwode to Macmunn, 17 May 1926, CAB25/78, authors A–D, PRO. Quote, Preston (note 28) p.58.
30. Kressenstein from Clive Garsia to Liddell Hart, 10 May 1934, Liddell Hart Papers, 1/306/4, LHCMA.
31. CAB24/4, G-199, 1 March 1918, p.3, PRO. For nature of coast see W. Lindsell, 'Military Administration in the Palestine Campaign', *Jnl of the Royal Artillery* (1928–29) p.378. For Rarotongans see Archibald Wavell, *Allenby: A Study in Greatness* (NY: Oxford UP 1940) p.263. There are 1993 Gregg Revival reprints of *A Study in Greatness* and Wavell's second volume *Allenby in Egypt* (1944), with new prefaces by Brian Holden Reid. Both volumes were also reissued by White Lion in 1974 as the single title *Allenby: Soldier and Statesman*.

ALLENBY AND THE PALESTINE CAMPAIGN 85

32. R. Tourret, *Hedjaz Railway* (Abingdon: Tourret Publishing 1989) pp.74–5. There is also a detailed study by William Ochsenwald entitled *The Hijaz Railroad* (UP of Virginia 1980).
33. Anglesey (note 5) p.141.
34. For Baku's fall see David Fromkin, *A Peace To End All Peace: Creating The Modern Middle East 1914–22* (London: Penguin 1991) pp.359–60 and Lionel Dunsterville, *The Adventures of Dunsterforce* (London: Edward Arnold 1920) Ch.7.
35. Liman von Sanders continually complains of this neglect in his account of the campaign, *Five Years in Turkey* (Annapolis, MD: US Naval Inst. Press 1927).
36. W.E.D. Allen, and Paul Muratov, *Caucasian Battlefields: A History of the War on the Turco-Caucasian Border 1828–1921* (CUP 1953) pp.477–8.
37. Frank Weber, *Eagles on the Crescent: Germany, Austria and the Diplomacy of the Turkish Alliance, 1914–1918* (London: Cornell UP 1970) p.245.
38. Ulrich Trumpener, *Germany and the Ottoman Empire 1914–1918* (Princeton UP 1968) pp.103–4.
39. POW statements 1914–18, AWM30/B2.1-B2.14, AWM.
40. Col Hussein Husni Amir Bey, 'Yilderim' Pt.3 (unpub.; trans. by G.O.de R. Channer: copy in AWM45[5/1] 'Heyes Papers', AWM) Ch.4, 20 Sept. 1917. See also ibid. app. 4, Kress to GOC 4th Army, 21 Sept. 1917.
41. M. Larcher, 'La Campagne du Général de Falkenhayn en Palestine', *Revue Militaire Française* (Oct. 1925) p.46.
42. Hussein Husni (note 40) Pt.3, Ch.5.
43. See Hughes (note 8) Ch.2.
44. GOC-in-C Egypt to CIGS, 12 July 1917, CAB24/20/GT1413, PRO.
45. Ibid. p.1.
46. Chetwode seems to have been behind the Beersheba plan. In 'Notes on the Palestine Operation', 21 June 1917 (Chetwode Papers, PP/MCR/C1, folder 3, IWM) Chetwode says that Allenby adopted his plan on arriving in Egypt. Parts of Allenby's July report are copied straight from these notes of Chetwode's.
47. On 8 Nov. 1917 Clayton remarked on the strength of Gaza's defences (Clayton to Wingate, Wingate Papers, 146/8/63–65, Sudan Archives, Durham). Coldicott (note 25) p.37 was an EEF officer with the same opinion.
48. Anon. 'The Campaign in Palestine from the Enemy's Side', *The Jnl of the Royal United Services Institute* 67 (1922) p.508. Partial translation of Kress von Kressenstein, *Zwischen Kaukasus und Sinai: Jahrbuch des Bundes der Asienkämpfer 1921* (Berlin-Tempelhof) (henceforth Von Kressenstein). Franz von Papen, *Memoirs* (London: Andre Deutsch 1952) p.71.
49. Hussein Husni (note 40) Pt.3 outlines the rundown Turkish defences.
50. Von Papen (note 48) p.73.
51. Archibald Wavell, *The Palestine Campaigns* (London: Constable 1933) p.115.
52. Ibid. pp.112–13 and *Official History* II, pp.35, 42–3.
53. 'Notes on Foreign War Books', *Army Qtly* (April 1922) p.159 gives 23,000. Von Kressenstein (note 48) p.510 gives 140,000 in the EEF (p.508 for hospital figures).
54. P.W. Long, *Other Ranks of Kut* (London: Williams & Norgate 1938) p.174 for shortage of anaesthetics.
55. Hussein Husni Pt.1, Ch.4 (see note 40 above).
56. *Official History* II, pp.42–3.
57. Von Kressenstein (note 48) p.511.
58. Allenby to WO, 28 Nov.[1917], Gullett papers, AWM40/45, AWM.
59. Garsia to Hare, 8 June 1920, Hare Papers, 66/85/1, 3rd Gaza folder, IWM (Garsia had been a GSO1 with 54th Div.).
60. See Allenby's 12 July request (CAB24/20/GT1413), pp.4-5, PRO; *Official History* II, p.14 and table in Wavell (note 51) pp.112–13.
61. Comparing the *Official History* (II, pp.14–5) with Wavell (note 51) pp.112–13 there seems to be a slight discrepancy. The EEF ration strength for 5 Nov. 1917 gives 462 guns which equals full divisional complement plus 90 (heavy?) guns (in WO106/43, GHQ Egypt to WO, pp.2,737–8, PRO).

62. *Official History* II, p.15.
63. CAB23/13/210(a), 10 Aug. 1917, p.1, PRO.
64. William Robertson, *Soldiers and Statesmen* (London: Cassell 1926) Vol.II, p.173. Also in Robertson Papers, I/16/6a, 'Palestine', 19 July 1917. LHCMA.
65. *Official History* II, p.65.
66. Von Papen (note 48) p.74. Misc. Collection at IWM and letter written 30 Oct.–12 Nov. 1917 by a rating in HMS *Comet*, pp.14–17.
67. Clayton, 'Robert Nivelle and the French Spring Offensive 1917', in Brian Bond (ed.) *Fallen Stars: Eleven Studies of Twentieth Century Military Disasters* (London: Brassey's 1991) pp.58–9 and Larcher (note 41) p.51.
68. For the stamina of the Turks see Hans Kannengiesser, *The Campaign in Gallipoli* (London: Hutchinson 1928) pp.146-9.
69. Ronald Storrs, *Memoirs of Sir Ronald Storrs* (NY: Arno Press 1972) p.290 (diary entry for 19 Dec.).
70. Letter to wife, 2 Nov. 1917, Dawnay Papers, 69/21/2, IWM.
71. Letter to father, 9 Nov. 1917, Hare Papers, folder on 3rd Gaza, IWM.
72. 'Turkish Machine Gun Defences and Emplacements', Maj Pardoe, 11 Nov. 1917, AWM25/923/23. See also ibid 'Report for DMC, 3/12/17 by Australian and NZ Mounted Division' (both at AWM).
73. The Turks had to strip Gaza of all its wood and this and EEF shelling meant that Gaza was badly damaged. See pictures in 'Australian Light Horse in Sinai & Palestine' film in AWM 00042. See also IWM film 11.
74. 'Allenby's 1st Offensive', Gullett Papers, AWM40/58, AWM (gas used by XXI Corps at Gaza).
75. In Wavell's correspondence in the Allenby Papers Chetwode says Dawnay drew up the actual details (Chetwode to Wavell, 17 Feb. 1939, 6/VIII/31). Point also made by Chauvel in a letter to the Australian War Memorial, 1 Jan. 1936, p.3 (in Allenby Papers, 7/4/1). Writing to Edmonds, Chetwode said that he handed Allenby the plan as he got off the boat (Chetwode to Edmonds, 26 Sept. 1926 [?], Edmonds Papers, II/1/32). All at LHCMA.
76. See Dawnay to Edmonds, 25 April 1928, CAB45/78, authors A-D, PRO. Dobell having a part in the plan: Dawnay to Wavell, 20 Aug. 1926, Dawnay Papers, 69/21/5. For Mott: Dawnay to Col Aeron-Thomas, 7 July 1950, ibid., 69/21/3, IWM.
77. Chetwode to Garsia, April 1937 [?], ibid.
78. David Lloyd George, *War Memoirs* (London: Odhams Press 1938) Vol.II, pp.1,089–90.
79. Two 'cockney' privates took the surrender: see Shea Papers, folder 4/5, LHCMA.
80. Hussein Husni (note 40) Pt.4, Ch.4 says that only 3,000 men stood between the EEF and Jerusalem.
81. Report 15 to Mark Sykes by his secretary (Lt Albina), 15 June 1918, pp.8–9, FO800/221. See also pigeon message from Lt Alec Kirkbride (with Prince Abdullah), 14 May 1918 WO158/638 (both PRO).
82. Notes by Chauvel on Ch.36 of *Australian Official History* (note 22), Gullett Papers, AWM40/97, AWM. A.J. Hill, *Chauvel of the Light Horse* (Victoria: Melbourne UP 1978) p.145.
83. For instance Deut. 11:14 and Zech. 10:1.
84. C. Guy Powles, *The New Zealanders in Sinai and Palestine*, Vol.III of the *Official History of New Zealand's Effort in the Great War* (Auckland: Whitcombe & Tombs 1922) Ch.7 (hereafter *NZ Official History*).
85. Aust Mtd Div, GS April 1918, 'Ops East of Jordan/Es Salt', 29/4–4/5/18, p.6, WO95/4551, PRO.
86. Wavell (note 51) p.181.
87. Ryrie letter to wife, 10 April 1918, Ryrie Papers, MS986/485–643, NLA.
88. 4th Bn ICC, roll 179, 30 March 1918, AWM4[11/9], AWM.
89. *NZ Official History* (note 84) p.197 for pack guns. Ryrie letter to wife, 10 April 1918, Ryrie Papers, MS986/485–643, NLA.
90. *Statistics of the Military Effort of the British Empire during the Great War, 1914–1920* (London: HMSO 1922) p.280. The figure of 543 was high for the Palestine campaign.

91. HQ 2nd ALH Bde, WD 27 March 1918, 20.15hrs, WO95/4538, PRO.
92. 7th ALH Regt, WD (Amman), roll 162, 28 March 1918, AWM4[10/12], AWM.
93. *NZ Official History* (note 84) p.202.
94. Bakig, *Amman: Yesterday and Today* (London and Ipswich: W.S. Cowell 1983) Plate 5.
95. Ryrie to wife, 10 April 1918, Ryrie Papers, MS986/485–643, NLA.
96. There are photographs of *cacolets* in Ian Jones, *The Australian Light Horse* (Australia Time Life 1987) pp.84, 108. See also *Australian Official History* (note 22) p.577.
97. Notes by Chauvel on Ch.35 of ibid., Gullett Papers, AWM40/97, AWM.
98. Statement by Sgt Halpin (of ALH), made POW 1/5/18, AWM30/B2.11, AWM.
99. 'Allenby', Gullett Papers, AWM40/77, AWM. In personal correspondence with this author, Alec Hill (Chauvel's biographer, note 82), also points out that there was too much 'loose talk'.
100. Von Sanders (note 35) p.226.
101. See *Official History* II, p.392 and O. Welsch, 'Cavalry in the Palestine Campaign', *Cavalry Journal* 17 (trans. of article in *Militär-Wochenblatt*) (1927) p.299 for build-up on west bank.
102. Statement by POW Sgt Halpin, AWM30/B2.11, AWM.
103. '2nd Es Salt', Gullett Papers, AWM40/62, AWM.
104. 'Personal Note', ibid., AWM40/72, AWM.
105. Shea to Wavell, 10 May [1939?], Allenby Papers, 6/IX-X/40–41, LHCMA.
106. Personal correspondence, Alec Hill to author, 24 Oct. 1994.
107. 'Joint Note 12 Submitted to the Supreme War Council by its Military Representatives', 21 Jan. 1918. Copies in *History of the Great War, France and Belgium, 1918*, Appendices (London: HMSO 1935) app.9, para 19; WO106/729 and CAB25/68 (by H. Wilson dated 19 Jan. 1918).
108. A.J.P. Taylor, *English History 1914–1945* (Oxford: Clarendon Press 1983) p.140.
109. Summary of trip in W.K. Hancock and J.van der Poel (eds.), *Selections from the Smuts Papers* (Cambridge: 1966) Vol.3, Gen. Smuts' Mission to Egypt, pp.612–24.
110. Von Papen (note 48) p.76.
111. Allenby to Wilson, 5 June 1918, Wilson Papers, HHW2/33A/4, IWM. For Pathan discontent see reports in L/MIL/17/5/3919-3920, Oriental and India Office Collections, British Library, London.
112. GHQ Egypt to War Office, 1 July 1918, Milner Papers, III/B/140, Bodleian Library, Oxford (29% per cent figure here also).
113. For T.E. Lawrence's report on the battle of Tafilah see Malcolm Brown (ed.) *Secret Despatches from Arabia* (London: Bellew 1991) pp.175–9.
114. Feisal's Arabs were close on the heels of the EEF but 3rd ALH Bde were the first into Damascus, and the NAA was reliant on the success of the EEF for their advance from Dera'a.
115. T.E. Lawrence, *Seven Pillars of Wisdom* [1935] (London: Penguin 1962) pp.653–5.
116. H.S. Leeson *et al.* 'Anopheles and Malaria in the Near East', *London School of Hygiene and Tropical Medicine*, Memoir 7 (1950) p.6. My thanks to Dr Chris Curtis and Ms Mary Gibson at the London School of Hygiene and Tropical Medicine for their help explaining malaria to me. For an interesting general study of malaria see L.J. Bruce-Chwatt and J.de Zulueta, *The Rise and Fall of Malaria in Europe: A historico-epidemiological study* (Oxford: OUP 1980).
117. For casualties from malaria in 1918 see *Official History* II, p.597; *Australian Official History* (note 22), pp.773, 780 and Hill (note 82) p.183.
118. Translation of a document captured by DMC during operations 19–21 Sept. 1918, Clayton Papers, 694/6/6–8, Durham.
119. See H.A. Jones, *Official History of the War in the Air* (Oxford: Clarendon Press 1935 and 1937) Vols.V and VI.
120. For an account of the actions of armoured cars operating with the Arabs see S.C. Rolls, *Steel Chariots in the Desert* (London: Jonathan Cape 1937).
121. Discounting Lloyd George's time in the Militia in 1881–82: see John Grigg, *The Young Lloyd George* (London: Methuen 1973), p.44.

122. Terms used by Keith Simpson in, 'Frock Coats, Mandarins and Brasshats: The Relationship between Politicians, Civil Servants and the Military', *RUSI Jnl* 137/1 (Feb. 1992) pp.57–63.
123. Translated Turkish sources are hard to find, and the original documents are written in a form of the Ottoman language that requires knowledge of both Turkish and Arabic. The Armenian massacres have not encouraged access to Turkish archives, although the Turkish General Staff in Ankara recently sponsored and published two volumes on the campaign: *The Official History of the Ottoman Army in Sinai and Palestine* (1979 and 1986).
124. Reid, 'T.E. Lawrence and his Biographers', in Bond (note 2) p.227.

The British Expeditionary Force and the Difficult Transition to 'Peace', 1918–1919

IAN M. BROWN

During the Great War, the British Expeditionary Force (BEF) managed to develop a highly efficient and effective administrative infrastructure. By the summer of 1918, it became capable of supporting simultaneous offensive action by multiple British armies. From the Armistice on 11 November 1918, however, British administrators found themselves in the unenviable position of watching this infrastructure begin to collapse under the stress of the transition to peace; a problem made more acute by the temporary nature of the Armistice, and by the eight months of waiting for the Peace of 28 June 1919. This essay examines this deterioration in capability. Drawn extensively from archival sources, particularly the war diaries of British administrative officers, it briefly examines the state of British capability in 1918, and then looks to 1919 and the difficulties caused by the transition from the Armistice to the Peace.

Meeting the German Spring Offensive

On 1 January 1918 the BEF's commanders and administrators faced the task of preparing their units and formations for the assumed German spring offensive. Many of the most difficult problems had to be solved by the rear area administration. British rear area services had exhibited competence in 1917 when four very large offensives (Arras, Messines, Passchendaele and Cambrai) had been supported. This meant that the BEF's administration took the necessary steps to prepare for the spring of 1918 well ahead of time. During the winter, each of the five British armies prepared a defence in depth, usually in three defensive zones which roughly followed the German example of a defence-in-depth system. They then estimated their needs for a defensive battle and decided on railheads in the case of fighting in each defensive zone. These figures amounted to roughly 50 daily trains per army, depending upon its strength. Fifth Army (Gough), for example, gave a daily rail estimate of one-half supply train per division (the standard divisional pack), one-half supply train per corps for Corps Troops, one supply train per day for Army Troops, four ammunition trains per corps in the line, one engineering stores train per corps in the line, two roadstone trains per corps in the line, two roadstone trains for the Army Troops, and 14 ambulance trains in the first 24 hours of defensive fighting (this dropped to 12 per day for the next 48 hours).[1] These figures may be taken as reasonably standard throughout the BEF, since only the ambulance and ammunition trains might be expected to show great variance. Looking only at Fifth Army and Third Army (Byng), which ultimately bore the brunt of the first of the German offensives, they comprised seven corps in the line with 21 divisions between them, and 12 divisions in reserve positions.[2] Assuming a static defensive battle, the 103 daily trains required could be maintained – this should have been well within capabilities, given that this figure had been comfortably exceeded during Messines and Third Ypres (see Table 1). Unfortunately, a static defensive battle was not what the Germans planned for Fifth and Third Armies, and the rear areas of Fifth Army did not enjoy the rail network that supported the more northerly armies.

TABLE 1
DAILY TRAIN RATES IN SELECTED BRITISH OFFENSIVES

Offensive	Average Number of Divisions	Number of Trains Daily	Number of Trains Daily (@ 33 Divs.)
Messines	20	67.5	111.5
Third Ypres	19	64.5	112
Cambrai (attack)	25	51.5	68
Cambrai (defence)	28	77.5	91
1918 estimate	33	103	103

The history of the German Spring Offensives is generally well known.[3] From a British perspective, these offensives caused tremendous strains – threatening the vital centres of Amiens and Hazebrouck in March and April respectively. At the end of March, the Quartermaster General (QMG) reported that losses in motorised transport had been more severe than anticipated. Some 380 lorries and, most seriously, 80 Holt tractors had been lost.[4] While not a desperate loss, indeed they represent a tiny fraction of the motorised transport available, they proved more difficult to replace than artillery, since the delivery of replacements to France used space needed by other classes of supply – space that the submarine war had ensured remained in short supply. By 29 March the Germans held Bapaume, Albert, Péronne, Nesle, Ham, Chauny, Noyon, Roye and Montdidier. The British held new front lines, in some places 45 miles from where they had been eight days previously, with the Germans on the outskirts of Villers-Bretonneux and able to shell Amiens, only ten miles distant.[5] This meant that nearly all of Fifth and Third Army's railheads from a fortnight before had been captured, along with rolling stock and many miles of broad and narrow gauge railway track, and that north-south movement behind the front through Amiens was very hazardous.

Ammunition Expenditure, Spring 1918

The BEF expended an enormous quantity of ammunition in the spring. In the three weeks following the launch of the *Michael* offensive, the artillery used just under 5.5 million 18-pounder and nearly 1.5 million 4.5in howitzer shells.[6] This represented nearly the total number of 18-pounder shells available to the BEF just prior to the Somme Offensive 21 months previously. During April, 725 ammunition trains ran to the front[7] – nearly as many as ran during the whole five months of the Somme Offensive.[8] In both months combined, the BEF fired nearly nine million 18-pounder shells, and over 15 million shells in total, of which, heavy shells numbered nearly four million rounds.[9] In spite of such heavy expenditure, and with the exception of 9.2in howitzer shells (of which the BEF expended 50 per cent more than it received), the receipts of ammunition at the base ports significantly exceeded requirements – a clear sign that greatly increased production in France had been matched by an efficient and effective handling system in France. For example, the field artillery and what would later be called medium artillery (60-pounders and 6in howitzers) only expended between 62 and 70 per cent of receipts. The heavy artillery other than 9.2in howitzers required between 78 and 96 per cent of receipts.[10] In all, during the March and April offensives, the BEF's rear area services moved nearly 350,000 tons of ammunition, an average of more than 8,700 tons per day (higher in March), over tracks heavily congested by the dislocation caused by the German advance and by efforts to interdict vital junctions such as Amiens and Hazebrouck. Such traffic could not have been supported in 1916, and might not have been fully possible in 1917. The culmination of years of effort and reorganization, however, left the BEF in the enviable position of having that capability in 1918.

German Disruption Efforts

By 27 April, when the offensive on the Lys petered out, the Germans controlled Armentières, Bailleul, nearly the whole of the ground won during Passchendaele, and Estaires. Further, they were on the edge of Ypres in the north, only 2,500 yards from Béthune on the south, and 6,000 yards from the important rail centre of Hazebrouck in the centre of the battle area.[11] The Germans made great efforts to disrupt the BEF's lines of communication in May. The Director of Ordnance Service's War Diary for May makes this clear. The first entry on 21 May noted that No.12 Ordnance Depot at Blargies had been bombed overnight and 5,000 tons of ammunition lost. The next night, the Germans bombed No.20 Ordnance Depot at Saigneville and cost the BEF 60 million rounds of small arms ammunition.[12] The German bombing combined with the offensives to handicap the BEF, by ensuring that both of their major forward marshalling and switching yards remained partially interdicted until the summer, and by hindering moving traffic.

By May, the entire British transportation system had been reduced to a chaotic state. While actually stopping short of Amiens and Hazebrouck, the German March and April advances had significantly hurt the BEF's lines of communication by capturing several light rail systems, some broad-gauge engine depots, and by placing the main frontal lateral line under fire. In addition, the Germans mounted air attacks on the rear lateral line at Etaples and Abbeville. The rear line was, as a result, subject to minor delays while the front line remained usable but precarious.[13] As a result, a tremendous cumulative strain placed stress on the whole railway system. The front line could not be used fully, so the back line received more traffic. Minor delays on the back line added to congestion, which forced the administration to try to move more materiel by other means. This meant that the motorised transport took up a very heavy load and, in fact, this left the roads 'in a critical condition' due to the increased traffic.[14] Ultimately, this cumulative congestion forced the stoppage of all non-necessary rail traffic for three days in early June, and led to a conference at Calais to try to find a better way to utilise engines and rolling stock.[15] By the end of June, the QMG considered that the Germans had worked hard to hinder the delivery of supplies, their interdiction efforts targeting base ports, depots and lateral line constrictions, and causing a great deal of inconvenience, but that they never managed to stop the flow of supplies.[16] However, the QMG remained anxious because the Germans were obviously trying to pinch supply lines and there was an insufficient margin of safety.[17]

BEF '100 Days' Offensives

August 1918

In August the QMG looked back on the trials of the spring and made the ironic observation that they had helped to prepare the BEF's administrative services for the advances of the summer.[18] These began in earnest for the BEF on 8 August when the Australian and Canadian Corps spearheaded an assault by Fourth Army (Rawlinson) which eased the pressure on Amiens. Other sites might have been chosen, but the weak nature of the German defence and the vital importance of the Amiens marshalling yards made the location of the attack a wise one. The importance of the Battle of Amiens cannot be understated. This is clear from an appreciation of the German spring attacks in the south made by General Sir Henry Rawlinson, who felt that the loss of Amiens, 'would cut off the Armies in the North from Railway communication with the rest of France'.[19] This attack required quite an administrative effort, as the entire Canadian Corps (four over-strength divisions, and extra Corps' artillery assets) had to be moved from First Army (Horne) to Fourth Army in ten days with absolute secrecy. A planned deception misled the Germans as they believed the attack would be launched by First Army. The attack proved a complete operational success, and once it began to peter out, around 13 August, Haig made the strategic decision to change the axis of the BEF's attacks. By the end of August, the Canadian Corps had been returned to First Army and had begun offensive operations on the River Scarpe. In 1916, Haig could not have so easily switched the axis of his attacks, but the administrative excellence brought about by four years of hard-won experience made it a relatively simple matter by 1918. The advances in August had been well supported, and a policy adopted on 27 August of concentrating on the advance of broad gauge railways and roads had worked well.[20] By August 1918, all types of ammunition, with the exception of 6in howitzer, remained readily available, and the problems of previous years with bad fuses and high explosives no longer caused serious problems.[21]

September 1918

September 1918 proved a difficult month for the BEF, as the continued advance threw an increasing strain on the lines of communication. Bad weather slowed shipments to France, and the further the BEF advanced from their base ports, the more the 'logistic equaliser' came into play. (The 'logistic equaliser' is a term which refers to the relative difficulty of operating near to or far away from supply sources. The further one advances, the greater the difficulty in moving supplies forward, while the enemy's task becomes easier as he falls back on his sources of supply.) In addition, the enormous demands of formations in the fighting made this equaliser even more pronounced. For example, the first three days of the operations which forced the Canal du Nord (27 to 29 September) saw the expenditure of 62,813 tons of ammunition, an average of 20,937 tons per day.[22] The QMG had to handle this extra demand despite a serious shortage of rolling stock.[23] The final complication was the extra strain placed on the larger ports on the southern line of communications by the need to supply the American Expeditionary Forces – the smaller northern ports were not as suitable for supplying British needs in full – and the need to feed large numbers of liberated civilians.[24]

An idea of the power of British and Allied administrative superiority can be gained from the offensives launched in late September 1918. After the pause which followed the advances in August and early September, the Allied powers launched a series of concentric offensives. The first, involving the US First Army and French Fourth Army, opened on 26 September; the second, that of First and Third Armies on the Canal du Nord, on the 27th; the third, by the Groupe d'Armées des Flandres, on 28th; and the fourth, by Fourth Army and French First Army, on the 29th.[25] GHQ faced the task of providing support for three field armies launching attacks over a wide front almost simultaneously, at the end of supply lines stretched by the advances of the previous month – a very difficult task. Much of this only became possible as a result of the unification of Allied command under Generalissimo Ferdinand Foch. After his appointment,

> large scale strategical movements became common. French corps were moved to and from the British area, British corps were moved to and from the French area, and reserve armies composed of British, French, Americans and Italians were assembled from time to time and place to place as the situation demanded.[26]

October 1918

Such strategic power led to a marked Allied superiority in late 1918. In spite of their interior lines of communication, the Germans could not cope with the counter-offensives launched in rapid succession in late September, and indeed throughout the summer and autumn.

The serious logistic strain on the British continued in October, as all the British armies remained active and advancing. Indeed, the faster the Germans retired, the harder it became for the BEF to keep up, and the more the BEF began to experience some of the problems which would hinder them after the Armistice.[27] This caused considerable anxiety among the commanders chasing the Germans; Lt-General Sir Arthur Currie (GOC Canadian Corps) wrote in his diary on 20 October:

THE BEF AND TRANSITION TO PEACE 1918-19 95

... the fact remains that the enemy is making a very orderly and practically unmolested retirement. Our trouble is that the troops are very tired and that the getting forward of supplies is becoming very difficult owing to the distance away of railheads.[28]

This problem recurred immediately after the Armistice due to the great distance between base ports, railheads and the front lines. Because of the decision to concentrate on broad gauge railways wherever possible, light railways had ceased to play a role in movement of supplies and had been left behind while motorised transport took up the slack. This led to the breakdown of both machines and drivers due to chronic over-use, although the troops never suffered a serious lack of food. Ammunition remained plentiful at railheads. However, once moved forward and dumped, problems began, because artillery batteries moved rapidly forward in order to stay in touch with the advance.[29] As a result, numerous small dumps of ammunition remained throughout the British rear areas which had to be collected and moved forward again. This all combined to frustrate aggressive field commanders like Currie. In regard to the difficulties placed on the lines of communication, Lt-General Sir Travers Clarke (Haig's QMG in 1918) wrote to Lt-General Sir John Cowans (QMG of the Forces, War Office) on 6 October that, 'things are going well out here, but our department is stretched to the utmost; however, thanks to your help we have got all we want, and the troops are being very well catered to in every way'.[30] The aggressive commanders clearly wanted to push forward, but Travers Clarke's Q Branch had reached the limits of their capability.

The Armistice and Aftermath

Until the Armistice came into effect at 11.00am on 11 November, the strain on the road and rail transport services remained immense. Once the Armistice had been signed, the reduction of ammunition supply only meant a 10 to 15 per cent reduction in total military traffic. As a result, the Armistice merely provides a useful way-point in the study of British administration. It must be borne in mind that ammunition did not make up the majority of supply shipments to the front lines. Indeed, based on total shipments to France, it amounted to an overall total of roughly 10 per cent of supplies, perhaps as much as 15 per cent in 1917 and 1918. At that level of supply, forage for horses out-massed ammunition, and food for the men came close. Ammunition records, however, are quite complete and detailed, and ammunition expenditure harder to predict than food, so the delivery of ammunition challenged the administration in France more than most other classes of supply.

96 MILITARY POWER: LAND WARFARE IN THEORY AND PRACTICE

Rhineland Occupation Plans

With the Armistice, the BEF's administrative echelons suddenly had to deal with the questions surrounding the supply of the armies earmarked for the occupation of the Rhineland.[31] The armies of occupation had to be moved to the occupied zone, potentially large numbers of destitute civilians had to be cared for, and generous plans had to be made for returning British prisoners of war released by the Germans. Orders for military stores from England had to be cancelled and plans for the Army's maintenance revised. Provision had to be made for rapid demobilisation, even if only partial, which would add additional strain to the system. Finally, the QMG's Branch would have to be reorganised to supply two armies in Germany and the armies remaining behind in France and Belgium.

When the fighting ceased, the BEF initially planned to occupy their portion of the Rhineland with two armies (Second and Fourth), leaving the rest roughly where they had stopped on 11 November. This meant supplying eight corps and 32 infantry divisions at an extended distance from ports and railheads. Administratively this could not be done, for two main reasons. First, the boundary zone where the British and German armies had met formed a devastated area or gap of up to 20 kilometres in depth where the transportation infrastructure had been severely damaged by the fighting and by the efforts of German rearguards to deny the infrastructure to the BEF. This required a great deal of costly and time-consuming repair work. Second, the BEF had been operating through much of October and November at increasing distances from both railheads and base ports. In spite of tremendous efforts at repairing damaged and destroyed railway lines, and the very effective use of motorised transport to fill some of the gap, the BEF had practically reached its administrative limit. Indeed, it is unclear how much longer an advance could have been sustained, had hostilities continued.

Re-opening Belgian Railways

The BEF followed a sound and coherent policy in regard to re-opening lines across the inter-army gap. Almost immediately upon the Armistice, railway construction ceased in rear areas, and the assets thus freed began work on three main routes across the gap. Ultimately, reconnaissance led to an additional (fourth) route being chosen. In addition, the BEF undertook to repair such lines as were requested by Belgian authorities, where good reasons could be shown. For example, the QMG agreed to re-open lines which served the mining districts and those that moved coal to Brussels. The damage to the various means of communication in Belgium proved a severe handicap to the allies. German railway personnel abandoned their posts on the Belgian railways, and Belgian personnel did not know the extent of the damage to the rail net. Therefore, the BEF's administration had no firm idea of what kind of supply system could be maintained in forward areas. A measure of the difficulties faced can be had from A. M. Henniker's description in the Official History:

> Communication by telegraph or telephone across the devastated area hardly existed; the only way to obtain information and circulate instructions was by motor-car and despatch rider, and lack of petrol in Belgium at times brought these to a standstill. Two or three weeks were required to ascertain the position.... Meanwhile, the armies of the Allies had advanced across Belgium while the communications were still in a state of disorganization.[32]

Given that telegraph and telephone lines are far more easily laid than road or railway beds, the challenge to administrators must have been extreme. They had to improvise on a scale never experienced before. While improvisation had proven successful in 1914–15, Travers Clarke now faced a problem which was an order of magnitude greater: supplying five armies at extended distances from port and railhead with two of them on the move over land lines of communication two to three times the length faced in 1914–15 was clearly an enormous task. Further complicating matters, a regular passenger service had been reinstated between Paris, Boulogne, Calais, Lille and Brussels. These trains, moving faster than troop or supply trains, had priority on the lines they used, and this meant that the smooth system that had been developed during the war suffered. The passenger trains interrupted regular military services and meant that timings for military trains could no longer be so reliable. Even when carefully predicted, one late-running passenger train could dramatically disrupt schedules. The lack of lines over the inter-army gap exacerbated the problems when civilian trains ran to Lille or Brussels, and increased the load placed on the BEF's already-strained motorised transport echelons.

Canadian Corps' March to the Rhine, November–December 1918

A measure of the BEF's difficulty in supplying the troops on the march to the Rhine can be had from the example of the Canadian Corps. This Corps had been assigned to Second Army for the Rhineland occupation, and Corps headquarters issued orders for the move by 16 November.[33] By 23 November, the plans for the advance had been amended, and the decision made by GHQ that only Second Army could advance.

This amendment was made necessary by the difficulty of bringing forward the necessary supplies owing to the thorough destruction of railways and roads in the battle areas, and the immense amount of work required to effect temporary repairs sufficient to take care of the needs of the Army and of the Belgian population.

Weather and the deterioration of resupply forced the Corps to halt on 26 November. Daily rains began on that day, and, combined with the heavy traffic, led to a serious deterioration of the road conditions and compelled the Corps to restrict itself to first-class roads, rather than use side-roads. The march on 27 November proved a very trying one for the troops because of the traffic and mud, and reduced the first-class roads to a poor condition. This all conspired to make resupply very tenuous:

> [The] railhead was still west of Valenciennes, necessitating a haul of over 100 miles by road to the leading troops, and mention has already been made of the congestion of traffic on the roads. As a result, supplies had been reaching the Units later each day, and the safety margin ordinarily maintained, of one day's rations in hand, had been lost. The climax was reached on November 28th, when rations for that day were received just as the day's march was commencing – in fact some of the Units of the 1st Canadian Division had already passed the starting-point. As the same situation recurred on the 29th, it was necessary to cancel the march of the 1st Canadian Division for that day.

Currie's administrative staff coped by utilising the lorries of the Canadian Machine Gun Corps to bolster the movement of supplies. This allowed the march to continue on 30 November. The final stages of the Corps' march to Cologne took place between 4 and 12 December in bad weather and 'without incident or trouble other than that of supplies'. The two divisions of the Canadian Corps which occupied their section of the Rhineland had taken nearly one month to make an advance of some 80 to 90 miles, and only the strenuous efforts of the rear area services had allowed its completion. It must be assumed that other British formations had similar problems. Clearly, the BEF could not have remained, by December, the same efficient fighting formation that it had been on 11 November. However, the existence of an armistice meant that some offensive capability had to be maintained.

Demobilisation

Euphoric stories in the press and unrealistically optimistic promises by politicians got demobilisation off to a bad start, and the Army on the continent came to believe that the 'false start is the basis of all our difficulties'.[34] This caused further problems for the BEF, by increasing the expectations of the population in Britain without indicating the extent of the difficulties faced on the continent. The QMG's greatest problem had become the feeding and continued supply of British formations in France, Belgium and the Rhineland over rail lines in host countries which were desperate to return to civilian trade and traffic. The Armistice meant that the notional preference of military traffic was not applied in practice. In particular, civilian passenger trains, which ran at considerably faster speeds than military troop trains, tended to get preference and interfered with wartime practices on the railways.[35] This greatly hindered the BEF's and BAOR's administration. Haig wrote in early 1919 that,

> My opinion of the railway situation is that the French Gov[ernmen]t is now running too many *civilian* trains, and fast expresses, and that consequently our military traffic is suffering. The French railways at present are under manned, and a large number of lines in this part of France are still in an indifferent state of repair as the result of the war.... I do not admit for a moment that my Transportation branch is at fault. They do all that the French rail[roa]d people ask them to do. And the manner in which broken railway lines, telegraphs, stations etc. etc. have been repaired, and traffic handled under most difficult conditions is beyond all praise.[36]

The problem must have been grave, for Haig wanted a government delegation to come out to France and speak with the French minister for railways on this matter, but Haig did not enjoy great influence with David Lloyd George's government after the Armistice, and he had little sway, as a result, in Paris.

By 1 January 1919, some 100,000 British soldiers whose trades were needed at home had been demobilised from the BEF. These included engineers, builders, miners, and farmers, but not railway personnel. The plans drawn up as soon as late 1916 proved to be useful guides for what was to come. The decision had been made early on that the transportation system and demobilisation centres could not be expected to handle more than 50,000 men per week. This meant that the men could be reintroduced to Britain with some semblance of care and orderliness at a rate which did not overtax the diminished transportation capacity. The difficulty of demobilising a two million-man expeditionary force, which included two national armies (Australian and Canadian) requiring long distance shipping, proved enormous. When the demobilisation of the American Expeditionary Forces' two million men, all of whom had to be returned to the United States, is added in, the problem became even more complex. As of 1 October 1918, the British Army in all overseas theatres, including Dominion troops and Indian Army troops serving outside India, amounted to 2,931,560 men, the majority of these with the BEF. Six months later, on 1 April 1919, 1.45 million of those had been demobilised and the total size of the British Army at home and abroad had dropped to nearly half what it had been the previous October.[37] Some 900,000 of those demobilised came from the BEF, and this further taxed the transportation system, since these men had to be moved and supplied while such movement and supply remained unreliable.

Contingency Plans for Armistice Breakdown

From a military perspective, Clause F (section 34) of the Armistice is most important, but generally ignored. It reads: 'The duration of the Armistice is to be 36 days, with option to extend.' During this period, on failure of execution of any of the above clauses, the Armistice may be repudiated by one of the contracting parties on 48 hours previous notice.'[38] Although the Armistice did, as it turned out, ultimately end hostilities, this could not be guaranteed at the time and its signing did not mark the end of the War. Indeed, with the Armistice's validity only holding for 36 days, it had to be extended. The various parties signed extensions on 13 December, 16 January, and 16 February, with a further protocol added on 4 April. The need continually to extend the Armistice created uncertainty, and this uncertainty left the BEF's administration in an invidious position. The British government had promised rapid demobilisation, but two million men took a considerable time to return to civilian life. Further, they still had to be maintained in the field while waiting to demobilise, and two armies in the Rhineland needed to be fed at the end of supply lines which still stretched to the channel ports.

In fact, the commanders of the Rhineland occupation force, BAOR (British Army of the Rhine), had to face the very real prospect that the German government would not accept the terms presented at Versailles. In late May 1919, General Sir William Robertson (Commander-in-Chief, BAOR)[39] let Field-Marshal Sir Henry Wilson, the Chief of the Imperial General Staff (CIGS) at Versailles, know that he needed more railway personnel, clearly because of uncertainty about permanent peace. If Robertson had to face renewed hostilities, he needed the logistic capability to support his army in offensive operations. Wilson responded with an overview of the situation on 5 June, writing,

> My own opinion is that when two people want to sign a paper as much as do the Allies and the Boches it will take more than all the Powers in all the Capitals to prevent it. Therefore I personally think there is very little chance indeed of your having to move forward [to Berlin]. It is because of this that I keep on refusing to allow you to have the railway personnel etc. from France which you otherwise would undoubtedly require.[40]

THE BEF AND TRANSITION TO PEACE 1918-19   101

In this, Wilson held similar views to those of Lloyd George, who wrote years later of a meeting of the British Empire and Dominion representatives at Versailles, who apparently all felt some apprehension that the Germans might refuse to sign the Treaty. The Prime Minister wrote,

> Some speakers went so far as to insinuate that such was the French hatred of Germany, that they were hoping that such a refusal would be provoked by the harshness of the Treaty in order to justify a military occupation of the German capital. I was convinced at the time – and still am – that no responsible Frenchman had that thought in his mind.... But the apprehension of a refusal to sign undoubtedly influenced some of the speakers at this Cabinet Conference.[41]

However, 'very little' still implied that Robertson faced some chance of having to renew offensive operations, slim though it might have been. Indeed, after the war, Major General Henry T. Allen, US Army, wrote that, 'by June, 1919, the situation had changed so considerably that renewal of the war appeared as a distinct possibility'.[42] Robertson replied in such a way as to leave Wilson in no doubt about his limited capabilities, warning,

> What you say about the possibility of a further advance is what I expected; at the same time, a week or two ago Foch seemed very busy, and as you will remember, you also telegraphed me to get ready. I cannot get ready unless I am given the means, nor can I get ready at a moment's notice. So long as this is understood I shall be satisfied, and will do my best to conform to what is required of me.[43]

A week later, Wilson gave Robertson a date after which he would know about possible military action, but this also included a line which read, 'I am writing to the War Office to inform them of this [the date] and to tell them to let Asser know he may have to send you up the railway personnel at short notice.'[44] In his next letter Wilson enclosed an appreciation which he had sent to the Prime Minister on 16 June. In part this read,

> I think that our force of 39 Divisions is enough to accomplish the operation you wish carried out, viz the march on and the occupation of the Capital [Berlin], but if such a manoeuvre is not instantly successful in attaining your object I would be very anxious indeed as to what might follow.[45]

The Peace Treaty of Versailles, June 1919

Clearly, and in spite of what civilians would have liked to believe, for Robertson and the remaining commanders and staff officers of the BEF and BAOR, the war could not end until the Treaty had been signed by the

Germans. This occurred on 28 June 1919, and only then could Robertson put plans for the resumption of hostilities on the shelf and really get down to the business of final demobilisation and to the analysis of the war with a view to the future. The British Army realised quite well the difficulties it had faced after the Armistice. On the question of why the Allied armies did not simply advance to Berlin and dictate terms, the accepted answer, and the correct one, remained valid. Reflecting on this experience, seven years later, an officer observed that 'such an army could not have been maintained during its advance. It was with the utmost difficulty that the force that did go forward was fed until the railway system could be reconstructed behind it.'[46] Unfortunately, the Army had little influence over Prime Minister Lloyd George after the Armistice, so it had to cope as best it could on what it received – which is a British tradition.

The BEF, and British Army as a whole, learned a great deal from the administrative challenges of 1919 and later. The occupation of the Rhineland proved a tremendous strain on the resources available. Indeed, had more been required, for example because of a renewal of hostilities, it is unlikely that the administration could have delivered. This inability, however, resulted from the demands on the system made by the return to civil control, and the administration of the BEF and BAOR cannot be greatly faulted since they had little influence in the corridors of power at that time. A resumption of hostilities would have been very difficult, but it would also have implied a return of the railways to the control of the French *Commission Regulatrice* and to the administration of the British armies in Europe. They could rapidly have recovered much of the efficiency demonstrated in 1917 and 1918, had it been required. With the ultimate signing of the Peace of Versailles on 28 June 1919, such problems no longer mattered. After that time, British administration could concentrate on peacetime maintenance and the final demobilisation of all non-regular British soldiers and the return to a peacetime routine.

NOTES

1. A.M. Henniker, *Transportation on the Western Front, 1914–1918* (London: HMSO 1937) pp.355-8. This is one of the British Official Histories of the Great War compiled by direction of the Historical Section of the Committee of Imperial Defence and, as such, is in the same category of official histories as James E. Edmonds, *Military Operations: France and Belgium*, 14 vols. (London: HMSO various dates). Hereafter, Henniker's work will be abbreviated to *Official History (Transportation)* and other volumes of the Official History will be abbreviated with year and volume: e.g. *Official History (1918, 2)* will indicate Vol.2 of the five concerning 1918.
2. Tim Travers, *The Killing Ground: The British Army, The Western Front and the Emergence of Modern Warfare, 1900–1918* (London: Allen & Unwin 1987) p.272 (map).
3. Good short assessments of the German offensives are contained in Holger Herwig,

'Dynamics of Necessity: German Military Policy During the First World War', in Allan R. Millett and Williamson Murray (eds.) *Military Effectiveness* (Boston: Unwin Hyman 1988) Vol.1 and Travers (note 2). More extensive studies of the various offensive techniques can be had from Bruce Gundmundsson, *Stormtroop Tactics: Innovation in the German Army* (NY and London: Praeger 1989) and Timothy T. Lupfer, *The Dynamics of Doctrine: The Changes in German Tactical Doctrine During the First World War*, No.4 Leavenworth Paper (Ft Leavenworth, KS: Combat Studies Inst., US Army Command & Gen Staff Coll. 1981), though these tend to make an assumption that the German High Command was more effective than Allied commands because of their attempt to use maneuvre warfare in 1917–18.
4. Public Record Office, London (hereafter PRO), WO107/16 (letter 607), Travers Clarke to Cowans, 31 March 1918. See also, War Office, *Statistics of the Military Effort of the British Empire During the Great War, 1914–1920* (London: HMSO 1922) pp.593–4 for tables showing numbers of motorised vehicles in each theatre of war. Hereafter, abbreviated: War Office, *Statistics* (note 4).
5. See Sketch Map, *Official History (1918, 1)* p.532.
6. *Official History (1918, 2)* table, p.494.
7. PRO, WO95/38, QMG Branch, War Diary, 30 April 1918.
8. Figures for ammunition expenditure and estimates of the number of trains run have been drawn from PRO, WO95/3964–69, 'Inspector-General of Communication, War Diary, January to July 1916'.
9. *Official History (1918, 2)* table, p.494.
10. Ibid.
11. See Sketch Map, *Official History (1918, 2)* p.442.
12. PRO, WO95/59, Director of Ordnance Services, War Diary, 21 and 22 May 1918.
13. PRO, WO95/38, QMG Branch, War Diary, Explanatory Review, May 1918.
14. Ibid. May 1918 and 8 May 1918.
15. PRO, WO95/39, QMG Branch, War Diary, 5 and 7 June 1918.
16. Ibid. QMG Branch, War Diary, Explanatory Review, June 1918.
17. Ibid.
18. Ibid. Aug. 1918.
19. Imperial War Museum, London (hereafter IWM), HHW2/13, FM Sir Henry Wilson Papers, 'An Appreciation', 18 April 1918, by Gen. Sir Henry Rawlinson.
20. PRO, WO95/39, QMG Branch, War Diary, Explanatory Review, Aug. 1918 and 27 Aug. 1918.
21. The relative shortage of 6in howitzer shells must have been caused by the enormous expenditure of that shell in Aug. During that month, expenditure amounted to roughly double that of earlier in the year. Shipments of this particular shell, in fact, increased dramatically in Aug., so the factories must have been producing significant amounts in excess of requirements. For the 6in howitzer shell expenditure and shipments see War Office, *Statistics* (note 4), pp.420 and 434. For the assessment of fuses, and general availability of ammunition see *Official History (1918, 5)* p.595.
22. PRO, WO95/40, QMG Branch, War Diary, Explanatory Review, Sept. 1918.
23. Ibid. QMG Branch, War Diary, 19 Sept. 1918.
24. Ibid. Explanatory Review, Sept. 1918.
25. *Official History (1918, 5)* p.7.
26. *Official History (Transportation)* p.397.
27. PRO, WO95/40, QMG Branch, War Diary, Explanatory Review, Oct. 1918.
28. National Archives of Canada, MG30 E100 Vol.42, A.W. Currie Papers, Currie Diary, 20 Oct. 1918.
29. PRO, WO95/40, QMG Branch, War Diary, Explanatory Review, Oct. 1918.
30. PRO, WO107/16 (letter 631), Travers Clarke to Cowans, 6 Oct. 1918.
31. PRO, WO95/40, QMG Branch, War Diary, Explanatory Review, Nov. 1918.
32. *Official History (Transportation)* p.466.
33. Unless otherwise noted, all references to the Canadian Corps and the Rhineland occupation are from Lt-Gen. Sir A.W. Currie, *Canadian Corps Operations During the Year 1918,*

Interim Report (Ottawa: Dept of Militia and Defence 1919) pp.86–93.
34. IWM, 69/21/4, G.P. Dawnay Papers, 'Demobilization', early Jan. 1919.
35. *Official History (Transportation)* pp.466–7.
36. IWM, HHW2/7, Wilson Papers, Haig to Wilson, 11 Jan. 1919.
37. PRO, WO33/932, Report on Account of Army Expenditure, 1917–1922, p.4.
38. War Office, *Statistics* (note 4) p.727.
39. Robertson took up his appointment on 18 April 1919. William Robertson, *From Private to Field-Marshal* (London/Boston and NY: Constable/Houghton Mifflin 1921) p.357.
40. IWM, HHW2/1, Wilson Papers, Wilson to Robertson, 5 June 1919.
41. David Lloyd George, *Memoirs of the Peace Conference* Vol.1 (NY: Howard Fertig 1972) p.466.
42. Henry T. Allen, *My Rhineland Journal* (Boston/NY: Houghton Mifflin 1923) p.110.
43. IWM, HHW2/1, Wilson Papers, Robertson to Wilson, 6 June 1919. [full citation needed].
44. Ibid. Wilson to Robertson, 13 June 1919.
45. Ibid. Wilson to Robertson, 17 June 1919 enclosing Wilson to Prime Minister, 16 June 1919.
46. W.G. Lindsell, 'Administrative Lessons of the Great War', *Jnl of the Royal United Service Instn* 66 (Feb.–Nov. 1926) p.713.

'Small Wars' and 'Imperial Policing': The British Army and the Theory and Practice of Colonial Warfare in the British Empire, 1919–1939

T. R. MOREMAN

Following the Armistice in November 1918, the British Army quickly reverted to its traditional role as an 'imperial gendarmerie' maintaining colonial rule in the far-flung Empire. It was faced with a range of old and new threats to imperial authority in the immediate post-war period that offered British officers and men prospects for active service in conditions very different from those of the Western Front. In Ireland, Egypt, Iraq and India British troops and various locally-enlisted armed forces sought to contain nationalist resistance to imperial rule during this post-war 'crisis of empire'.[1] Similar operations continued intermittently during the 1920s and 1930s. These have been characterised under the heading of 'imperial policing', in which British armed forces contained internal threats to colonial authority by employing methods very different from normal military operations. 'Small wars' still persisted throughout the inter-war years, however, following this burst of activity in the early 1920s, though they were generally defensive or punitive operations to protect frontier regions from tribal aggression. Many of these were also fought in support of the civil authorities, though they were still conducted *á outrance*.[2] As Colonel C. E. Vickery noted in the *Army Quarterly* in 1923:

> The soldier of to-day may look round and bemoan the absence of any fresh countries which might afford a potential outlet for his energies and for his training. Certainly the halcyon years of 1880 to 1910 are gone and their equal will not be seen, but there will remain for many years wars and rumours of war on the frontier of India and elsewhere on the marches of the empire.[3]

Yet the manner in which the British Army and other imperial forces conducted these colonial military campaigns had attracted surprisingly little attention from either military or imperial historians, in contrast to that directed towards conventional European military campaigns.[4] As Ian Beckett has argued, low-intensity conflict has always enjoyed a relatively low status in the study of war, both among professional soldiers and new generations of academic military historians.[5] Apart from those interested in the origins of British counter-insurgency methods, colonial campaigns have attracted little attention from historians.[6] This article examines how the British Army approached the varying military requirements of colonial warfare – both 'imperial policing' and 'small wars' – paying particular attention to how it devised doctrine and specialised training for such operations in India, which have been overlooked hitherto.

The British Army and Its Imperial Role

The British Army was quickly demobilised, reduced to pre-1914 strength and plunged without a break into world-wide garrison, occupation and police duties. As Brian Bond has observed, the return to its imperial role was emphasised by a clause in the Ten Year Rule which specifically stated that no Expeditionary force would be required for the Continent in the near future.[7] The imperial commitment and the needs of home defence determined the post-war structure of the British Army. It had to find a large garrison for India for internal and external defence, a garrison in Egypt for safeguarding the Suez Canal, garrisons for several Crown Colonies and Protectorates as well as smaller forces for the defence of ports, dockyards and fuelling stations on which trade and the Royal Navy depended. In addition, troops briefly occupied new mandates granted to Britain following the First World War in the Middle East, although these were eventually turned over to the RAF, which employed its new doctrine of air control using aircraft, armoured cars and local levies to maintain order.[8] Throughout the inter-war period the regiments of the British Army were periodically rotated through garrisons which on 1 January 1938 included Gibraltar, Malta, Cyprus, Palestine, Egypt, the Anglo-Egyptian Sudan, India, Burma, Singapore, Hong Kong, Shanghai, Tientsin and Bermuda, in strengths varying from one company to 55,000 officers and men.[9]

To carry out these duties and to provide enough units and manpower to maintain garrisons overseas at sufficient strength, the Cardwell system was re-adopted by the British Army. Those units at home and abroad were ideally to be kept at equal strength so drafts and reliefs could be provided for regiments deployed in India and the Colonies.[10] Infantry units detailed for tours of foreign service in the British Empire during the normal course of peacetime service served overseas for periods of up to 16 years, mostly in India. In the case of

British cavalry regiments the normal tour of overseas duty was 14 years.[11] Cross-posting between units and volunteers, however, meant that some British officers and men remained overseas for even longer periods.[12] The majority of those battalions posted overseas immediately following the First World War were filled with young, poorly trained and inexperienced young soldiers whose rudimentary training was predicated on a conventional European conflict. Few officers or men with training and experience in colonial warfare remained, following the interruption of 1914–18.[13]

Training for Colonial Warfare

The British Army faced a fundamental dilemma as to the kind of war for which it should train, organise and equip in the post-war period, given its disparate colonial and continental roles. In an Empire of such vast extent, imperial troops on tours of foreign service or forming part of an expeditionary force had to be prepared to fight in different climates and terrain, against 'civilised', 'semi-civilised' or 'savage' opponents, whose tactics, organisation and armament varied considerably. During the 1920s potential opponents included the Soviet Union and Afghanistan as well as the tribes of Iraq, Arabia, Kurdistan and the North-West Frontier of India. As Lt-General Sir Archibald Montgomery-Massingberd observed in a lecture given at King's College, London, in December 1927: 'We have to be prepared to fight in every part of the globe and under the most varying conditions.'[14] It also had to prepare for carrying out duties in aid of the civil power in British or mandated territory. Moreover, the possibility of a continental conflict could not be entirely ignored, and required radically different military organisation, equipment and training. The 1934 edition of *Training Regulations* was far more explicit regarding the differing operations for which the British Army had to prepare:

> In a world-wide Empire the Army may be called upon to fight in developed or undeveloped countries, and under every condition of climate and ground. In India, and in certain other parts of the Empire, the garrisons are faced with specific military problems, but, broadly speaking, there is no single predominant objective towards which the training of the Army can be categorically directed.

It identified four broad categories of military activity in which British armed forces might engage: imperial policing, minor expeditions carried out on a peace establishment, major expeditions that might or might not include the Territorial Army, and finally a national war involving full mobilisation.[15] These different commitments demanded wide variations in training in leadership, minor tactics, administration and the employment of modern weapons. The sheer variety of possible opponents and terrain meant that it was very difficult to rationalise such disparate experience, as so many variables existed.[16]

The military establishment in the United Kingdom adopted the view that, as no definite threat existed to direct instruction, it was inadvisable to train the British Army for a specific type of war or for operations in any one type of terrain. It considered that the broad principles of war, if intelligently applied, were sufficient to direct all kinds of warfare – indeed, the lesser was contained in the greater. Training for conventional European warfare therefore formed the main topic of study during individual and collective training carried out each year in the United Kingdom. This was regarded as a solid foundation on which specialised training could be added as required when units were on overseas service. Even this training was hampered, however, by the fact that many units on the British establishment were badly under-strength and their ranks filled by young, partially trained soldiers, because of the Cardwell system. As a result, training at depots and units concentrated primarily on bringing these men up to an acceptable standard of discipline, skill-at-arms and fieldcraft before they were sent overseas to replace time-expired soldiers and casualties in battalions on foreign service. As Brigadier Archibald Wavell observed in a lecture given at the Royal United Service Institution in May 1933, 'Our business at home is to fix these essential qualities in the man. Abroad, we may specialise: in mountain warfare on the North-West Frontier of India; in police duties in certain other garrisons; and so forth.'[17]

The attention of most officers and military intellectuals in the United Kingdom was also preoccupied by conventional European warfare, generally paying only lip-service to imperial requirements.[18] Despite the fact that colonial warfare was the main practical collective experience of the inter-war army, little or no attention was directed towards training before units or personnel were sent overseas. This was understandable to an extent. Few training areas existed in the United Kingdom suitable for realistic mountain, desert or jungle warfare training, and, given this fact, few efforts were made to carry out instruction. On occasion, imaginative officers enlivened the usual run of military training by addressing operations against second class and irregular enemies. Brigadier Wavell, for example, conducted 'savage warfare' exercises for 5th Brigade at Aldershot, simulating bush warfare operations against the 'Wah Wah' tribes that inhabited the 'inaccessible jungles' between Camberley and Bracknell. Those men chosen to act as the 'savage enemy' enthusiastically entered into the spirit of the occasion, bedecking themselves with 'authentic' war paint and native costume, much to the horror of the Regimental Sergeant Major.[19]

Field Service Regulations, 1920

The British Army lacked any official detailed study of how to conduct either 'small wars' or 'imperial policing', as it had always emphasised practicality rather than theory in this type of operation.[20] The 1920 edition of *Field Service Regulations* (*FSR*) formed the foundation upon which the training of the British Army was based. This emphasised the applicability of the principles of war – maintenance of the objective, offensive action, surprise, concentration, economy of force, security, mobility and co-operation – to all forms of conflict. It also contained a 28-page chapter on 'Warfare against an Uncivilized Enemy', which discussed general principles governing 'savage warfare' as well as including detailed sections on mountain, bush and desert warfare against comparatively poorly-armed opponents. This was a relatively new addition to *FSR*, having been included only since 1912, when the military authorities in India persuaded the General Staff to make additions covering local requirements in the subcontinent.[21] *FSR* pointed out that:

> In campaigns against savages, the armament, tactics, and characteristics of the enemy, and the nature of theatre of operations demand that the normal application of the principles of regular warfare be considerably modified; the modifications in this chapter are such as experience has shown to be necessary.

FSR placed a premium on self-reliance, vigilance and judgement as the chief requirements for overcoming the peculiar difficulties inherent in 'savage warfare', as well as stressing the importance of a vigorous strategic and tactical offensive when conducting such operations. It also briefly discussed the problems encountered when operating in undeveloped countries against opponents enjoying certain natural advantages, and the precautions which imperial troops needed to obey in order to overcome them. The manual also recommended that careful study be made of the theatre of operations, also of the mode of fighting, customs and characteristics of the likely enemy. The brief sections on mountain, bush and desert warfare were so condensed, however, that they afforded little detailed insight into the conduct of these different operations for the junior British officers and NCOs, whose training was predicated on conventional European warfare. Moreover, these outlines were so general that it proved difficult to standardise training between units and formations in peacetime training or under wartime conditions.[22] Later editions of *FSR* contained a similar chapter on colonial warfare, of equally limited use for troops on foreign service.[23]

The obvious limitations of *FSR* as a source of detailed guidance for colonial warfare meant that additional sources of information were required. Major-General Sir Charles Callwell's *Small Wars: Their Principles and Practice*, originally published in 1896, remained a key text for young subalterns and regimental officers proceeding on foreign service.[24] This seminal work identified fundamental principles underlying colonial warfare, although many of its tactical prescriptions were now out of date. It provided useful principles for use in countering guerrilla warfare, as well as discussing the peculiar difficulties of various forms of colonial conflict. Indeed, Callwell has been hailed as the most significant early theorist of modern counter-insurgency.[25] During the inter-war period this classic work formed part of the curriculum at both the Staff College at Camberley and at the RAF Staff College at Andover.[26] At least three other unofficial publications existed in this field, written by British officers before the First World War, but these were rather dated and it is difficult to know how easily available they were to units preparing for overseas duty.[27]

Duties in Aid of the Civil Power

Those British Army units overseas which fell directly under War Office control were primarily employed on 'imperial policing' duties between 1919 and 1939, rather than in 'small wars', after the initial post-war burst of activity. In Egypt in 1919, Palestine in 1929 and Cyprus in 1931, troops were employed on several occasions on 'duties in aid of the civil power', to contain outbreaks of resistance to imperial rule. Such duties were very different from normal military operations, requiring instead the employment of minimum force and close civil-military co-operation. Units in garrisons faced by possible internal discontent had to adapt quickly to local requirements and train accordingly, employing instructions issued by the responsible local military authorities. Apart from those manuals which dealt with the employment of troops in suppressing riots, there was little official guidance for dealing with organised threats to imperial rule.[28] However, in the 1920s several unofficial articles, written by British officers eager to record their personal experiences, appeared in the service press, discussing the recent employment of British troops in this role.[29] It is not perhaps surprising that the only manual produced by the War Office specifically for colonial military requirements was devoted to duties in aid of the civil power under circumstances hitherto neglected in training literature. *Notes on Imperial Policing 1934* provided guidance on operations to maintain or restore internal security within colonial or mandated territory under British rule, that was threatened by widespread organised internal disorder. It was intended to be read in conjunction with *Duties in Aid of the Civil Power* and was largely based on lessons learnt during post-war internal security operations. The manual pointed out that 'The enemy, although possibly well-armed, has usually no open and recognized military organization, and acts largely by subterranean methods, offering no opportunity of locating or defeating his forces by the ordinary methods of war.' It acknowledged that situations might arise in which disturbances could 'no longer be dealt with by a series of isolated acts in aid of the civil power and that their suppression demands a concerted military plan of operations'. The manual laid down principles governing operations of this nature, and covered area deployment, intelligence gathering and the conduct of drives, cordons and searches.[30]

In May 1934 a lengthy study written by Major-General Sir Charles Gwynn (Commandant of the Staff College 1926–30) and entitled *Imperial Policing* was also published. It contained a range of case studies of recent operations in which troops had supported the civil administration.[31] On a few other occasions local commanders produced their own training guidelines specifically suited to local requirements where a definite threat was perceived. Lt-General Sir John Dill, GOC British Forces in Palestine and Trans-Jordan, for example, issued tactical notes on the recent lessons of the 1936 Palestine Rebellion for the use of formations and units serving in that country. In this publication Dill openly acknowledged the usefulness of *Notes on Imperial Policing 1934.*[32]

Local Armed Forces in Africa

The British Army was spared the immediate demands of 'small wars' or maintaining order within colonies and protectorates in Africa. In the 1920s and 1930s no British regulars were maintained south of Khartoum, although over 12,000 British-officered indigenous troops were deployed in the colonies.[33] Units such as the Royal West African Frontier Force (WAFF), King's African Rifles (KAR), Somaliland Camel Corps and the Sudan Defence Force were a cheap and highly effective response to local military requirements.[34] These para-military and military units were trained and led by British officers and senior NCOs 'seconded' for short tours of duty to either the Colonial Office or Foreign Office, and instruction generally followed the same lines as that of the British Army. As the 1925 edition of *Regulations for the King's African Rifles* laid down:

> Training is not to be confined to the tactics suited to purely local conditions. The various battalions of the King's African Rifles are liable to be called upon to serve anywhere, and they must be prepared to meet an enemy trained in modern warfare and armed with modern weapons, as well as foes employing various forms of native tactics at comparatively close quarters in the bush. No one system of tactics, therefore, is universally applicable, and in this respect F.S. Regs., Volume II. (Operations). Chapter XIV, (Warfare against an Uncivilized Enemy) should be carefully studied.[35]

112   MILITARY POWER: LAND WARFARE IN THEORY AND PRACTICE

In practice, however, during the inter-war years the commanding officers of the WAFF, KAR and the Somaliland Camel Corps concentrated primarily on bush warfare, with tactics little altered from those developed in the late nineteenth century.[36] Training was based on *FSR* and special guidelines for the use of British officers and NCOs, published by the Colonial Office. These elaborated upon the instructions in *FSR*, providing more in depth information on operations against both 'savage' and 'civilised' troops.[37] British officers and senior NCOs attached to these local forces learnt valuable lessons during their tour of duty regarding bush tactics, but there is little evidence to suggest that the lessons were taken back and applied in training the British Army. A generally dismissive attitude amongst British Service officers regarding service with African troops, and a belief that it could not be compared to training for modern war, meant that valuable lessons regarding this class of warfare were ignored.[38]

The Army in India and the Defence of the British Raj

The Army in India gave British Army officers and men a greater opportunity of seeing active service during the inter-war period than anywhere else in the British Empire. The security of the Subcontinent represented the largest and most significant 'small war' problem for the imperial armed forces. It involved British and Indian Army troops in a series of military operations during the inter-war years, ranging from minor skirmishes to major campaigns on the frontiers, and also internal security duties. The garrison of India formed the single largest and most important overseas deployment for the British Army. In 1923 the British component of the Army in India comprised 8 cavalry regiments, 45 infantry battalions and 55 batteries of field artillery, totalling approximately 70,000 troops.[39] This figure gradually declined to 2,798 officers and 40,938 other ranks by May 1939, but it still remained the most significant overseas deployment of the British Army.[40] British regiments normally served tours of duty on the Indian establishment of six to ten years, during which they were paid for and came under the direct control of the Indian military authorities as regards their organisation, equipment and training, before they either returned to the United Kingdom or else were posted to another colonial station.[41] The Indian military authorities had a far more pragmatic attitude regarding training for colonial warfare than the War Office in London, due to its peacetime duties of controlling the trans-border Pathan tribes on the North-West Frontier and ensuring Internal Security in the rest of India. As a distinct long-term commitment existed for both British and Indian troops, training in the Subcontinent did not slavishly follow that of the rest of the British Army, but instead specifically took colonial warfare into account. As

R. Haycock has observed, British arms in India developed in a manner distinct from that of the army in Britain.[42]

The Lessons of Waziristan: Mountain Warfare on the North West Frontier

The control of the trans-border Pathan tribes on the North-West Frontier, in the mountainous belt of no-man's-land between Afghanistan and the administrative border, was the most insistent military problem in India. It led to repeated military operations during which imperial troops employed specialised principles and minor tactics appropriate to the terrain and to the guerrilla tactics used by the tribesmen. During the nineteenth century these specialised principles and tactics had been developed and used first by the localised Punjab Frontier Force and the Army in India. The conduct of what was viewed as tribal warfare, mountain warfare, hill warfare, or more commonly as frontier warfare, posed a range of military problems very different from conventional military operations in Europe or other 'small wars'. Operations in tribal territory were hampered by limited intelligence, climatic extremes and scarcity of water and food, which severely complicated the transport, supply and administration of imperial troops. In comparison the local population was ideally adapted to fighting under such conditions. As Charles Callwell noted, 'Hill warfare may fairly be said to constitute "a special branch of the military art" and indeed "almost the most trying which disciplined soldiers can be called on to undertake"'.[43]

The Army in India initially employed the same training manuals as the rest of the British Army, and shared a common school of military thought with the latter for all its different roles; this was in accordance with the principle laid down by the Imperial Defence Conference of 1909 that standard regulations and training manuals should be adopted as the basis of organisation, administration and training throughout the Empire.[44] However, between 1914 and 1918 the inherent dangers of relying on general principles and on the limited section in *FSR* on mountain warfare were demonstrated on several occasions as trained and experienced regulars troops were sent overseas.[45] In the immediate post-war period the dangers were driven home during the Third Afghan War (1919) and the ensuing tribal rising in Waziristan. Heavy casualties were inflicted on the raw, ill-trained Indian troops comprising the Derajat Column by Mahsud and Wazir tribesmen during punitive operations in Waziristan during the winter of 1919–20. During the heaviest fighting ever seen on the North-West Frontier, imperial troops were nearly defeated by well-equipped and trained *lashkars* (groups of armed tribesmen) which included a significant number of ex-servicemen.[46] Writing at the height of the fighting on 13 January 1920,

Major-General S. H. Climo, the GOC Waziristan Field Force, observed:

> I doubt it is understood how desperate the fighting has been during these operations.... It is, perhaps, to be expected that those who do not know India and the frontier, and even some who have fought on the frontier in pre-war days, but lack the knowledge and imagination to realise that conditions have altered with the great improvement of the armament of the tribesmen, cannot understand or believe the standard of training that is required for the Infantry in the conditions that now prevail on the Frontier to-day. To such, the belief is natural that the mere frontier tribes cannot be formidable opponents to modern troops nor can they believe that the standard of training or method of tactics that succeeded in the great war can, in former cases, be insufficient for and, in the latter case, be inapplicable to a Frontier campaign.[47]

This fighting graphically demonstrated that conventional tactics and training were simply inappropriate and that specialised training was urgently needed by imperial troops deployed to fight in tribal territory. During the ensuing operations Indian troops in the Derajat Column rediscovered the time-honoured principles and minor tactics of hill warfare, but at a heavy cost in lives, money and prestige. To meet the demand for training a Mountain Warfare School opened at Abbottabad to instruct officers and impart a common tactical doctrine, and a range of pamphlets was published as a stop-gap measure.[48] During the early 1920s intermittent guerrilla warfare in Waziristan confirmed the need for training in frontier warfare, as further untrained units were deployed in the North-West Frontier Province (NWFP). As the future Field-Marshal Viscount Slim noted, 'On every village green in England monuments were rising which proclaimed that the war was over, yet here I had only to raise my eyes to see once more the piled sandbags, the rough stone parapet, and writhing strands of barbed wire.'[49] On numerous occasions British and Indian troops suffered losses at Pathan hands that were primarily attributed to poor training.[50]

The Waziristan operations of 1920–24 and the permanent deployment of large numbers of imperial troops in close proximity to the trans-border Pathan tribes in the NWFP confirmed the need for specialised training in mountain warfare for the Army in India. As a result it was now accepted by the General Staff in India that the general principles of war and a small section on mountain warfare in *FSR* formed an insufficient basis for training troops stationed in the NWFP. Such views were openly supported by officers writing in the service press. In an article published in the *Journal of the United Service Institution of India* (*JUSII*), Colonel C. Kirkpatrick complained that the section on mountain warfare was outdated and pointed out that the Mahsuds and Wazirs could no longer be regarded as 'savages' in a purely military sense, either as regards their armament or their tactics. As the tribesmen continued to mutilate dead and wounded, however, specialised tactics were still required by imperial troops operating in tribal territory.⁵¹ Moreover, the need for training was accentuated after practical experience and trials demonstrated that the employment of much of the new military technology developed during the First World War was impossible on the North-West Frontier.⁵² The infantryman and pack mule reigned supreme in frontier warfare. Writing in 1925 one officer concluded:

> The use of the Lewis gun enables a reduction in the strength of piquets and to increase fire effect: the motor vehicle and the tractor may speed up operations: wireless telegraphy may add the personal touch: the glider may become the infantry of the air to assist the infantry of the ground: yet the age long principle remains that it is the soldier who will win or lose the frontier.⁵³

Manual of Operations on the North-West Frontier of India

The lessons of Waziristan were incorporated in a new manual compiled at Army Head Quarters during 1924 and intended to complement *FSR* and the training manuals for the various arms of the service. The General Staff in India clearly recognised the need to lay down more definite rules than those in *FSR*, so as to ensure uniformity in training and in war between units and formations. Although the revised 1924 edition of *FSR* still included a chapter on warfare in 'undeveloped' and 'semi-civilised countries', with a brief section on mountain warfare, it directed readers to a new manual under preparation in India for further detailed guidance.⁵⁴

The *Manual of Operations on the North-West Frontier of India* reflected the important changes that had occurred in the conduct of frontier warfare since tribal territory had been flooded with modern rifles after the beginning of the First World War. No fewer than 35,000 copies were printed and by October 1925 had been issued to units serving throughout the subcontinent, after which it formed the basis of training in hill warfare for the Army in India. Its contents reflected the Indian Army's extensive experience of conducting military operations against the trans-border Pathan tribes, and brought up-to-date the existing doctrine and system of training caused by improved tribal tactics, leadership and equipment and changes in the organisation, training and equipment of imperial troops. It represented a significant improvement over solely relying on *FSR* as the basis of all training, although it still discussed the conduct of mountain warfare with close reference to the principles of war. The *Manual* included chapters describing the trans-border Pathans and tribal territory, fighting troops and their characteristics, protection on the march and when halted, the organisation and protection of the lines of communication, the conduct of the attack and withdrawal for all three arms of service, foraging and demolitions, as well as administrative routine in camp and on the line of march. It emphasised the importance of specialised training for all three arms, especially with regard to the individual skills of self-reliance, vigilance and initiative, which were judged essential in overcoming the peculiar difficulties encountered when fighting in tribal territory. A section of the manual discussed the use of the RAF in tribal territory in co-operation with troops and even went on to cover the employment of tanks in hill warfare, even though they were as yet unavailable in India. Particular importance was attached to close co-operation between the infantry and mountain artillery to counter increasingly well-armed tribal *lashkars*. Imperial troops serving in tribal territory had to be repeatedly warned to maintain alertness despite prolonged periods without contact with hostile tribesmen. Officers were encouraged to read histories of past campaigns. It was suggested that, wherever possible, training should take place in country approximating to the frontier hills. The *Manual* pointed out, however, that valuable instruction could be given by means of sand models, maps and cinema films.[55]

Training for Mountain Warfare

In *The Manual of Operations on the North-West Frontier in India* the General Staff promulgated and disseminated a clearly thought-out formal doctrine for frontier warfare, and they then instituted a thorough training programme based on its guidelines, to ensure its acceptance throughout the Army in India. Training was combined with frequent opportunities to gain practical experience of this class of warfare. Throughout the remainder of the inter-war period Indian regiments served a tour of duty of two years out of every six in the Covering Troops Districts, allowing them steadily to build up a cadre of trained and experienced officers and men. In comparison, British infantry units only served a one-year and comparatively infrequent tour of duty in the area.[56] While stationed in the border cantonments, imperial troops trained intensively in mountain warfare based on *Manual of Operations on the North-West Frontier*, supervised by the staff and senior officers of the formations to which they belonged. Standing Orders were also periodically issued by those formations permanently stationed along the border, to provide additional sources of guidance for units during peacetime training and while on active service.[57] These official sources of tactical guidance were complemented by a range of unofficial books, written by experienced soldiers and published in Britain and India, which were available to any motivated British officers interested in teaching the subject to their units.[58] Training in frontier warfare also formed part of the curriculum at the Staff Colleges at both Camberley and Quetta during the inter-war period.[59]

The Army in India became highly proficient in mountain warfare by the late 1920s as a direct result of specialised training combined with frequent opportunities for gaining practical experience.[60] Tours of duty in the Covering Troops Districts were regarded as providing particularly valuable and highly realistic training under 'semi-active service' conditions. Whenever imperial troops left the safety of their perimeter camps they went fully armed and loaded in anticipation of surprise attacks. Indeed, the Pathan tribes were popularly regarded as the best tactical 'umpires' in the world, ready to exploit the slightest mistake committed by unwary troops in order to secure valuable rifles.[61] As one officer later observed:

> There was no pretence at all about our daily military training. Any fool could see the practical necessity of it, and examples were always occurring to show the penalty of neglect. There was not an atom of useless training on the frontier. Everything we did and learned fitted into the essential job of living among a wily and warlike enemy.... One bit of slackness, one violation of the 'golden rules' of frontier warfare, or one moment's relaxation of vigilance, and retribution would fall quickly upon the offending body of soldiers. They were always round our camps and columns, well armed and tough, just waiting for the moment when the soldier would slip up.[62]

Instruction in mountain warfare was facilitated by the availability of exercise areas encompassing a wide variety of terrain suitable for training. The newly-formed Waziristan Military District included parts of tribal territory, containing old battlefields and many local tribesmen who were willing to discuss with British officers former military operations from the viewpoint of the 'other side of the hill'.[63] In Kohat District training areas ideal for battalion training existed within the administrative border at Chichanna, Dhoda and Siab, Alizai, Khwaja Kizar and Chillibagh, while manoeuvres at brigade level were carried out by the local garrison near Balyamn and Shinwari.[64] While units stationed on the frontier trained for hill warfare, the training of the Field Army was predicated on conventional 'open warfare', albeit against opponents envisaged as having lower scales of equipment and poorer training than in Europe.[65]

The emphasis on specialised training in frontier warfare was frequently criticised by British Service officers serving in India, whose attention had been given to preparing for a conventional European warfare. These 'Aldershot type' officers were highly critical of the frontier as a training ground and of the apparently outmoded tactics that were employed by imperial troops.[66] As Lt-General Sir Frederick Morgan noted in his memoirs:

Frontier warfare had become, over the generations, a matter of extreme formalism, comparable with the wars of stereotyped manoeuvre in Europe in the seventeenth and eighteenth centuries. To many of us who were unhampered by practical experience or preconceived notions it seemed as if the rules of the game had taken charge to the extent of obscuring any well defined-strategic object.[67]

However, it was a class of warfare that simply could not be ignored by imperial troops without risking significant casualties, given that the principles and minor tactics required in tribal territory were so radically different from conventional warfare. As one anonymous Indian Army officer pointed out in the *JUSII* in April 1930:

> There are two forms of warfare to be taught in India, viz, open warfare and mountain warfare. Except for those stationed on the frontier the former of course requires the most attention, but mountain warfare should never be entirely neglected in view of the fact that wherever the Army in India fights in the future it is almost certain to be in mountainous country. In addition, about a third of our Army in India is presently stationed on the frontier and practically every unit takes a turn of duty there sooner or later. It has been argued and will continue to be argued to the end of all time, particularly [by] those whose knowledge or mountain warfare is limited, that such training is unnecessary and even detrimental, but the undoubted fact remains that troops unaccustomed to and untrained for warfare in mountainous country are at a very great disadvantage until they have learnt the 'tricks of the trade' and are physically fit to climb mountains, which they can never be so long as they confine themselves entirely to foot-slogging on the plains.[68]

The General Staff in India also recognised that more attention needed to be devoted to training British units than to Indian, as mountain warfare was not regarded as British troops' particular strong point.[69] British battalions were generally unprepared for operations in tribal territory, with prior training predicated on conventional 'open warfare' or internal security duties. Intermittent tours of frontier duty prevented them from accumulating an experienced cadre of 'frontier hands', thus placing greater reliance on 'on the job' training. Several books were written with British units directly in mind, to assist instruction. The most important of these was written by General Sir Andrew Skeen and published in 1932, specifically for the 'junior officer ... of the British Service in particular, as he is less likely in his wider range of service to be trained for the local problem which all officers in India have to keep in mind'.[70] This 136-page minor classic, entitled *Passing it On: Short Talks on Tribal Fighting on the North-West Frontier of India*, was widely read, especially after the Commander-in-Chief ordered that it should be issued to officers' and NCOs' libraries of all units serving in India. This ruling aimed to ensure that officers and NCOs would benefit directly from the advice of the Indian Army's most experienced frontier soldier, regarding the principles, minor tactics and administrative arrangements required in hill fighting.[71] Despite such measures it was necessary for British units to be 'shepherded' by more experienced Indian units when they first served on the North-West Frontier. Although some units did become quite efficient, this was the exception rather than the rule.[72] The tactical competence of British units serving in tribal territory was often very different from their more professional Indian counterparts for other reasons. One officer summed up the essential problems encountered when British units arrived on the frontier:

> How good or bad these regiments were on the frontier depended on just one thing, and that was how ready they were to learn. All the Indian and Gurkha regiments spent two years in every six on the frontier and had a large proportion of older men experienced in frontier warfare and the ways of the Pathan. Brigadier and Staff of the Razmak, Bannu and Wana brigades had all spent many years in Waziristan or elsewhere on the frontier. They all said the same, and we all came to know it. If a British regiment arrived at Razmak, or better still at Bannu prior to its march up to Razmak, and said: 'We are new to this. You are not. Please teach us!' then it would soon be a regiment well able to look after itself and take a share of responsibility in mobile columns, piquetting and so on. But let a regiment think that it knew, and that it was too famous to have to learn, to think that the Highlands of Scotland bore any real resemblance to the mountains of Waziristan, and that regiment might have trouble. And during its year in Waziristan it would be of little use to anyone, and often a liability.[73]

The adaptability of British officers and men to local requirements was therefore the key. A combination of cap-badge rivalry between regiments, a rapid changeover in personnel during their period of service in India, the comparative 'amateurism' of British officers, and racism, often militated against the assimilation from experienced Indian units of the military skills required on the frontier. Much depended on the attitude of individual commanding officers, as to whether valuable lessons would be gleaned from their more experienced and better-trained Indian colleagues. Sometimes close ties developed, like that between 2nd Battalion The Northamptonshire Regiment and 1/9th Gurkha Rifles while serving in Waziristan.[74] Some units never learned and suffered unnecessary casualties as a result. During the 1936–37 Waziristan Campaign 1st Battalion The Argyll and Sutherland Highlanders, for example, paid a high price for failing to adapt quickly to local conditions and to maintain sufficient alertness.[75]

The conduct of military operations against the trans-border Pathan tribes on the North-West Frontier remained a subject of close study by the military authorities in India throughout the inter-war period. As Captain D. M. Kennelly observed in an article in the *Journal of the Royal Artillery*:

> Training for mountain warfare cannot remain stationary. With each year the danger on the North-West Frontier of India increases; the tribesmen are becoming better armed and better acquainted with our manner of dealing with them. Every endeavour should be made to counter this increase in efficiency on their part by new methods of training.[76]

During the 1930s the conduct of frontier warfare underwent various changes as the Army in India re-organised and adopted new equipment. Accordingly on several occasions various amendments to *The Manual of Operations on the North-West Frontier of India* were suggested by Northern Command.[77] The 1935 Mohmand Operations finally prompted the military authorities to begin preparation of a new manual of frontier warfare, after light tanks, medium artillery and large-scale night operations were employed in hill warfare for the first time.[78] The new work was intended for officers of both the Army and the Royal Air Force. As General Sir William Bartholomew observed, 'It is most comprehensive and much larger than the old manual, but I think that it is right that this should be so. It is intended primarily for the use of officers of both services at Home and in India who have no knowledge of the Frontier or of Frontier fighting.'[79] *Frontier Warfare (Army and Royal Air Force) 1939* represented the most comprehensive manual for colonial warfare ever devised by the British military authorities. It provided the Army in India with a comprehensive and up-to-date written doctrine of frontier warfare employing both aircraft and ground troops that remained in use until the end of the British Raj.[80]

Jungle Warfare on the NE Frontier and in Burma

In comparison, the conduct of military operations on the remote jungle-covered North-Eastern frontier of India and in Burma received scant attention from the Army in India. During the post-war period both areas presented an immediate source of concern to the imperial authorities. Between November 1917 and March 1919, punitive operations were undertaken against the Kuki tribes on the North-East Frontier of India by elements of the Assam Rifles and Burma Military Police, rather than by regular troops.⁸¹ This established a pattern that was followed for the rest of the inter-war years, with military police forces carrying out most operations while regular troops carried out internal security duties. The Assam Rifles – a paramilitary force originally raised under civil control to prevent tribal raids and carry out punitive expeditions at a far cheaper cost than regular troops – operated from the Indian side of the border. It consisted of five battalions, composed of Gurkhas and local tribesmen, under the command of Indian Army officers seconded for short tours of duty. This force was retained under the direct control of the civil and political authorities and provided escorts, performed outpost duty and conducted minor punitive expeditions against the Naga, Chin, Kuki and Lushai tribes who inhabited the wide tract of densely wooded and jungle covered hills. Although the training, equipment and economy of the battalions closely resembled that of the regular Indian Army, special attention was paid to jungle warfare, based on a special code of training evolved as a result of near constant practical experience.⁸² As Major A. Vickers noted:

> To those military officers serving in the local forces which picket the wild and inaccessible frontier tracts inhabited by divers and little-known savage tribes, of the head-hunting variety, the truth is quickly brought home that it is unwise to make war upon these people without special training at the hands of those who have been and have seen. Regular battalions triumphant in the field of modern war and proud of their tactical knowledge and experience of frontier fighting on the Afghan borders would at first be at a loss how to proceed and would have to 'find themselves' anew under the novel conditions of the North-Eastern frontiers.⁸³

The Burma Military Police – a paramilitary force also trained and led by British officers seconded from the Indian Army – similarly gained extensive experience of military operations in the jungle-covered mountainous frontier tracts of Burma while keeping the peace among the turbulent hill tribes. A special training manual published for the Burma Military Police in 1902 remained the main source of guidance for training in jungle warfare. In this booklet, Captain A. W. Taylor (an officer of 10th Gurkha Rifles with Burma Military Police experience) pointed out that the Drill Book offered most British officers without prior experience of fighting on Burma's frontiers little guidance for that particular form of warfare. He pointed out:

> I do not attempt to lay down any hard and fast rules as to how operations should be conducted, for circumstances alter cases more than ever in jungle-fighting and so much must depend on the class and tactics of the enemy to be encountered, the magnitude of the

operations rendered necessary and, above all, the nature of the ground to be operated over. I merely offer these notes as a rough guide to such as may care to use them, and with the hope that some more experienced officer may take the subject up and improve on it.[84]

He explicitly recognised the need for a standard doctrine, because of the constant changeover of British officers which frequently caused confusion in the minds of NCOs and other ranks regarding tactics. Otherwise jungle fighting experience was not retained or disseminated in any formal way for the benefit of the rest of the Army in India.

The Moplah and Burma Rebellions

The Moplah rebellion, in Malabar in southern India in August 1921, provided the Army in India with its first brief experience of jungle fighting following the First World War.[85] Except for 3/70th Burma Rifles, composed of Chin-Kachin troops recruited from Burma, and Gurkha battalions which assisted during the final stages of suppressing the revolt, this type of warfare was completely new to all the troops deployed, and who therefore had to devise appropriate tactics while the operations were in progress.[86] In some quarters the importance of training in this class of warfare for imperial troops was recognised. An account of the Moplah operations appeared in the *JUSII* in January 1926, written by Captain W. St. J. Carpendale of 1st King George's Own Gurkha Rifles, who believed:

> Owing to the conditions under which the Army in India may be called upon to fight being so numerous, the enemy's mode of fighting and the theatres of operations so diverse, it is considered that the operations in Malabar in 1921–22 present so many useful lessons to those who have never taken part in jungle warfare, or duties in aid of the civil power.[87]

Despite this recognition of the importance of such specialised training, operations undertaken in Burma against bands of dacoits or punitive columns on the North-Eastern frontier during the 1920s remained the preserve of the Assam Rifles and Burma Military Police battalions. The British garrison and the Burma Rifles trained solely for Internal Security duties. In 1928 a revised booklet on jungle warfare was published at Rangoon for British officers serving with the Burma Military Police, compiled by Captain J. W. Young of 2/10th Gurkha Rifles, because experience had indicated many amendments were necessary in the procedure detailed in the earlier manual.[88] It pointed out:

> It will be understood that, while the principles of War as detailed in F.S.R. remain unchanged, in undertaking campaigns in an

undeveloped and uncivilized country, as is met with on the frontiers of Burma, the armament, tactics and characteristics of the tribes, and the nature of the theatre of operations, will necessitate considerable modifications in the methods of application of those principles. The modifications referred to hereafter are such as have been found necessary in the operations against these tribes and the instructions embodied herein, are intended to supplement, and in no way supersede, those contained in F.S.R. and the Training Manuals.[89]

An abridged version was also published as an article in the *JUSII* the same year, although it is impossible to gauge how widely this was read by British officers serving in the subcontinent.[90] The only units trained in jungle warfare in Burma during the 1920s and 1930s remained the officers and men of the Burma Military Police, who were regularly tested on infantry tactics in jungle warfare during annual inspections.[91] Those British and Indian troops deployed during the 1930–32 Burma Rebellion did so without any specific training. However, experience and general skills learnt by imperial troops on the North-West Frontier were deemed relevant to the fighting. An editorial in the *JUSII* observed:

It is a far cry from the gaunt hills of the North-West frontier to the wet jungles of Burma, but the training, sense of responsibility, leadership and initiative which frontier fighting inculcates in the minds of junior leaders are equally necessary for bush-fighting. The battalions from India, therefore, who perhaps have paid more attention to the Afridi or Mahsud than to the Burman dacoit, should find no difficulty in adjusting themselves to an unexpected sphere of operations.[92]

To satisfy the immediate demand for information on bush fighting from Indian units the same journal republished an article on fighting on the North-East Frontier originally published in 1922, written by an officer serving in the Assam Rifles.[93] Apart from this measure little was done to implement jungle training in the regular army.

The frontier battalions of the Burma Military Police were reorganised and renamed the Burma Frontier Force on 1 April 1937, following the creation of a separate Army in Burma. These battalions, distributed along the frontier between the Chin Hills in the North-West and the Southern Shan States in the East, and having a combined strength of 7,716 officers and men, remained solely responsible for watch and ward of the frontier tribes.[94] As Burma was not regarded as being under threat of external attack, those regular British, Indian and Burmese units located in the Rangoon and Maymyo districts were still trained, organised and equipped as a police force for their primary task of maintaining internal order.[95] Even the four battalions of the Burma Rifles, composed of Chin, Karen and Kachin recruits, became 'regularised' during the 1930s, largely forgetting the skills and lore required to live and fight in the jungle.[96] Their training was based primarily on support to the civil power, open warfare and even mountain warfare on the North-West Frontier of India, despite the fact they never had an opportunity of serving there. During its annual training camp in the North Shan States in March 1940, for example, 4th Burma Rifles spent much of its time practising piquetting drills and building perimeter camps.[97]

Aid to the Civil Power

The maintenance of law and order within India and duties in support of the civil power was always regarded as the main function of the British component of the Army in India.[98] In the post-war period within India the Non-Cooperation, Khilafat and Sikh Gurdwara reform movements posed a growing threat to colonial rule, in addition to recurring agrarian, industrial, ethnic and communal disturbances which threatened public order. The lessons of the Amritsar massacre in April 1919 were carefully learnt and British troops were routinely trained in internal security duties and drilled in 'Aid to the Civil Power' throughout the inter-war period. Training was based on a range of manuals specifically prepared by the General Staff in India, which complemented those produced by the War Office. Units were regularly exercised in internal security duties and support of the civil power, using scenarios likely to arise locally and often involving close co-operation with the civil and police authorities.[99] Troops were specifically trained in the dispersal of unlawful assemblies, methods of co-operating with the police in carrying out cordons, searches and arrests, patrolling on foot and in motor transport, dealing with individual acts of violence and disarming hostile rioters. In addition, British officers were given lectures and conducted discussions on Indian law, past riots and the application of perceived lessons to local circumstances. Large-scale models of nearby cities and towns were also utilised for training purposes. Tactical exercises without troops (TEWTs) were also held in localities where rioting was likely to break out, with officers wearing mufti to prevent causing alarm.[100] The numerous articles published in the service press bears witness to the interest maintained by officers of both the British and Indian service in this particular aspect of military work.[101]

Conclusion

During the inter-war period British officers and men on tours of foreign service gained considerable practical experience of 'imperial policing' duties within the Empire and of 'small wars' on its peripheries, yet, outside India, lessons learned in operations were not systematically recorded for those who might face similar problems in the future. It appears almost paradoxical, given that 'imperial policing' was the British Army's main task and that it had conducted 'small wars' for over a hundred years, that it devoted so little attention to theory, or to preserving the lessons in manuals or specialised training.

The fundamental reasons for this neglect were the British Army's strong institutional and professional resistance to studying colonial warfare and to training for its specific military requirements. The sheer diversity of conditions and opponents encountered within the British Empire presented a near-impossible problem to those responsible for devising training appropriate to all the conditions likely to be met by imperial troops. Indeed, most outbreaks which did occur were so localised and of such short duration that the Army did not require to develop and implement specialised training. As the War Office lacked a definite threat and thus a specific type of operation for which it could organise, train and equip in the British Empire, it instead concentrated on training for conventional military operations under modern conditions.

The myopic professional viewpoint adopted by the War Office and by many British Service officers was a further important factor. As Major-General Sir Charles Gwynn noted in 1934: 'To minds trained to think in terms of the events of the Great War, the police duties of the Army, even when they take the form of small wars, may appear of insignificant importance.'[102] To serious 'modern' professional British Service officers, 'small wars' were regarded as little more than an embarrassment or an aberration from training for conventional military operations. As a result they were treated as an afterthought rather than as a lasting commitment for the British Army. These soldiers nearly always judged colonial experience against the rather inappropriate yardstick of European military professionalism. To such critics 'imperial policing' and 'small wars' employing apparently outmoded tactics taught few lessons of lasting significance for the British Army. What could a serious professional soldier learn of lasting value from operations against poorly-armed and ill-disciplined 'savages', who knew nothing of modern military skills? Indeed such operations were seen as exerting a positively harmful influence on the Army's preparedness for conventional military operations. The predominant view that the lesser was contained in the greater was reinforced by the fact that training for conventional European warfare was professionally more rewarding. The British Army clung to the view that a European conflict rather than imperial policing was its real concern. As Ian Beckett has observed, most armies perceive themselves to exist primarily to wage a conventional war, whatever their other experience, and during this period the British Army was no exception.[103]

The War Office and British Army as a result of these factors retained a pragmatic, *ad hoc* approach to imperial roles. They produced few training manuals that preserved or disseminated the lessons of operations conducted in the British Empire for the British Army. As T. R. Mockaitis has observed, they suffered from 'historical amnesia', reinforced by an institutional distrust of doctrine.[104] Apart from a brief section included in *FSR* they largely ignored the conduct of 'small wars'. Those officers interested in the conduct of such operations had to rely on the increasingly out-dated *Small Wars: Their Principles and Practice*. The only real attempt by the War Office to discuss colonial requirements was published as late as 1934 and dealt with the 'imperial policing' which now represented the main task of British troops in areas of the Empire other than India. The study of other forms of colonial operation, such as bush or desert warfare, were generally ignored. Indeed, the British Army had little incentive to train for such tasks as bush warfare remained the responsibility of locally-enlisted armed forces with a purely regional role.

The British and Indian components of the Army in India received the most detailed training in colonial military operations. As a definite long-term local commitment existed, the virtually autonomous military authorities in India developed a well thought-out approach to both the theory and practice of colonial warfare as compared with the British Army. As a result of the commitment of large numbers of British and Indian troops to tribal control and of the strategic importance of the North-West Frontier, the General Staff in India devoted considerable attention to devising and implementing training in frontier warfare. They recognised that although the principles and minor tactics of colonial warfare were generally simple enough, specialised training and practical experience was required to make imperial troops proficient and thus prevent unnecessary casualties. This must be regarded as an important reflection of military professionalism devoted solely to local military requirements. T. R. Mockaitis is simply incorrect in a recent study to assert that: 'In the bump and shove of military life on the Northwest Frontier and in Burma and Palestine, soldiers were left to the time-honoured method "making it up as they went along".'[105]

By 1939 a comprehensive range of training manuals was available to British officers, incorporating the lessons from a wealth of frontier fighting experience and describing in elaborate detail the principles and minor tactics of frontier warfare. Similar attention was devoted to internal security duties, in which British units were heavily involved and in which they maintained a high reputation for impartiality. The General Staff in India ensured that there would be no repetition of Amritsar by producing special training guidelines dealing with theory and practice of such duties. In Burma and on the North-Eastern Frontier, however, reliance on localised forces meant that regular troops were denied experience and training in jungle warfare. The virtual independence from the War Office which the General Staff in India enjoyed, and the competition which existed between officers of the British and Indian Services, however, meant that lessons learnt regarding colonial warfare were not widely circulated outside the Subcontinent. Similarly compartmentalisation and decentralisation of responsibility to other colonial armed forces meant that information regarding training for local requirements was seldom passed on to other areas: it remained locked into one compartment of the imperial structure and when British officers left for pastures new they quickly forgot what they had learnt.

The concomitant of this haphazard, patchy and *ad hoc* approach to the theory and practice of colonial warfare in the British Empire was that the lessons of successive operations were quickly forgotten by British Army units when they returned from foreign service to the United Kingdom and trained for a conventional war in Europe. Unless retained in the minds of a cadre of experienced long-service officers and NCOs within each unit, in a form of oral tradition, the lessons were lost, as there was no official means of recording and disseminating them. Moreover, even on tours of foreign service, frequent changes between garrisons, roles and a constant interchange of personnel within British units, meant it was difficult to maintain a high level of expertise in any one class of colonial warfare.[106] As a result of lack of suitable theoretical training, British Army units sometimes suffered an unnecessarily high casualty rate on active service. A premium was placed instead on 'on the spot' training and rapid adaptation to local circumstance, but for this to be effective much depended on the attitude of officers in individual units. In comparison, Indian and other locally-enlisted troops were often far more proficient than their British counterparts, as they had far greater experience and training in one particular form of colonial warfare. Moreover, the general lessons learnt regarding living, moving and fighting in mountains, jungles and deserts – of equal value for conventional military operations in similar terrain – were squandered by the British Army as a whole. In particular, the British and Indian Armies paid a very high price for neglecting special training in jungle warfare. In the long term, however, operations in which British troops fought irregulars in difficult terrain provided an invaluable fund of experience and a solid base for the British authorities when dealing with counter-insurgency operations after the Second World War.[107]

128 MILITARY POWER: LAND WARFARE IN THEORY AND PRACTICE

NOTES

1. See K. Jeffery, *The British Army and the Crisis of Empire 1918–22* (Manchester: UP 1984).
2. Maj-Gen H. Rowan-Robinson, *The Infantry Experiment* (London: William Clowes 1934) pp.9–10.
3. Lt-Col C.E. Vickery, 'Small Wars', *Army Quarterly* 6/2 (1923) p.307.
4. D.C. Gordon, 'Colonial Warfare, 1815–1970', in R. Higham (ed.) *A Guide to the Sources of British Military History* (Berkeley, CA/London: U. of California Press 1975) p.302 and H. Strachan, *European Armies and the Conduct of War* (London: Allen & Unwin 1983) p.76.
5. I.F.W. Beckett, 'Low-Intensity Conflict: Its Place in the Study of War', in D.A. Charters, M. Milner and J.B. Wilson (eds.) *Military History and the Military Profession* (London: Praeger 1993) pp.121-2.
6. See J. Pimlott, 'The British Experience', in I.F.W. Beckett (ed.) *The Roots of Counterinsurgency: Armies and Guerrilla Warfare, 1900–1945* (London: Blandford Press 1988) and T.R. Mockaitis, *British Counterinsurgency 1919–1960* (London: Macmillan 1990).
7. B. Bond, *British Military Policy between the Two World Wars* (Oxford: Clarendon Press 1980) p.38.
8. See D.E. Omissi, *Air Power and Colonial Control* (Manchester UP 1991).
9. Memo by the Secretary of State for War, 10 Feb. 1938, Public Record Office, Kew W033/1502 (hereafter PRO).
10. Bond (note 7) pp.26, 99.
11. *The Army in India and its Evolution* (Calcutta: Supt of Govt Printing 1924) p.61.
12. Brig. G. Blight, *The History of the Royal Berkshire Regiment (Prince Charlotte of Wales') 1920–1947* (London: Staples Press 1953) p.127 and F. de Butts, *Now the Dust has Settled. Memories of War and Peace, 1939–1994* (Padstow: Tabb House 1995) p.11.
13. Vickery (note 3) p.308.
14. Lt-Gen Sir A.A. Montgomery-Massingberd, 'The Rôle of the Army in Imperial Defence', *Army Quarterly* 15/2 (1928) p.247.
15. *Training Regulations 1934* (London: HMSO 1934) p.1.
16. Strachan (note 4) p.77 and D. French, *The British Way in Warfare 1688–2000* (London: Unwin Hyman 1990) p.142.
17. Brig. A.P. Wavell, 'The Training of the Army for War', *Jnl of the Royal United Service Instn* [hereafter *JRUSI*] 78/510 (1933) p.255.
18. Gordon (note 4) p.298.
19. MRAF J. Slessor, *The Central Blue: Recollections and Reflections* (London: Cassell 1956) p.128. See also Field-Marshal Earl Wavell, *The Good Soldier* (London: Macmillan 1948) pp.129–34.
20. K. Jeffery, 'Colonial Warfare 1900–1939', in C. McInnes and G.D. Sheffield (eds.), *Warfare in the Twentieth Century* (London: Unwin Hyman 1988) p.31 and I.F.W. Beckett, 'The Study of Counter-insurgency: A British Perspective', *Small Wars and Insurgencies* 1/1 (April 1990) p.49.
21. Gen O.M. Creagh, 'The Army in India and the New Field Service Regulations', *Army Review* 4 (1913) p.34. See *Field Service Regulations, Part I Operations. 1909 (Reprinted with Amendments 1912)*, (London: War Office 1912) pp.191–212.
22. *Field Service Regulations Vol.II Operations (Provisional)*, (London: War Office 1920).
23. See ibid. Vol.II *(Operations)*, (London: War Office 1924) pp.212–42, ibid. (London: War Office 1929) pp.204–12 and ibid. – *General* (London: HMSO 1935) pp.176–86.
24. Col C.E. Callwell, *Small Wars: Their Principles and Practice* (London: HMSO 1906).
25. Beckett (note 20) p.47.
26. A.D. English, 'The RAF Staff College and the Evolution of British Strategic Bombing Policy', *Jnl of Strategic Studies* 16/3 (Sept. 1993) p.420.
27. See C.B. Wallis, *West African Warfare* (London: Harrison & Sons 1905), Lt-Col W.C.G. Heneker, *Bush Warfare* (London: Hugh Rees 1907) and G. Casserly, *Manual of Training for Jungle and River Warfare* (London: T. Werner Laurie 1915).

'SMALL WARS' AND 'IMPERIAL POLICING' 1919-1939   129

28. *Duties in Aid of the Civil Power 1923* (London: Official 1923) and *Duties in Aid of the Civil Power 1937* (ibid. 1937).
29. See Brevet-Major A.W. Lee, 'Reflections on the Recent Disturbances in Palestine August, 1929', *Army Quarterly* 20/1 (1930) pp.45–51 and Lt-Col H.M. Burrows, 'The Control of Communal Disturbances in Walled Cities', *JSRUSI* 9/515 (1934) pp.565–72.
30. *Notes on Imperial Policing 1934* (London: War Office 1934).
31. Maj-Gen Sir C.W. Gwynn, *Imperial Policing* (London: Macmillan 1934).
32. *Notes on Tactical Lessons of the Palestine Rebellion* (London: No Imprint 1937) p.1.
33. D. Killingray, The Colonial Army in the Gold Coast: Official Policy and Local Response, 1890–1947 (London: PhD thesis 1982) p.14.
34. See J. Lunt, *Imperial Sunset: Frontier Soldiering in the 20th Century* (London: Macdonald 1981), Lt-Col H. Moyse-Bartlett, *The King's African Rifles: A Study in the Military History of East and Central Africa, 1890–1945* (Aldershot: Gale & Polden 1956) and Col A.H.W. Haywood and Brig. F.A.S. Clarke, *The History of the Royal West African Frontier Force* (ibid. 1964).
35. *Regulations for the King's African Rifles* (London: Waterloo & Sons 1925) pp.18–19.
36. Killingray (note 33) pp.237–8 and Lunt (note 34) pp.206–7.
37. See *Notes on Training in Bush Warfare* (London: Colonial Office 1922) and *Notes on Training in Bush Warfare Reprinted and Amended 1930* (ibid. 1930).
38. Lunt (note 34) pp.xv–xvi.
39. Bond (note 7) p.32.
40. 'Return of British Troops on the Indian Establishment 1st May 1939, 18th May 1939', India Office Library and Records (hereafter OIOC) L/WS/1/142.
41. *The Army in India and its Evolution* (Calcutta: Supt of Govt Printing 1924) p.61.
42. R. Haycock, 'British Arms in India', in G. Jordan (ed.) *British Military History. A Supplement to Robin Higham's Guide to the Sources* (NY/London: Garland 1988) p.457.
43. Callwell (note 24) p.286.
44. Col D.E. Robertson, 'The Organisation and Training of the Army in India', *JRUSI* 69/474 (1924) p.326.
45. *Report of a Conference of General Officers held at Delhi 22nd to 24th February 1917 under the direction of His Excellency the Commander-in-Chief in India* (Delhi: General Staff, India, hereafter GSI 1917) pp.21–6.
46. T.R. Moreman, '"Passing it On": The Army in India and the Development of Frontier Warfare, 1849–1947 (PhD thesis, King's College London 1996) pp.175–94.
47. 'Waziristan Force Weekly Appreciation for week ending 13th January 1920', PRO WO 106/56.
48. See Mountain Warfare School, Abbottabad, *Synopsis of Lectures 1920 (Revised 1921)* (Rawalpindi: Fazal Elahi 1921), *Notes on Mountain Warfare* (Calcutta: Supt of Govt Printing 1920) and S.H.C., *Mountain Warfare Notes* (Poona: Scottish Mission Press 1921).
49. Field-Marshal Sir W. Slim, *Unofficial History* (London: Cassell 1959) p.101.
50. See *Despatch by His Excellency General Lord Rawlinson of Trent on the Operations of the Waziristan Force for the period 1st April 1921 to 31st December 1921* (Simla: GSI 1922) p.5 L/MIL/7/16930, OIOC.
51. Col C. Kirkpatrick, 'Some Thoughts on Frontier Fighting', *Jnl of the United Service Institution of India* [hereafter *JUSII*] 54/236 (1924) pp.326–7.
52. Moreman (note 46) pp.203–17 and Col F.S. Keen, 'To what extent would the use of the latest scientific and mechanical methods of warfare affect operations on the North-West Frontier of India?' *JUSII* 53/233 (1923) p.215.
53. Capt. M.C. Gompertz, 'The Application of Science to Indian Frontier Warfare', *Army Quarterly* 10 (1925) p.133.
54. *Field Service Regulations Vol.II (Operations)* (London: War Office 1924) p.215.
55. *Manual of Operations on the North-West Frontier of India* (Calcutta: Govt of India 1925).
56. Lt-Col H.B. Hudson, 'Those Blue Remembered Hills' (unpub. TS Memoir 1980) p.70, Hudson MSS Photo. Eur.179 and Col H.R.C. Pettigrew, '"It Seemed Very Ordinary" Memoirs of Sixteen Years Service in the Indian Army 1932–47' (unpub. TS Memoir 1980) p.65, Imperial War Museum 84/29/1.

57. See *Standing Orders for Frontier Warfare. 16th Infantry Brigade 1924* (Ahmednagar: No Imprint 1924), *Kohat District Standing Orders for War and for Local Columns* (Lahore: Model Electric Press 1927) and *Landi Kotal Standing Orders for War 1936* (Landi Kotal: Risalpur Press 1936).
58. See *"Frontier", Frontier Warfare* (Bombay: Thacker 1921), *Notes on Frontier Warfare* (Aldershot: Gale & Polden 1922), Col J.P. Villiers-Stuart, *Letters of a Once Punjab Frontier Force Officer to his Nephew giving his Ideas on Fighting on the North West Frontier and in Afghanistan* (London: Sifton Praed 1925) and Maj. D.B. Mackenzie, *Mountain Warfare on the Sand Model* (Aldershot: Gale & Polden 1936).
59. Maj.-Gen. J. Smyth VC, *Milestones* (London: Sidgwick 1979) p.97 and Gen. Ismay, *The Memoirs of General the Lord Ismay* (London: Heinemann 1960) p.38.
60. C. Chenevix Trench, *The Indian Army and the King's Enemies 1900–1947* (London: Thames & Hudson 1988) p.120.
61. Lt-Col O.D. Bennett, 'Some Regrettable Incidents on the N.-W.F.', *JUSII* 63/271, (1933) p.194, Lt-Gen Sir P. Neame VC, *Playing with Strife: The Autobiography of a Soldier* (London: Harrap 1947) p.134 and Smyth (note 59) p.63.
62. R. Hilton, *Nine Lives: The Autobiography of an Old Soldier* (London: Hollis and Carter 1955) pp.104-5.
63. See Capt R.E. Wood, 'Life on the Frontier', *Royal Engineers Jnl* 42 (1928) p.243 and 'W', 'Mahsud Waziristan 1919–20', *JUSII* 60/259 (1930) pp.193–200.
64. *Military Report on the Kohat District* (Simla: GSI 1928) p.65.
65. See *Report on the Staff Exercise and Manoeuvres held under the orders of the G.O.C.-in-C Northern Command, India 22nd November to 30th November 1925* (Calcutta: Govt of India Central Publication Branch 1926) and *Eastern Command Manoeuvres* (Simla: GSI 1925).
66. J. Masters, *Bugles and a Tiger* (London: Michael Joseph 1956) p.252.
67. Lt-Gen F. Morgan, *Peace and War: A Soldier's Life* (London: Hodder 1961) p.90.
68. 'An Infantry Officer', 'Collective Training in a Battalion', *JUSII* 60/259 (1930) p.128.
69. G. Moore, *'Just as Good as the Rest'. A British Battalion in the Faqir of Ipi's War Indian N.W.F. 1936–37* (Huntingdon: Privately Printed 1979) p.8.
70. Gen Sir A. Skeen, *Passing it On: Short Talks on Tribal Fighting on the North-West Frontier of India* (Aldershot: Gale & Polden 1932).
71. Indian Army Order 80. Books – 'Passing it On' by Gen. Sir Andrew Skeen, 2nd Dec. 1932, L/MIL/17/5/274, OIOC.
72. Lt-Gen G.N. Molesworth, *Curfew on Olympus* (London: Asia Publishing House 1965) p.85 and Brig. J.H. Prendergast, *Prender's Progress: A Soldier in India, 1931–47* (London: Cassell 1979) p.57.
73. Pettigrew (note 56) p.65 See also pp.88–9.
74. Brig. W.J. Jervois, *The History of the Northamptonshire Regiment: 1934–1948* (London: Regimental History Committee 1953) p.24.
75. M.F.K. Betty, 'Waziristan, 1937', in C.H.T. MacFetridge and J.P. Warren (eds.) *Tales of the Mountain Gunners* (Edinburgh: William Blackwood 1973) p.118 and Prendergast (note 72) p.90.
76. Capt. D.M. Kennelly, 'Artillery Support of Pickets in Mountain Warfare', *Jnl of the Royal Artillery* 57/2 (1930–31) p.253.
77. *AHQ India, Training Memorandum No. 2 Collective Training period 1930–31* (Simla: Government of India Press 1931) p.6.
78. *AHQ India, Training Memorandum No. 12 Collective Training period 1935–36* (Delhi: Manager of Publications 1936) p.2.
79. Bartholomew to Wilson, Feb. 1937, L/WS/1/257, OIOC.
80. *Frontier Warfare – India (Army and Royal Air Force)*, (Delhi: Defence Dept 1939).
81. See *Despatch on the operations against the Kuki tribes of Assam and Burma, November 1917 to March 1919* (Simla: Government Monotype Press 1919).
82. See Maj. A. Vickers, 'Wardens of the North Eastern Marches', *JUSII* 52/228 (1922) pp.246–52 and Col L.W. Shakespear, *History of the Assam Rifles* (London: Macmillan & Co. 1929).

83. Maj. A. Vickers, 'Concerning fighting on the North-Eastern Frontiers of India', *JUSII*, 52/227 (1922) p.157.
84. Capt. A.W. Taylor, *Jungle Warfare: the conduct of small expeditions in the jungles and hilly tracts of Burma, and a system of drill and musketry instruction connected therewith, for the use of officers of the Burma Military Police* (Rangoon: Supt Govt Printing Burma 1902) p.1.
85. See *Report by His Excellency General Lord Rawlinson of Trent on the Operations in Malabar for the period 20th August 1921 to 25th February 1922* (Simla: GSI 1922).
86. Lt-Col A.C. Mackinnon, 'The Moplah Rebellion, 1921–22', *Army Quarterly* 7/2 (1923) p.268.
87. Capt. W.S. Carpendale, 'The Moplah Rebellion 1921–22', *JUSII* 56/242 (1926) p.76.
88. Capt. J.W. Young, *Manual of Jungle Warfare for Officers of the Burma Military Police* (Rangoon: Supt Govt Printing and Stationary Burma 1928).
89. Ibid. p.1.
90. Capt J.W. Young, 'Notes on Jungle Warfare', *JUSII* 58/251 (1928) pp.338–63.
91. *Manual for the Burma Military Police* (Rangoon: Supt Govt Printing & Stationary Burma 1931) p.40.
92. 'Editorial', *JUSII* 61/264 (1931) p.283.
93. Maj A. Vickers, 'Concerning fighting on the North-Eastern Frontiers of India', *JUSII* 61/264 (1931) pp.371–6.
94. *Report on the Administration of the Burma Frontier Force for the year 1938* (Rangoon: Supt Govt Printing & Stationary Burma 1939) p.6.
95. H.Q. Army in Burma, 'Progress Report No.1, 16th Nov. 1937', L/WS/1/261, OIOC and Col W. Hingston, *Never Give Up, being Volume V The History of the King's Own Yorkshire Light Infantry* (London: Humphries & Sons 1950) pp.40–5.
96. Lt-Col B. Oatts, *The Jungle in Arms* (London: Kimber 1962) p.40.
97. Lunt (note 34) p.358.
98. D.E. Omissi, *The Sepoy and the Raj: The Indian Army 1860–1940* (London: Macmillans 1994) p.216.
99. *Training and Manoeuvre Regulations 1923 (With additions for India)* (Calcutta: Supt of Govt Printing 1924) p.10. See *Exercise on a Situation of Internal Security and Martial Law fully explained in Detail* (Lahore: 'Civil and Military Gazette' Press 1923).
100. AHQ India, *Training Memorandum No. 14 Collective Training period 1936–7* (Delhi: Mngr of Publications 1937) n.100 p.8 and *Notes on Internal Security Training* (Simla: Defence Dept. 1937).
101. See Capt and Brevet Maj. H.P. Radley, 'The Suppression of Riots', *JUSII* 58/250 (1928) pp.28–37 and Maj. T.A. Lowe, 'The Cawnpore Riots from Company Commander's Point of View', *JUSII* 64/274 (1931) pp.360–70.
102. Gwynn (note 31) p.7.
103. Beckett (note 5) p.123.
104. Mockaitis (note 6) p.189.
105. T.R. Mockaitis, *British Counterinsurgency in the Post-Imperial Era* (Manchester UP 1995) p.133.
106. Col H.E. Franklyn, 'Training Troops on Foreign Service', *JRUSI* 9/515 (1934) p.558
107. Pimlott (note 6) p.38.

Montgomery, Morale, Casualty Conservation and 'Colossal Cracks': 21st Army Group's Operational Technique in North-West Europe, 1944–45

STEPHEN HART

The aim of this essay is to examine Field-Marshal Montgomery's conduct of the 1944–45 North-West Europe campaign in the light of two interlinked influences: conducting a campaign in a way designed to maintain the morale of your own troops, and with great concern to avoid heavy casualties. These influences respectively may be termed the maintenance of morale and casualty conservation. These two concerns were interconnected, since avoidance of heavy casualties bolstered the morale of 21st Army Group's non-regular soldiers during the decline in morale caused by active operations, whilst high morale facilitated a superior battlefield performance, and this probably contributed to reducing casualties. Although these influences have been recognised in the historiography of the campaign, they have not received the attention justified by their significance.

It will be argued here that morale maintenance and casualty conservation were the paramount influences on Montgomery's operational conduct of the campaign. Moreover, it will be suggested that the other aspects of Montgomery's operational method can only be understood in the light of these two factors: his approach can only be comprehended as the totality of all the characteristics of which it was comprised. Too often, isolated features of Montgomery's generalship (such as his caution) have been criticised without due consideration to how this related to all the other characteristics of his approach, and especially to the two influences under consideration here. Indeed, these criticisms often fail to give due regard to the actual situation facing the British Army in 1944. When these morale and casualty influences are taken into account, it is clear that Montgomery, despite his undeniable operational flaws, such as his inability to master exploitation, was the most competent of the British generals in Europe, especially with regard to the art of the practicable. Montgomery's approach was an appropriate way of achieving Britain's war aims, given the relative capabilities of the British Army against the determined and skilled *Wehrmacht*. These aims sought victory over Germany with tolerable casualties, but with a high military profile within a larger Allied effort. Montgomery sought to nurture his limited, fragile resources into a sustained adequate combat performance which would slowly grind the enemy into submission by the inexorable logic of an attritional war of *matériel*.

This essay examines Montgomery's operational conduct as Commander-in-Chief of the Anglo-Canadian 21st Army Group, which comprised 2nd British and 1st Canadian Armies. In Normandy, Montgomery was also temporary Land Forces Commander controlling all Allied troops in the theatre. After 1 September 1944, however, although promoted Field-Marshal, he reverted to being 'merely' an army group commander within a theatre now deploying three army groups (two of which were American), all under the operational command of the American General, Dwight D. Eisenhower, acting as a dual Supreme Allied, and Land Forces, Commander. This command context permeated Montgomery's conduct of the campaign. The concept of the operational level of war is used here in the sense of the 'area between strategy and tactics which denotes the fighting of battles in a given theatre of operations in pursuit of the political objective of the war',[1] and as the 'gr[e]y zone once called Grand Tactics, the tactics of large formations', such as army groups, armies and corps.[2]

All commanders of armies are concerned with the morale of their forces and the casualties that result from using this force. The key issue, however, is how important were these two considerations in relation to all the other influences on a commander's conduct of a campaign, such as military and political objectives, relative force strengths, doctrine, and the actual unfolding operational situation? In North-West Europe morale and casualty influences were extremely significant in relation to these other considerations.

Montgomery's Operational Methods: 'Colossal Cracks'

Montgomery's operational method was encapsulated by his expression 'Colossal Crack': '[When] I am ready I ... hit hard, and quickly',[3] and '[I] concentrate great strength at some selected place and hit the Germans a colossal crack'.[4]

His operational methods were characterised by massive set-piece battles based on concentration and massed artillery firepower (supplemented by aerial bombing) and on integrated use of tactical air power. Montgomery would only commence these set-piece battles after very careful preparation and massive concentration of resources. He would conduct these battles cautiously and methodically, with close regard to the logistical situation, and would 'grip' them according to a previously prepared 'Master Plan'. Operationally, Montgomery would seek to maintain the initiative and remain balanced: respectively, to force the enemy merely to react to his moves, and to have his forces so deployed that any sudden enemy move could be countered rapidly. 'Colossal Cracks' was an attritional method based on *matériel* which eschewed operational manoeuvre. These methods had been disseminated through the British Army after the successes in North Africa, with Montgomery particularly inculcating his subordinate commanders in 21st Army Group with these techniques.

Some historians have criticised Montgomery's approach as being excessively cautious, attritional, and reliant on massed firepower at the expense of operational manoeuvre.[5] Whilst these criticisms have some validity, an appreciation of the appropriateness of Montgomery's approach is facilitated by consideration of the issues of morale maintenance and casualty conservation.

Morale Maintenance

This analysis will now demonstrate that Montgomery was extremely concerned with maintaining the morale of his troops. His abiding concern with the 'maintenance of morale'[6] was clear to James Grigg, the Secretary of State for War, who observed that Montgomery's technique 'rested on the supreme importance of morale in war'.[7] Montgomery's wartime lectures and writings consistently demonstrated this concern:

> [The soldier's] training is the most important consideration in the fashioning of a fighting army. All modern science is directed towards his assistance but on his efforts depends the outcome of the battle. THE MORALE OF THE SOLDIER IS THE MOST IMPORTANT SINGLE FACTOR IN WAR.[8]

The doctrine espoused by Montgomery, when Chief of the Imperial General Staff (CIGS) at 'Evolution', the 1946 annual War Office exercise, repeated this view: 'without a high morale no success can be achieved in battle.'[9] This concern with morale refutes Thompson's accusation that in North-West Europe Montgomery was just a 'general manager' of a campaign reduced merely to overwhelming weight of *matériel* – of machines rather than of men.[10]

Recognition that simple weight of *matériel* was not enough to convince senior Allied commanders that victory was assured, illustrates the appropriateness of Montgomery's belief that the army's morale was one of the keys to victory. Indeed, the success of 'Overlord' seems more certain with hindsight than it did at the time. Then, its success was as uncertain as the vast risks involved were clear. For Britain's war weariness in 1944 has often been underemphasized: civilians found it harder to endure the German V-weapon onslaught with the same stoic resilience as they had the earlier *Blitz*. Equally, the foreboding with which senior Allied commanders viewed 'Overlord', the culmination of three years' desperate toil, has often been underestimated, with the CIGS General Sir Alan Brooke confessing on 5 June 1944 that 'it may well be the most ghastly disaster of the whole war'.[11] While there is some validity in the portrayal of the Second World War as one essentially of industrial production, what really mattered, however, at least for the Anglo-Canadian forces in 'Overlord', was how well these non-martial soldiers used their array of machines.[12]

A key issue here is what Montgomery really felt about the true capabilities of his troops. Sir Michael Howard has argued perceptively that Montgomery's concern to maintain his forces' morale prevented him from expressing negative thoughts about the real capabilities of the British soldier relative to that of the enemy. Both Howard and Max Hastings rightly argue that Montgomery privately was only too well aware of the limitations of his troops. Therefore, much of the praise he lavished on his soldiers was rhetorical, and hence statements of his like 'the British soldier is the finest fighting man in the world, if properly led' cannot be taken simply at face value.[13] Indeed, Howard makes the crucial point that 'in the Second World War this was not true. Mont[gomer]y knew that this was not true, and by far the most difficult part of his job ... was to make the British Army, the British public, and everyone else believe that it was [true].'[14] This statement encapsulates what morale maintenance meant to Montgomery.

Despite being well aware of the British Army's limitations in 1944, Montgomery was still genuinely proud of his troops. That the British Army had got from its 1940 nadir to a point in 1944 where it could take on the highly effective *Wehrmacht*, and consistently win, was a tremendous achievement, of which British commanders were justly proud. Yet, Montgomery was sufficiently professional to realise that there was far to go before the British Army could defeat the enemy without overwhelming superiority in *matériel*.

The situation facing Britain in 1943–44 provided little opportunity for the army to make much progress toward the herculean task of defeating the Germans on equal terms, even if this had been an objective. For Britain, however, that the war was won was more significant than the combat performance with which this was achieved. Montgomery's purpose in Normandy was not to prove 'the superiority of [his troops] ... to those of Hitler',[15] but rather to do *now* the best with whatever weapon war-weary

Britain could muster: to somehow 'persuade [his troops] to do ... just enough' to secure victory whilst avoiding a repetition of the slaughter of the Great War.[16] Moreover, since there probably would be no second chance if 'Overlord' failed, this weapon would have to be nursed until final victory over Nazi Germany was achieved. Its morale would have to be nurtured until weight of numbers succeeded in bringing the enemy to collapse. That Montgomery accomplished precisely this in North-West Europe was a considerable achievement.[17]

Montgomery had long appreciated the overwhelming significance of success in battle to the maintenance of high morale:

> Morale is based on ... [the] troops [having] complete confidence in their higher commander; they must know that the battle is safe in his hands, that he will not sacrifice their lives needlessly, that success will always crown their efforts. If this state exists, the troops will have the highest morale.[18]

Other factors that had long been recognised as being important in maintaining morale included: good leadership; firm discipline; effective and realistic training; physical fitness; and good man-management, in the sense of 'removing all discomforts [and] ... unpleasantness', especially by getting hot tea forward to the troops.[19] The terrible demands that combat placed on soldiers would be ameliorated as far as operational conditions permitted. If these elements were coupled with repeated success, then it was possible, Montgomery believed, to sustain high morale among his troops. When high morale was coupled with material advantage, British troops could defeat consistently the best of the *Wehrmacht.*

Morale Problems Within 21st Army Group

This analysis will now examine the morale of 21st Army Group's forces during the campaign. It will be shown that serious morale problems existed within Montgomery's command, but (despite this) that his forces advanced into Germany with their morale still intact. In this campaign, as in the Second World War generally, the morale of the British Army was clearly more fragile relative to the German Army's high and resilient morale. Alistair Horne's recent analysis concluded that Montgomery fought the campaign 'with a much more "flawed weapon" ... than has been realised'.[20]

This deficiency was not surprising, since the British Army of 1939–45 was a mass-conscripted civilian army, based on a tiny peacetime cadre. Many of its regular officers had had Empire-wide experience of peacetime soldiering which might have prepared them better for a major modern European war. Its personnel came from a society with no particularly strong martial tradition, and so they lacked the fanaticism and willingness to risk death which characterised much of the German Army. The same also applied in a more extreme form to the Canadian Army. Anglo-Canadian troops, while undoubtedly extremely brave, could not always be expected to meet the sacrificial, super-human efforts frequently demanded of their German foes.[21]

On D-Day, 21st Army Group's morale was clearly very high, but during the first five weeks' bitter fighting, its fighting edge was blunted. That this well-conditioned weapon was blunted was partly due to features particular to the Normandy battles, including: inability to absorb replacements in reserve; effective enemy resistance; the defensibility of the *bocage* terrain; the enemy mortar and sniper menaces; superior enemy armour; lack of successful advances; local reverses which necessitated incurring further casualties re-attacking objectives previously gained; and heavy casualties, especially among officers. Collectively, these factors took a serious toll on 21st Army Group's forces, and by mid-July serious morale problems were appearing in several divisions. Many British officers recognised that these problems existed, but refused openly to admit it, preferring euphemisms like 'stickiness'. However, these problems were observed frankly by Brigadier James Hargest, the respected New Zealand army observer at XXX Corps: 'the troops have not the spirit essential to Victory.... I realise that the enemy's morale is lower but ours frightens me.'[22]

By mid-July morale problems were evident within Lt-General John Crocker's I British Corps, holding the eastern flank beyond the Caen Canal. Crocker informed his superior, the Canadian Lt-General Henry Crerar, that 3rd British Infantry Division, after fighting continuously since D-Day, recently had shown 'signs of ... exhaustion'.[23] Morale problems were also appearing the 2nd and 3rd Canadian Infantry Divisions. Both had spent long periods in the front, suffering heavy casualties, so that by late July they were barely battleworthy. The latter soon 'lapsed into ... despondency', failing in Operation 'Spring'.[24] These problems forced Lt-General Guy Simonds, the commander of II Canadian Corps, to use the inexperienced troops of the newly-arrived 4th Canadian and Polish Armoured Divisions for the second phase of his 8 August 'Totalize' attack. Their inexperience contributed to the operation's failure, which also resulted from dismally ineffective use of the massive firepower available.

Morale problems were also prominent in the three veteran North Africa formations – particularly the 7th Armoured and 51st (Highland) Infantry Divisions. Montgomery brought these forces back to provide backbone for 21st Army Group's largely inexperienced troops, but in Normandy this seemingly sensible decision proved to be a serious mistake. On 24 July 1944, Crocker informed Crerar that 51st Division was 'not ... fit for battle'.[25] Indeed, both divisions 'did badly ... in Normandy',[26] according to Major-General G. L. Verney, 7th Armoured's commander from 4 August 1944. The latter demonstrated the 'bifurcation' of initial dashing recklessness, giving way to excessive caution, which resulted partly from British reaction to German tank superiority. This 'stickiness' prompted Montgomery in early August to instigate widespread sackings within the division's senior command after its failure in Operation 'Bluecoat'.[27]

Over-caution was also evident within the Guards Armoured and 43rd (Wessex) Infantry Divisions. Indeed, by mid-August significant morale problems had emerged in as many as nine of 21st Army Group's 16 divisions: in the worst scenario only seven divisions were completely reliable for offensive operations. In these circumstances, divisions with morale problems could not be allowed to become completely unbattleworthy. This imperative – to nurture the failing morale of such formations – was constantly at the back of Montgomery's mind.[28]

The spectacular Anglo-Canadian advances of late summer 1944 initially caused a surge in morale, but then an incredible wave of over-optimism, bordering on hysteria, swept through all Allied forces in the theatre: the belief was widespread that the war was virtually won and would be over in days. Consequently, according to Lt-General Sir Richard O'Connor, the VIII Corps commander, 'nobody was ... prepared to take the same risks as they had earlier'.[29] This caution may have been a contributory factor in the failure to link up with the airborne forces dropped during Operation 'Market Garden'. That autumn, there existed a continuing need to nurture the Polish Armoured Division, whose effectiveness was hampered by shortage of replacements. Consequently, the division was placed in reserve to train and reorganize, rather than being wrecked in active operations, so that later it would become 'a really effective fighting formation'.[30]

Despite these morale problems, 21st Army Group's morale fabric remained intact throughout the campaign, as demonstrated by the successful completion of the terribly harsh February 1945 'Veritable' offensive in the Reichswald. This achievement was due principally to Montgomery's careful husbanding of his forces.

The Effect of Morale Maintenance on Montgomery's Conduct of the Campaign

This analysis now examines the effect of morale maintenance on Montgomery's conduct of the campaign. His approach nurtured his forces toward an adequate but sustained combat performance, recognising that this, 'assisted by competent generalship',[31] was enough to win a war of attrition in the long run, given Allied material superiority. He understood that his forces, despite their weaknesses, could defeat the *Wehrmacht* if –

but only if – they were properly trained and rehearsed, truly motivated, cautiously led, carefully handled and husbanded, and backed by copious *matériel*.[32]

It is significant to note that while limitations in morale were a factor in the genesis of a firepower-laden approach based on *matériel*, such weaknesses were also unfortunately perpetuated by the attritional approach that derived from them. Although this approach helped to nurture morale by avoiding imposition of extreme demands on British troops, the existence of massive firepower made most soldiers believe that they could 'dispense with anything resembling personal fanaticism on the battlefield'.[33] 'Colossal Cracks', therefore, were a product of, and appropriate response to, morale maintenance concerns, but (paradoxically) also perpetuated the very fragility of morale that lay behind its evolution: Montgomery's method was, inevitably, a two-edged sword.

Montgomery's determination to sustain high morale through uninterrupted success meant that he ensured that any operation he launched would enjoy the best possible chances of success. He would only launch attacks after careful preparation, and after large material superiority had been concentrated. He would 'not have any failures' because he would 'limit the scope of any operation to that which can be done successfully. I do not launch [it] until I am ready.'[34] This striving to ensure that battles would never be lost sometimes meant that potential (but risky) opportunities to win battles were missed. This caution has often been criticised, with some justification, but the logic of attrition suggested that as long as the Allies avoided defeats, and thus sustained their own morale, sheer weight of numbers eventually would secure victory.

Some cynics have dismissed Montgomery's cautious approach as being designed merely to secure his own reputation, and indeed his vanity and seedy glory-grabbing fostered such suspicions. Eisenhower informed General George C. Marshall, the US Army Chief of Staff, that:

> [General Montgomery] is unquestionably able, but very conceited. ... he is so proud of his successes to date that he will never willingly make a single move until he is absolutely certain of success – until he has concentrated enough resources so that anybody could practically guarantee the outcome.[35]

Such critics failed to recognise (as Montgomery did) that a commander's reputation was inextricably linked to the morale of his troops. This enabled him simultaneously to serve his vanity and also be professional, by exaggerating his confidence for his troops' benefit. Montgomery was, however, too monkishly devoted to the professional art of war merely to pursue personal glory alone.

Overall, Montgomery's cautious firepower-reliant approach, engendered by morale maintenance concerns, was largely justified, since the 1943–45 experiences on both the Eastern and Western fronts had demonstrated that simple numerical superiority was not enough to ensure Allied successes over the *Wehrmacht*. The German Army, despite numerical inferiority, was able to inflict local defeats on the Allies on both fronts, as at Targul-Frumos (2–4 May 1944), and Villers Bocage (13 June 1944). In North-West Europe, these defeats often occurred after Allied tactical audacity which left forces without adequate artillery fire-support. Equally in these years, both German and Russian forces displayed an increased reliance on concentrated firepower. Furthermore, Anglo-Canadian numerical advantage often seemed greater on paper than it actually was in combat. Given the tactical techniques of 'Colossal Cracks', particularly the echeloning in depth of assault formations, together with casualty conservation concerns, Anglo-Canadian forces often only deployed at any given time a fraction of their strength at the point of combat. Furthermore, Allied equipment was generally inferior to that of the enemy. Continual Allied success, therefore, was far from guaranteed simply by weight of numbers, and hence Allied commanders had to avoid morale-damaging setbacks. Given these factors, it was a creditable achievement that Montgomery ensured all his European battles were at least marginally successful. Not once was a rupturing of his forces' carefully nurtured morale risked by audacity which allowed the Germans to inflict a major setback.

In Normandy, Montgomery did not blunt his Army Group on several spectacular victories, but ensured it would achieve every task set it throughout the campaign. He was unwilling to launch attacks lacking the most favourable circumstances for success, such as insufficient build-up of artillery shells, instead postponing them until conditions improved. Montgomery complained to Major-General Sir Frank Simpson, the Director of Military Operations, about the storm of late June 1944: 'In ships off the beaches is everything I need to resume the offensive with a bang ... I must have ... more artillery ammunition.' Without this Montgomery concluded: 'I shall have to postpone the attack.'[36] Postponement was also likely if there was bad weather preventing use of the awesome power of Allied tactical air forces: Montgomery announced concerning the 'Epsom' offensive that 'each ... day of bad weather will mean a further postponement of a day'.[37]

Both operationally and tactically, Montgomery's soldiers went into battle with all material support possible: artillery, armour (including specialised equipments), tactical airforces and strategic bombers. This reliance on machines had significant implications for the operational approach of 21st Army Group. Due to the desire emanating from all command levels for maximum possible support, there was simply not enough artillery, ammunition or specialised armour to go round. Maximum support could neither be given simultaneously to both armies within 21st Army Group, nor to separate thrusts within the same army. On 16 October 1944, Operation 'Constellation', the eastward attack toward the River Maas by VIII Corps (of 2nd Army), was halted when Montgomery shifted the weight of 2nd Army westward to support 1st Canadian Army's clearance of the Scheldt estuary. Operationally, this feature may have enabled the Germans to maintain the integrity of their very hard-pressed front by constantly shifting reinforcements from one threatened sector to the next: concentration permitted counter-concentration against it, as 'Veritable' demonstrated. Simultaneous full-scale attacks by both 21st Army Group's armies, even with reduced scales of support, might have brought the Germans more rapidly to collapse.

The imperative to avoid heavy casualties as a prerequisite for sustaining the fragile morale of non-regular troops illustrates the interlinkage between morale maintenance and casualty conservation. Montgomery, like his senior colleagues, recognised this necessity: 'Soldiers will follow you if they know you will not waste their lives.'[38] One of Montgomery's officers in North Africa commented that the troops 'liked serving under [him as they] had a better chance of surviving'.[39] Similarly, Brigadier Edgar Williams, 21st Army Group's Chief Intelligence Officer, observed: 'We were always very aware of the doctrine, "let metal do it rather than flesh". The morale of our troops depended upon this. We always said: "Waste all the ammunition you like, but not lives"'.[40]

The fear of severe casualties expedited degeneration into 'stickiness', whilst sustaining casualties steadily unravelled the basic fabric of a unit. The devastating effect on morale that severe casualties caused among infantry battalions was illustrated by a report on 6th Duke of Wellington's Regiment, which stated that the unit was in 'complete disorganization ... because all the key men have gone'.[41]

Casualty Conservation

The second foundation of Montgomery's operational approach in this theatre was casualty conservation: his caution and reliance on firepower can only be understood fully in the light of his concerns to avoid heavy casualties. Prior to Carlo D'Este's work in 1983, the campaign's historiography showed only limited awareness of this issue. D'Este emphasised the effects that manpower shortages had on the campaign from the end of June 1944, suggesting that the problem was a new, temporary phenomenon resulting principally from the War Office's faulty estimation of infantry wastage rates. In reality, the manpower crisis was a long-term problem which had long been foreseen. This analysis will show here that this crisis was extremely serious, had been long anticipated, and had a profound impact on Montgomery's conduct of the campaign.[42]

There were four principal, interconnected, factors behind Montgomery's fervent desire to attain victory in North-West Europe with tolerable casualties: morale maintenance, the manpower shortage, the 'shadow of Passchendaele',[43] and Britain's political or grand strategic objectives and war aims. Montgomery understood that by 1943 Britain was suffering a chronic manpower shortage throughout its war effort, and that there would be a serious infantry-reinforcement problem for his command. Like many of his peers, Montgomery also had been profoundly influenced by the horrors of the trenches of the Great War, and in this war was determined to avoid repetition of such slaughter. Finally, he appreciated clearly the campaign's political dimension. Britain had gone to war, apart from resisting Nazi aggression, to protect her influence on the Europe that would emerge after the War. Emerging victorious was insufficient to secure these aims, for if Britain so emerged but with its Army destroyed, then Britain's influence on post-war Europe – already waning as that of the two nascent superpowers rose – would be further diminished.

The Manpower Problem

The United Kingdom by 1943 had an acute manpower shortage which could not satisfy the demands of war production and the armed services. Intakes of new recruits into the Army were insufficient to meet predicted wastage, especially in the case of infantry: and this problem would be acute for 21st Army Group. This situation had been long foreseen, with United Kingdom Home Forces expressing fears in December 1943 that the number of men they would have to draft to 21st Army Group as reinforcements would exceed their total fit personnel.[44] On 19 March 1944, Montgomery wrote to Lt-General Sir Ronald Weeks, the Deputy CIGS:

> The situation [concerning] reinforcements is not good. But we must take things as they are and find the best answer.... We have got to try and do this business with the smallest possible casualties. If we play our cards properly, ... we could do it fairly cheaply.[45]

Indeed, in March it was recognised that even if the five home service divisions defending the British Isles were broken up for reinforcements, there would still be by the year's end a shortage of 40,000 infantry. Further steps were immediately taken to retrain as infantry men from other branches, and two operational divisions were scheduled for cannibalisation.

That Home Forces had been bled dry of draft-quality infantry long before 21st Army Group reached France illustrates the extent of the manpower shortage. By 7 August 1944, Home Forces had been reduced to being merely an army of young boys and old men, with a mere 2,654 fully trained draft-quality infantry under its command. The only source of reinforcements now available for Montgomery in France would be the meagre monthly output of new infantry recruits (and those retraining) who had finished their training programmes.[46]

The fear that 21st Army Group's reinforcement pool might run dry constantly haunted Montgomery's conduct of the campaign. The fact that the British reinforcement pool only once temporarily dried up was due largely to the cannibalization of two divisions. However the Canadian pool ran dry between 12 August and 23 September, when the total Canadian infantry reinforcements available was markedly less than the infantry deficit within 1st Canadian Army. At its peak, on 2 September, the Canadian infantry manpower deficit of 3,917 (a staggering 19 per cent of War Establishment) dwarfed the paltry 618 reinforcements available.[47]

'The Shadow of Passchendaele'

Many of the senior officers of 21st Army Group had witnessed the slaughter of 'the poor bloody infantry' in the First World War and were determined in this war to avoid the slaughter which, they believed, had so damaged inter-war Britain. This concern – 'the shadow of Passchendaele' as Henry L. Stimson, the American Secretary for War put it – fostered a British grand strategic approach which sought to weaken the Germans on the peripheries, rather than pay the 'Butcher's Bill' of engaging the enemy's main forces.[48]

Montgomery and his senior commanders were determined that 21st Army Group's infantry would not be treated as cannon fodder, although in North-West Europe, like most campaigns, the vast majority of casualties fell on the infantry arm. Richard O'Brien, who served under Montgomery, believed that the latter 'was determined not to repeat the mistakes made by the First War generals. This may be the main explanation of the caution he showed in preparation for his battles.... He wanted always to lose as few men as possible.'[49] Montgomery did not waste his men's lives by continuing attacks which incurred heavy casualties but no longer stood a reasonable chance of success, halting 'Epsom', 'Goodwood' and 'Spring' for this reason.

The Political/Imperial Dimension

The last aspect of the manpower shortage lay in the realm of Britain's political objectives in the Second World War. By 1944, the British leadership realised that if Britain emerged after Germany's defeat with virtually no army, then Britain's say in post-war Europe would be diminished. Similarly, the CIGS Brooke was determined to see Montgomery head the campaign not just because of the latter's operational abilities, but also because both men concurred on Britain's political war objectives. Montgomery's actions, especially his carping over the command set-up, reflected his determination 'to maintain the course of the campaign ... on lines most suitable to Britain'.[50] Although Montgomery's pride was at stake with the command issue, so too was his ability to protect the British Army's interests within the campaign: his egotism, however, has obfuscated appreciation of the influence of British aims on his behaviour.

Montgomery's pursuit of British interests prompts consideration of whether he received any formal instructions from the British government concerning his conduct of the campaign. There is no evidence for any such instructions, but then they were probably unnecessary. It is inconceivable that a commander as senior as Montgomery, and as close to Brooke, would not have been aware of the British government's agenda. Moreover, Montgomery shared the arrogant Imperial outlook of the British *élite*, as his treatment of Canadian commanders demonstrated. Indeed, despite claiming to be an apolitical general, Montgomery was much concerned by this political dimension: he was greatly influenced when Field-Marshal Jan Smuts, the South African Prime Minister, urged him in May 1944 to 'speak out' once the war was over, on Britain's role in Europe.[51] Montgomery noted:

> Smuts is worried that we may lose the peace. Britain, with American aid, won the Great War ... but when it was over we were tired and we stood back, allowing France to take first place in Europe; the result was the present war. We cannot allow Europe to disintegrate: Europe requires a structure ... Britain must stand firm as the corner stone of the new structure ... Britain must remain strong.[52]

Churchill was particularly conscious of this dimension, 'greatly fear[ing] the dwindling of the British Army ... in France as it will affect our rights to express our opinion upon strategic and other matters'.[53] By the time of Germany's defeat, American forces outnumbered the Commonwealth's best effort for a force by three to one. Churchill, obsessed with 'bayonet' strength, was determined not to see 21st Army Group's 16 divisions (at its 1944 peak) dwindle. In late 1944 he attempted to halt the disbandment of 50th (Northumbrian) Infantry Division which the reinforcement shortage had made imperative. That Brooke clearly shared Churchill's position is demonstrated by his response to Major-General John Harding's proposal that Italy should become an all-British front by denuding 21st Army Group: Brooke enquired whether it was 'advisable that the offensive ... responsible for the final defeat of the Germans [should be left] entirely to the Americans'.[54]

One facet of this British political viewpoint was the avoidance of heavy casualties. According to Major-General Kenneth Strong, Chief Intelligence Officer at Supreme Allied Headquarters (SHAEF), Churchill intervened directly in the conduct of the campaign by requesting:

> That if possible Eisenhower should avoid too many British casualties; British losses had been severe, and Britain was being assaulted by the V weapons. Eisenhower understood ... but [said] if Britain wished to be in the van of the battle, as Montgomery had suggested, British casualties could not be avoided.[55]

Montgomery's conduct of the campaign reflected the casualty dilemmas facing him. He recognised that playing a prominent role in the military defeat of Germany would help secure a significant role in influencing postwar Europe. However, maintaining such a high operational profile was likely to result in severe casualties, and due to the manpower shortage, this would force further disbandments within his meagre total of divisions. The fewer the divisions with which Britain emerged after the war, the smaller her influence on Europe was likely to be in the face of the military might of the two emerging superpowers. Striving to achieve this political goal by assuming a high operational profile might emasculate the British Army and hence destroy the chance of achieving these goals. The paradox facing Montgomery was that of achieving this high profile without incurring severe casualties.

Unfortunately, Montgomery also faced another dilemma. The longer the war lasted, the smaller would be Britain's effort compared with that of the Americans, as the latter's numerical might was increasingly deployed. Consequently, the British were more interested in achieving victory quickly than the Americans, and hoped victory could be obtained during 1944. However, 21st Army Group had insufficient resources to achieve this by itself, nor could Montgomery afford the casualties that would be incurred in the attempt. Should this attempt fail, Britain's emasculated army could not secure the post-war influence which the British government desired. Montgomery's atypically bold 'Market Garden' offensive was an attempt to solve both these dilemmas: the operation, by exploiting as fully as possible a moment of German weakness, grasped a golden opportunity for Britain to take the key role in defeating Germany in 1944 without incurring severe casualties.

Montgomery, the military professional and yet also the British political champion, was in a double dilemma: how to strive to win both the war and the peace (by seeking a high profile and an early victory), without destroying his forces and thus the chances of achieving these aims. His solution was to strive to remain as Land Forces Commander after Normandy. By commanding all forces in the theatre, any success, irrespective of the nationality of the forces achieving it, would reflect on him and hence on Britain. He could also ensure that operations conformed to a theatre strategy which, in allocating priority to the northern axis of advance towards the Ardennes, would secure a key profile for 21st Army Group: a profile which would incur only marginally higher casualties, as the Americans would still be making the larger (but less glorious) contribution to the Allied effort. The operational logic of a northern attack against the Ruhr, the key German industrial centre, was combined with pursuit of both British interests and Montgomery's own glory. The ambiguities in this British position, and mutual misunderstandings and suspicions, haunted Anglo-American relations throughout the campaign.

Montgomery woefully failed, however, to appreciate the impact of public opinion on the campaign, failing to grasp that American numerical superiority meant that there had to be an American Land Forces Commander. After Eisenhower assumed his dual command functionm on 1 September, Montgomery insubordinately campaigned to be reinstated as Land Forces Commander. When this proved impossible, he strove successfully to have American formations placed under his 21st Army Group command. This enabled him to enjoy the military profile that his own dwindling forces, and his avoidance of casualties, would not permit.[56]

Casualty Conservation and Montgomery's Conduct of the Campaign

This analysis now examines the manner in which these casualty concerns influenced Montgomery's conduct of the campaign. The existence of a casualty conscious approach was deduced by senior German commanders in the theatre. On 10 July, General Geyr von Schweppenburg, commanding *Panzer Gruppe West*, observed that the Allies were striving 'to wear down their enemy with their enormous material superiority. It will never be known whether Montgomery had received private instruction from his Government to avoid ... another blood-bath such as they had suffered in the First World War.'[57]

Another German report of November 1944 also concluded that 'instead of attacking energetically [the Allies] ... smash the enemy [with] ... heavy weapons and ... occupy ground without ... fight[ing] for it, thereby avoiding heavy casualties'.[58] A similar awareness was evident among senior British commanders, with Brooke noting of Cassino in March 1944:

> [Lt-General Sir Bernard] Freyberg has been fighting with a casualty-conscious mind. He has been sparing N[ew] Z[ealand] infantry and hoping to accomplish results by use of heavy bombers and artillery, without risking too much infantry. As a result he has failed. [He has]

had instructions from [his] Government not to risk losing too many soldiers as [their] casualties were already very high.[59]

In an apparently whimsical culinary metaphor, Brooke observed perceptively the operational side-effects of using such methods: 'it is hard in war to make omelettes without breaking eggs, and it is often in trying to do so that we break most eggs!'[60] He recognised that using such methods meant that opportunities were often wasted, and this, unfortunately, may have actually prolonged the war and hence led to more casualties. This paradox consistently dogged casualty-conscious methods.

Given the importance that Montgomery attached to casualty conservation, and his belief in a unity between strategy and operations, it is not surprising that his Normandy theatre strategy reflected these concerns. The fact that the Americans were given the larger role in breaking out, reflected the fact of their greater resources, and ability to absorb casualties. Montgomery's strategy did not necessarily mean that the Anglo-Canadian role would result in fewer casualties, since he fully recognised that these troops would face the greatest concentration of enemy forces. However, his increased emphasis, after the invasion, on the holding role of these forces – attracting German armour to the eastern, British, sector – at least avoided massive attacks and made it feasible to call off high-casualty operations without significant detriment to the overall operational situation.

Casualty concerns also profoundly influenced the operations which unfolded in pursuit of Montgomery's Normandy strategy. During the first few days of the invasion, 21st Army Group failed to exploit the surprise which it had gained and capture Caen easily before the German defences solidified. Immediately after this, Montgomery was prepared to push 2nd Army hard to capture this strategically vital town, and hence suffered very heavy losses. During Operation 'Epsom', the late-June attempt to encircle Caen from the west, infantry casualty rates reached Great War dimensions at 50 per cent.[61] However, after Caen was captured on 9 July, Montgomery did not continually smash 2nd Army against the strong German defences, although he claimed to be doing precisely this.

It was reinforcement shortages that forced Montgomery to adjust his operational intentions. Before D-Day, Montgomery had been determined to reach Falaise rapidly, to gain airfields and room both for manoeuvre and for logistical build-up. However, after incurring severe casualties capturing Caen, he was less determined to advance further south unless this could be achieved without such losses, as his 10 July orders to 2nd Army, made clear: 'The south side of the [River] Orne opposite Caen will be secured and a bridgehead thus gained, if this can be done without undue losses; I am not prepared to have *heavy* casualties to obtain this bridgehead, as we will have plenty elsewhere.'[62]

Casualty conservation influenced Montgomery's operations most specifically in the 18 July 'Goodwood' attack. General Sir Ronald Adam, the Adjutant-General, had warned Montgomery that sufficient infantry reinforcements could no longer be guaranteed. This enabled the ambitious Lt-General Sir Miles Dempsey, commanding 2nd Army, to persuade Montgomery reluctantly to launch an all-armour outflanking assault east of Caen. An attack was necessary to keep German armour tied down to the British flank, and 'Goodwood' was sensible because Dempsey could afford to lose armour but not infantry. However, it contravened Montgomery's policy of not employing an all-armoured corps.[63] This policy reflected both the poor previous performance of Allied armour in break-in operations, and the realities of post-1943 warfare which required strong infantry support and intimate infantry-tank co-operation. Indeed it was largely shortage of infantry which caused the failure of 'Goodwood'.

Operationally, these casualty concerns meant that Allied commanders called off attacks which met strong resistance and suffered high casualties without success; instead these attacks were repeated later when circumstances were more favourable. On 24 July 1944, Montgomery ordered VIII Corps to attack down the Falaise road, stipulating that 'if the form is not too good, we can always withdraw into our own lines ... and repeat the operation a few days later'.[64] These concerns were also manifested in Montgomery's 'alternate thrusts' approach, in which consecutive attacks were launched at different points of the front so that the enemy, in being compelled to shift forces around, would become unbalanced and this weakness could be exploited. This reflected attempts to achieve penetrations without having to engage the strongest enemy forces.

Casualty conservation also explains much of the relatively poor combat performance of Anglo-Canadian forces in this campaign, particularly their consistent failure to achieve decisive penetrations despite marked numerical superiority. In reality, however, due to attempts to minimise casualties, only a fraction of Allied forces engaged the enemy at any one time. Moreover, as Trevor Dupuy has shown, there were diminishing returns for a numerically superior force, due to the effects of 'friction', and of 'negative-challenge', where the very fact of numerical advantage often encouraged a mediocre combat performance. Therefore, the emphasis which subsequent analyses of the campaign place on crude comparisons of strengths may be quite misleading.[65]

Paradoxically, 21st Army Group's substantial numerical superiority was scarcely an advantage: its senior commanders faced such a reinforcement shortage, and had such an aversion to using troops as 'cannon-fodder', that they could not accept the prolonged killing-matches necessary to break the

Wehrmacht's determined resistance in Normandy. Indeed, one might speculate that Anglo-Canadian progress in Normandy would have been much quicker than it actually was if 2nd Army had had abundant manpower reinforcements, and (like the Germans or the Soviets in 1941–42) less of an aversion to incurring casualties. Continually launching forces against the German front would almost certainly have caused it to collapse earlier than it actually did – assuming that such ruthless methods had not first caused a collapse in Allied morale. It seems probable, however, that the sensitive morale of Montgomery's forces would not have withstood this callous use of soldiers' lives long enough to achieve a German collapse. Therefore, Montgomery's methods, whilst undeniably crude, were an appropriate use of the raw material available to him

Casualty conservation and morale maintenance, however, were not merely dogmas, but were also weighed in Montgomery's mind against other operational considerations. Occasionally he was prepared to accept heavy casualties if this was operationally vital. On 16 October 1944 he ordered that operations to open Antwerp's port now be pursued with the utmost vigour irrespective of casualties. Similarly, Montgomery still launched his great 'Veritable' offensive, realising that 'Grenade', the assault's American southern pincer, had been delayed by the enemy's deliberate flooding of the Roer valley, and that his forces would consequently suffer heavier casualties. When constraints of build-up and casualties precluded major operations, Montgomery maintained the initiative by a raiding policy, ordering the exhausted 1st Canadian Army in mid-August to launch single battalion attacks, the scale being deliberately limited to keep casualties down. However, despite these qualifications, within Montgomery's conduct of 21st Army Group, casualty conservation generally assumed too strong a significance in relation to other valid operational considerations: there was an imbalance in his technique.

It is germane to consider the appropriateness of alternative approaches for securing low casualties, such as bold, aggressive methods. Despite its appearances, 'Colossal Cracks' was not merely an attritional technique, but rather an essential precursor to achieving fluid operations, where superior Allied mobility would decisively defeat the Germans: attrition and manoeuvre were not necessarily diametrically opposed. Moreover in Normandy, terrain and force-to-space densities severely limited manoeuvre opportunities, whilst attempts at mobile warfare before the German Army had been devastated by attrition, were extremely risky: luckily for Patton's seemingly *Blitzkrieg*-style break-out during Operation 'Cobra', this prerequisite had already been achieved.

Conclusion

In conclusion, historians cannot fully comprehend Montgomery's handling of 21st Army Group in North-West Europe without giving due consideration to the influences of morale maintenance and casualty conservation. Montgomery's firepower-reliant attritional methods rightly reflected these two constraints. His approach appropriately used the raw materials available to Britain in 1944, nurturing the fragile morale of these non-regular soldiers toward a sustained adequate combat performance based on superiority in *matériel*. Moreover, these methods were an appropriate way of achieving British war aims. These aims sought to win the war with tolerable casualties, as part of a larger Allied effort, and, politically, to do so with such a high profile that British influence on post-war Europe would be secured. However, there were flaws inherent in Montgomery's 'Colossal Cracks' approach. This technique perpetuated the very structural weaknesses within the British Army from which it had derived, and occasionally reflected an excessive emphasis on morale and casualty concerns to the detriment of other valid operational considerations. Yet, these weaknesses were – paradoxically – closely bound up with the strengths of Montgomery's methods. Overall, the advantages of 'Colossal Cracks' clearly outweighed the inherent flaws. Even though the weakness of this technique may have slightly prolonged the war (hence making the casualty conscious motivations behind it partly self-defeating), the strengths of 'Colossal Cracks' ensured that the British Army succeeded in defeating their tenacious enemy. All factors considered, 'Colossal Cracks' was undoubtedly a winning method, despite also being a somewhat flawed one: a double-edged and rather fragile sword. Yet it had taken heroic efforts to get the British Army from its 1940 nadir to a point in 1944 where it could, using Montgomery's methods, defeat the efficient *Wehrmacht* within a larger Allied effort. There simply had not been enough time, and probably not enough ability and experience, to surmount the operational side-effects inherent in Montgomery's approach. It is quite clear that for the 1944 British Army no more viable weapon than 'Colossal Cracks' could have been forged: with this technique the British Army emerged victorious in May 1945.

MONTGOMERY, MORALE ... AND 21ST ARMY GROUP

NOTES

The author would like to thank the Trustees of the Liddell Hart Centre for Military Archives for permission to quote from copyright material.

1. J.J.G. Mackenzie and Brian Holden Reid (eds), *The British Army and the Operational Level of War* (London: Tri Service Press 1988) p.i.
2. John English, *The Canadian Army and the Normandy Campaign* (London: Praeger 1991) p.xiii.
3. Imperial War Museum (hereafter IWM), Papers of FM Bernard Law Montgomery [BLM/] 41/5, 'Some Notes on Morale in an Army', Aug. 43; also quoted in Stephen Brooks (ed.) *Montgomery and Eighth Army* (London: Bodley Head 1991) p.268, doc. 102.
4. IWM, BLM/126/35, M535, letter from Montgomery to Brooke [CIGS], 17 Nov. 1944; also quoted in Nigel Hamilton, *Monty: the Field Marshal 1944–76* [Vol.III] (London: Hamish Hamilton 1986) p.141.
5. Montgomery's critics include: J. Ellis, *Brute Force: Allied Strategy and Tactics in the Second World War* (London: Deutsch 1990); R.W. Thompson, *Montgomery the Field Marshal: a Critical Study* (London: Allen & Unwin 1969); M. Blumenson, 'The Most Over-Rated General of World War Two', *Armor* (May–June 1962) pp.4–10; Maj-Gen. J.F.C. Fuller described 'Colossal Cracks' as 'asinine', *The Second World War: a Strategical and Tactical History* (London: Eyre & Spottiswoode 1948) p.304.
6. Liddell Hart Centre for Military Archives (hereafter LHCMA), Papers of FM Alanbrooke [AP/] 7/3/12, War Office Exercise 'Evolution', Aug. 1946, pp.3, 7, 39–40.
7. P.J. Grigg, *Prejudice and Judgement* (London: Jonathan Cape 1948) p.422.
8. IWM, BLM/161, Montgomery's 'Morale in Battle', April 1946, sect. 9, para. 59, emphasis in original.
9. LHCMA, AP/7/3/12, Exercise 'Evolution', p.7.
10. Thompson (note 5) pp.23–4.
11. LHCMA, AP/3B/XII, Notes on My Life, entry 5 June 1944.
12. (Key) IWM, BLM/74/5 (and /90/8) Montgomery's Notes for Mansion House Speech, 24 March 1944. (Production) BBC Television, 'White Heat: People and Technology', 8pm 10 Oct. 1994.
13. Montgomery quoted in Michael Howard, 'Monty and the Price of Victory', *Sunday Times*, 16 Oct. 1983, p.42.
14. Ibid.
15. Max Hastings, *Overlord: D-Day and the Battle for Normandy* (London: Pan ed. 1984) p.372.
16. Ibid.
17. Ibid. p.369.
18. IWM, BLM/41/5, Some Notes on Morale.
19. IWM, BLM/[no number], Montgomery's Address to Middle East Staff College, Haifa, 21 Sept. 1942; original draft, IWM, Belchem papers; also quoted in Brooks (note 3) pp.54–5. For list of factors, see IWM, BLM/161, Morale.
20. Alistair Horne and Brian Montgomery, *The Lonely Leader: Monty 1944–1945* (London: Macmillan 1994) p.xxii.
21. Montgomery stated 'we British are a martial but not a military race', Churchill College Archive, Cambridge (hereafter CCA), Papers of P.J. Grigg [Grigg/] 11/1, Montgomery's Guildhall Address, 18 July 1946.
22. Public Record Office, Kew (hereafter PRO), CAB106/1060, reports by Brig. Hargest; also quoted in Carlo D'Este, *Decision in Normandy* (London: Collins 1983) p.282. (Stickiness) J.B. Salmud, *The History of the 51st Highland Division* (Edinburgh: Blackwood 1953) p.155; also quoted in D'Este (note 22) p.275. (Bocage) Hastings (note 15) pp.43, 175–7. (Snipers) Ibid. p.248.
23. National Archives of Canada, Ottawa (hereafter NAC), Papers of Gen. H.D.G. Crerar [CP/]8, [file] 6-10-9, folios 4–5, Crerar's Memo of Conversation with Crocker, 1015 hours, 24 July 1944, p.2.
24. IWM, BLM/119/7, letter from Dempsey to Montgomery, 6 July 1944, enclosing letter from

Crocker to Dempsey of 5 July; Nigel Hamilton, *Monty: the Master of the Battlefield 1942–44* [Vol.II], (London: Hamish Hamilton 1983) pp.714–15. ('Spring') NAC, CP/3, 5-0-3V1, folios 88–9 letter from Simonds to Dempsey, 27 July 1944.
25. NAC, CP/8, 6-10-9, Crerar's Memo of Conversation with Crocker, 24 July 1944. (Montgomery's request) Hastings (note 15) p.55.
26. Verney diary, quoted in D'Este (note 22) pp.272–4.
27. English (note 2) p.290. (Over-confidence) PRO, CAB106/1060, Hargest (Caution) D'Este (note 22) pp.272, 423; Hastings (note 15) pp.311, 345. (German tank superiority) PRO, WO205/422, Immediate Report No.6 'Impressions of the Fighting in Normandy', GOC 7AD, 17 June 1944; Maj. J. How, *The British Breakout* (London: Kimber 1981) pp.86–7. (Sackings) Michael Carver, *Out of Step: Memoirs of a Field Marshal* (London: Hutchinson 1989) p.196.
28. (Guards) LHCMA, Papers of Gen. O'Connor [OCP/] 5/1, Nairne's questions; LHCMA, Papers of John North [JNP/], II/3/24 and /197a, letters from North to Belchem, 23 Jan. 1953, and to Liddell Hart, 10 Nov. 1953. (43rd Div) LHCMA, OCP/5/3/18, Report Corps Psychologist; 5/4/103, Notes on Ryan's *A Bridge Too Far*. (11th Armoured) OCP/5/3/14, DO393, letter from O'Connor to Roberts, 8 July 1944; and OCP/8, Comments on Senior Commanders; B.H. Liddell Hart, *The Tanks* II (London: Cassell 1959), p.347. (Other divisions) IWM, BLM/115/33, M137, Message Montgomery to VCIGS [Nye], 2 Sept. 1944.
29. LHCMA, OCP/5/4/103, Notes on 'Market Garden'. (Optimism) CCA, Papers of Ronald Lewin [RLEW/], 8/15, Notes on RUSI conference; and letter from Gavin to Lewin, 28 Feb. 1978. LHCMA, the Papers of Maj.-Gen. G. Turner Cain, Narrative, p.33. Thompson (note 5) p.174.
30. NAC, CP/2 1-0-2-1, letter from Simonds to Crocker, 12 Oct. 1944.
31. Hastings (note 15) p.373.
32. IWM, BLM/74/5, Mansion House Speech, emphasis in original.
33. Hastings (note 15) p.372.
34. IWM, BLM/41/5, Some Notes on Morale, Aug. 1943.
35. Butcher Diary, appendix, letter from Eisenhower to Marshall, 5 April 1943, quoted in Hamilton (note 24) pp.210–11 n.1; also quoted in Omar N. Bradley and C. Blair, *A General's Life* (London: Sidgwick & Jackson 1983) p.165.
36. IWM, Montgomery-Simpson Correspondence [MSC/], /20, letter Montgomery, 20 June 1944; also quoted in Hamilton (note 24) p.682.
37. PRO, WO205/5B, M25, Message Montgomery to De Guingand, evening 20 June; also quoted in Hamilton (note 24) p.683.
38. Montgomery, IWM/90/9, Montgomery Speech to [21st Army Group] Staff, 28 March 1944.
39. Paul Johnson, 'What Makes a Great Commander?', *Daily Mail*, 20 Nov. 1993, p.8.
40. Williams interview, Hastings (note 15) p.180.
41. CCA, Grigg/9/8/12(B), Report on State of 6 DWR as of 30 June 1944.
42. John Peaty, drafts for PhD Dissertation, U. of London.
43. Stimpson, cited Thompson (note 5) p.26, quoting Robert E. Sherwood, *White House Papers* II (London: Eyre & Spottiswoode 1949).
44. PRO, WO199/1334, Memo, Director Military Production [DMP] to C-in-C Home Forces [CiC,HF], 28 Dec. 1943.
45. PRO, WO285, Dempsey Papers, /2, letter from Montgomery to Ronald Weeks (DCIGS), 19 March 1944.
46. PRO, WO166/14174, Memo CinC, HF to War Office, 7 Aug. 1944.
47. NAC, Stuart Papers, AG(Stats), 13 Oct. 1944.
48. Thompson (note 5) p.26, quoting Sherwood (note 43). Brian Holden Reid, 'Alexander', in John Keegan (ed.), *Churchill's Generals* (London: Weidenfeld 1991) p.109.
49. Richard O'Brien, cited in T.E.B. Howarth (ed.) *Monty at Close Quarters: Recollections of the Man* (London: Leo Cooper with Secker & Warburg 1985) p.51.
50. Thompson (note 5) p.20.
51. IWM, BLM/73, Montgomery's Diary, entry 17 May 1944; also quoted in Hamilton (note 24) p.590.
52. IWM, BLM/73, Montgomery's Diary, entry 15 May 1944.

53. PRO, WO216/101; also quoted in D'Este (note 22) p.265; Hamilton (note 3) p.158.
54. LHCMA, AP/3/B/XIII, Notes on My Life, commentary on entry, 23 Aug. 1944.
55. Kenneth Strong, *Intelligence at the Top* (London: Cassell 1968) p.149; also quoted in D'Este (note 22) p.266.
56. Thompson (note 5) p.182.
57. Ibid. p.86, quoting Freiherr Leo Geyr von Schweppenburg, *Spectator*, 5 June 1964.
58. PRO, WO208/3193, MIRS Special Tactical Study No.5829 'German Views on Allied Combat Efficiency', 17 Nov. 1944, p.2.
59. LHCMA, AP/3/B/XII, Notes on My Life, entry 31 March 1944 and 1950s commentary; and D. Fraser, *Alanbrooke* (London: Collins 1982) pp.403–4.
60. Ibid.
61. PRO, WO171/291, War Diary, 'A' Branch 8 Corps; IWM, Macmillan Papers; D'Este (note 22) pp.244–5;
62. LHCMA, AP/14/27, folio 12, emphasis in original. (Less determined) Dawnay Interview, Hamilton (note 24) p.662.
63. David Irving, *The War Between the Generals* (London: Allen Lane 1981) pp.190–1; D'Este (note 22) p.260; Hamilton (note 24) p.732; LHCMA, Liddell Hart Papers 1/230/22A and/16; John Baynes, *The Forgotten Victor: General Sir Richard O'Connor* (London: Brassey's 1989). (Armoured Corps) PRO, WO179/2579, Headley Court Conference, 31 Jan. 1944.
64. LHCMA, AP/14/28, folio 'g', M514, letter from Montgomery to Simpson, 24 July 1944.
65. Trevor N. Dupuy, *Understanding War: History and Theory of Combat* (London: Leo Cooper 1992). Liddell Hart suggested that in Operation 'Bluecoat' the Allies possessed an effective superiority as great as 30:1, 'New Warfare – New Tactics', *Marine Corps Gazette* 39/10 (Oct. 1955) pp.10–14.

'Tommy is No Soldier': The Morale of the Second British Army in Normandy, June–August 1944

DAVID FRENCH

Morale is a problematic concept, a fact tacitly acknowledged in 1949 by the War Office when it produced a short, unpublished, study of the morale of the British Army during the Second World War. Its author, Lt-Colonel J. H. Sparrow, acting with the caution of the astute barrister he was, produced a long list of factors which had some bearing upon morale, but provided only a bland definition of the subject he was analysing, arguing that it was 'the attitude of the soldier towards his employment as a soldier'.[1] In Sparrow's defence historians of the British troops who fought in Normandy have done little better. The only aspect of the morale of 21st Army Group which has received detailed investigation has been the problem of battle exhaustion and neuro-psychiatric casualties in the Canadian formations which fought in Normandy.[2] The quotation which serves as the title for this essay, taken from a captured German letter which was incorporated into a SHAEF G-2 report in August 1944, has served to summarise the existing, albeit rather scant, historiography on the question. The official British history of the campaign did not analyse the morale of the troops who served in Normandy. Most of the leading unofficial accounts of the campaign manage to imply, without ever stating explicitly, that morale was at best mediocre and in some units downright poor and suggest that the British Army only won because it was able to employ overwhelming material superiority against the Germans. This essay will investigate the morale of the British formations allotted to 2nd Army between June and August 1944. It will explore the limitations of the evidence which some historians have used as a surrogate for an analysis of British morale during the campaign, and it will present fresh evidence, which, although it is incomplete and in many respects imperfect, provides a fuller picture of the many variations in British morale during the course of the fighting in the bridgehead.

MORALE OF SECOND BRITISH ARMY 1944   155

Existing Assessments of Morale

Many accounts of the morale of British formations in Normandy rely upon three pieces of evidence.³ The first was a report produced by Panzer Lehr Division which, although conceding that British tank crews showed a good offensive spirit, asserted that

> The fighting morale of the British inf[antry] is not very great. They rely largely on the art[iller]y and airforce s[u]p[port]. In the case of well-directed art[iller]y fire by us they often abandon their pos[itio]n in flight. The enemy is extraordinarily nervous of close combat. Whenever the enemy inf[antry] is energetically engaged they mostly retreat or surrender.⁴

The second was a report written by Brigadier James Hargest, the official New Zealand observer with 2nd Army, who noted on about 10 July that

> Speaking to other officers I come to these conclusions.
>
> The morale of the infantry officer and soldier is not high. This applies to new troops as well as veterans. Officers are not keen on patrol work as an example.
>
> Even senior officers grumble about being too long in line and have opinion that they are being 'used'.
>
> The number of 'bomb-happy' casualties is very high. In the attack by 2 S[outh] W[ales] B[orderers] on 9 July the casualties were nearly 50 per cent – shell shock (50 of 100).⁵

The third piece of evidence was the collapse of 6th Duke of Wellington's Regiment (DWR), of 47th Brigade, 49th (West Riding) Infantry Division, following its unsuccessful attack on Le Parc de Boislande on 17 June, which was recounted in a report written by the battalion's new commanding officer, Lt-Colonel A. J. D. Turner, on 30 June. Turner admitted that 'I have twice had to stand at the end of a track and draw my revolver on retreating men.'⁶

Such evidence cannot be accepted as a surrogate for an analysis of the morale of the British formations in 2nd Army, because it suffers from multiple flaws. First it fails to recognize that morale changed during the course of the campaign. The Panzer Lehr report only covered the period from 6 to 30 June. Hargest's report ended in mid-July when he was killed, and Turner's report only pertained to a single battalion in late June. Second, as one historian has noted, the Panzer Lehr report contained at least an element of propaganda. Senior German officers were concerned about the morale of their own troops and highlighting supposed weaknesses in British morale helped to encourage their own men.⁷ Third, most of this evidence was drawn from a restricted number of formations. Before 30 June Panzer Lehr only encountered veteran divisions from 8th Army, 7th Armoured Division, and the 50th and 51st Infantry Divisions. Similarly, Hargest spent most of his time in Normandy attached to either 50th (Northumbrian) Division or 7th Armoured Division and only briefly witnessed operations by two unbloodied formations, 11th Armoured and 49th Infantry Divisions.⁸ They thus give little sense of the fact that morale in these veteran divisions was probably lower than in the unbloodied divisions. Finally, although Turner's report does apply to an unbloodied unit, a closer study of the circumstances surrounding the disintegration of the morale of 6th DWR suggests that the battalion's experience was in some respects untypical of most British infantry battalions engaged in Normandy. Its collapse owed a good deal to bad luck and was not symptomatic of the fact that the morale of British infantry units was unsteady from the very beginning of the campaign.

The experience of 6th DWR was untypical in that it suffered casualties at a much higher rate over a much shorter time than most other battalions in Normandy. Entering the line on 14 June, with a war establishment of 861 all ranks, by the end of the month it had lost 350 other ranks and only 12 of the battalion's original 38 officers remained. In that time its original Commanding Officer had been dismissed, a temporary replacement had come and gone, and by the end of the month it was commanded by its third CO. As Turner emphasised in his report, the virtual destruction of the battalion's leadership cadre *over such a short period* was crucial in undermining the battalion's morale. A survey of the officer casualties suffered by nine other infantry battalions which also served in Normandy showed that they suffered losses of a comparable magnitude, *but that they were spread out over the entire period of the campaign.*⁹ This was crucial to their survival as functioning military units because it ensured that replacements could be fitted into these units piecemeal and have at least a minimal opportunity to get to know their men. This was not the case in 6th DWR where, by the end of June, half of the battalion were strangers and 60 per cent of the officers did not know their men.¹⁰

The battalion's demise began on 17 June, when, in its first operation, it attacked and occupied Le Parc de Boislande. Despite the fact that the battalion had the support of four field regiments, two medium regiments, a heavy mortar company and a squadron of tanks, this was an expensive operation. While one of its flanking units, 10th Durham Light Infantry lost only 23 casualties, 6th DWR suffered 110 casualties, including 20 men killed. The battalion's losses occurred because the barrage moved too fast and one company was caught in the open and suffered heavy casualties from

German mortar fire. Before these losses could be made good the battalion dug in. It was then subject to intermittent shelling during the night, and at 1400hrs on 18 June the Germans mounted a counter-attack, supported by mortars and artillery, which drove the battalion from its position. That evening the survivors marched to Chateau Bronay to lick their wounds and await the arrival of reinforcements to make good their losses, leaving behind much burnt-out equipment, and most of their shovels and entrenching tools. That was to prove a grievous piece of ill-luck because on 20 and 21 June, just as the battalion was attempting to absorb nearly 200 reinforcements, it was twice subjected to heavy German shelling which cost 40 more casualties. It was the experience of being subjected to heavy shelling, coming so unexpectedly at the very moment when all ranks thought they had been granted a temporary reprieve, and when they were helpless either to protect themselves by digging in or to retaliate, that temporarily broke the battalion's morale.[11]

On 11 July, 6th DWR, less those men who had joined it as reinforcements since D-Day, were sent back to England, ostensibly because the battalion commander had reported that it had to be reorganised and retrained before it could again be committed to action, and there was no space to do that in the bridgehead.[12] The battalion undoubtedly needed time to re-organised and absorb reinforcements, but it is debatable whether it also had to be sent back to England. At least one other unit endured a similarly catastrophic introduction to battle but was successfully rebuilt in the bridgehead. On 24 June, 43rd Reconnaissance Regiment suffered even heavier losses than 6th DWR when the troopship carrying the regiment sank off Ouistrehem with the loss of 150 wounded and 180 men missing. These losses were quite properly described by the unit's padre as 'staggering'. But after landing in Normandy it remained in the bridgehead, and following an inspection by 2nd Army's adviser in psychiatric medicine, Major J. Waterson, it was rebuilt with reinforcements, and committed successfully to action at the beginning of August.[13] Probably 6th DWR did not deserve to bear the stigma of being returned to England and Field-Marshal Lord Carver may be right to suggest that Montgomery sent them home as evidence that his failure to achieve a swift breakout from the bridgehead was not for want of trying.[14]

Desertion/AWOL

A fuller, albeit still incomplete picture of the morale of the British formations in Normandy can be created using three other indicators. These are statistics gathered concerning men who deserted or who went absent without leave (AWOL), statistics for self-inflicted wounds and statistics for men diagnosed as suffering from 'exhaustion'. Although, as the following analysis will demonstrate, these pieces of evidence have many imperfections, they do have two advantages not possessed by the evidence examined above. They do not pertain merely to an unrepresentative sample of units in 2nd Army, but cover all, or nearly all of them, and they are continuous over time, thus enabling a picture to be produced which charts changes in morale between the landing in June and the breakout in late August.

Table 1 (see Appendix to this essay, p.172) shows the number of men convicted by court martial for desertion and AWOL between February and September 1944. The discrepancy in the figures for convictions for AWOL and desertion is testimony to the fact that commanding officers retained considerable discretion about how to treat miscreants. Before D-Day they were prepared to take a comparatively lenient attitude towards those soldiers who absented themselves from their units, preferring to charge them with the less serious offence of being absent without leave, rather than with the more serious charge of desertion. However, following the landing, they took a more dim view of men who absented themselves, and were more willing to prosecute them with the full force of military law by proffering the more serious charge of desertion. They were actively encouraged to do so by the Judge Advocate General's department in 2nd Army. In July, believing that it had detected too much laxity, it decided 'to remind unit commanders of their responsibility in charging deserters'.[15]

The figures also suggest that, as the fighting in Normandy intensified in July and August after the initial landing, so morale subsided and the number of convictions for desertion, rose accordingly. However, the total number of cases of desertion and AWOL between June and September, 978, can hardly be considered excessive in light of the fact that by late July 2nd Army consisted of approximately 420,000 men. Similarly, although in 21st Army Group as a whole the number of court martial convictions, most of which were for AWOL or desertion rose in the summer of 1944, it did so from only 0.077 per 100 men in May 1944 to 0.189 per 100 men in August.[16]

Tables 2 and 3 demonstrate that there was no significant difference in the conviction rates for desertion/AWOL between those divisions which had already seen action in North Africa and Italy and those which were first committed to battle in Normandy, with the exception of 50th Division, which had the highest average rate of convictions for all formations.

There was undoubtedly much feeling in 50th Division that they had been unfairly treated, that they had already done all that could reasonably be asked of them in North Africa and Italy, and that it was unreasonable to expect them to lead the invasion. The men of 2nd Devons (50th Division) 'admitted that they were not amused by the prospect'.[17] The wife of a newly-joined officer noted that many veterans in the unit were suffering from battle fatigue, an emotion which was heightened because many of their families believed that they had now done their share of fighting and should not be exposed to danger a second time.[18] This was not a problem unique to this unit. Shortly after returning from Italy in early 1944 several senior NCOs of 1st Royal Tank Regiment, another veteran 8th Army unit, were encouraged by their wives to ask to be transferred to units less likely to be in the front line.[19] In May 1944, when Montgomery visited units of 50th Division, some troops showed their displeasure by booing him.[20]

Tables 2 and 3 also indicate that soldiers convicted of desertion/AWOL on active service tended to be infantrymen. The three British armoured divisions listed suffered on average eight convictions for desertion/AWOL each per month between June and August 1944, whereas by contrast, the seven infantry divisions listed each experienced on average 22 convictions per month. This was hardly surprising. In Normandy the infantry accounted for less than 25 per cent of 21st Army Group, but suffered 71 per cent of its casualties.[21]

A review of the cases of men found guilty of desertion showed that the main cause was battle stress, perhaps endured over a prolonged period and culminating in the death of a close friend, and sometimes aggravated by family problems, the serious illness of a close relative, inadequate training or transfer from one unit to another with a consequent lack of identification with the new unit.[22] The case of two riflemen who deserted from 1st Battalion The Rifle Brigade (7th Armoured Division) in July 1944 exemplifies several of these factors. Both had already endured a great deal of active service, having served throughout the North African campaigns. One had learnt of the death of his mother shortly before D-Day and the other had left behind his pregnant wife. Shortly before they deserted, their truck had been blown up by a mine.[23]

The effective collapse of the regimental system by 1943–44 was another source of instability. Newly-joined replacements, flung into battle for the first time and unaware of what was happening around them, figured prominently among deserters.[24] Competent and well-respected officers could play a major role in sustaining their men but conversely their departure could undermine morale. Deserters were also more likely than other soldiers to have suffered from psychological disabilities before they enlisted. A study of 200 deserters from 21st Army Group suggested that only 43 per cent of them had 'normal stable personalities', 21 per cent were classified as being immature, 5.5 per cent were 'dullards', the same proportion were psychopaths who exhibited anti-social tendencies, and a quarter of them had, according to the psychiatrists who examined them, inadequate personalities.[25]

Self-Inflicted Wounds

Self-inflicted wounds (SIWs) were only a very minor problem in the British Army during the Second World War. Until 1944–45 no more than 20 soldiers serving overseas were found guilty of this offence by courts martial. However, in 1944–45, 208 soldiers were convicted of injuring themselves with intent to avoid duty, a figure which might indicate some deterioration in morale.[26] This figure pertained to all units overseas, not just to 2nd Army. According to the unpublished history of 2nd Army, in the 13 weeks between D-Day and to 30 September, that is to say the period covering the landing, fighting in the bridgehead and breakout, self-inflicted and accidental wounds accounted for an average rate of 1.77 per 10,000 men per week admitted to hospital, compared to 7.71 per 10,000 per week who were admitted to hospital after having been wounded in battle.[27] Self-inflicted wounds were probably confined to other ranks. Of the 35 cases treated by medical units in VIII Corps between 16 June and 18 August, not one involved an officer.[28]

In statistical terms, therefore, SIWs were a small problem, but by July it seemed to be sufficiently serious for the Assistant Adjutant General to appoint an experienced officer, Major A. T. A. Browne, to investigate the extent of the problem with a view bringing those guilty before a court martial. To facilitate Browne's work, all suspected cases were sent to No.110 British General Hospital. Not surprisingly, Browne discovered that the problem was largely confined to infantry battalions. 279 cases were from the infantry, compared to only 109 from all other arms of the service. Most infantry battalions only had a small number of reported cases, 89 having three or fewer, and only 25 reporting more than four. Those units with the highest number of reported cases were 11th Royal Scots Fusiliers in 49th Division (11 cases), and 2/5th Lancashire Fusiliers in 59th (Staffordshire) Division, 5th Wiltshires in 43rd (Wessex) Division, and 1/4th King's Own Yorkshire Light Infantry, in 49th Division, each of which had eight cases.[29] None of these units was a veteran 8th Army battalion.

However, before this raw data can be accepted at face value as showing that a very small minority (of mostly infantry soldiers) preferred to injure themselves rather than face the rigours of the battlefield, two caveats must be entered. The total of 388 cases listed by Browne is almost certainly not an accurate reflection of the extent of this problem. In an unspecified number of instances, Browne was unable to find sufficient evidence or witnesses to recommend that the Judge Advocate General bring a prosecution.[30] Some battalion officers were undoubtedly reluctant to report men they believed had wounded themselves, whether from compassion for men who had clearly done their best, or because a prosecution might reflect badly on their unit.[31] In 8th Middlesex, the machine-gun battalion of 43rd Division, the case of a driver who had shot himself in the arm was hushed-up by the battalion officers. They asked their men to attribute the wound to 'an unknown, trigger-happy Yank', because the driver involved was the last survivor of three brothers who had served in the regiment and the soldier had just received a letter from his mother telling him of her fears for her only remaining son.[32]

If these instances suggest that the official figures for SIWs may have underestimated the extent of the problem, a second factor suggests that the figures may actually inflate it. Browne was ordered to investigate not only SIWs, which may indeed have been an indicator of fragile morale, but also cases of accidental woundings, which might not be. British Sten guns and German Luger pistols were notorious for having insecure safety-catches and often wounded those who handled them carelessly. Even experienced soldiers could on occasions forget to unload weapons before cleaning them. No figures are available to show the extent of this problem, but the case of the officer who accidentally wounded himself with a German pistol, or the trooper who blew himself up when priming a grenade in 2nd Northamptonshire Yeomanry could not have been unique.[33]

In view of these caveats, only two things were certain; the actual number of cases of SIWs will probably never be known with any accuracy, but it is apparent that the problem was most serious in infantry battalions. Browne's opinion was probably correct; although the GOC-in-C Lt-General Sir Miles Dempsey was concerned about SIWs in July, they did not present a serious threat to the morale or discipline of his army.[34]

'Exhaustion'

When 2nd Army landed in Normandy it did so in the knowledge that many soldiers would be unable to withstand the psychological traumas of combat, and in the belief that it had already done a great deal to minimise the scope of this problem. The experience of the Army in dealing with the victims of 'shell-shock' during the First World War had been crystallised in 1922 in the Report of the War Office Committee of Enquiry into 'Shell-Shock'. It had asserted that all men would suffer from 'shell-shock' if they spent too much time exposed to danger, but that there were several ways of minimising the numbers of those who suffered breakdowns. First, the men most predisposed to breakdown were unlikely ever to make efficient soldiers and should not be enlisted. Second, those men who were enlisted must be properly trained before being sent into battle. Third, officers had to do all they could to maintain high unit morale and discipline. Fourth, it was vital to minimise unnecessary physical discomforts, and rest and recreation were essential. And finally, regimental officers and medical officers had to cooperate closely to watch their men carefully so that they could save those on the point of breakdown by giving them a brief rest. Facilities for the treatment of 'shell-shock' cases should exist in every division so that casualties could be treated and returned to duty as rapidly as possible.[35]

The inter-war army had no difficulty in trying to maintain high unit morale and good discipline, but, being short of recruits, especially for the infantry, it did not enjoy the luxury of rejecting men who might be predisposed to breakdowns. This neglect continued in the early years of the war and little attempt was made to subject recruits to psychiatric screening, although men who were obviously so lacking in intelligence that they could not be trained were discharged.[36] The Army did still try to maintain a high standard of paternal officership and unit administration, although it found it increasingly difficult to do so given the rapid expansion of the junior officer corps.[37] However, from about 1941 onwards increasing numbers of recruits and serving soldiers were screened to identify those who, according to the prevailing Freudian beliefs of many psychiatrists, were predisposed by their childhood experiences to break down under stress. They were weeded out of combat units and posted to other jobs.[38] By 1943 official medical policy increasingly emphasised personnel selection as the best way to reduce 'exhaustion' casualties. In May 1943 the Army Bureau of Current Affairs issued a pamphlet entitled *Casualty Report* which underlined this, stating that 'We can do very little in an actual battle area to limit the stresses and strains or to alter the adverse environment; and, given sufficient stress and sufficient strain, any person *may* breakdown. We can, however, and we should, sift out those who are likely to break down early....'[39] In the months before D-Day most formations carried out an extensive programme of 'weeding'.[40] Between October 1943 and April 1944, VIII Corps psychiatrist, for example, examined nearly 600 men and recommended that 85 per cent of them be given psychiatric treatment or transferred to other, usually noncombatant employment.[41]

But as it was recognised that screening could not be totally effective, and as experience in North Africa and Italy had pointed towards the efficacy of giving men who did break down early treatment as near to the front line as possible, each corps in 2nd Army had a consultant psychiatrist.[42] He was responsible for overseeing the work of the Corps Exhaustion Centre which was formed from a field dressing station.[43] Corps psychiatrists tried to return as many men as quickly as possible to the front line and advised on how those who could not be returned to their unit might be usefully employed elsewhere in the army.[44] This meant, according to one psychiatrist, that, 'the principle of treatment in the Army does not aim at a therapeutic attack on the neurosis, but is a social management of psychoneurotics'.[45] To this end, the use of the term 'shell-shock' was banned as it was desirable that psychiatric casualties should not be labelled in such a way as to suggest they were suffering from a form of mental illness. Officially, psychiatric casualties were identified as suffering from 'exhaustion', and that became the catch-all label for all soldiers suffering from stress-related neuropsychiatric conditions.[46] Unofficially, front-line soldiers often referred to such men as being 'bomb-happy'.[47] The majority of troops diagnosed as 'exhaustion' cases were in fact suffering from chronic anxiety manifested through uncontrollable tremors, a pronounced startle reaction to war-related sounds and a profound loss of self-confidence.[48]

Initially, as Table 4 illustrates, the pre-Invasion policy of weeding out men supposedly predisposed to suffering from 'exhaustion' appeared to work satisfactorily. There were no reported incidents of 'exhaustion' on D-Day or D+1 and for the rest of the first week of fighting only three per cent of total battle casualties were 'exhaustion' cases. However, the percentage of 'exhaustion' casualties then began to creep upwards; it reached 11 to 13 per cent in the second week of the campaign and 23.8 per cent in July, falling in the following six weeks to 14.2 per cent of total battle casualties.

However, these figures are an incomplete reflection of the real extent of 'exhaustion' in 2nd Army. First, the great majority of 'exhaustion' casualties, like the great majority of deserters or victims of SIWs were drawn from infantry battalions. Between 26 and 30 June during Operation 'Epsom' 15th (Scottish) Infantry Division had 152 'exhaustion' casualties, of whom 140 were drawn from its nine rifle battalions, even though the infantry only accounted for about a quarter of the division's total strength.[49] Similarly, During Operation 'Goodwood' the majority of 'exhaustion' cases came not from the three armoured divisions spearheading the offensive, but from the infantry divisions operating in support on their flanks.[50] Second, most exhaustion cases were other ranks, rather than officers. Between 29 June and 13 July, for example, VIII Corps exhaustion centre dealt with 928 cases, of whom only 21 were officers.[51]

Third, these figures probably overstated the number of 'exhaustion' cases in June and early July and conversely understated their numbers in the second half of July and August. Before D-Day Corps psychiatrists had been enjoined not to permit the indiscriminate evacuation of 'exhaustion' casualties,[52] but the first link in the chain of diagnosing whether or not a soldier was suffering from 'exhaustion' was not the psychiatrists but the Regimental Medical Officers (RMOs) and the unit commanders, and they were given very imperfect guidance as to how they should act. In March 1944 the Deputy Director of Medical Services in XII Corps frankly recognised that, 'there is no sharp line between minor cases of "Exhaustion" and men who merely need a night or two of good sleep under sedatives without requiring evacuation'. He ordered RMOs confronted by possible exhaustion cases to adopt a comparatively permissive treatment regime and to

> be guided by these considerations; (a) the man's usefulness in his present condition at the front, (b) that early evacuation, treatment and return to the line before a breakdown occurs is preferable to evacuation after breakdown, when the prognosis is so much worse, (c) that men who are evacuated will go to Div FDS only a few miles away and have a good chance of returning to their Units in a few days.[53]

By D+8, XXX Corps had opened the first Corps Exhaustion Centre in the bridgehead and by the end of the month other corps had followed suit and all were implementing this treatment regime. On 2 July, for example, the Assistant Director of Medical Services (ADMS) of 50th Division told his medical officers that, 'Officers Commanding all units may use 200 F[iel]d Amb[ulance] for borderline cases, i.e. officer or man who has had a trying time and requires a few good nights' sleep or the officer or man who has been showing signs of jumpiness or emotion. Prevention is better than cure and such cases tackled early will be back with their units within a few days.'[54]

The incidence of 'exhaustion' cases was within the range for 'exhaustion' casualties which 2nd Army's adviser on psychiatric medicine had predicted before the invasion. But nonetheless the apparently sharp rise in July caused many commanders considerable concern.[55] By early July it was becoming apparent that this permissive regime was producing problems of another kind. Some hard-pressed RMOs were evacuating suspected 'exhaustion' cases without first subjecting them to a rigorous examination and, because Corps medical facilities were still very limited in the bridgehead, most cases could only be kept in France for a couple of days before they were evacuated to England and thus lost to 2nd Army. Some senior commanders began to suspect that, 'the incidence of psychiatric disabilities was exorbitant, and that evacuation across the Channel constituted an easy means of escape for those of poor morale'.[56] But in reality, many regimental officers and RMOs found it extremely difficult to distinguish between psychological casualties and men who were simply frightened. Lt-Colonel E. Hutcheon, the commanding officer of 21st Light Field Ambulance which acted as an exhaustion centre for VIII Corps in July 1944, noted that between 10 and 13 July, 280 cases of 'exhaustion' reached his unit. In his opinion regimental officers and RMOs had been negligent in allowing at least 70 per cent of them to leave the front line. They were no more physically exhausted than other walking wounded 'and in the majority of cases, less, while their anxiety was not above a normal apprehension of participating in a battle'.⁵⁷ Hutcheon was not alone in believing this. Lt-Colonel Frank Richardson, the commander of 160th Field Ambulance which acted as an exhaustion centre for 49th Division, had decided nearly three weeks earlier that '[There are] Too many cases of EXHAUSTION. The soldiers showed a tendency to talk too glibly of such conditions and RMOs are being advised to ensure that this does not become a popular and easy means of escape from unpleasant situations.'⁵⁸

In early July there was, therefore, an attempt to reduce the number of 'exhaustion' cases leaving the front line. Some senior combatant officers thought that 'exhaustion' should be treated as a disciplinary rather than a medical problem. Lt-General Sir Richard O'Connor, the commander of VIII Corps, believed that 'there were genuine cases of shell shock but the great majority were merely frightened of shelling, & wanted an excuse to get out of it. The shelling was horrible, & most frightening, but if people were allowed to leave the battlefield every time they were frightened the army would have disintegrated in no time.'⁵⁹ He ordered his divisional commanders to court martial for desertion any soldiers who were discovered to have feigned 'exhaustion' as a way of escaping from the front line.⁶⁰ Major-General Gordon MacMillan, the GOC of 15th Division, agreed that some RMOs, 'under pressure of work, [were] sending men back merely to get them out of the way', and ordered that any NCO who was evacuated for 'exhaustion' and subsequently returned to his unit should be stripped of his rank 'as I do not consider that a man who has been so affected can possess the stamina necessary in a leader'.⁶¹ In 53rd (Welsh) Infantry Division an order was issued that 'exhaustion' cases were to be dealt with by platoon commanders, who were told to send men in need of rest to their unit's transport lines, rather than allow them to be evacuated through medical channels.⁶² Lt-Colonel George Taylor, commanding 5th Duke of Cornwall's Light Infantry in 43rd Division followed a similar policy, minimising the number of official 'exhaustion' cases in his battalion by ordering that such men should not be evacuated beyond the unit's own transport lines, where they were treated by the RMO before being returned to duty.⁶³

Military doctors were part of the chain of command and could only bow to such pressure. On 3 July the Deputy Director of Medical Services (DDMS) of 2nd Army, Brigadier E. Phillips, ordered RMOs to examine suspected 'exhaustion' cases with the same thoroughness as other sick or wounded soldiers and, 'to use his professional judgement to exclude minor cases which do not require evacuation and malingerers from the more serious type'.⁶⁴ Colonel Melvin, the ADMS of 50th Division, reviewed his permissive policy at the end of July when he instituted an inquiry into the morale of 56th and 231st Brigades because he was 'concerned about the number of young men leaving the battle on the excuse that they are "Exhausted"'.[65] At the end of the month a meeting between the psychiatrists and the Judge Advocate General's department in 2nd Army agreed that the policy to be aimed at was that no soldier should be allowed to leave the battlefield without the authority of his commanding officer.[66] RMOs were instructed in August that 'Exhaustion cases were really a question of man-management rather than a purely medical concern.'[67]

If the incidence of exhaustion is examined on a formation by formation basis, several factors concerning the relationship between morale and 'exhaustion' come to light. Different divisions were prone to suffer bouts of 'exhaustion' casualties at different times. Montgomery had especially asked that 50th, 51st Infantry and 7th Armoured Divisions be brought back from Italy to spearhead the invasion. But it soon became apparent that these divisions were producing more than their fair share of 'exhaustion' casualties. By 18 June, only four days after XXX Corps Exhaustion Centre had opened, it had admitted 63 exhaustion cases from 7th Armoured Division and 40 from 50th Division. No fewer than 75 of these men had already taken part in at least one campaign, 25 had already been wounded and 65 already had a history of neurotic reaction to stress during the war.[68]

Such formations contained too many men like the following:

> xxxxxxxx Pte J. G. 7th A[rgyll] & S[utherland] H[ighlanders]. Age 25. Service 4½ yrs. Previous campaigns in France and Middle East. Jittery from the start. Broke down and cried during counter-attack. Evacuated in a 'miserable tremulous' condition. Improved with narcosis therapy but is still depressed, apathetic and anxious. Feels guilty about coming overseas again, leaving his wife, who is 'fed up with him'. May return to duty, but only after lowering category to B1.[69]

Some senior officers, like O'Connor, were surprised at this, believing that the period of leave they enjoyed between returning to Britain and embarking for the invasion 'would set them up a bit'.[70] Soldiers in these formations who broke down did so because they had experienced too much combat-related stress, a fact supported by a comparative study of the incidence of 'exhaustion' cases in 6th Airborne and 51st Infantry Divisions prepared by Major D. J. Watson, the 2nd Army's adviser in psychiatric medicine. Both divisions had landed on D-Day and were fighting in the same part of the bridgehead but Normandy was the 6th Airborne's first battle, whereas 51st (Highland) Division had fought in North Africa and Italy. As Table 5 shows, the veterans of 51st Division were far more prone to become 'exhaustion' victims than the men of 6th Airborne. One factor which may have contributed to the comparatively high incidence of 'exhaustion' in 51st

Division was the fact that many of its veterans were suffering under an additional handicap. Malaria was so endemic in 50th and 51st Divisions that before D-Day doctors in both formations insisted that all personnel must take a course of mepacrine, and this treatment continued throughout the Normandy campaign.[71] However, it was not always effective, as shown by the case of a private in 8th Durham Light Infantry tried for cowardice in July. The court found him guilty despite the fact that he had been sent to hospital with malaria in the bridgehead and had not fully recovered when he committed the offence.[72]

Some unbloodied formations did in fact suffer considerable numbers of 'exhaustion' casualties in their very first large-scale operation, but most seem to have conformed to the experience of 6th Airborne, in that their losses from 'exhaustion' were, over the longer term, below those of 2nd Army's veteran divisions.[73] Attempts to weed out men predisposed to breakdown and to inoculate the rest against the traumas of battle by training them in live-firing exercises in Britain did have some perceptible, albeit limited success. But the Normandy campaign also exposed the limitations of over-reliance on the notion that some men were 'predisposed' to breakdown. One psychiatrist who treated patients evacuated from Normandy became convinced that

> It has been a common experience to find that the majority of cases breaking down under battle conditions could not be called psychoneurotics in the proper sense of the word. Most of these soldiers were physically exhausted by long periods without sleep, and may have developed symptoms such as tremor by this alone, even without the alarming experience of battle. These cases reacted well to simple sedation which gave them the necessary physical rest, and they were soon fit to return to the unit.[74]

Psychiatry was an inexact and evolving science. In the course of the campaign it became clear that the rate of 'exhaustion' casualties increased over time if units were not regularly relieved and rested, and doctors and commanders were coming to recognise that predisposition was not a magic key to reducing 'exhaustion' casualties. At the end of the war a study conducted by two Canadian psychiatrists who examined 200 soldiers who had fought throughout the North-West European campaign indicated that some men who had significant neurotic traits had still performed well in combat over a prolonged period.[75] Other factors, especially good unit leadership and the knowledge that one was fighting alongside men one knew, could keep in the front line even soldiers who were predisposed to breakdown. These facts were underlined by the high incidence of reinforcements amongst 'exhaustion' cases or when whole sub-units temporarily broke down because a respected leader had been killed.[76] Reinforcements were particularly vulnerable because they were 'bereft of that sense of security which comes of knowing their mates and leaders'.[77] A final precipitating factor which could produce breakdown was ignorance of the tactical situation in which troops found themselves. One psychiatrist found in talking to large numbers of 'exhaustion' cases that, 'Their officers had not given them a clear idea of the plan and objective of the action in which they were participating', and concluded that in such situations, 'morale is bound to crack easier because the man feels insecure, [and] become[s] extremely anxious about all that is happening around him'.[78]

This rediscovery of the principles of the 1922 'Shell-Shock' report had important implications for how 'exhaustion' casualties were treated. Some divisional commanders came to understand that there was something they could do in the 'actual battle area to limit the stresses and strains or to alter the adverse environment'. In August 1944 Major-General Evelyn Barker, GOC 49th Division, established a board of enquiry to discover why some units in his division had a much lower rate of 'exhaustion' than others. Thereafter, and as far as the exigencies of the campaign and the growing shortage of infantry replacements allowed, he tried to give his infantry battalions at least brief rest periods.[79] Similarly, Major-General L. O. Lyne, commanding 59th (Staffordshire) Infantry Division, established a divisional reinforcement group to give drafts who were strangers to the division a few days to acquire a sense of attachment to the division before going into action.[80]

Forward psychiatry undoubtedly played some part in minimising the manpower loss caused by 'exhaustion'. By the beginning of August, when the system was in full operation, 'exhaustion' casualties were usually bathed, sedated for 36 hours and allowed, 'a couple of days lounging about in a reassuring atmosphere while barbiturate detoxication occurs'. They were also interviewed by a psychiatrist who explained to each patient why he had broken down, 'accentuating the "exhaustion" factor and the fact that it is now necessary to ensure he gets deep sleep'.[81] This was followed by two days of 'rehabilitation' when casualties were subjected to the gradual reimposition of military discipline. On discharge those men who were thought to have recovered were either returned to their units or sent to a reinforcement camp, whilst those men who were not sufficiently recovered to return to the front line were sent to 2nd Army Rest Centre for further rehabilitation, or medical recategorisation prior to being employed on the lines of communication.[82]

It is difficult to place any precise figure on how many men were 'saved' to fight another day by being giving a brief spell in a divisional or corps exhaustion centre, but the figure almost certainly increased as the campaign progressed. In late June, for example, No.35 Casualty Clearing Station had so little accommodation that it could only hold cases for 48 hours. A mere 15 per cent of 'exhaustion' cases could be returned to their units and the rest had to be evacuated to England.[83] However, by the end of July facilities had improved, some divisions had opened their own divisional exhaustion centres where it was possible to hold cases for between 7 and 14 days in the bridgehead, and the proportion of men who could be returned to some form of duty, although not necessarily in the front line, rose.[84] In 1987 the Director of Army Psychiatry (DAP) asserted that 70 per cent of 'exhaustion' cases were returned to duty.[85] This is a slightly higher figure than that accepted by other authorities. R. H. Ahrenfeldt, author of *Psychiatry in the British Army in the Second World War*, thought that in the first month of the campaign the average rate of return from Corps Exhaustion Centres was between 30 and 40 per cent, but when divisional centres began to open in July they were able to return 60 per cent of their cases to duty.[86] The unpublished official history of 2nd Army gave a slightly different but not necessarily contradictory figure, suggesting that only about a third of exhaustion cases returned to full duty in the front line.[87] The DAP's figure presumably included not only those men who returned to combat, but also those who were placed in a reduced medical category and found other useful employment elsewhere. A report compiled by 21st Army Group covering the period from 6 June to 25 July broadly supports this hypothesis. It indicated that of the 65 per cent of exhaustion cases who were returned to some form of duty in the theatre, half of them went back to the front line.[88] There are no comprehensive figures for relapse rates. The DAP believed that no more than 7 per cent of those who were treated later relapsed.[89] However, it is likely that the figure was higher for those men who were returned to front line units. In mid-October 1944, of 107 'exhaustion' cases admitted to No.39 British General Hospital no fewer than 43 per cent had previously been treated for exhaustion.[90]

Conclusions

During the Second World War many senior British officers had qualms about the steadiness of their troops when pitted against the German army, but these qualms antedated not only the Normandy campaign, but also the war itself. In the 1920s and 1930s the Army developed a doctrine based upon gaining victory through the application of mechanised firepower as a means of restoring mobility to the battlefield. Generals knew they could never again be as profligate with their mens' lives as their predecessors had been in 1914–18. The major lesson which the British Army had drawn from the First World War was that in future it would have to win its battles by the deployment of overwhelming firepower, not by repeating the extravagant use of manpower which had characterised the attritional warfare of the Western Front campaign. In the 1920s, building on its experiences of 1917–18, the Army developed a doctrine which emphasised the importance of combined arms operations to generate overwhelming firepower and so reduce casualties.[91] The Army's reliance upon overwhelming *matériel* in Normandy was not, therefore, a product of a sudden realization during the Second World War that, man for man, British soldiers were no match for their German counterparts. The writer who insisted that 'despite his heavy equipment, "Tommy is no soldier"', had simply misunderstood the main line of development of British operational doctrine over the preceding quarter of a century.[92] A measure of the success of this doctrine was shown by the comparative casualty rates for the Army during the two World Wars. In the whole of the First World War approximately 5.8 men per 1,000 per month were killed on the battlefield, compared to only 3.6 per 1,000 per month during the Second World War. Similarly, only 13.5 men per 1,000 per month were wounded in North-West Europe in 1944–45, compared with 28.1 men per 1,000 per month in the whole of 1914–18.[93] Much of the evidence which has hitherto been most frequently cited as a surrogate for an analysis of the morale of 2nd Army in Normandy is misleading, and the resulting bleak picture of fragile morale among the teeth arms of the British units in Normandy requires considerable qualification. The evidence scrutinised in this essay for desertion and AWOL, self-inflicted wounds and battle exhaustion, provides a fuller picture, but even it requires considerable interpretation and cannot be taken at face value. The 11th Royal Scots Fusiliers, for example, had the highest *reported* rate of self-inflicted wounds of any British unit in the bridgehead, and yet it was singled out by the doctor in charge of its divisional exhaustion centre for its very low rate of 'exhaustion' cases.[94] Conversely, in July the 2nd East Yorks had the second fewest number of exhaustion casualties in any of the nine infantry battalions in 3rd Infantry Division, but it also had the highest number of reported self-inflicted wounds.[95] The 50th Division had a reputation for having a low incidence of 'exhaustion' cases, but it had the highest number of desertions of any formation in 2nd Army.[96] A study by three psychiatrists of 103 soldiers under sentence for desertion in No.3 Military Hospital at Bayeux in October 1944 indicated that a quarter of them had been suffering from severe 'exhaustion' at the time of their offence.[97] All this suggests that if unit commanders forbade men to become exhaustion casualties or tried to stamp out desertions or self-inflicted wounds, men would find another way of leaving the battlefield.

Whether men who broke down on the battlefield were punished or treated as psychological casualties largely depended upon the judgement and knowledge of their regimental superiors. Men who broke down but who were well-known to their officers were more likely to be treated as medical casualties, especially if the latter believed they had done their best and had reached the limit of their endurance. Conversely, men who refused to obey the orders of officers whom they hardly knew were more likely to be punished. This was illustrated by the case of a corporal and six private soldiers in 2/6th Staffordshire Regiment in 59th Division, who were found guilty of mutiny when they refused to obey an order to advance issued by their company commander. The latter had only joined the battalion on 13 July, barely two weeks before the offence was committed on 2 August, and three of the accused were even more recent reinforcements.[98]

There is no single, reliable and conclusive indicator of the morale of 2nd Army. But if morale can be taken to connote the willingness of soldiers to fight rather than absent themselves from the battlefield, then it appears that tentative conclusions can be drawn about the morale of 2nd Army. Generalisations across the army, or even across single divisions are hazardous. Morale was a dynamic force which changed over time. On the eve of the invasion a War Office survey of morale indicated that, although the troops were confident of the eventual success of the operations, 'most soldiers seem to be well-aware that they are not likely to be a "walk-over"'.[99] After D-Day, following the euphoria of the successful landing and the consolidation of the bridgehead, morale dipped significantly in the first half of July when the campaign seemed to be developing into 'an infantry slogging match', only to pick up again at the end of July and in early August, as the German defences progressively collapsed and the pace of 2nd Army's advance quickened.[100] Comparisons between British and German morale are problematic, not least because German medical officers did not officially recognize psycho-neurotic conditions. After inspecting a captured German hospital in Normandy, Brigadier Bulmer was 'left with the impression that many psycho-neurotics are masquerading under a diagnosis of organic disease such as "commotic cerebri", a heart disease, gastritis, etc'.[101]

Morale was not uniform throughout the Army. It was more fragile in veteran divisions brought back from Italy than it was in those divisions which came to Normandy fresh. Unsurprisingly, it was most fragile in infantry battalions, because infantrymen were exposed to the most discomfort and maximum danger on the battlefield. It was probably strongest in those battalions which, through luck, were able to retain a cadre of officers and NCOs who were known to their men and who took a personal interest in their welfare. Finally, the typical deserter, 'exhaustion' case or victim of a self-inflicted wound was an other-rank infantryman who had recently joined an infantry battalion as a reinforcement or a veteran soldier who was asked to take part in one battle too many.

APPENDIX

TABLE 1
NUMBERS OF CONVICTIONS BY COURTS MARTIAL
FOR DESERTION AND AWOL AMONG FORMATIONS OF 2nd ARMY

Date (1944)	Desertion	AWOL
February	3	32
March	19	145
April	7	105
May	33	246
June	15	79
July	132	27
August	352	15
September	237	31
Total	798	857

Source: PRO, WO171/182. War diary, Deputy Judge Advocate General, 21st Army Group, April–Dec. 1944. The formations concerned were HQ 2nd Army, I, VIII, XII and XXX Corps Troops, 7th, 11th and Guards Armoured Divisions, 3rd, 15th, 43rd, 49th, 50th, 51st and 53rd Infantry Divisions, 3rd and 4th AGRA, 1st and 6th Airborne Divisions.

As Courts Martial usually tried cases in arrears it seems appropriate to include figures for September on the grounds that men tried in September probably committed their offences during the battle for the bridgehead.

TABLE 2
DESERTION/AWOL CONVICTIONS IN 'VETERAN' DIVISIONS IN NORMANDY

Division	June	July	August
7th Armoured	3	13	24
50th Infantry	2	73	150
51st Infantry	2	6	1

Source: PRO WO171/182. War diary, Deputy Judge Advocate General, 21st Army Group, April–Dec. 1944.]

MORALE OF SECOND BRITISH ARMY 1944   173

TABLE 3
DESERTION/AWOL CONVICTIONS IN 'GREEN' DIVISIONS IN NORMANDY

	June	July	August
Guards Armoured	2	3	12
11th Armoured	4	2	10
15th Infantry	8	23	61
43rd Infantry	6	1	27
49th Infantry	1	8	21
53rd Infantry	6	8	15
59th Infantry	2	1	42

Source: PRO WO171/182. War diary, Deputy Judge Advocate General, 21st Army Group, April–Dec. 1944. 3rd Division has been omitted as there are no continuous runs of figures for that formation.

TABLE 4
'EXHAUSTION' CASES IN SECOND ARMY

Date	A	B	C
6–24 June	928	11.1	1.67
24 June–29 July	6288	23.8	3.14
29 July–16 Sept.	2199	14.2	1.17
Total	9415		

Column headings: A = total number of exhaustion cases; B = exhaustion cases as a percentage of total battle casualties; C = weekly exhaustion rate per 1,000 men.

Source: HQ, Second Army, *An Account of the Operations of Second British Army in Europe, 1944–45*, Vol.1 p.482.]

TABLE 5
COMPARATIVE INCIDENCE OF 'EXHAUSTION' CASES IN 6th AIRBORNE AND 51st HIGHLAND DIVISIONS

	A	B	C
6th Airborne Week ending:			
17 June 1944	1871	54	3
24 June 1944	229	29	13
1 July 1944	164	10	6
51st Highland Week ending:			
17 June 1944	205	30	15
24 June 1944	394	35	9
1 July 1944	177	76	43

Column headings: A = total battle casualties; B = exhaustion cases; C = exhaustion cases as a percentage of battle casualties.

Source: PRO, WO177/321. Major D.J. Watson, Monthly report for June 1944 by psychiatrist attached to 2nd Army, 7 July 1944.

174 MILITARY POWER: LAND WARFARE IN THEORY AND PRACTICE

NOTES

Research for this essay was made possible by a Small Personal Research Grant of the British Academy. I am grateful to the following for permission to quote from manuscripts to which they own the copyright: Crown Copyright material appears by permission of Her Majesty's Stationary Office; Browne MSS (Mrs Madeline Browne); Grigg MSS (The Master and Fellows of Churchill College, Cambridge); Adam MSS, Dempsey MSS, Liddell Hart MSS, Pyman MSS, O'Connor MSS (The Trustees of the Liddell Hart Centre for Military Archives, King's College London).

The quotation in the title is from Public Record Office WO219/1908. SHAEF Operational Intelligence Section, Intelligence Notes, No.21, 3 Aug. 1944.

1. PRO, WO277/16. Lt-Col J.H. Sparrow, *Morale* (London: War Office 1949) p.1. Sparrow had served in the Adjutant General's department at the War Office and acted as secretary to the Morale Committee of the Executive Committee of the Army Council. He was a practising barrister who later became Warden of All Souls College, Oxford.
2. T. Copp and B. McAndrew, *Battle Exhaustion. Soldiers and Psychiatrists in the Canadian Army, 1939–1945* (Montreal and Kingston: McGill-Queen's UP 1990) pp.109–127; T.J. Copp, 'Battle Exhaustion and the Canadian Soldier in Normandy', *British Army Review*, 85 (1987), pp.46–54. I am most grateful to Dr Brian Holden Reid for bringing this article to my attention. In addition R.H. Ahrenfeldt, *Psychiatry in the British Army in the Second World War* (London: RKP 1958) pp.175–7 contains some brief references to the Normandy campaign.
3. See, for example, R. Lamb, *Montgomery in Europe, 1943–45: Success or Failure* (London: Buchan & Enright 1983) pp.105–6, 109–12; M. Hastings, *Overlord. D-Day and the Battle for Normandy* (London/NY: M. Joseph/Simon & Schuster 1984) pp.147–50; C. d'Este, *Decision in Normandy* (London/NY: Collins/E. Dutton 1983) pp.279–84, 295–6.
4. Liddell Hart Centre for Military Archives (hereafter LHCMA). Dempsey MSS. Second Army Intelligence Summary No.46, 20 July 1944. Appendix C. Translation of enemy document. Panzer Lehr Div. Subject: Report on experience.
5. PRO, CAB 106/1060. Reports from Normandy, 1944. 6 June–10 July, by Brig. James Hargest, New Zealand Army observer with XXX Corps.
6. Churchill College Cambridge (hereafter CCC), Grigg MSS PJGG 9/8/12. Montgomery to Grigg, 2 July 1944 and enc. Lt-Col A.J. Turner, Report on state of 6th DWR (49 Div) as on 30 Ju[ne].
7. Lamb (note 3) p.106.
8. PRO, CAB 106/1060. Reports from Normandy, 1944.
9. See PRO, WO171/1372. War Diary 4th Somerset Light Infantry, 1944; PRO, WO171/1365. War Diary 11th Royal Scots Fusiliers, 1944; PRO, WO171/1228 War Diary 7th Duke of Wellington's Regiment, 1944; PRO, WO171/1262 War Diary 2nd Argyll and Sutherland Highlanders, 1944; PRO, WO171/1275 War Diary 9th Cameronians, 1944; PRO, WO171/1396 War Diary 1st Worcesters, 1944; PRO, WO171/1289 War Diary 8th Durham Light Infantry, 1944; PRO, WO171/1286 War Diary 4th Dorsets, 1944.
10. CCC, Grigg MSS PJGG 9/8/12. Montgomery to Grigg, 2 July 1944 and enc. Lt-Col A.J. Turner, 'Report on state of 6 DWR (49 Div) as on 30 Jun[e]'; PRO, WO205/81. Brigadier, Staff Duties, Main HQ, 21st Army Group to Chief of Staff, 3 July 1994.
11. This account of the operations of 6th DWR draws upon PRO, WO166/15096. War Diary 6th DWR, 1944 and App. B, 'One damn thing after another'; PRO, WO177/399. Medical War Diaries Assistant Director of Medical Services (ADMS) 49th Div., 1944; PRO, CAB 106/963. Reports, etc. on the fighting in Normandy, 1944. Immediate Report No.13. Capture of Le Parc de Boislande, 17 June 1944; PRO, WO171/666. War Diary 147th Inf. Bde, 1944.
12. CCC, Grigg MSS. 9/8/12. Montgomery to Grigg, 2 July 1944 and enc., Lt-Col A.J.D. Turner, 'Report on state of 6 DWR (49 Div) as on 30 Jun[e]'; PRO, WO205/81. Brigadier, Staff Duties, Main HQ, 21st Army Group to de Guingand, 3 July 1944.
13. Maj.-Gen. H. Essame, *The 43rd Wessex Division at War 1944–1945* (London: William Clowes 1952) pp.16–17; R. Doherty, *Only the Enemy in Front (Every other beggar*

behind...) *The Recce Corps at War 1940–46* (London: Tom Donovan 1994) pp.163–5; E. Gethyn-Jones, *A Territorial Army Chaplain in Peace and War: A County Cleric in Khaki 1938–61* (East Wittering, Sussex: Gooday 1988) pp.89–100; PRO, WO177/321. Maj. D.J. Watterson, Weekly report by psychiatrist attached to 2nd Army for week ending Saturday 24 June 1944, 28 June 1944.
14. Lamb (note 3) pp.109–10.
15. PRO, WO177/321. Maj. D.J. Watson, Monthly report for June 1944 by psychiatrist attached to 2nd Army, 5 Aug. 1944.
16. PRO, WO163/53/AC/G(44)39. War Office Committee on Morale in the Army. Tenth Quarterly Report, June–Aug. 1944, 15 Nov. 1944. PRO, WO177/321. Medical war diaries of Deputy Director of Medical Services (DMS) 2nd Army. App. H. Hygiene, 29 July 1944. These figures can also be compared with the astronomical figures for desertion in the Union and Confederate armies during the American Civil War in B. Holden Reid and J. White, "'A mob of stragglers and cowards": desertion from the Union and Confederate Armies, 1861–65', *Journal of Strategic Studies* 8/1 (March 1985) p.64. On 1 Feb. 1865 the Union Army had 338,536 absentees compared to 630,924 men on duty. The Confederates had 194,494 absentees and 160,198 men on duty.
17. D. Houldsworth, *One Day I'll Tell You* (Marlborough, Wilts.: Heraldry Today 1994) p.3. On 7th Armoured Div. see LHCMA, Liddell Hart MSS 1/56/6. Maj.-Gen. D. Belchem to Liddell Hart, 7 Aug. 1952.
18. Houldsworth (note 17) pp.4–5.
19. M. Carver, *Out of Step: The Memoirs of a Field Marshal* (London: Hutchinson 1989) p.178.
20. Houldsworth (note 17) p.12.
21. J. Ellis, *The Sharp End of War: The Fighting Man in World War Two* (London: David & Charles 1980) pp.176–7.
22. PRO, WO277/7. Brig. A.B. McPherson, *Discipline* (London: War Office 1950) p.37.
23. PRO, WO71/919. Proceedings of a Field General Court Martial of Rifleman A and Rifleman B, 1944. [These proceedings are listed in the Public Record Office catalogue under the names of the accused. I can see no good purpose in causing embarrassment to them or their descendants by revealing their identities and have therefore chosen to maintain their anonymity.]
24. LHCMA, Pyman MSS 4/42. HQ, Second Army, *An Account of the Operations of Second British Army in Europe, 1944–45* (Germany 1945) Vol.1, p.464.
25. PRO, WO291/1141. Army Operational Research Group Report No.9/51. A study of the subsequent career of deserters from the BLA released from military prisons and detention barracks under suspended sentence. July 1951.
26. PRO, WO277/7. McPherson (note 22) App. 1 (a). Court Martial Convictions, home and overseas (British other ranks), 1 Sept. 1939 to 31 Aug. 1945.
27. LHCMA, Pyman MSS 4/42. HQ, Second Army (note 24) p.159.
28. PRO, WO177/434. Medical War Diary DMS VIII Corps, 18 Aug. 1944.
29. Imperial War Museum (hereafter IWM), Browne MSS IWM 86/4/1. Maj. A.T.A. Browne to HQ, Lines of communication, 21st Army Group. Report relative to suspected Self-Inflicted Wounds and negligent wounding cases passing through 110 (British) General Hospital, 24 Aug. 1944.
30. IWM, Browne MSS IWM 86/41/1. Lt-Col A.T.A. Browne, 'Destiny. Portrait of a Man in Two World Wars.'
31. Maj. A.T.A. Browne to HQ, Line of Communication, 21st Army Group. 'Subject – SIW or wounds caused by negligent handling', 28 Aug. 1944.
32. J. Thompson, *The Imperial War Museum Book of Victory in Europe. The North West European Campaign 1944–45* (London: Sidgewick & Jackson/IWM 1994) pp.200–01.
33. K. Jones, *Sixty-Four Days of a Normandy Summer: With a Tank Unit after D-Day* (London: Robert Hale 1990) p.63, 126; IWM, Browne MSS IWM 86/4/41. Maj. A.T.A. Browne to HQ, Line of Communication, 21st Army Group. Subject – SIW or wounds caused by negligent handling, 28 Aug. 1944.
34. Browne (note 30).

35. Parliamentary Papers, Vol.xii, 1922. [Cmd 1734] *Report of the War Office Committee of Enquiry into 'Shell-Shock'*, passim.
36. Brig. J.R. Rees, 'The development of psychiatry in the British Army', in *Military Neuropsychiatry. Proceedings of the Association December 15–16, 1944 New York* (Baltimore: William & Wilkins Co. 1946) pp.48–53.
37. PRO, WO163/53/AC/G(44)22. War Office Committee on Morale in the Army. Eighth Quarterly Report, Nov. 1943 to Jan. 1944, 25 May 1944.
38. Copp and McAndrew (note 2) pp.109–10. A similar policy was pursued in the RAF. See A.D. English, 'A predisposition to cowardice? Aviation psychology and the genesis of "lack of moral fibre"', *War and Society* 13/1 (1995) pp.18–20.
39. This policy was explained to the troops in an Army Bureau of Current Affairs pamphlet, *War Casualty Report*, No.44, 15 May 1943.
40. PRO, WO177/316. Medical War Diary DMS 21st Army Group, 11 March 1944.
41. PRO, WO177/343. Maj. R.J. Phillips, VIII Corps psychiatrist, Psychiatric Monthly Report, May 1944.
42. LHCMA, Sir R. Adam MSS ADAM V/6. Adam to Corps District, District, Divisional and Area Commanders, Dec. 1943.
43. PRO, WO177/316. Medical War Diary DMS 21st Army Group, 25 Feb. 1944 and Minutes of a conference of DMS 21st Army Group held at St Paul's School at 10.00hrs 29 Feb. 1944; PRO, WO177/321. Second Army Medical Plan, No.2, 18 April 1944.
44. PRO, WO177/409. Medical War Diary ADMS 53rd Div. RAMC Administrative Instruction, 14 Feb. 1944. App. A.
45. A.P. Thorner, 'The treatment of psychoneurosis in the British Army', *Int. Jnl of Psychoanalysis* (1946) p.57.
46. PRO, WO177/343. VIII Corps Medical Standing Orders, 5 June 1944; PRO, WO177/405. Medical War Diary ADMS 51st Division. Handling of psychiatric battle casualties, 15 May 1944.
47. M. Lindsay, *So Few Got Through* (London: Collins 1946) p.13.
48. Copp article (note 2) pp.46–7.
49. PRO, WO177/343. Cases admitted to exhaustion centres (35 & 1 FDS) from units under command VIII Corps, period 26 to 30 June 1944 (inclusive) – up to midnight 30 June 1944.
50. PRO, WO177/321. Medical war Diary DMS 2nd Army. App. H. Hygiene, 29 July 1994.
51. PRO, WO177/343. Maj. R.J. Phillips, Corps Psychiatrist, VIII Corps. 'Cases admitted to exhaustion centre (No.1 FDS) period 2359hrs 7 Jul 1944 to 2359hrs 13 Jul 1944.'
52. PRO, WO177/409. Medical War Diaries ADMS 53 Div. 53rd Div. RAMC. Administrative Instruction, 14 Feb. 1944. App. A.
53. PRO, WO177/321. DMS XII Corps to Senior Medical Officers, XII Corps, 9 March 1944. Similar orders were issued by the DMS of VIII Corps. See PRO, WO177/343. VIII Corps Medical Standing Orders, 5 June 1944.
54. PRO, WO177/402. Medical War Diary ADMS 50th Div. Col J. Melvin to OC all medical units and RMOs, 2 July 1944.
55. PRO, WO177/321. Maj. D.J. Watterson, Report by psychiatrist attached to 2nd Army for month of July 1944, 5 Aug. 1944.
56. Ibid., Monthly report for June 1944 by psychiatrist attached to 2nd Army, 7 July 1944; PRO, WO177/316. Medical War Diary DMS 21st Army Group. Notes on visit to beachhead by Col R.F. Walker, DMS HQ 21st Army Group, 4 July 1944.
57. LHCMA, O'Connor MSS. 5/3/18. Maj. H.R. Leslie to O'Connor and enc, 21 July 1944.
58. PRO, WO177/750. 160 F[ield] Ambulance. (12 to 20 June 1944). Report by Lt-Col F.M. Richardson, 21 June 1944.
59. LHCMA, Sir R. O'Connor MSS 1/5. O'Connor to Major Nairne, n.d. but c.1970–72.
60. Ibid. 5/3/18. O'Connor to Adair, Roberts, Thomas and MacMillan, 21 July 1944; O'Connor (note 59).
61. LHCMA, O'Connor MSS 5/4/14. Maj.-Gen. MacMillan to O'Connor, 22 July 1944.
62. PRO, WO177/409. 53 Div. Medical Admin. Instruction number 3, 13 Aug. 1944.
63. Brig. George Taylor, *Infantry Colonel* (Southampton/Worcester: Self-Publishing Assoc. 1990) p.29.
64. PRO, WO177/321. DMS, 2nd Army, 2nd Army Medical Admin. Instruction, 3 July 1944;

PRO, WO177/405. Medical War Diary ADMS 51st Div., 11 July 1944; PRO, WO177/377. Medical War Diary ADMS 3rd Div., 3rd British Div. Medical Admin. Instruction number 2, 11 July 1944.
65. PRO, WO177/402. Medical War Diary ADMS 50th Div., 31 July 1944.
66. PRO, WO177/321. Maj. D.J. Watson, Monthly report for June 1944 by psychiatrist attached to 2nd Army, 5 Aug. 1944.
67. PRO, WO177/409. Medical War Diary 53rd Div., 11 Aug. 1944.
68. PRO, WO177/321. Maj. J.J. Wishart, XXX Corps Exhaustion Centre, Psychiatric summary week ending Sunday 18 June 1944, 21 June 1944.
69. PRO, WO177/321. Maj. D.J. Watson, Monthly report for June 1944 by psychiatrist attached to 2nd Army, 7 July 1944.
70. O'Connor (note 59).
71. PRO, WO177/405. Medical War Diary ADMS 51st Div., 21 April, 2 & 6 May, 17 July 1944. In the three months ending 30 June 1944, there were 161 fresh cases of malaria and 509 men suffered a relapse.
72. PRO, WO171/914. Proceedings of a Field General Court Martial of Pte C, 1944.
73. Both 43rd and 49th Divs seem to have suffered from an above-average rate of exhaustion cases in their first battles. See PRO, WO177/343. Maj. R.J. Phillips, Corps Psychiatrist, VIII Corps. Cases admitted to exhaustion centre (No.1 FDS) period 2359hrs 7 Jul 1944 to 2359hrs 13 Jul 1944' and PRO, WO177/399. War Diary 49 Div ADMS. Entry for 3 July 1944.
74. Thorner (note 45) p.52.
75. Majors T. E. Dancey and B. H. McNeel, 'The personality of the successful soldier', *American Journal of Psychiatry* 102 (1945–46) pp.337–42.
76. Referring to 43rd Wessex Division in early July Major R.J. Phillips, VIII Corps psychiatrist, remarked on 'the number of cases arriving [at VIII Corps Exhaustion Centre] – from same companies, platoons, sections, often accompanied by NCOs or even officers, that not only had individual morale gone, but group morale as well'. See PRO, WO177/343. Maj. R.J. Phillips, Corps Psychiatrist, VIII Corps. Cases admitted to exhaustion centre (No.1 FDS) period 2359hrs 7 July 1944 to 2359hrs 13 Jul 1944.
77. PRO, WO177/321. Maj. D.J. Watson, Monthly report for June 1944 by psychiatrist attached to 2nd Army, 7 July 1944; PRO, WO177/321. Ibid., Monthly report for June 1944 by psychiatrist attached to 2nd Army, 5 Aug. 1944.
78. Phillips (note 76).
79. Between 2 and 30 July these figures varied from a high of 38 (1st Tyneside Scottish) to a low of 1 (7th DWR). See PRO, WO177/399. Medical War Diary ADMS 49th Div. Entry for 1 Aug. 1944; PRO, WO177/750. Medical War Diaries 160 Field Ambulance. App. A. Analysis of exhaustion cases. Periods 2–20 July and 25–31 Jul 1944; IWM, Bucknall MSS IWM 80/33/1/folder 12. Maj.-Gen. Barker to Lt.-Gen. Bucknall, 4 Aug. 1944.
80. Watson (note 77), 5 Aug. 1944.
81. PRO, WO177/343. Treatment in Corps Exhaustion Centre of psychiatric battle casualties, June 1944.
82. Watson (note 80).
83. PRO, WO177/321. Maj. D.J. Watterson, psychiatrist attached to 35 CCS, Psychiatric summary week ending Sunday 19 June 1944; Wishart (fnote 68).
84. PRO, WO177/321. Brig. E. Phillips, DMS 2nd Army, to senior medical officers, 2nd Army, 30 June 1944; PRO, WO177/321. Medical War Diary DMS 2nd Army (note 50).
85. 'Comment by the Director of Army Psychiatry, British Army', in Copp article (note 2) p.53.
86. Ahrenfeldt (note 2) p.175.
87. HQ, Second Army (note 22) Vol.1, p.481.
88. LHCMA, de Guingand MSS IV/4/3. Anon., *The Administrative History of the Operations of 21 Army Group on the Continent of Europe 6 June 1944–8 May 1945* (Germany 1945) p.27.
89. See note 85.
90. PRO, WO32/11550. Report on a visit to 21st Army Group, BLA by Director of Army

Psychiatry and consultant psychiatrist to the Army, Oct. 1944.
91. This is a theme I intend to explore in more detail in my book *Raising Churchill's Army. The Combat Effectiveness of the British Army in the War Against Germany, 1939–1945* (OUP forthcoming). See the comments by the CIGS, Gen. Sir George Milne, to the General Staff Conference in Jan. 1927 in PRO, WO279/57. Report on the Staff Conference held at the Staff College, Camberley, 17 to 20 Jan. 1927 under the orders and direction of the CIGS. See also B. Holden Reid, *J.F.C. Fuller: Military Thinker* (London: Macmillan 1987) pp.56–174.
92. PRO, WO219/1908. SHAEF Operational Intelligence Section, Intelligence Notes, No.21, 3 Aug. 1944.
93. LHCMA, de Guingand MSS IV/4/3. Anon. *The Administrative History of the Operations of 21 Army Group*, App. M. 'Casualties – British in North-West Europe. First and Second World Wars. Mean monthly rates per 1,000 strength.' The best study of British operational doctrine in Normandy is S.A. Hart, 'Field Marshal Montgomery, 21st Army Group, and North-West Europe, 1944–45' (PhD, U. of London 1995).
94. PRO, WO177/750. Medical War Diary 160 Field Ambulance, 25–30 June 1944.
95. PRO, WO177/377. Medical War Diary ADMS 3rd Division. Exhaustion, sick and wounded table, period 1–3 July 1944; IWM, Browne MSS IWM 86/4/1. Report relative to suspect Self-inflicted wounds and negligent wounding cases passing through 110 (British) General Hospital, 24 Aug. 1944.
96. O'Connor (note 59).
97. See note 90.
98. PRO, WO71/902. Proceedings of a Field General Court Martial of L/Cpl C and Privates D, E, F, G and H, 1944.
99. PRO, WO163/53/AC/G(44)22. War Office Committee on morale in the army. Eighth quarterly report. Nov. 1943–Jan. 1944, 23 May 1944.
100. Watterson (note 55).
101. PRO, WO177/316. Medical War Diary DMS 21st Army Group. Brig. E. Bulmer, Quarterly Report of Consulting Physician, 21st Army Group, 1 July 1944 to 30 Sept. 1944.

The British Army and Approaches to Warfare since 1945

JOHN KISZELY

Over the past decade, the British Army has formally adopted a manoeuvre-oriented approach to warfare which seeks to defeat the enemy by methods other than attrition alone. This essay examines the nature of this approach and traces its evolution in the British Army since the end of the Second World War.

The British Army's desire to go down a less attritional route in its conduct of operations is born of a recognition that approaches to warfare can be described, relatively, in terms of the degree to which the enemy's defeat is sought through his attrition (the incremental destruction or wearing away of his forces), with differing approaches lying on a continuum from the highly attritional at one end, to the non-attritional at the other. Since attrition is a mutually wearing-away activity, the highly attritional approach is normally favoured by the side having, or perceiving itself to have, superiority in men and matériel, and thus the ability to win a contest of stamina. At its extreme, firepower is moved to engage the enemy's strength, and remains there until he is exhausted and succumbs. General Erich von Falkenhayn's attempt at Verdun in 1916 '…to bleed the French army white'[1] is often cited as an example. The attritional approach is therefore characterised by firepower, concentration of force, and by little movement once battle is joined.

The antithesis of this is, in theory, a non-attritional or, in practice, a minimum-attritional approach, traditionally favoured by the belligerent who is weaker in men or materiel. He must avoid the mutually wearing test of stamina, and rely on evading the enemy's strength while attacking his vulnerabilities and breaking his cohesion in order to allow his defeat or destruction in detail. He may also be able to achieve this by focusing on the enemy's moral cohesion – his will to resist. Since the main means of achieving this is through manoeuvre, either mental or physical, this approach is sometimes described as 'manoeuvre warfare' or 'the manoeuvrist approach'. The ability to carry out this approach successfully depends on at least six prerequisites not required by the attritionalist.

Prerequisities of the Manoeuvrist Approach

The first is intelligence good enough to identify not just the enemy's strengths, but also the critical weaknesses and vulnerabilities of his whole system. This is easier said than done. It requires focus on the specific enemy at the specific place and time, an intimate knowledge of his system (in its widest sense), and an ability to get inside his mind. This is a world away from the approach which is satisfied by a 'relative strengths' comparison of hardware.

The second is the ability to act faster than the enemy can react, sometimes called high tempo – tempo being the rate or rhythm of activity relative to the enemy. This allows us to manoeuvre: to move into a position of advantage relative to the enemy either to apply force, or to threaten the application of force, thus forcing a reaction which we can exploit further. High tempo is achieved by a fast decision-action cycle (or 'OODA loop' – based on the requirement in any situation to Observe, Orient, Decide and Act), by a high standard of tactical drills (thus reducing the need for orders) and by fast, mobile weapon-platforms. Since tempo is relevant only in comparison to our opponent, an important way of raising our tempo is to lower his – for example by deception and surprise, since these force on him the uneconomical use of time.

Fundamental to the achievement of high tempo and, therefore, the third prerequisite, is decentralised command. Clearly a command system in which decisions are only allowed at a high level, or which requires proposed decisions to be passed upwards for ratification, will result in slow tempo. But so that activity is focused and not dissipated or mutually interfering, there are two fundamental principles which must be followed: all subordinates must work within the commander's overall intent; and, in turn, the commander must clearly specify that intent, together with the mission of each subordinate, and the focus (or main effort) of the activity, but leave to the subordinates the method of achieving their mission. In short he must tell them 'what' and 'why', but not 'how'. Finally, to work effectively, decentralised command requires openness, honesty and mutual trust between commanders at all levels.

The fourth prerequisite is for an all-arms, joint service and combined (multinational) approach, not just to maximise our own potential, *per se*, (equally desirable, arguably, for the attritional approach) but to provide the maximum overmatch of our strengths on the weaknesses of the enemy's system, while preventing him from doing the same to us.

Fifth, the manoeuvrist approach requires a rather different type of commander. The attritional approach requires a commander to have a few qualities in large measure: physical courage, tenacity, discipline, and the ability to plan in detail, but with limited amounts of imagination (too much imagination being dysfunctional). The manoeuvrist approach, by contrast, requires a commander who is focused above all on mentally outmanoeuvring his opponent. To achieve this, the commander must be cunning and devious, a creative thinker able to apply originality and imagination to problem-solving. He must have the ability instantly to recognise fleeting opportunities; and having done so, to have the initiative to decide, act and communicate his orders, and to do so quickly. He must develop intuition, and he must be able to judge and take risks.

The last prerequisite is room to manoeuvre, in space, time and method. A commander who is given narrow boundaries, little time and tight political constraints (e.g. in Rules of Engagement – when, and when not, to shoot) may be forced to adopt a more attritional, direct approach.[2]

Avoiding the enemy's strengths and attacking his weaknesses can be seen simply in terms of the enemy's armed forces, or it can be seen at a deeper level in terms of the enemy's whole system in relation to our own. We may perceive that our enemy has a comparative inability to fight in certain terrain or to generate forces quickly; we choose to fight him in that terrain or before he can generate his forces. Our enemy may favour a highly structured, centrally-controlled warfighting style but cannot match our tempo; we would welcome – indeed try and create – a fluid, chaotic battlefield. Our enemy's strength in conventional warfare may over-match our own; we avoid his strength by choosing another form of warfare, for example guerrilla warfare. Our approach is therefore to drag the enemy into the arena of our choice, to fight the battle of our choosing rather than his.

Of course attrition and manoeuvre are opposites only in the sense of being alternative approaches to warfare at opposite ends of a spectrum. All warfare in practice is a combination of both attrition and manoeuvre, with the most appropriate balance or harmony being determined by the circumstances. There are, therefore, degrees to which any given approach can be described as attritional or manoeuvrist.

Sun Tzu, Liddell Hart and Fuller

There are obvious similarities between 'manoeuvre warfare' and Liddell Hart's 'indirect approach' – his emphasis, for example, on avoidance of the enemy's strength, dislocation of the enemy, deception, and that 'the true aim in war is the mind of the hostile ruler not the body of his troops'.[3] Liddell Hart, of course, projected his theory on to a far broader plane than just manoeuvre warfare theory. As Mearsheimer has pointed out, '...the indirect approach ... was such a loosely defined, and flexible concept that it could be used to suit almost any purpose'.[4] Just as Liddell Hart's indirect approach owes much to Sun Tzu, (rather more than Liddell Hart might wish to admit) so, too, can many of the antecedents of manoeuvre warfare be found in Sun Tzu. The advocate of an attritional approach would have no difficulty with the thesis that the acme of skill is to fight and win a hundred battles. What could be better? But Sun Tzu's point was that '...to fight and win one hundred battles is not the acme of skill; to subdue the enemy without fighting is the acme of skill'.[5] It would, however, surely be a misinterpretation of Sun Tzu to suggest that he was implying that defeating the enemy without any fighting whatsoever is often, if ever, possible.[6] Liddell Hart may himself have been guilty at times of such a misinterpretation. Sun Tzu is, of course, advocating the minimum of fighting in accomplishment of the enemy's defeat, in order to preserve our own strength. There are also direct parallels here with Major-General J. F. C. Fuller's perspective. He wrote:

> There are two ways of destroying an organisation:
>
> (i) By wearing it down (dissipating it).
>
> (ii) By rendering it inoperative (unhinging it).
>
> In war, the first comprises the killing, wounding, capturing and disarming of the enemy's soldiers (body warfare). The second, the rendering inoperative of his powers of command (brain warfare). Taking a single man as an example, the first method might be compared to a succession of slight wounds which eventually cause him to bleed to death; the second – a shot through the head.[7]

Both Liddell Hart and Fuller emphasised that the disruption of the enemy's cohesion was unlikely to be a substitute for battle, but should be a precursor to it. In Fuller's view, '...as our present theory is to destroy "personnel", so should our new theory be to destroy "command", not after the enemy's personnel has been disorganised, *but before it has been attacked....*' (his italics).[8] For Liddell Hart; 'In most campaigns the dislocation of the enemy's psychological and physical balance has been the vital prelude to a successful attempt at his overthrow.'[9] Fuller also neatly encapsulated the concept of tempo so central to a manoeuvre-orientated approach: 'If you can move five times as fast as your enemy, then whilst the military hour will remain sixty minutes for him, it will be reduced to twelve minutes for you, and every mile will become less than two furlongs'.[10]

Attritionalist Legacy of the Second World War

Although some British commanders in the Second World War showed themselves adept at a manoeuvrist style of warfare and had the room for manoeuvre in which to demonstrate their skill, the British Army tended to fight its battles by building up matériel superiority and fighting in an attritionalist style, often for very good reasons, for example at the Second Battle of El Alamein. Nevertheless, in 1939–41 the Army had suffered defeats at the hands of the German Army which had demonstrated the effectiveness – given the right circumstances – of the manoeuvrist approach, exemplified by what came to be termed *Blitzkrieg*. Furthermore, the British Army took some trouble to subject it to analysis.[11] It was perhaps surprising, therefore, that after 1945 the Army did not itself seek to adopt a less attritional, more manoeuvrist approach – but there is little evidence that it did so.

There are at least two reasons why this did not happen. First and foremost, winners of wars do not as a rule perceive a necessity to change; that is the not inconsiderable prize of the runner-up. Second, opinion was sharply divided on the relative merits of fluid, mobile operations as against operations based on a highly structured approach founded on centralised command and detailed orders. Nowhere was this more so than amongst those who had fought in the Western Desert. Many blamed the British Army's lack of success in 1941 and 1942 on doctrine which had forsaken the well-tried, tightly controlled battlefield for one exalting manoeuvre, dispersion and loose control.[12] In their eyes, success had only been redeemed by a return to tight control and to the 'teed up', 'tidy' battlefield[13] advocated by General Montgomery. It is not the purpose here to examine the reasons for failure of the manoeuvre school in the desert, only to note that at the end of the war many veterans and commentators believed that, ultimately, success had been retrieved by Montgomery's highly centralised approach, where superior matériel was applied against the enemy's strength in accordance with a rigid master plan. And Montgomery was wont to emphasise (sometimes despite the facts),[14] that his master plans had always worked, just as he had said they would. As Chief of the Imperial General Staff (CIGS) in the immediate post-war years, Montgomery's view, not unnaturally, carried considerable weight, and his admirers occupied influential posts in the Army for many years after the war. Staff College instruction at the time, unsurprisingly, emphasised a highly controlled style of warfare[15] which sought to impose order on the battlefield, moving firepower to destroy enemy strengths, rather than a style aimed at flourishing in situations of chaos and uncertainty.

Furthermore, the attritional approach appeared to many to be entirely compatible with the British Army's main role as the British Army of the Rhine (BAOR). A large proportion of the army settled down in West Germany to confront the Russian, and subsequently Warsaw Pact forces, limited by constraints which allowed little room for manoeuvre. A strategy of forward defence for reasons of political necessity within the NATO alliance resulted in a linear and heavily positional General Defence Plan, with lateral movement constrained by several national corps deployed shoulder-to-shoulder in what became known as the 'layer cake' deployment. Formations and units found themselves planning positional battles and a slogging match – how best to *absorb* the shock of the enemy attack rather than *avoid* it, and requiring defence of ground to the last man. Although substantial elements of the British Army were deployed elsewhere, for example East of Suez, training emphasis at the Staff College and at arms schools was firmly on the type of warfare anticipated in Europe.

There were, however, critics of the attritional approach. Some were theorists such as F. O. Miksche and Tom Wintringham, whose books[16] had been popular during and after the war. But books with titles such as 'How to Reform The Army' would undoubtedly have been of limited popularity with the military establishment, even if their authors had not been civilians, foreigners and socialists, or in some cases all three. Other critics had closer connections with the Army, such as the retired general, Sir Giffard Martel, who had been one of the advocates of mechanisation in the inter-war years and had had pre-war experience of the Soviet Army. Martel criticised '...the position war complex which seized us at the end of the War' and advocated that '...mobility must have top priority. It replaces the numerical strength of the Russian masses ... [our tanks] must be able to move rapidly between enemy columns or round their flanks, attack them in rear, and they must be prepared to spend a week behind enemy lines.'[17]

The Armoured Division in Battle, 1952

It is difficult to judge the degree of sympathy for views such as this in the Army, but there were certainly elements, particularly among the Royal Armoured Corps, for whom this must have struck a chord. The 1952 Army pamphlet *The Armoured Division in Battle* stands out as an example of what today might be termed 'manoeuvrist' thinking:

> The ultimate aim is to break the enemy's will to fight. All operations must be directed towards that supreme aim....
>
> [The Armoured Division's] first characteristic is mobility ... it is by the judicious exploitation of this characteristic that the full power of the division in the battlefield can make itself felt. [Firepower, or

'hitting power', was only the third characteristic].

So long as the higher commander can keep his mass of armoured firepower mobile on the battlefield, so long will he hold the advantage.... The armoured division should not be required to occupy for any length of time a sector of a static defensive system.

[In pursuit] Wherever the enemy is met and cannot be bypassed, he must be manoeuvred out of position where possible. Otherwise he must be attacked with a very rapidly mounted assault....'[18]

It was, however, a far cry from what was written in a doctrinal publication to what was actually done on the ground. First and foremost, the British Army had a strong antipathy for doctrine. The Army was a collection of fiercely independent clans. Each of the combat arms believed that not only was it 'Queen of the Battlefield', but also that it *virtually alone* could win the battle. Within each arm, each regiment believed that it was the best, and that it was the best because of the special and different way it did things. To be forced to abandon this special way and conform to someone else's was seen as wholly detrimental and something to be resisted at all costs. In any case, to most officers there was no such thing as 'doctrine', only 'pamphlets' – and they were, at best, a basis for discussion, and for quoting in promotion exams. Instead there was an ethos – a generally accepted way of approaching matters – which viewed tactics as being the opinion of the senior officer present: an agreeable state of affairs (for the senior officer, at least.)

There were other structuralist factors which militated against a change to a more manoeuvre-orientated approach to warfare. Such a concept would require a manoeuvre-equipped army. By 1950, though, the British Army had reduced the number of its armoured divisions from 14 to one, and was relying heavily on lorried infantry. Although some increases in the armoured strength did take place, it was not universally welcomed. Any change to the infantry/armour balance threatened to be expensive, not only in money, but also in upsetting the regimental system, and thus endangering the number of infantry cap badges – a far more important factor for infantry officers. And, as they do today, senior officers (not just in the infantry) still associated themselves very closely with the regiment into which they were commissioned.

A manoeuvre-oriented concept would also require a higher standard of training, higher arguably than might be expected from a conscript army, and conscription was a central tenet of government policy of both Conservative and Labour governments until the late 1950s. Furthermore, it would require the close integration of all arms at a time when each arm was fiercely proud of its independence and often suspicious of at least one, if not all, of the other arms.

Armour and Infantry Views

The two manoeuvre arms – armour and infantry – viewed the battlefield in very different ways. Since the infantry had, with few exceptions, to fight on their feet, being delivered to the battlefield by lorry, their view of warfare was positional and attritional: victory would be gained by well-planned, set-piece battles combined with an aggressive spirit and courage. Focus for the infantry tended to be on ground – its seizure or defence – rather than on destruction of the enemy. As Montgomery had emphasised, 'The first aim of an attack is to capture ground; the second is to hold it.'[19] Moreover, at the same time that the pamphlet, *The Armoured Division in Battle*, was constantly urging speed, mobility and what in effect was high tempo, the Infantry equivalent made comparatively little mention of these factors. Speed *during* the attack was emphasised, and as a means of gaining surprise, but not as a means of developing momentum or in the sense of developing a rate of activity higher than that of the enemy, that is, tempo. There was also a warning that speed should not be achieved at the expense of tidiness: 'An operation which starts untidily will finish untidily and may have serious results.'[20] Moreover, infantry divisions had only one integral regiment of tanks, and these were distributed to infantry regiments for use as dug-in, anti-tank defences, although further tanks might be attached to the division as a counter-attack force.[21] The two arms thus had at this time very different approaches to the conduct of operations, and by its very size the Infantry's view tended to be the one that was more widely held in the Army as a whole.

Last, the move to a more manoeuvre-oriented doctrine would require a radical change to the command and control system from the existing one, based on command by detailed orders in accordance with a master plan, to one based on broad direction and minimum orders, without which a manoeuvre-oriented concept would be doomed to failure. It is easy to underestimate the enormity in change of ethos that this requires in an army. It strikes at the heart of its attitude to discipline and hierarchy, its perception of martial qualities, its recruiting and training policy, the expectations it has of its soldiers and their ability to think independently, and its view of the relative merits of perfection and speed. On all of these, the British Army as a whole held strong and fixed views.

The degree to which the Army was wedded to the set-piece rather than fluid operations was underlined in 1951 by Lt-Colonel Michael Carver, a wartime armoured brigade commander (and future Chief of Defence Staff).

The tendency of training in peace, or in England in war-time, to hold extensive post-mortems after exercises, to stress the importance of careful planning and detailed foresight, and to see that everyone is in the picture, important as these factors are, led, and still leads, to the lengthy and detailed conferences and 'O' groups and the meticulous planning which is so often criticised by Americans and causes so ponderous a functioning of the military machine. Contrast it with Rommel's method of command and note the results.[22]

Although this theme was taken up in the 1952 pamphlet *The Armoured Division in Battle*,[23] it was not enough to make and sustain the radical change required. As the years passed and the number of tactical nuclear weapons grew and nuclear strategy developed, so the concept of operations for British forces grew to centre on 'canalising or compressing the enemy into killing zones (KZs) (conventional or nuclear), and using obstacles and conventional fire to hold him there long enough to destroy him with nuclear weapons ... Counter-attack after nuclear release will primarily be by nuclear fire.'[24] The concept, therefore, centred around positional warfare and attrition. Indeed, 'The broad picture of the battle is one of constant attrition so that the further the enemy penetrates our position the more he will be worn down until he is finally in a position to be destroyed.'[25]

The Attrition/Manoeuvre Debate, 1950s and 1960s

This attritional approach to warfare was not seriously challenged in Britain for many years. In part this may be attributed to the fact that, in comparison with today, few academics concerned themselves with military affairs, and those who did, concentrated on the nuclear debate rather than styles of warfighting. Debate in the area of attritional and anti-attritional approaches to warfare was not, however, entirely moribund, continuing sporadically throughout the post-war years. In Britain it was largely centred in contributions to the *Journal of the Royal United Service Institution (RUSI Journal)*, albeit limited to a small group of people. Much of this debate centred not so much on the concepts themselves as on reassessments of the World Wars and of the inter-war armoured argument, and especially on the claims made by Liddell Hart, in particular, about the universal application of his theory of the indirect approach. Liddell Hart, as Mearsheimer and Brian Bond, among others, have pointed out,[26] did not suffer from false modesty, or modesty of any sort, often argued a case well beyond its logical conclusion, exaggerated his own importance in affairs, and tended to personalise arguments with his critics. This produced long-running and sometimes vindictive feuds such as that with John Terraine over 'The Basic

Truths of Passchendaele' (1959),[27] with arguments expressed in strong or mocking tones. Another critic, the late Brigadier Shelford Bidwell, notably characterised the indirect approach as being 'like that degenerate art of Malay self defence called "bersillat", which appears to consist of agile moves and menacing gestures'.[28] Terraine's rejoinder in 1971 (after Liddell Hart's death) dismissed the indirect approach as 'a delusion', and interpreted Fuller as having '...pronounced the deadly epitaph of "the strategy of the indirect approach"...'.[29]

Moreover, these claims and counter claims often tended to take arguments to their extreme, advocating for example, that either attrition or manoeuvre *alone* could win, or implying that the 'indirect approach' claimed to have abolished the requirement for any attrition.[30] Clearly, in practice, all war is a combination of manoeuvre and attrition in varying degrees, and the argument was over the balance between the two. Grossly exaggerated arguments with a high emotional content did not help to resolve the issue.

Finally, the more the arguments centred around the claim that manoeuvre alone could provide victory, the further the concept was led away from the German interpretation of a manoeuvre doctrine which held that the culmination of manoeuvre was encirclement and *annihilation* rather than piecemeal fighting, let alone bloodless victory.[31]

It is notable that few participants in this debate were serving officers – unsurprisingly, perhaps, since this was essentially a historical debate between historians. But few serving Army officers, particularly middle ranking or junior officers, contributed in writing to debate of any sort in (or even subscribed to) the main professional publications, the *RUSI Journal* or the much less influential *Army Quarterly*.[32] Had they done so, the debate might have moved forward to examine the theories in the light of current circumstances. The *British Army Review* had a wider (and free) circulation in the Army and was actively supported, but during the period, any warfighting subjects addressed were generally at the tactical level. It is also notable how few serving officers had works of any sort published during this period. In part this may have been due to a trait noted by Sir Michael Howard that

> The sceptical, inquiring, implacably agnostic spirit of the scientist ... is not the normal cast of mind of the military profession. The disciplined acceptance of traditional values and of traditional solutions is the natural product of a military environment, and the problem of combining this attitude with the scientist's scepticism and agnosticism lies at the root of military education and of military training at every level.[33]

It was also the case, however, that little official encouragement was given to Army officers to enter public debate of any sort, and that the requirement to have any work for publication 'cleared' with the Ministry of Defence was seen as an active disincentive, a view not dispelled by the zealous nature with which this role was carried out.[34]

Lessons for NATO from Vietnam and the Middle East

However, certain factors and events started to cause approaches to warfare to become an issue in the late 1960s and early 1970s. One of the first of these was the US Army's experience in Vietnam. How could it be, many asked, that a world superpower with seemingly unlimited supplies of weaponry, ammunition and matériel could be defeated by a Third World country with an apparently third-rate army? Some of those who sought to answer this question noted that ultimately it was a failure of will on the part of the US government, not the destruction of US forces in the field, that had secured victory for North Vietnam. At the same time they noted that the US Army had never been able to bring to bear the full potential of its combat power because of attacks on its own cohesion, and because it had been drawn into battles for which it was unsuited. It was conclusively not the case, as claimed by the US military, that 'The solution in Vietnam is more bombs, more shells, more napalm....'[35] Echoing Falkenhayn, General William C. Westmoreland had stated his policy with clarity: '...we'll just go on bleeding them until Hanoi wakes up to the fact that they have bled their country to the point of natural disaster for generations'.[36] Not least, commentators increasingly called into question the validity of applying to warfare industrial measurements of success such as 'body-count', so favoured by Secretary of Defense Robert S. McNamara. McNamara had probably been right when he had said 'Every quantitative measurement we have shows that we're winning this war.'[37] But as is so often the case in warfare, it was what had not or could not be measured that counted.

Clearly there were lessons to be drawn for NATO's approach to warfare on the Central Front from both an industrial approach to warfare[38] and from the vulnerability of democracies to battle casualties in the media age. But other factors came to challenge the credibility of NATO's strategic posture. Many of these came from a step change in the degree and type of scrutiny of the Soviet Union and its armed forces. Until the late 1960s this scrutiny was largely the preserve of government intelligence agencies, using classified information and operating to a strictly enforced 'need-to-know' principle. There could be little informed public debate. However, some academics on both sides of the Atlantic concerned themselves with the Soviet armed forces, not least Professor John Erickson at Edinburgh University, and also a group of academic staff at the Royal Military Academy Sandhurst. In 1971 this group was formalised into the government-sponsored Soviet Studies Research Centre which became a focus for analysis of the Soviet military, using open-source material, of which there was a surprisingly large amount.[39] Increasingly authoritative articles appeared, such as that in 1971 on the Soviet 'desant' capability,[40] and in 1975 on the Soviet concept of operations.[41] These articles questioned the validity of NATO plans based on a positional and largely linear concept. The 1975 article spelt it out:

> ...the Russians would ... launch a number of frontal attacks on the main enemy defences to keep them occupied, to harass them and to make them uncertain of where the main blow was to fall. By contrast, the bulk of Soviet forces, moving round the flanks, would seek to avoid contact with the enemy until the encirclement was virtually complete.

The early 1970s were also replete with commentary on the Arab-Israeli wars, in particular those of 1967 and 1971, examining how a much smaller force – and one, it was noted, with British and US equipment – had spectacularly defeated a larger and Soviet-equipped force. Emphasis was placed on the fast-moving, fluid nature of battles, the suitability to it of the Israeli command system and ethos, and the significance of the Israeli Army's rate of activity relative to that of its opponents. Note was also taken of the Israeli emphasis on the perceived success of attacking the enemy's cohesion and the perceived failure of frontal attacks,[42] and of the late General Yitzhak Rabin's remark that 'we use our armour like a mailed fist, thrusting with speed and massive momentum, deep into the enemy's territory, not to take his positions, but to throw him off balance and make his positions untenable'[43] – even if, as Field-Marshal Lord Carver has pointed out, this was not always the case in practice.[44] Whatever the dissimilarities of circumstances, there was no shortage of pundits seeking to draw parallels with NATO's Central Front.

The US Operational Doctrine Debate from 1976

Although some ensuing discussion was taking place in the United Kingdom, notably in the *RUSI Journal* and the *British Army Review*, rather more debate was taking place in the United States. Following the publication of the US Army's new operational doctrine in 1976, some commentators criticised the emphasis in it on firepower at the expense of manoeuvre. One of the earliest and most vociferous of these was William S. Lind, then a legislative aide to Senator Gary Hart, who in 1977 publicly deplored what he called a change towards what might be seen as a 'Maginot mentality',[45] suggesting that US Army doctrine was being driven by German political insistence on forward defence, and that it should adopt what he called a 'manoeuvre doctrine'.[46]

In the same year Steven Canby wrote about '...infantry versus armoured-style of warfare, and firepower versus manoeuvre. In the first, war is attrition; in the second, war is the avoidance of costly battle with the aim of unravelling the opponent's ability to organise himself and to act', and alleged that 'NATO is using the paraphernalia of armour in an infantry mode of warfare based on the primacy of *firepower* [his italics] on the battlefield.'[47] Edward Luttwak in an article in 1979[48] argued that this attritional approach was an American style in warfare, based on a self-image of superiority in matériel and on the application of firepower, as opposed to what he called 'manoeuvre warfare' which sought to achieve disruption, and in which forces were structured and configured not to maximise their own all-round capabilities, but to exploit weaknesses particular to the enemy. The article became celebrated not so much for these views as for the remarkable attack it made on the US Army. Criticising the 'systems analysis' techniques based on mathematical models which treated warfare as a cumulative exchange of firepower, Luttwak added, 'To their great discredit, the uniformed military have chosen to play the bureaucratic game, and now have their own models, suitably rigged. Instead of resisting the pressure to conform, and elevating their intellect to the study of war ... the military waste their talents on studies and models which are based on premises which are false, and which they *know* [his italics] to be false.... Unfortunately, the tactics of bureaucratic conflict in the Pentagon are of no use on the battlefield.' This can have done little to advance his cause within the Pentagon.

Closer study of the Soviet approach to warfare also highlighted the emphasis placed on *levels* of war, and in particular on the level between tactics and strategy known as the operational level. This view of warfare in levels was not, of course, new, nor was the recognition of a level or levels between the tactical and the strategic – particularly in the Russian and German armies. Although Britain's tradition had been largely in small wars and imperial policing, with a resulting lack of scale of operations, Liddell Hart and Fuller had both acknowledged the existence of and developed a concept for what they called 'grand tactics' as early as the 1920s;[49] but although the concept had received passing mention in a doctrinal publication in 1935, it had not been properly understood and had subsequently been dropped from British doctrine.[50] (There are suggestions both that it was a victim of the long-running feud between supposedly progressive and traditionalist factions in the inter-war years, and that the British regimental system tended to restrict thinking to the tactical level.) In the late 1970s, and early 1980s, though, attention was redirected on the operational level, not least in the UK by the Soviet Studies Research Centre,[51] and in the US by the Army's annual Operational Research Symposia, and Tactics and Military Posture Symposia.[52] Wider public attention was drawn by several commentators, including Luttwak with his 1980 article, 'The Operational Level of War'.[53]

In it Luttwak postulated that a view of warfare which acknowledged only two levels – tactical and strategic – would lead to the attritional style of warfare he had discussed the previous year. Without an intermediate level, with its campaign plan and strategy, effort would be expended on cumulative battles, the sum of which (if successful) would result in the destruction of the enemy. Commanders of whatever sized unit or formation would be engaged in similar tasks: how to mass the maximum quantity of firepower on the largest-available target array, and having done so, how to do it again. The same alternative as before was posited, but under a different name, 'relational-maneuver', the goal of which was the incapacitation of enemy forces or structures – 'systemic destruction', rather than 'cumulative destruction' – with an emphasis on high tempo.

Two notable events in the United States followed these debates. First, the Army's new operations doctrine, 'Air Land Battle',[54] published in 1983, included much of the spirit of manoeuvre warfare or 'relational-maneuver' without mentioning them by name, accepted the operational level of war, and adopted a decentralised command and control system.[55] Second, a course – the School for Advanced Military Studies (SAMS), designed to educate and train high grade officers in operational art – was founded in 1982 at the Army Command and General Staff College at Fort Leavenworth. In addition, in 1984 came the publication of a book, *The Defense Reform Debate*[56] sponsored by West Point, which included some highly critical views analysing the military issues involved.

It was not only the US Army which was moving to a less attritional warfighting style. By 1981 the US Marine Corps, later to fully embrace the concept, was including lectures on the subject in the curriculum of its Amphibious Warfare School, and some USMC officers co-operated with William Lind in the production of his book *Maneuver Warfare*,[57] published in 1985. This book became increasingly read in British military circles, particularly at the Army Staff College at Camberley, and stimulated considerable debate on the subject.

Race to the Swift, 1985

Also published in 1985 was an in-depth analysis of many of the ideas surrounding manoeuvre warfare, *Race to the Swift* by the late Brigadier Richard Simpkin.[58] A retired British Royal Tank Regiment officer Simpkin had previously produced two books[59] examining Soviet and NATO concepts of armoured warfare. *Race to The Swift* examined what he termed 'attrition theory' and 'manoeuvre theory' and their application, and is a seminal work. His brilliant analysis, especially in relating approaches to warfare in terms of the dynamics of physics, is marred by some complex prose, as a result of which the book has had a less wide readership than it deserves. Among many British Army officers it has gained for manoeuvre theory a reputation as being impenetrably obscure.

Simkin provocatively labelled those who favoured an attritional approach as 'addicts of attrition' – an implication that those who become accustomed to an attritionalist approach find difficulty in giving it up – and he makes a suggestion that this may be a British trait, or at least a trait of the British military.[60] There is nothing new in the thesis that a particular style in warfare can become addictive in the sense of being difficult to change even when the changing nature of conflict demands, and that this is particularly applicable to positional and attritional warfare.[61] Nor is it new to suggest that this can become a national style in warfare,[62] nor that for periods in the past it has been, in a sense, the British way in warfare.[63] For much of its history the British Army has fought from a position of superiority in matériel, the majority of its wars in the late nineteenth and early twentieth centuries being small imperial conflicts where 'Whatever happens we have got/The Maxim Gun – and they have not.'[64] But to what extent could an affinity with an attritional style be said to be an inhibiting factor in the move to a less attritional approach since 1945?

Certainly there are many examples that might suggest that the British way in warfare since 1945 has been the very antithesis of attritionalist: the Malayan counter-insurgency, the Borneo confrontation, the anti-Mau Mau campaign in Kenya, operations in Muscat and Oman, even the Falklands War.[65] (Northern Ireland, perhaps, less so, since although some elements of the army were involved in mentally and physically out-manoeuvring the terrorist organisations, the majority were involved in defensive and reactive tasks, with limited room to manoeuvre in time, space and political constraints.) Indeed the whole ethos of SAS operations throughout the period epitomises a manoeuvrist approach.

Attritional Concepts and Culture

But, as has been noted earlier, the theatre which tended to dominate British doctrine and training tended to be BAOR. Here several factors combined to influence the British concept of operations to remain essentially attritional rather than manoeuvrist. First, throughout the post-war period until the mid-1980s, the Army was primarily equipped with a series of slow, heavily armoured, well-gunned tanks – the Centurion, Conqueror and Chieftain –

designed to be able to slog it out with opponents. At the same time the infantry was equipped not with a fighting vehicle (with a gun), but with an armoured taxi, the wheeled Saracen and subsequently the tracked 'AFV 432', designed to carry its passengers from position to position to fight on their feet.[66] Furthermore, with Warsaw Pact air superiority anticipated, and very limited air defence assets, a concept which did not rely on much movement around the battlefield had its attractions. Much faith was placed in well-reconnoitred and well-prepared battle positions on natural and manmade obstacles, with a tactical emphasis on the holding of ground. This appeared to be, but of course was not, synonymous with defeating the enemy. Finally, warfighting was reduced to the implementation of a General Deployment Plan – a stately quadrille which relied on everyone knowing the steps in advance – with very limited manoeuvre, particularly above the tactical level.

There were also cultural factors which militated against change in doctrine in the British Army. First, as Henry Stanhope has suggested, 'Historically, the Army has resisted change until its trenches have been overrun, after which it has retreated in orderly fashion, regrouping and defending new positions. It opposed the innovations introduced by Cardwell and Haldane, but ever since has fought strongly to retain them.'[67] In this respect, one of the proudest boasts of the British Army – its record of success – appeared to it a convincing reason to remain the same, and not to change. The British Army is inspired by strongly held mores, not least, as noted earlier, its attachment to a regimental system and a deep suspicion of anything seen as challenging it. Its self-perception is that the roots of its strength lie in its heritage and traditions, and that these have given it an unrivalled record of success over many centuries. Its most dearly-held qualities tend to be those exhibited in its mythology (often as represented in pictures hanging in regimental messes) and in its most dearly held triumphs, notably those against overwhelming odds, where the day was saved by a combination of physical courage, unquestioning discipline, *sang-froid* and firepower: for example, Agincourt, Hougoumont Farm and the Squares at Waterloo, the Thin Red Line in the Crimea, Rorke's Drift, Dunkirk, Kohima and Imphal. This suggests that the British Army perceived itself as having derived considerable success from, and having an affinity with, a positional, firepower culture, with command by detailed orders, obeyed to the letter. (Great positional disasters which lack the redeeming features of recorded acts of individual courage tend to be quietly forgotten.) To forsake this battle-proven approach for an untried alternative required a considerable leap of faith. As the *Official History* of the First World War had observed in connection with a proposal for new, dispersed, defensive tactics on the 1918 Western Front: 'The British soldier prefers to fight in line. An old NCO of

1914 summed up the new system in discussion with an officer; 'It don't suit us. The British Army fights in line and won't do any good in these bird cages.'[68]

Furthermore, although the British Army had shown itself to be particularly adept at set-piece operations, this came at a price. As Correlli Barnett has noted,

> The British Army was good at the rigidly controlled, elaborately organised, set-piece attack in which all its commanders believed.... There was therefore a rigidity, an emphasis on hierarchy and strict control from the top which tended to inhibit initiative and swift exploitation....[69]

Barnett is not alone. W. G. F. Jackson, wartime soldier and later four-star general, remarked of the Italian Campaign,

> It was one of the weaknesses of the British Army command and staff training that so much emphasis was placed on the foresight needed to be ready for the major, set-piece offensive ... that shorter term opportunities for decisive action in the mobile phases of a campaign are lost.[70]

And Lt-General Sir Francis Tuker, wartime divisional and corps commander, wrote of the Staff College before the Second World War,

> Excellent staff officers emerged, men capable of the highest efficiency, exemplified by such projects as "Overlord", but inevitably there came forth astonishingly few capable fighting commanders for a war of manoeuvre.[71]

This is not to suggest that the British soldier is incapable of expertise in mobile, fluid operations. As Field-Marshal Lord Carver has observed,

> It is quite wrong to assume that this is a national trait – the stolid, phlegmatic Briton and the rest. When trained for mobile and rapid warfare the Briton is second to none. The main reason is that we have not, even yet, [1951] sloughed off the effects of the 1914–18 War.[72]

But when *not* 'trained for mobile and rapid warfare' it may have seemed more sensible to place one's faith in the tried-and-tested, set-piece method. After a particularly heroic but unsuccessful stand by a British brigade in the Western Desert, Rommel remarked, 'This brigade was almost a living embodiment of the virtues and faults of the British soldier – tremendous courage and tenacity combined with a rigid lack of mobility.'[73]

Chivalry and Self-Sacrifice

A further factor in the British Army's self-image connected with a positional and attritional culture was, and is, a sense of chivalry and self-sacrifice. John Keegan has written of the chivalrous, ritualistic code of honour associated with the phalanx fighter who fought face-to-face, as opposed to what he calls the horse hordes, for whom 'there was absolutely no hint of ritual or ceremony.... The horse people fought to win – quickly, completely and quite unheroically.'[74] If so, the British Army's tradition and heritage is very much that of the phalanx fighter. Many of the Army's greatest heroes, according to its own and the nation's mythology (again, regimental pictures are a guide), have been individuals or groups prepared, like Horatius at the Bridge, to make the supreme sacrifice ('And how can man do better than facing fearful odds/ For the ashes of his fathers and the temples of his gods'):[75] Charles Gordon at Khartoum, the Last Stand of the 24th Foot at Isandhlwana, the Last Stand of the 44th Foot at Gandamak, the 66th Foot Back to Back at Maiwand, Captain Lawrence Oates (the 'Very Gallant Gentleman') in Antarctica, the men of the 74th Highlanders standing firm on the decks of the sinking troopship *Birkenhead*: ('Thank heaven for those undegenerate souls/Who sank aboard the 'Birkenhead' in Simon's Bay'.)[76] Positional warfare – standing and fighting – allowed considerable scope for the display of such qualities.

Other elements of chivalry were very much part of this ethos. The concept of 'a fair fight' held that the opponent must not be placed at a disadvantage, but must be allowed equal terms, with the contest decided by the display of knightly qualities such as courage, stamina and 'pluck'. Opponents who would not observe these courtesies were objects of derision: 'The Boers are not like the Sudanese who will stand up to a fair fight. They are always running away on their little ponies.'[77] Pitting strength against weakness was, *per se*, often treated with suspicion. General Tuker noted, 'It is an extraordinary obsession in British commanders' minds that they must challenge the enemy's strength rather than play on his weaknesses. Perhaps it is a little bit unsporting to pit strength against weakness.'[78] There was also an aversion to taking the easy way out, since to do so was showing a lack of courage and self-sacrifice. 'Stout fellows, these soldiers', observed Vice-Admiral John de Robeck at the Gallipoli landings, 'They always go for the thickest part of the fence.'[79] Some operations of war such as pursuit – kicking a man when he's down – clearly ran counter to this ethos, and not surprisingly the British Army has rarely shown itself adept at pursuit. The Prussian tradition of 'pursuit to the last breath of man and beast'[80] was decidedly un-British.

Although much of this reflects essentially Victorian and Edwardian values, some of them permeated into the mid-twentieth century epitomised by much children's literature. One of the most popular children's books of the 1940s and 1950s has the hero offering the following philosophy:

> I teach a boy to be a man, for without that essential qualification he will never be anything. I teach sportsmanship according to the British idea.... I teach that decent behaviour wins in the end as a natural order of things ... (the basic principles of decent behaviour being) courage, loyalty, fair play, knight errantry.[81]

Although the British Army of today would certainly be proud to be associated with these qualities, the manoeuvrist approach is very much that decent behaviour is *not* the deciding factor in war; on the contrary, it suggests that success in war depends on commanders who are devious, cunning, ruthless, always on the lookout for an unfair advantage, and far from not kicking a man when he's down, look to put the man down before kicking him – the very antithesis of 'Gentlemen of France, fire first!' – unless the latter was a ruse to allow the French to be charged while they were reloading. This is not to suggest that a strong ethical basis is unnecessary as a foundation for military activity, nor to argue that a manoeuvrist approach is incompatible with such an ethical basis nor, indeed, that the British Army did not or does not contain officers capable of combining the two. But it does suggest that overemphasis on the one may be at the expense of the other, and that such overemphasis may have occurred up to the middle of this century, or later.

Lack of an Agreed Military Vocabulary

A further, and rather more prosaic factor which might have inhibited the British Army in its adoption of a different approach to warfare, is the lack of a commonly-agreed military vocabulary. Michael Elliott-Bateman and Jonathan Moore have suggested[82] that such a vocabulary is a necessary first step to any meaningful discussion of sophisticated military concepts, and that whereas some armies – notably the German Army – have a strong tradition of precision in their military language, the British Army does not. The British Army's glossary of military terminology was, until recently, confined largely to relatively low-level procedural and technical terms. This would appear to have allowed considerable latitude in definition of conceptual terms, in stark contrast to the immensely detailed and prescriptive regulations governing the procedures to be followed in written staff work[83] – 'minor staff duties' – in the past, the object of so much of the Staff College instructors' attention and red ink. However, this absence of a conceptual glossary is perhaps more indicative of the relative absence of anything other than superficial conceptual discussion, either at the Staff

College (until recently), or in the Army at large, the lack of such a glossary being both cause and effect. Instead, labels have been bandied about, often foreign ones (for instance, *auftragstaktik, schwerpunkt, beweglichkeit*), with little understanding of their underlying meaning or implication. 'Manoeuvre Warfare' comes into this category, the term having had no official Army-wide definition until 1996.

NATO Exercises in West Germany

Finally, a manoeuvre-oriented approach requires commanders trained to think in terms of outmanoeuvring an opponent, and for a time during the post-war period this received less emphasis than it might have. Many exercises became two-sided in name only, instead becoming highly choreographed demonstrations. Nowhere was this more so than in West Germany where the priority was seen to be to demonstrate to the media – and through it to audiences on both sides of the Iron Curtain – that NATO worked: that its reinforcement plans were efficient and that its tactics were effective. Furthermore, environmental pressures constrained the extent of free play, since battles could no longer be allowed to take place wherever the forces happened to meet, but only in those parts of the German countryside where damage was acceptable. These battle sites became fewer in number and smaller in size, and exercise planners increasingly had not only to steer exercising troops into them, but very often to take commanders to reconnoitre them before the exercise. These commanders could thereafter be judged on their choreographical skills, but not on their capability to out-think their opponents, nor in their capacity for originality and improvisation. Furthermore, since mistakes could not be afforded, command by detailed orders was required. Ironically, training had come to mirror operations – both had become a stately minuet. Not unnaturally, this tended to favour officers who thrived in these circumstances.[84] Although such environmental pressures remain, preventing off-road, tracked manoeuvre except in designated training areas, the development of laser technology now allows highly realistic two-sided exercises, for example at the British armoured training area in Canada. In addition, indoor simulators permit commanders and staffs at unit and formation level to pit their wits against each other in challenging, two-sided wargames.

The Bagnall Manoeuvrist Reforms, 1980s

The eventual change in the British Army to a self-consciously manoeuvrist approach and a decentralised command system ('mission command') was less the result of theories or the product of debate than of one officer's dynamism. When he took command of 1st British Corps in 1981, Lt-

General Sir Nigel Bagnall strongly advocated a less positional, more mobile style of warfare, a greater appreciation of the importance of speed in battle procedure, and the importance of standard operating procedures throughout the corps.[85] His Corps *Battle Notes* (echoing the spirit of *The Armoured Division in Battle 1952*) stressed that

> Wherever possible orders should be given as a single directive.... The mission should leave the subordinate commander as much freedom of execution as possible and should contain only those constraints essential to cooperation with other units.... Dithering over details, when these are not fundamental to the task, leads to delay and lost opportunities.[86]

The section on command and control concluded, 'These requirements demand small, hard headquarters swift in reaction and movement.'[87] In addition, he instituted standard operating procedures common to all units and formations, since no such thing existed. Bagnall was openly critical of the over-literal interpretation of forward defence, 'the battle of attrition which we could never hope to win', and defensive thinking: 'The British Corps [have] been schooled for years in restrictive thinking of a static defence.'[88] Such criticism, so necessary as a first step to reform, was unusual in a serving officer – not least because it could have been interpreted not only as disloyalty, but as detrimental to morale and as giving solace and encouragement to the enemy.

As commander of the NATO Northern Army Group 1983–85, Bagnall instituted for the first time an Army Group plan for general deployment based on manoeuvre at Army Group level, rather than one based on a series of corps battles, largely in isolation. As Chief of the General Staff 1985–88 he was also to preside over the formation, for the first time in the British Army, of an Army-wide doctrine, and to establish at Camberley an operational level course – the Higher Command and Staff Course – similar to the SAMS course at Fort Leavenworth. Both the doctrine and the course recognised the operational level of war, and acknowledged the centrality of a manoeuvre-oriented approach to warfare, although the latter concept was only translated into lower-level doctrine and fully embraced into the exercises of the Army Command and Staff Course in 1994. Here manoeuvre warfare was defined as 'a warfighting philosophy which seeks to defeat the enemy by shattering his moral and physical cohesion – his ability to fight as an effective, coordinated whole – rather than to destroy him physically through incremental attrition'.[89]

However, it was recognised that the term 'manoeuvre warfare' could be misleading, and that the term 'manoeuvrist approach' better encapsulated the idea of the mental activity required to outmanoeuvre an enemy commander. This was, in turn, defined as

> an approach to operations in which shattering the enemy's overall cohesion and will to fight is paramount. It calls for an attitude of mind in which doing the unexpected, using initiative and seeking originality is combined with a ruthless determination to succeed.[90]

The concept is now also incorporated into Royal Air Force and Royal Navy doctrine.[91]

Better understanding of manoeuvre warfare or the manoeuvrist approach was greatly facilitated at the British Staff College by a series of books published in the United States by young US Army officers, notably *The Art of Maneuver*[92] by Robert Leonhard, and *Maneuver Warfare: An Anthology*[93] edited by Richard Hooker. Both books advocated a more manoeuvre-oriented approach by the US Army.

Conclusions

Several conclusions offer themselves as a result of this brief survey. The first is that the military – any military – is an inherently conservative organisation, and expectations of precipitate change or reform from within a military organisation may be misplaced. The British Army is no exception to this. The majority of the period covered, however, was perhaps exceptional in the lack of change in circumstances and context in which the Army found itself, and thus it became accustomed to little or no change. The same could not be said of the last five years, and during this period the Army has taken considerable initiative to make necessary changes in its structure and doctrine.

The second conclusion might be that discouragement of debate, real or perceived, is not conducive to the evolution of change or reform. Although questioning or discordant voices can sometimes be uncomfortable to a hierarchical organisation, they play an important part in effecting change. The fact that West Point commissioned the book *The Defense Reform Debate*, containing highly critical commentaries, is significant. Serving officers have much to contribute to intellectual debate and require encouragement to publish their works if the potential of their contribution is to be realised.

Disadvantages of 'Manoeuvre Warfare'

With exceptions, though, it has also been the case that much of the literature about 'manoeuvre warfare' tends to be written by enthusiasts, many of whom are so keen to advocate the concept that they fail to mention its disadvantages and attempt to give it (like Liddell Hart with his indirect approach) a universal applicability. Clearly such disadvantages exist, even in an era where casualty-avoidance has almost become a principle of war. Attrition with long-range, stand-off precision weapons against an enemy who cannot reciprocate may be the most cost-effective approach as regards casualties (his bodies; our bullets); a manoeuvrist approach may involve an unacceptable level of risk (it is inherently more risky); we may lack the necessary room to manoeuvre; or our troops may lack the training or equipment necessary to achieve higher tempo than our opponent, or may be incapable of operating except by detailed order. All these factors might steer us towards a necessarily attritional approach. Furthermore, as Martin van Creveld has pointed out, 'A great victory like Cannae takes both a Hannibal and a Varro.'[94] (Gaius Terentius Varro, the incompetent Roman commander).

The Operational Level

Also highlighted by this survey has been the significance of the recognition of the operational level of war, and of operational art, in the development of a more manoeuvre-orientated approach to warfare. At the tactical level, warfare is largely about battles – by definition attritional affairs – and consideration of warfare exclusively at the tactical level can obscure the desirability of *avoiding* battles which becomes apparent at the operational level. This can breed an approach which sees virtue only in fighting and attrition – avoidance of battle being synonymous with running away. Furthermore, operational art encourages focus on defeat of the enemy by targeting his Centre of Gravity (the Clausewitzian notion of the hub or source of the enemy's strength), approached indirectly by way of a series of stepping stones (or Decisive Points) – in other words a manoeuvrist appproach. It is probably equally true, though, that over-emphasis on the operational level, and on mobility at the expense of firepower, can cause an army to lose the low-level aggression so necessary to success in battle. Clearly a balance is required; yet to shift a cast of mind from, for example, an attritional approach, requires a certain amount of imbalance, and fine judgement is needed as to when balance should be restored.

Knowledge of the Enemy

Noteworthy, too, has been the role of close scrutiny of the potential opponent in moving away from an attritional approach. A deep knowledge of and fascination with an adversary is both the cause and effect of a move to a manoeuvrist approach. It is a *cause* because such fascination leads you to consider how your opponent will react to your actions several moves ahead, as in chess, and therefore how you can outmanoeuvre him. Lack of knowledge of the enemy, on the other hand, tends to direct attention on our own activity regardless of the enemy, and therefore leads to consideration of war as a one-sided activity. Deep knowledge of the enemy is also an *effect* of the manoeuvrist approach, as evidence of the interest which an army has in outmanoeuvring its opponent, and its awareness that such knowledge is the starting point. According to Field-Marshal Slim this has not been a conspicuous British trait in the past: 'We, the British at any rate, are not very good at that: we don't study our enemy enough.'[95]

Theory and Doctrine

This account has also highlighted the British Army's uneasy relationship with theory and doctrine. A strong preference for the empirical approach, together with a certain amount of intellectual laziness, has often caused theory to be viewed as an unnecessary encumbrance, and this has resulted in a tradition of scepticism of the need for doctrine, and in resistance to it. Official acknowledgement of its necessity is not synonymous with its universal acceptance. As Barry Posen has pointed out, 'changing doctrine takes time; it disorients a military organisation'.[96] Undoubtedly some will find it hard to assimilate, and others will be over-ready to embrace it as a substitute for thought, and happy to apply it as a template, just as the concept of operations for a single theatre – BAOR – came to be applied at times as a universal warfighting doctrine for the Army as a whole. There is a further danger: that the official sanction required to implement doctrine can transform it into dogma and ossify it; but without that official sanction it is liable to become ignored and irrelevant. Moreover, if too much criticism of it is encouraged, the doctrine may lack credibility; but if some criticism is not made, it will not remain dynamic. This is not a new challenge for military leaders, but it still remains very much a challenge. What is also important is, like Sir Michael Howard,[97] to have a healthy scepticism that one's doctrine, whatever it is, will be appropriate for the next conflict, and to concentrate on being able to adapt to the necessary doctrine faster than our opponent, and then to focus not so much on maximising our capabilities as on tailoring them to exploit our specific enemy, at the specific place and time. There is no universally-applicable doctrinal panacea: 'The law is in the circumstances.'[98]

The Future. All-Arms, Joint and Combined

For much of the period the degree to which the Army's approach could be described as all-arms, let alone joint or combined, has been limited. However, all-arms training has recently been greatly enhanced by an Army-wide doctrine and by the institution of an all-arms training centre at Warminster. Joint training should be similarly enhanced by the imminent

BRITISH ARMY APPROACHES TO WARFARE SINCE 1945   203

advent of a joint doctrine, and by the institution of both a Joint Services Command and Staff College and a single Permanent Joint Headquarters. Although the amount of combined (multinational) training and operations has greatly increased recently, it is here that there is perhaps the greatest scope for development in the future.

Cultural Changes

Also highlighted has been the concept of a national style of warfare in terms of a positional or mobile approach, and a suggestion that, in this century at least, the British Army has more often shown a closer affinity with a positional than with a mobile culture. Although the extent to which Simpkin's term 'addicts of attrition' is applicable to the British Army is debatable, what is clearer is that the shift from a positional to a mobile culture requires a profound change of ethos. It involves forsaking the well-ordered, tidy, essentially linear battlefield, with its emphasis on phases, balance and detailed orders, where position gives security, where movement is seen as danger, where risk is avoided and where there is a continuous quest for certainty – a Jominian view, at least in part – and adopting a Clausewitzian view of the battlefield as 'the province of chaos and uncertainty' and 'of the play of chance and probability in which the creative spirit is free to roam'.[99] Here no plan survives contact with the enemy, security is gained through high tempo, command is by minimum orders, movement spells opportunity, and calculated risk is positively welcome. The former seeks order, certainty and perfection; the latter happily trades perfection for speed, seeks to be at home in chaos and uncertainty, and to be able to operate through it as one works through interference on a radio net. The difference between the two in the mental approach required by commanders is considerable.

Summary

In summary, several prerequisites for a manoeuvrist approach were identified at the outset: good intelligence, the ability to generate high tempo; a decentralised command system; an all-arms, joint and combined approach; commanders set on outmanoeuvring opponents; and room to manoeuvre. This survey has suggested that these prerequisites were not notable in the British Army for most of the Cold War period and that the result was an approach to warfare which tended towards the attritional and positional. Various factors – not least the end of the Cold War itself – have been identified which have contributed to the development of these prerequisites, and to the possibilities which this offers to the British Army's approach to operations, now and in the future.

NOTES

The ideas expressed in this essay are purely personal and do not necessarily reflect HM Government policy.

1. '...so werden sich Frankreichs Kräfte verbluten...', *Deutsche Militärgeschichte in sechs Bänden* (Munich: MGFA Hrsg 1983) p.510.
2. Martin van Creveld, *Air Power and Manoeuvre Warfare* (Maxwell, AFB, AL: Air UP 1994) pp.3–7, suggests six 'central themes' for successful manoeuvre warfare: 'Tempo', '*Schwerpunkt*', 'Surprise', 'Combined Arms', 'Flexibility' and 'Decentralized Command'.
3. B.H. Liddell Hart, *Strategy: The Indirect Approach* (London: Faber 1967) p.219.
4. J.J. Mearsheimer, *Liddell Hart and the Weight of History* (London: Brassey's 1988) p.215.
5. Sun Tzu, *The Art of War* (trans. by Samuel B. Griffith, OUP 1963) p.77.
6. Similarly, Napoleon's claim that on occasions he had destroyed the enemy merely by marches was made possible by the threat of annihilation posed by the position of advantage gained by the march. The *coup de grâce* was not required.
7. J.F.C. Fuller, *On Future Warfare* (London: Sifton Praed 1928) p.93.
8. Ibid. p.94.
9. Liddell Hart (note 3) p.25.
10. J.F.C. Fuller, *Lectures on FSR III* (London: Sifton Praed 1932) p.32.
11. Tactics of the German Army (WO 20/GS Publication/1250, London 1944).
12. J.P. Harris, *Men, Ideas and Tanks* (Manchester UP 1995) p.307.
13. B.L. Montgomery, *Some Brief Notes For Senior Officers on the Conduct of Battle* (Eighth Army 1942) pp.8–14.
14. But, at the time, for good reason: '...when the troops see that the battle has gone exactly as they were told it would go, the increase in morale and the confidence in the higher command is immense – and this is a most important factor for the battles to come'. B.L. Montgomery, *Memoirs of Field-Marshal Viscount Montgomery of Alamein* (London: Collins 1958) p.88.
15. Staff College Course Records 1945–53 (unpub.). Instruction neatly compartmentalises warfare into four distinct and separate phases: Advance, Attack, Defence, Withdrawal. This remained the approach until NATO doctrine (ATP 35(A)) was formally adopted at the Staff College in 1990.
16. F.O. Miksche, *Blitzkrieg* (London: Faber 1941) and T. Wintringham, *Deadlock War* (ibid. 1940) and *How to Reform The Army* (ibid. 1940).
17. G. Martel, 'Tank Policy', *RUSI Journal* 95/3 (Aug. 1951) p.449.
18. *The Armoured Division in Battle* (WO Code 8715, 1952) pp.7–10 and 49.
19. B. Montgomery, *The Infantry Division in Battle* (21st Army Group Pamphlet 1944, unpub.) para.19.
20. *The Infantry Division in Battle* (WO Code 8476, 1950) p.21.
21. Staff College Course 1953, Records Vol.9, Defence Demonstration, p.3 (unpub.).
22. M. Carver, 'Tanks and Infantry – The Need for Speed', *RUSI Journal* 95/3 (Aug. 1951) p.453.
23. 'Except at the beginning of major operations, there is rarely time for the issue of written orders in confirmation, or indeed of confirmation by signal.... The whole procedure of command and control is a very personal affair demanding a quick grasp of the situation, clear cut decisions, mutual confidence and absolute brevity.' *The Armoured Division in Battle*, pp.28–9.
24. Guidance on the Conduct of Operations of A Battle Group in North West Europe, (Army Code 70494, Jan. 1969) pp.4–5.
25. Ibid.
26. Mearsheimer (note 4); B. Bond, 'Further Reflections on the Indirect Approach', *RUSI Journal* 116/4 (Dec. 1971) p.69.
27. B.H. Liddell Hart, 'The Basic Truths of Passchendaele', ibid. 104/4 (Nov. 1959) p.433.
28. R.G.S. Bidwell, 'The Five Fallacies. Some Thoughts on British Military Thinking', ibid. (Feb. 1967) p.54.
29. J. Terraine, 'History of the "Indirect Approach"', ibid. 116/2 (June 1971) pp.44–9.
30. R.G.S. Bidwell, *Modern Warfare* (Allen Lane 1973) pp.193–215.

31. 'Zweck des Angriffen, den Feind zu vernichten...', *Truppenführing 1962* (HDv 100/1) p.149.
32. For a notable exception, see Maj. R.S. Evans, RTR, 'The Need for Offensive Operations on Land', *RUSI Journal* 121/3 (Sept. 1976) pp.28–33.
33. M. Howard, 'Military Science in an Age of Peace', ibid. 118/4 (Dec. 1973) p.3.
34. '...that tiresome process of bureaucratic interference in the publication of the works of British Army officers which has reached such ludicrous proportions today...', B. Holden Reid, *War Studies at the Staff College 1900–1930*, 'Occasional' No.1 (London: HMSO 1992) pp.18–19.
35. Brig.-Gen. de Puy, quoted in Neil Sheehan, *A Bright Shining Lie* (London: Cape 1988) p.619.
36. Westmoreland, quoted in ibid. p.643.
37. McNamara, quoted in ibid. p.290.
38. See e.g. D.C. Watt, 'Lessons of the American Defeat in Vietnam', *RUSI Journal* 118/2 (June 1973) p.38, 'America's European allies have to ponder over the consequences of the American industrial approach to war and the dangers of imitating it.'
39. See e.g. the USAF's Soviet Military Thought series, V. Savkin, *The Principles of Operational Art and Tactics* (Moscow 1972, trans. and pub. by USAF 1985).
40. C.N. Donnelly, 'The Soviet Concept of the Desant', *RUSI Journal* 116/3 (Sept. 1971) pp.52–6.
41. C.N. Donnelly and P.H. Vigor, 'The Soviet Threat to Europe', ibid. 126/1 (March 1975) p.72.
42. M. van Creveld, 'Two Years After: The Israeli Defence Forces 1973–75', ibid. 127/1 (March 1976) p.31.
43. Ibid.
44. M. Carver, *The Apostles of Mobility* (London: Weidenfeld 1979) p.95.
45. A phrase echoed by a former CINCENT in 1986. See F.M. von Senger and Etterlin, 'Race to the Swift: A Review Article', *British Army Review* 82 (April 1986) p.29.
46. W. Lind, 'Some Doctrinal Questions for the United States Army', *Military Review* 57/3 (March 1977) pp.54–65.
47. S.L. Canby, 'NATO: Reassessing the Conventional Wisdoms', *Survival* 18/4 (July–Aug. 1977) pp.164–8.
48. E.N. Luttwak, 'The American Style in Warfare and The Military Balance', *Survival* 21/2 (March–April 1979) pp.57–60.
49. C. Bellamy, *The Evolution of Modern Land Warfare* (London: Routledge 1990) p.60.
50. Ibid. pp.60–79.
51. C.N. Donnelly 'The Soviet Operational Manoeuvre Group: A New Challenge for NATO', *Int. Defense Review* 9 (1982) pp.1177–86. The reasons for the impact of this article are well described in Bellamy (note 49) p.122.
52. J.L. Romjue, *Active Defense to Air Land Battle* (Tradoc Historical Office 1984) p.16.
53. E.N. Luttwak, 'The Operational Level of War', *Int. Security* 5/3 (Winter 1980/81) pp.61–79.
54. US Army Publication, FM 100-5, *Air Land Battle*, 1983.
55. Romjue (note 52) pp.58–61.
56. A.A. Clark (ed.), *The Defense Reform Debate* (Baltimore, MD: John Hopkins UP 1984).
57. W.S. Lind, *Maneuver Warfare* (Westview Special Studies 1985).
58. R.E. Simpkin, *Race to the Swift* (London: Brassey's 1985).
59. Idem, *Tank Warfare* (Brassey's 1979) and *Red Armour* (ibid. 1984).
60. Simpkin (note 85) p.20.
61. See M. Elliott-Bateman, *Defeat in the East* (OUP 1967) pp.39–78.
62. See Luttwak (note 48).
63. See B.H. Liddell Hart, *Paris or The Future of War* (London: Kegan Paul 1935) pp.7–15, and Maj. R.A.D. Applegate and J.R. Moore, 'Warfare – An Option of Difficulties: An Examination of Forms of War and the Impact of Military Culture', *RUSI Journal* 135/3 (Autumn 1990) pp.13–20.
64. H. Belloc, *The Modern Traveller* (Edward Arnold 1898) Pt.6.
65. Although see S.S. Fitzgibbon, *Not Mentioned in Dispatches* (Cambridge, UK: Lutterworth Press 1995).
66. The British Army is now equipped with the much faster and more agile Challenger tank and Warrior IFV.

67. H. Stanhope, *The Soldiers* (London: Hamish Hamilton 1979) p.321.
68. J.E. Edmonds, *The British Official History: France and Belgium 1918* (London: Macmillan 1935) pp.257–8, quoted by Wintringham, *Deadlock War* (note 16) p.177.
69. C. Barnett, *Britain and Her Army 1509–1970: A Military, Political and Social Survey* (Allen Lane Penguin Press 1970) p.404.
70. W.G.F. Jackson, *The Mediterranean and the Middle East*, Vol.VI, Part 2 (London: HMSO 1986) pp.18–19.
71. F. Tuker, *Approach to Battle* (London: Cassell 1963) p.145.
72. Carver (note 22).
73. B.H. Liddell Hart, *The Rommel Papers* (London: Collins 1953) p.222 and E. Rommel, *Krieg Ohne Hass* (Verlag Heidenheimer Zeitung 1950) p.149. And, of course, the word for movement which Rommel uses – *beweglichkeit* – means not so much the physical act of movement as the mental desire to manoeuvre.
74. J. Keegan, *A History of Warfare* (London: Hutchinson 1993) p.213.
75. Macaulay, 'Horatius at the Bridge', *The Lays of Ancient Rome*, quoted by J. Richards, 'Popular Imperialism and the Image of the Army in Juvenile Literature' in J. Mackenzie (ed.) *Popular Imperialism and the Military 1850–1950* (Manchester UP 1992) p.22.
76. Sir Henry Yule, 'The Birkenhead', *The Great Poetry Book*, Vol.II (Educational Book Co. 1905) p.289.
77. Kitchener, quoted by N. Dixon, *On The Psychology of Military Incompetence* (London: Futura 1976) p.55.
78. Tuker, *Approach to Battle* (note 71) p.121.
79. De Robeck, quoted by Liddell Hart (note 3) p.12.
80. Quoted in D.W. Fraser, *Knight's Cross: A Life of Field Marshal Erwin Rommel* (Harper-Collins 1993) p.181.
81. P.B. Ellis, and P. Williams, *By Jove, Biggles: The Life of Captain W. E. Johns* (London: W.H. Allen 1981) pp.218 and 221, quoted by Mackenzie (note 75) p.22.
82. M. Elliott-Bateman, and J. Moore, 'Language: The First Problem of Military Reform', *Defense Analysis* 3/4 (Dec. 1987) pp.361–6 and M. Elliott-Bateman, 'Vocabulary: The Second Problem of Military Reform – II Tactics, ibid. 6/4 (Dec. 1990) pp.329–50.
83. See *Staff Duties in the Field* (WO Code 8457, rev. 1962).
84. See Dixon (note 77) esp. pp.238–56.
85. He acknowledged the influence, in particular, of Gen. von Senger und Etterlin, the then CINCENT, who was also a collaborator of Richard Simpkin. Script: *1 (BR) Corps Study Day 11 Feb 1981* (Army TDRC) (unpub.).
86. 1 British Corps Battle Notes (45309 G3 EPS, dated Oct.1981) p.1–3–1.
87. Ibid., p.1–2–4.
88. N.T. Bagnall, 'Concepts of Land/Air Operations in the Central Region: 1', *RUSI Journal* 129/3 (Sept. 1984) pp.59–62, based on a lecture given at RUSI, 23 May 1984.
89. Taken from USMC *FMFM-1*, 1989.
90. *Design For Military Operations – The British Military Doctrine* (Army Code 7145, 1996).
91. *RAF Air Power Doctrine* (AP 3000, HMSO, 1993) and *The Fundamentals of British Maritime Doctrine* (BR 1806, HMSO 1995).
92. R.R. Leonhard, *The Art of Maneuver* (Novato, CA: Presidio Press 1990).
93. R.D. Hooker, *Maneuver Warfare: An Anthology* (ibid. 1993).
94. van Creveld (note 2) p.209.
95. W.J. Slim, Lecture 8 April 1952: 'Higher Command in War', *Military Review* (May 1990) p.15.
96. B. Posen, *The Sources of Military Doctrine* (Ithaca, NY: Cornell UP 1984) p.30
97. Howard (note 33) p.3. 'I am tempted indeed to declare that whatever doctrine the Armed Forces are working on, they have got it wrong. I am also tempted to declare that it does not matter that they have got it wrong. What does matter is their capacity to get it right quickly when the moment arrives.... It is the task of military science in an age of peace to prevent the doctrine being too badly wrong.'
98. Attributed to US industrialist, Mary Parker Follett.
99. C. von Clausewitz, *On War* (eds. Michael Howard and Peter Paret, Princeton UP 1976) p.89.

Manoeuvre Theory in Operations Other Than War

J.J.A. WALLACE

The adoption of Manoeuvre Warfare Theory by the British and other armies will have a dramatic impact on their conduct of conventional war. Its influence is all-pervading, carrying with it not just tactical innovation but changes to their very military culture. It demands a fundamentally different approach to military problems, not just by adopting the Manoeuvre Theory tools such as 'mission-style' orders and 'reconnaissance pull', but through institutionalising the acceptance of risk and the delegation of decision-making. But cultural change, necessarily going deeper than procedural change, carries an attendant risk. Culture is less easy to adapt to foreign circumstances. Will a theory, arguably first formalised in doctrine by the German and later Russian armies, and refined in the large conventional battles of the Second World War, prove appropriate to today's western forces with more global responsibilities and faced with the ever less predictable nature of Operations Other Than War (OOTW)?

This question is all the more significant at a time when doctrine is set to play a more dominant role in shaping military culture. The British Army in particular has relied heavily on experience to create its military culture in the past and particularly in its approach to counter-insurgency. The largely unbroken experience of 'small wars', colonial policing and then the post-1945 counter-insurgency campaigns, made it both the pioneer and master of this form of warfare. But governments are now less eager to enter into low intensity conflicts and determined to limit both the size and duration of their commitment when they must. Armies must rely more on doctrine than experience and must therefore ensure that that doctrine is appropriate.

The aim of this essay is to determine the applicability of Manoeuvre Theory to military operations in Operations Other Than War.

Manoeuvre Warfare

In describing the theory of Manoeuvre Warfare, Richard Simpkin said that 'At root manoeuvre theory has nothing to do with vast numbers of men and machines charging about the countryside. Manoeuvre theory is about amplifying the force which a small mass is capable of exerting; it is synonymous with the indirect approach.'[1] Liddell Hart stressed in the theory of the Indirect Approach that it was not enough that it have 'geographical indirectness', but that it must have a 'psychological indirectness to upset the opponent's balance and create the conditions for a decisive issue'.[2] These statements provide the essence of the theory and an essential start point. The significance of the indirect approach is the focus on attacking the cohesion of the enemy force with the aim of achieving a catastrophic collapse. Military operations therefore aim not only at dislocating his forces and resources, but also at 'creating a picture of defeat'[3] in the opposition's mind, rather than simply wearing him down by attrition.

Purists would argue that attrition has no place in either the Indirect Approach or Manoeuvre Theory. But this is to deny the nature of war. Geography, politics, relative strengths and a host of other factors will determine to what degree the proponent of any theory can apply it on the battlefield in a particular set of circumstances. As illustrated below, solutions to military problems will nearly always see a mix of attrition and manoeuvre theories. What is important is the emphasis given to both. The proponent of Manoeuvre Theory will approach a problem from the right-hand side of the continuum. Attrition will not be the focus of his plan. Instead he will use it more deliberately, in pursuit of destroying cohesion, while placing emphasis on surprise, tempo and simultaneity.

FIGURE 1

Attrition/Manoeuvre Continuum

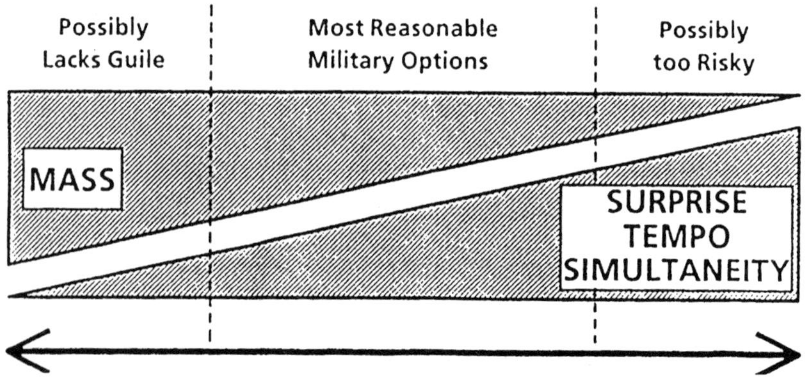

| Possibly Lacks Guile | Most Reasonable Military Options | Possibly too Risky |

MASS

SURPRISE
TEMPO
SIMULTANEITY

Key Elements of Manoeuvre Warfare

Surprise takes a central place because of the dependence of the theory on attacking the enemy's mind and getting inside his decision cycle. It therefore requires more than surprise in the literal sense of distraction or disguise of our own operations as we mainly use it. Instead we need to set the preconditions for psychological surprise both before and throughout the operation by ensuring we take 'the line of least expectation'.[4] Aiming to place our strength against his weakness is a factor of surprise as much as relative strengths, as it presupposes that his strength will be placed along his 'line of natural expectation'.[5] This acknowledges that the 'strength of an opposing force ... [is] fundamentally dependent upon stability of control, morale and supply'.[6] It is the psychological effect of upsetting this stability that is the surprise sought by the proponent of Manoeuvre Theory. This places great importance on our own intelligence to establish his 'line of natural expectation', so that it can be avoided or exploited by way of deception, itself a neglected art in most attrition-based armies.

Tempo is essential to the theory. However although a factor of speed, it is more than that. Speed in itself may render no advantage if the enemy's current action remains valid. However if we can move through more activities (cycles) than the enemy, so that his current or impending actions are no longer relevant, we have achieved tempo. This is the basis of the 'Boyd Cycle' explained in Lind's account of Manoeuvre Theory.[7] It again attacks the enemy's cohesion, his stability, and aims to cause paralysis of the mind through a feeling of suddenness or being trapped.[8] Tempo will be achieved by the sum of incremental time advantages which accrue through both a more aggressive approach and the application of the tools of Manoeuvre Theory. Being 'reconnaissance pulled' will exploit opportunities more quickly and the use of 'mission-style' orders will further assist tempo by pushing decision-making down to the lowest level.

Simultaneity,[9] or actions throughout the enemy's depth concurrent with the main activity, makes a significant contribution to tempo. As well as its physical impact on the thickness of the enemy defence as resources are diverted to deal with it, it has an exponential effect on the span of decisions to be made by the defender. It causes him to concentrate not just in a linear dimension, but in depth and even volume. On the conventional battlefield this is achieved by the use of forward detachments, offensive air, parachute or heliborne forces, electronic warfare and Special Forces (SF) operations in depth.

It is important to realise that tempo and surprise are complementary. The greater the tempo that can be generated the more likely the enemy is to be surprised and more significantly kept in a state of surprise – while the corollary is also true, in that surprise will give momentum to tempo.

The conduct of Manoeuvre Theory employs two major components: the holding force and the manoeuvre force. The balance of combat power in each cannot be prescribed, but the decision (dislocation) will usually be achieved by the manoeuvre force, while the holding force conducts economy of force operations.

An important characteristic of Manoeuvre Theory is the acceptance of risk. The main risk is that of over-extending the manoeuvre force. But there is also an inherent threat to control in maintaining tempo and employing the Manoeuvre Theory tools of 'reconnaissance pull' and 'mission-style' orders. If the aim is to achieve catastrophic collapse in the enemy, the danger is that the proponent of Manoeuvre Theory may in the process risk it himself.

In summary, this is a method of warfighting which seeks to avoid man's predilection for seeking battle for battle's sake or as an alternative to not thinking of, or risking, a smarter way. While it aims to maximise the combat power of a small force, it employs attrition as a means rather than an end. The emphasis is on dislocating the enemy through tempo and surprise, aiming as much at his command and control as at his forces. If successful it will achieve results more quickly and at lower cost than an attrition approach – desirable features in conventional war, but becoming essential in OOTW. However there is an attendant risk in the need for bold action and devolved decision-making that may be inconsistent with the very political environment at the operational and even tactical levels of OOTW.

Defining Lower Levels of Conflict

There has always been difficulty in adequately defining the lower end of the conflict spectrum. For years both US and UK definitions of low intensity conflict were inadequate. British doctrine included civil disorder and subversion, which by definition did not automatically involve force, but omitted intervention operations; while US doctrine also encompassed too much, even including obviously non-warlike activities such as disaster relief. US doctrine itself admitted to the term being a 'misnomer', not referring to any point within the spectrum of intensity of conflict, but to those activities in that 'ambiguous environment' between peace and war.[10] This adequately reflects the character of OOTW for the purpose of this essay, except to add that they should involve armed conflict, and have a distinct political dimension, which will impact on all levels of operations.

Military Operations in OOTW

To test the validity of the doctrine to OOTW, what is more useful than defining it, is to identify which operations the military will conduct in this environment. Traditional peacekeeping and support for the police during civil disorder should be excluded here, as not necessarily involving military forces deployed to fight. These are deployments where the presence of military force poses a threat of subsequent military operations. They therefore fall below the threshold at which a war-fighting doctrine like Manoeuvre Theory should come into play and deserve unique treatment. It is the difference between peacekeeping and peacemaking. By the same argument internal security operations are included as the application of armed force against insurgents who are by definition themselves in a state of armed insurrection. It is an important distinction, resisting dilution of a war-fighting doctrine on the one hand and acting as a precaution against the misuse of military force on the other. The types of military operations relevant to OOTW therefore become:

   a. Counter-Insurgency. This includes internal security and counter–terrorism.

   b. Intervention Operations. These include rescue missions, short-term offensive operations to achieve or protect political aims and peacemaking.

In attempting to put the role of the military in OOTW into perspective, the final draft of FM100-20 asserts that 'at the operational and strategic levels military operations in OOTW are best understood as indirect operations conducted for military political and psychological effects'.[11] This more subordinate, clearly supportive function, will cause a fundamental shift in the role played by the military in OOTW. If 'the separation of military means and political considerations, especially at the operational level is a basic and closely held tenet of conventional warfare'[12], it is not the case in OOTW. Here political imperatives invariably affect the planning and conduct of military operations not only at the operational, but even at the tactical level. This is an important factor not only in determining the nature and scope of military operations in OOTW, but the appropriateness of doctrine covering them. The doctrine must not jeopardise short term political objectives and must be wholly compatible with the long term political aim. But there is a more difficult consequence of this fact.

Although anathema to the soldier in its raw statement, it is a fact that one of the essential differences between general and limited war and OOTW is that 'defeat may be a legitimate outcome'.[13] This is not to suggest that tactical defeats are acceptable, although there may be restrictions on the degree to which victory can be pursued at the tactical level. But where the survival of the state is not at risk, the political aim may be simply to buy time to address political or socio-economic issues. Alternatively, it may be to apply only enough force to make the insurgents negotiate on the government's terms. 'Victory' may therefore not always be synonymous with 'winning' in the traditional military sense. This concept is most relevant to counter-insurgency where it will be discussed further, but it will also have an impact on other operations in OOTW.

Counter-Insurgency

Revolutionary warfare so epitomises Manoeuvre Theory that it is said that they share a common ancestor in Sun Tzu.[14] The similarities go much further than the obvious analogy of the application of strength against weakness in the tactics of revolutionary war. The study of successful revolutionary wars and insurgencies shows that the insurgents invariably held the initiative, forcing their opponents to be reactive. This edge of initiative rested in most cases on the key elements of Manoeuvre Theory – surprise, tempo, and simultaneity.

Insurgent Strategies

The insurgent achieves surprise by the denial of intelligence. This is possible for an enemy who by definition has at least the passive support of a large part of the population. This allows the guerrilla to achieve J. F. C. Fuller's 'moral surprise'[15] of the conventional battlefield – where the enemy does not know you are coming – on nearly every occasion. The security forces become tied to the reactive tactics of cut off or damage limitation, as the enemy melts back into the civil population.

In this case speed is not a function of relative mobility, but a product of surprise. If 'surprise can give momentum to movement'[16] on the conventional battlefield, then it has an even higher co-efficient here. The lack of warning time, and therefore response time, and the equally short withdrawal route for the guerrilla, mean he can usually operate inside the security forces' decision cycle, despite his inferior physical mobility. This provides an element of the tempo of guerrilla operations at the tactical level. However the guerrilla is expert at achieving tempo in its true meaning, in that his strategy and even tactics aim to move through activities at such a rate as to make the security forces' responses inappropriate. This is particularly valuable in this form of conflict as it provides not just a tactical edge, but strategic advantage in an environment where any inappropriate actions by the security forces are sure to attract adverse publicity. He practises the technique at all levels simultaneously, the tactical, operational and strategic, where his readiness to move up or down through revolutionary phases gives further impetus to tempo. But military operations are very much a means to an end for the insurgent; it is on the political plane that the decision is sought.

With the possible exception of proponents of the Foco Theory,[17] revolutionaries have generally recognised the need to infiltrate the key organs of government and society. Sun Tzu advocated the subversion of government officials, and the use of fifth columnists and spies. Marx and Lenin saw the importance of winning those groups that are critical to government legitimacy, while the Vietnamese refined the theory even further in their total people's war with the dual political and military arms of their Dau Tranh Strategy.[18] This provides the simultaneity within the political arm of his strategy. If possible he will achieve simultaneity in his military operations, by concentrating for occasional spectacular operations while all the time continuing the individual or small group attacks at the village guerrilla or terrorist level.

The Viability of Attrition Theory

Counter-Revolutionary Warfare (CRW) operations since the Second World War have seen a mixture of attrition and manoeuvrist approaches. However, attrition would seem to be failing or have failed to achieve a favourable outcome in nearly every case, while failure to adopt a manoeuvre approach from the outset unnecessarily prolonged other insurgencies. Space does not permit the cataloguing of all the lessons drawn from these campaigns, but highlighting a few critical issues shows the bankruptcy of an attritional approach.

A major reason for the failure of counter-insurgency campaigns has been the eventual loss of support for the conflict by the domestic populations of both the supported and supporting countries and inevitably by their security forces. The subsequent collapse of the security forces reinforced the concept that the centre of gravity in a counter-insurgency operation is often public opinion, both domestic and international. This centre of gravity is more vulnerable for security forces employing an attritional approach because of what Liddell Hart identified as the 'boomerang effect'. He maintained that even in victory, an attrition warfare approach had a 'boomerang effect' on morale because of the soldiers' aversion to the cost of winning, and that this effect was compounded over time.[19] There can be no denying that believing that the answer to insurgency was in the one word 'firepower' and with phrases like 'find 'em and fight 'em', General William C. Westmoreland exercised an attritional approach in Vietnam.[20] It is also true that he won the conventional war. But even after the very significant victory over the 1968 Tet offensive, the success was forfeited because of the South Vietnamese and American public perception of the cost. Liddell Hart's theory was given a new dimension by the advent of the television war. But television is now a reality in OOTW and makes Van Creveld's observation that 'He who loses to the weak loses and he who triumphs over the weak also loses'[21] even more poignant.

But the central dilemma in applying attrition theory to counter-insurgency has been that it is conceptually inappropriate. It has been widely accepted that failure in CRW campaigns can often be attributed to an inability to match the enemy's concept with our own – trying to play chess while the opposition is playing poker, as the late Sir Robert Thompson once observed.[22] This is relevant at all levels. Strategically there has been a concentration on military means when the enemy was pursuing political and/or diplomatic objectives. The proponent of attrition has a perceptual problem in identifying this subtlety because having deployed force, he will be preoccupied with employing it. The Israelis fell into this trap in their 'Peace For Galilee' operations in 1982 – persisting in indecisive military operations while the Palestinians won the moral and political high ground, as David became Goliath.[23]

At the operational and tactical levels a similar dilemma is faced. Having deployed highly trained troops and conventional firepower and support, the commander with an attritional approach feels compelled to use them. This is despite their inappropriateness to countering the enemy's tactics, which will inevitably see him avoiding battle when the odds are not in his favour. The result, usually encouraged by the insurgent, is an escalation in the level of violence, inevitable civilian casualties and as occurred in South Vietnam and on a smaller scale intermittently in Northern Ireland, propaganda success for the opposition. This danger of force being used because it is there, is particularly relevant to the revolutionary warfare phases one and two. If, as predicted, we can expect the insurgent of the future to avoid phase three and remain at phase two,[24] attrition theory becomes even more irrelevant to future counter-insurgency.

Applying Manoeuvre Theory

The key lesson from successive CRW campaigns has been that the strategic centre of gravity is often public opinion, usually domestic and international, and that the operational centre of gravity is the link between the people and the insurgent.[25] This essential first step is much more likely to be grasped by the commander approaching the problem from a manoeuvrist perspective than one coming from an attritional culture with its focus on the enemy forces. Thereafter Manoeuvre Theory ensures that the tactics adopted are appropriate.

It is helpful from the outset to consider counter-insurgency operations within the Manoeuvre Theory framework of holding and manoeuvre force operations. One Israeli commentator has labelled the objectives in counter-insurgency as being either 'moderate' or 'extensive'. Moderate objectives are those which are 'not', of themselves, designed to solve the underlying problem which insurgency represents. Instead they seek only to attain marginal gains in terms of compellence [sic] and deterrence, or perhaps just point scoring ... for sympathetic public attention at home and abroad.'[26] These are the aims of the holding force operations of counter-insurgency and cover the great bulk of military operations from vehicle checkpoints to most offensive operations. Thinking of them as holding operations is important from both a practical and psychological perspective. From a practical point of view it establishes their relative priority and ensures that military operations do not become an end in themselves – do not become the focus of activity or drive the campaign. Psychologically it prepares those who are to conduct the military operations so that they enter into them with the correct perspective, with realistic individual and group expectations. With what the Americans call 'the right vision of success'. This will both ensure that force is used appropriately and ameliorate Liddell Hart's 'boomerang effect', but most importantly it meets the enemy concept head-on, by acknowledging the protracted nature of the military role.

Extensive objectives call for counter-insurgency operations and political initiatives of a more specific nature. 'At their most ambitious their purpose is to achieve ... politicide [sic] of the adversary: his elimination as an independent actor. Hence they aim to inflict extensive if not complete damage on the insurgent forces and their infrastructure.'[27] These are the manoeuvre force operations of counter-insurgency. They will be a careful mix of political and military activities designed to be decisive, if not in the immediate term, at least in seizing and keeping the initiative. The main effort will be in political measures, as only these can hope to address the root cause of an insurgency by redressing the grievances, re-educating the population or defeating insurgent propaganda. The major problem with this critical facet of CRW operations has historically been that governments and security forces were reactive. Almost accepting literally that counter-insurgency simply meant countering insurgent initiatives.[28] Conceiving these operations within a manoeuvrist framework, as manoeuvre force operations, demands a different approach. It places the focus of these operations on the 'mind' of the enemy, at the strategic level his policy and strategy, and demands we pre-empt it with our own policy and strategy. It requires that we seek to place our strengths, the legitimacy of the government and control of communications, against his weaknesses in these areas. However, it eschews the trap of seeing our military strength as something to pit automatically against his, because of its inconsistency with the political intent. Deep military operations, deep into his infrastructure rather than geographically deep, will also play an essential role. But to achieve most effect, both the government and the security forces need to maximise the potential of the main elements of Manoeuvre Theory, particularly surprise and tempo.

In the decisive battle for the hearts and minds of counter-insurgency it is Manoeuvre Theory's psychological surprise, rather than surprise in time and space at the tactical level, which is pre-eminent. This is because it can be applied more readily at the more decisive operational and strategic levels and directly attacks the acknowledged centre of gravity. In this regard pre-emption is probably the key element of surprise, particularly through pro-active psychological operations, both domestic and international. The worst situation for the government is to become responsive in its information activities, as this is to surrender the initiative. The insurgent must also be surprised by having the points – and even potential – points of grievance pulled from under him before he can fully exploit them. This requires a pro-active programme of social and political reform or public information, as appropriate, and an effective amnesty policy.

Surprise at the operational and tactical levels may be more difficult to achieve and less decisive. However it should be pursued vigorously and tactical successes attributed due weight for their relative value as part of the holding force operations within the overall strategy. In achieving the holding force objectives in counter-insurgency it is enough that the insurgents' operations are thwarted or at least disrupted. This requires giving priority to intelligence activities and particularly countering of the insurgents' intelligence system. Deception becomes an important tool of surprise through infiltration of the enemy by pseudo teams[29] or agents, the use of electronic warfare (EW) and our own protective security measures. At the tactical level the security forces must exploit their relative mobility to mount random checkpoints, ambushes and deep raids, as appropriate to the theatre of operations. Each one is not decisive in itself, but together they help to steal the initiative, to disrupt the enemy's plans, threaten his security, and most importantly, contribute to the picture of defeat in his mind.

The protracted nature of counter-insurgency may seem to negate the need for a warfighting doctrine that emphasises speed and tempo. However, it actually invites the pure application of the terms as intended in the theory. Speed is relative. Exploiting the security forces' natural advantages in mobility, through for instance the use of helicopters, will generate tempo at the tactical level. The 'reconnaissance pull' of Manoeuvre Theory is more correctly 'intelligence pull' in CRW.[30] The more extensive and effective the intelligence network, the greater the tempo that can be generated at both the operational and tactical levels. However, equally important is the ability of the government and security forces to move through cycles more quickly than the insurgent. Types and styles of operation must be changed continually, not giving the insurgent the time to adjust his tactics. The security forces must be prepared and willing to transit through levels and stages of the insurgency campaign and then confront him there with appropriate policies and tactics that retake the initiative.

Simultaneity is all the more important in counter-insurgency because any field left unworked by the government will be exploited by the insurgents. This reinforces the need for active public relations both domestically and internationally, targeting insurgent aims and the infrastructure throughout its depth. It also requires infiltration of the insurgent organisation and at the tactical and operational levels, deep operations. These, which may be a role for special forces, aim to keep the insurgent on the defensive, to deny him freedom of movement and keep him dispersed within the areas he controls.

The Risk

The most obvious risk in employing Manoeuvre Theory in the highly political atmosphere of counter-insurgency is relying on the delegated decision-making implicit in the theory. However regardless of their specific nature, counter-insurgency operations are usually conducted at a very low level. The commander of the Northern Ireland team or the section/squad commander on jungle patrol, will often be faced with decisions in the heat of the moment and without any recourse to higher authority. In these circumstances the only effective control that can currently be exercised by senior commanders is through rules of engagement (ROE) and rules for opening fire (RFOF), (in Northern Ireland the 'Yellow Card'). However, the application of Manoeuvre Theory and its tools would ensure that the commander's purpose, invariably incorporating the political intent, would be communicated down to the lowest levels. It would not take the place of ROE or RFOF, but would be an addition to them. Thus the theory's tools actually provide extra safeguards for the political aims.

The other area of concern is that 'reconnaissance' or 'intelligence pull' might result in lack of control at lower levels, again risking political objectives. However, both the structure of the theory and procedural measures guard against this. Those forces subject to be 'pulled' in this environment are the manoeuvre force elements, while the majority of military operations are holding force ones. The intelligence 'pulling' manoeuvre forces will be controlled at a high level, if only to protect sources. At the same time the authority to mount manoeuvre force operations such as SF strikes in internal security or selected deep offensive operations in CRW, will similarly be held at a high level, usually the operational level of command. While perhaps limiting the free operation of the theory, these procedures cannot be ignored in this environment and certainly do not invalidate it.

Intervention Operations

Intervention operations have become a common feature of OOTW since the mid-1970s. They have varied in nature from punitive raids and rescue missions to operations to overthrow rogue regimes; while in Beirut a multinational force (MNF) peacekeeping operation became intervention, as it was dragged into peacemaking. In 1992 the UN Secretary-General indicated his support for a peacemaking role for UN forces[31] and since then this task for western military forces has grown in importance exponentially. The reluctance of governments to place forces in a situation where they might become involved in a protracted insurgency means peacemaking operations in OOTW will most likely involve very limited objectives. These may be to open ports, airports or even roads, to guarantee relief supplies or secure the evacuation or temporary safety of refugees. Nonetheless the danger will always be that such operations might be subsumed by an extant insurgency – undoubtedly the worst case for an intervention force.

Intervention will therefore continue by design, to involve the projection of a force into another country in operations of limited duration and with limited military objectives, to serve both short- and long-term political aims. The long term aims will vary considerably. However, short-term political objectives will almost invariably include the need for demonstrable success, and to minimise both casualties and collateral damage and time in country. This calls for the military plan to combine speed and minimum force in an operation with a high political profile.

Key Requirements

The degree of speed required will vary in each case, and in peacemaking in particular, may be relative, but it will always be a factor. The requirement is implicit in the nature of an operation that by definition violates national integrity and will be demanded by both domestic and international opinion. In addition, military success may depend heavily on speed. Where the release of hostages or evacuation of expatriates is the aim the requirement is obvious. If seizure of the machinery of government is the objective, it must be done before the regime can mobilise its own defence or support, or escape to face the attacker with at best a prolonged search and at worse an insurgency. In peacemaking operations pre-emption will be a valuable tool, because the application of minimum force early at a decisive point may obviate the need for more force later.

Minimum necessary force is another relative but important factor. Long-term political objectives in particular will seldom if ever be served by excessive civilian and even opposition security force casualties. Even in a punitive raid the force used must not exceed the tolerance of either international or domestic opinion. This principle must be retained not only in planning the operation but also in executing it, and particularly in responding to changes in the situation. The temptation to take purely retaliatory action in response to operational setbacks must be resisted by both politicians and soldiers, if the original political intent is to be protected.

The political intent must be clear and detail both short and long term objectives. Political direction must be exercised efficiently so that it remains valid in what will inevitably be a fast-moving scenario, both politically and operationally. This is obvious in a raid scenario, but equally applicable in peacemaking where local attitudes and intentions towards the intervention force can change rapidly on the basis of either a single local incident, international press reports, or even rumour. It will often mean the local commander has the best idea of what constitutes an appropriate military response, even for political ends.

The Viability of Attrition Theory

In studying previous military intervention operations, it is possible to identify both attrition and manoeuvre philosophies. The concepts for Entebbe, Operation 'Eagle Claw',[32] Son Tay (1970) and arguably Kolwezi (1978), utilised the longest way round and/or speed with varying degrees of success to exploit both tempo and surprise rather than mass. However, the US operations in Grenada (1983) and Panama (1989) used the concept of overwhelming force, which, although perhaps appropriate in the circumstances, was nonetheless a mass solution. Aspects of other operations, such as *Mayaguez* (1975) and the USMC intervention (1982) in Beirut, also reflect the attritional doctrine on which the US and many other western armies were based, making attainment of surprise, tempo and simultaneity extremely difficult.

In many operations there is little doubt that a sense of urgency in execution was either overlooked in the plan or lost in execution. Both *Mayaguez* and Grenada could be said to be successful only because the opposition either released or decided not to harm hostages.[33] The lack of speed in execution has often been attributed to a combination of operational concepts that saw forces so dispersed that they were easily checked by inferior forces, and tactics which relied less on manoeuvre and simultaneity and more on fixing the enemy with ground fire until they could be dealt with by air or naval gunfire. Intelligence oversights and failures in nearly every operation left the ground formations blind. Speed was also affected by what has been described as a bureaucratic 'mind-set', that saw even certain tactical decisions referred up for at least confirmation by at times the highest levels of government.[34] The propensity to do this was obviously exacerbated by the highly charged political atmosphere. But far from reflecting definitive command arrangements, this over-direction on the one hand, was often operating in parallel with very confused chains of command at lower levels.

The separation of planning and conduct, sometimes necessary to obtain speed in initial deployment, meant that even senior tactical commanders were often not fully aware of the political intent.[35] The *ad hoc* nature of a joint force, frequently thrown together at short notice, was often further complicated by lack of time for rehearsal and being forced to use dispersed concentration areas. This meant that chains of command were not always clear or responsibilities for command fully grasped. On other occasions a preoccupation with security, forced a compartmentalisation of rehearsal and training, and denied participants the reason behind what they were doing. While the US in particular has introduced both procedural and organisational reforms to mitigate their effect, such problems will continue to have an effect on the planning and conduct of future intervention operations.

Although there has doubtless been an underlying understanding of the rule of minimum force in each of these operations, the availability of force sometimes saw initial political objectives placed at risk to meet either military expediency or politically initiated retaliation. The Israeli operations in Lebanon in 1982, the US intervention in Beirut, *Mayaguez* and to a lesser extent Grenada, contained vestiges of this. However, Panama was the notable exception. Here the successful application of mass achieved simultaneity and tempo in a spectacular way. Overwhelming force secured a quick victory at minimum cost. Unfortunately, there are several factors which suggest this approach will not be appropriate in the future.

Despite most Western armies having tried to leave their light and SF forces unscathed by the recent universal troop reductions, accompanying cuts in naval and air forces mean the strategic lift to project these forces is unlikely to be available when required. The problem is exacerbated by the inevitable improvement in the capability of the likely opposition as Eastern armouries empty, thus demanding even higher force levels in the projected force if an attritional approach is to be pursued. Add to this the fact that intervention operations are increasingly being mounted in urban areas,[36] which demand even more troops, and the mass solution, even for the US, seems to have even less utility in the future.

Applying Manoeuvre Theory

Manoeuvre Theory has more utility in these circumstances because its conceptual basis is that it aims to maximise the effectiveness of what political imperatives and lift capability will inevitably cause to be a relatively small force. The theory's focus on the mind or command and control of the opposition, rather than his forces, is an intrinsic safeguard against the unnecessary use of force, thus protecting political aims. A mission rather than enemy orientation and reliance on surprise, tempo and simultaneity rather than raw combat power, mitigate against the spectre of television images of bloody prolonged battles, while also providing a viable solution to the particular tactical problems.

Surprise must be a paramount factor in intervention because without it the only alternative to achieve tempo is recourse to firepower, which will risk political objectives. The initial problem is that Fuller's 'moral surprise' will usually be forfeited by the mandatory negotiation phase that precedes these operations. In addition, long approach routes, the vulnerability of a force landing over a sea or air gap and the predictability of the likely points of entry, will usually simplify the problem of defence for even the most ragtag opposition. In these circumstances commanders must maximise the potential of any indirect approach. The tactician using Manoeuvre Theory will naturally seek this and then support it with a deception plan that focuses on both the enemy military and political command and control. Using Manoeuvre Theory, the aim will be not merely to distract, but to cause a dilemma in the higher government and military decision-making and prolong that dilemma as long as possible.

Once landed, the force is restricted in achieving tactical surprise because the objective will usually be undeniable and, in Third World countries, the routes to it are often limited. With surprise essential but denied in the traditional sense, it must be re-established by achieving tempo. What is being sought is to exploit the inter-relationship between surprise and tempo. To achieve incremental time advantages that will surprise him and through tempo keep him in a state of surprise. This utilises the true meaning of surprise in Manoeuvre Theory. By seeking to place our strength against his weakness, to chose his line of least expectation, we will not only reduce casualties, but create a tempo that achieves psychological surprise.

The speed of initial deployment and build-up, are factors of tempo. But more important are the tactics and organisational factors that generate it. Tactics which emphasise avoidance of strength, such as infiltration, should be exploited to their limit, because accepting strength-on-strength engagements will certainly risk tempo or even defeat in an inevitably light force. It has been relatively easy to introduce agents and SF into a country under civilian cover right up to the assault, and greater use could be made of this 'indirect approach'. But ground force tactics should also use an infiltration technique in conjunction with the 'reconnaissance pull' of Manoeuvre Theory. Commanders may find that the only usable tactical intelligence is what they gain from their integral reconnaissance. This is not only due to the characteristic inadequacy of technical intelligence in these operations, but also because the government may be reluctant to approve advance force operations during the negotiation period. However time will not permit the commander to direct his reconnaissance assets in the traditional way. Instead he must accept being 'pulled' by his reconnaissance in an effort to establish the tempo so essential to success. At the same time he must maintain flexible tactical groupings that allow him to exploit gaps and seize opportunities as they occur. Both the concept and tactics should allow the development of a 'main effort' that marshals not just the firepower of the force, but its mobility assets. The potential contribution of armour to tempo should not be underestimated in these operations. The mere appearance of even a troop of tanks might achieve tempo with much less force than a company of infantry having to fight its way forward.[37]

Inefficient command and control has been identified as one of the most significant weaknesses in several intervention operations. It was not just the tenuous nature of communications, always stretched in this environment, but the inability to adjust plans quickly to changing situations.[38] However if a plan formulated in contact with the enemy is unlikely to survive the first shot, what chance is there for one framed in a possible intelligence vacuum some hundreds or perhaps thousands of kilometres away? Manoeuvre Theory anticipates change and demands the ability to respond to it in its adherents. The 'mission-style' order with its emphasis on what the subordinate is to achieve rather than how, provides this flexibility and is essential if tempo is to be maintained in these operations. The need to frame the commander's intent also imposes a necessary discipline on government to establish clearly its purpose in deploying the military, as well as constraining the force to tactics and actions that support that purpose. Another function of the mission and intent is what Lind called the 'glue' holding the force and plan together.[39] This unifying purpose and hands-off yet implicit control, is a necessary safeguard against the problems inherent in throwing available forces from three services together at short notice or without rehearsal.

Simultaneity can both contribute to tempo and help obviate the need for force. By disrupting his defence in depth it causes him to deploy units from his front line and so helps establish the gaps for the manoeuvre force. This is particularly important where limited resources or geography may restrict the axes available to the main force and risk its becoming bogged down. However it can also contribute to the picture of defeat in the opposition's mind by seizing objectives critical to success and defending them until link-up with the main force is achieved. These may be the tasks of SF forces or agents inserted in advance of the main force and is an action that also protects victory for the intervention force – a major political consideration. Well-timed political or diplomatic initiatives and psychological operations should be an integral element of simultaneity, if we are not to fall into the attrition trap of concentrating only on the opposing military forces. Political initiatives should seek to isolate the opponent diplomatically and so deny him last minute moral or material support. Simultaneity might even extend to flooding the Government with spurious diplomatic initiatives or deadlines to further complicate or slow its decision-making process and so sharpen its dilemma.

The strength of Manoeuvre Theory here is the synergistic effect of surprise, deception and simultaneity for its contribution to tempo, the essential element in an intervention operation. But if Kolwezi, Mogadishu and Entebbe and even Son Tay attest to the possibilities, 'Desert 1' (the ill-fated attempt to rescue the Iranian hostages in 1980) reveals that the theory carries with it both a political and military risk.

The Risk

The mix of delegated decision-making and the availability of greater than normal combat power at very low levels, does risk actions by junior commanders jeopardising the political aim. But both the tools and structure of the theory carry their own safeguards. The use of the commander's intent, inevitably reflecting the political outcome required, should ensure that delegated decisions do not compromise the mission. In addition, soldiers practised in Manoeuvre Theory will automatically identify their roles as either holding or manoeuvre force ones and so be more likely to choose the appropriate level of force, rather than trying to win the fight everywhere. When we superimpose over this the normal use of ROE, we have by applying Manoeuvre Theory, arguably reduced the political risk, not increased it.

The military risk is of overextending the manoeuvre force and therefore not only compromising the mission but inviting destruction of the force. This risk is usually exposed by the need for a complex plan to support the operation, as was the case in Operation 'Eagle Claw', or the imposition of long turn-arounds as the force is built up, as occurred in the *Mayaguez* raid. These elements in a plan strike at the very heart of Manoeuvre Theory as they threaten both the potential mass (the threat) and the tempo of the manoeuvre force. For planners and commanders schooled in Manoeuvre Theory, balancing this risk is the art of applying it, and they would be much better able to do it successfully than officers trained in the attritional approach which refuses to acknowledge that military operations can be launched without perfecting elaborate details. It is no coincidence that the two most successful intervention operations of the last two decades have been executed by Germany (Mogadishu, 1977) and Israel (Entebbe, 1976), both nations with a strong Manoeuvre Theory tradition.

Conclusion

Manoeuvre Theory's attraction in both general and limited war is that it eschews accepting battle for battle's sake and aims to achieve victory with less force, more quickly and at less cost. Philosophically it therefore promises to reconcile the dilemma that the increasing need to use force to resolve tensions in OOTW is accompanied by a growing public and political expectation that operations will be of short duration and minimise collateral damage and casualties. In practice the theory's emphasis on surprise, tempo and simultaneity rather than raw force militates against the excessive use of force, while also providing a sound doctrinal basis for the concepts and tactics to be employed in OOTW.

In counter-insurgency a military schooled in Manoeuvre Theory is much more likely to grasp the essential precondition of any successful campaign, namely that it requires an integrated political and military response. Manoeuvre Theory's common ancestry with many revolutionary theories means it is a conceptually more appropriate doctrine for CRW. Our strategy will match the opposition's. This approach thus removes one of the most common reasons for the failure or unnecessary prolongment of CRW campaigns, that we have simply been fighting the wrong war. Seeing counter-insurgency operations within the context of manoeuvre warfare also places the part played by the military in perspective, as a holding force role. This correctly shifts the responsibility for finding a solution to the government, but also gives the military a realistic expectation of success and so better prepares the soldier mentally for the prolonged nature of counter-insurgency.

Every intervention operation has an imperative for speed, whether it is politically or tactically driven. The traditional response has been to achieve this either through concepts of mass, or through tactics that relied on early recourse to firepower. With the possible exception of Panama, these have only been marginally successful and often imperilled political aims in the process. In the future even the US will be unable to rely on mass to overwhelm the opposition in all but special circumstances. Manoeuvre Theory's emphasis on tempo and surprise aims to maximise the potential of what will inevitably be light and perhaps smaller forces deployed on these operations in the future and so offers the best basis for tactical doctrine.

However it is the unique politico-military nature of OOTW that demands a warfighting doctrine based on Manoeuvre Theory. The use of 'mission-style' orders, which in this environment must incorporate the political purpose in deploying military force, ensures that the soldier is constrained to meet that purpose. Importantly, though, it also demands a discipline of politicians and commanders at the strategic and operational levels, to have clear in their minds the purpose in deploying the military. This lends substance to the concept, often illusive in practice, that operations in this environment require an integrated political and military response. This is a concept that will become even more crucial to success in the post-'Cold War' period, which is already demanding joint and combined operations in increasingly complex scenarios, and ones that exhibit the most challenging aspects of both intervention and counter-insurgency operations.

NOTES

1. Richard E. Simpkin, *Race to the Swift*, Future Warfare Series, Vol.1. (London/Washington DC: Brassey's 1985, 1988) p.133.
2. B.H. Liddell Hart, *Strategy – The Indirect Approach*, 3rd ed. (London: Cassell 1954) p.288.
3. Simpkin (note 1) p.225.
4. Liddell Hart (note 2) pp.205–6.
5. Ibid. p.184.
6. Ibid. p.25.
7. William S. Lind, *Maneuver Warfare Handbook* (Boulder, CO: Westview 1985) pp.4–6.
8. Liddell Hart (note 2) p.337.
9. The term is used here in its accepted military meaning. Note that Simpkin (note 1, p.148) states that 'The Russians regard two actions as simultaneous if one follows the other within the enemy's response time at the level affected.'
10. *Operations in Low Intensity Conflict*, FM-100 Series, Dept. of the Army/Dept. of the Air Force, Dec. 1989 (Final Draft) p.vi; *The Design for Military Operations: The British Military Doctrine* (Revised ed. 1996) pp.3–43.
11. *Operations in Low Intensity Conflict* (note 10) p.vi.
12. Grant T. Hammond, 'Low Intensity Conflict: War By Another Name', *Small Wars and Insurgencies* 1/3 (Dec. 1990) p.270.
13. Arthur V. Grant, 'Strategic Decisions: The Mire of Low Intensity Conflict', *Comparative Strategy* 10 (1991) pp.167–8.
14. Simpkin (note 1) p.311.
15. Ibid. p.182.
16. Liddell Hart (note 2) p.337.
17. The Foco Theory is based on the presumption that if a government lacks legitimacy, action by even small armed groups will of themselves lead to mass rebellion.
18. *Operations in Low Intensity Conflict* (US Army and General Staff College 1992) pp.31–4.
19. Liddell Hart (note 2) p.186.
20. Sir Robert Thompson, *Make for the Hills* (London: Leo Cooper 1989) p.151.
21. Martin van Creveld, *The Transformation of War* (NY Free Press 1991) p.174.
22. Thompson (note 20) p.153.
23. R. Cohen-Almagor, 'The Intifada Causes, Consequences and Future Trends', *Small Wars and Insurgencies* 21 (April 1991) p.24.
24. Simpkin (note 1) p.289.
25. Sir Robert Thompson, *Defeating Communist Insurgency*, Studies in International Security 10 (London/NY: Chatto/Praeger 1966) p.56.
26. Stuart A. Cohen and Efraim Inbar, 'Varieties of Counter-insurgency Activities: Israel's Military Operations Against the Palestinians, 1948–90', *Small Wars and Insurgencies* 2/1 (April 1991) p.43.
27. Ibid. p.43.
28. Thompson (note 25) p.50.
29. Pseudo teams are teams of security force personnel who adopt the guise of the enemy and are introduced as guerrilla teams within guerrilla controlled areas. They were used

successfully in Kenya and Malaya.
30. J.R. Paget, 'Revolutionary Warfare and Manoeuvre Warfare: Its Relevance and Relationship', *Central Region vs Out-of-Area: Future Commitments* (eds) Maj.-Gen. J.J.G. Mackenzie and Brian Holden Reid (London: Tri-Service Press 1990) p.152.
31. Report of the Sec.-Gen. on the Work of the Organization, 'An Agenda For Peace' (UN June 1992) pp.10–13.
32. The codename for the abortive 1980 attempt to rescue US hostages in Tehran.
33. Despite the fact that ensuring the safety of American citizens on Grenada was the first of three strategic objectives, the last group of students was not secured until day four of the operation. See Daniel P. Bolger, *Americans at War 1975–86* (Novato, CA: Presidio Press 1988) pp.295 and 349.
34. As examples, the tactical deployments and even use of fire support by 24th MAU in Beirut were referred to the White House. (See Richard A. Gabriel, *Military Incompetence – Why the American Military Doesn't Win* [NY: Hill & Wang 1985] p.134.) The bombing runs against the Kompong Song port facilities, originally conceived to support the raid on Tang Is, were alternatively switched on and off by direct intervention of the White House. (See Christopher Jon Lamb, *Belief Systems and Decision Making in the Mayaguez Crisis* [U. of Florida Press 1989] pp.107–20.)
35. The Longmore Commission into the Beirut intervention reported that 'perceptions of the basic mission varied at different levels of the chain of command.' Gabriel (note 34), p.135.
36. Richard Szafranski, 'Thinking About Small Wars', *Parameters* 20/3 (Sept. 1990) p.43.
37. The appearance of tanks at the Governor's residence in Grenada allowed the siege of its SEAL defenders to be raised with little more than a demonstration. (See Gabriel [note 34] p.168.)
38. Ibid. p.147.
39. Lind (note 7) p.14.

The Buffalo Thorn:
The Nature of the Future Battlefield

ALISTAIR IRWIN

Among the innumerable wonders of the African plant kingdom, *Ziziphus mucronata* (the Buffalo Thorn) is one of the more humble. Its stems grow and extend in zigzag fashion. At each tack the stems sprout two thorns. One projects sharp and rapier-like in the direction of growth; the other, shorter but no less sharp, curls back towards the tree's roots, as if it were the toe of a caliph's slipper. The Zulus see in this tree an allegory of life. The zigzags represent the unpredictable and unexpected twists and turns in a man's life. The longer thorns thrusting confidently into the future represent the opportunities of life, the chances which, if seized, will bring benefit and reward. And the retrospective, hook-like thorns are all those traditions, prejudices and experiences that tie man to his past. In the Buffalo Thorn the professional soldier may recognise the Zulu's allegory of life; he may also see a representation of *la vie militaire*.

The general's first duty is to win his nation's battles. He cannot be certain when and where these will take place, since the zigzags of global geopolitics have none of the elegant symmetry of the Buffalo Thorn. The general's second duty is to prepare himself and his men as best he can in the periods of peace that precede conflict. It has been a frequent criticism by historians and contemporary commentators that generals have performed this second duty imperfectly; when battle came it was not the battle for which they had prepared. So initially at least many generals have also failed in their first duty. The professional soldier has to pay as much attention to the future, the thorns of opportunity, as to the lessons of the past, the thorns of wisdom – but of inertia too. Keeping the perspectives of the past, present and future in balance is one of the more demanding tricks that the soldier must master.

Never was this more important than in the 1990s, since it seems possible that the turn of the century will witness one of those defining moments which change the character and form of warfare so profoundly that it will be neither appropriate nor sufficient to continue to prepare for battle as we have done in the latter decades of the twentieth century. Such moments have occurred in the past. The appearance successively of iron weapons, the horse, gunpowder, breech-loading rifles and guns, the mass production of the industrial age, air power, mechanisation and nuclear weapons have all forced dramatic reviews of the conduct of war. The advent of what some refer to as Information Age warfare[1] demands a similar review. Such is the purpose of this essay, which will attempt to articulate a view of future warfare, its character and how to engage in it. In order to avoid stretching the reader's credulity well beyond its natural limits, and so as to maintain a recognisable link with the familiar territory of today, we shall set our sights on 2025 as the year of future war.

It was George Eliot who said that 'among all forms of mistake, prophecy is the most gratuitous' and it is with no little humility that one approaches the task of describing tomorrow's wars. Whether it be H. G. Wells[2] B. H. Liddell Hart[3] or Martin van Creveld,[4] the military soothsayer may at worst entertain and at best provoke debate. Rarely will he persuade: The *Army Quarterly*, reviewing J. F. C. Fuller's *The Foundations of the Science of War*, commented that the danger, 'is that the young might take it too seriously',[5] implying the unwelcome danger that this might challenge their elders to abandon entrenched positions. The future cannot be proved. Trends may be called in evidence and even these may prove unreliable witnesses. And when it comes to technological innovation, what trend advertised the advent of, for example, the aeroplane? What new artefact of war may we expect to see within the next 25 years? The *Design for Military Operations: British Military Doctrine*[6] has it thus:

> Predicting the future of modern warfare is a notoriously unreliable process. Armies must, however, plan and train for future conflict on the basis of some indication of the likely nature of war. A middle course must be steered between experience (armies are often accused of training for the war they fought last) and projections of futuristic weapons (whose technology may be unproven and whose cost may be prohibitive).

It is with these strictures in mind that we might now peer into the future, assuming, as a soldier must, that armed conflict will continue to be an inevitable part of the human condition.

The Dogs of Future War

As to its form, there can be less certainty. As the world approaches the millennium it is instructive to take an inventory of the means currently available for prosecuting war. At the epicentre are modern forces equipped with the latest high technology fighting and communications systems. Foremost among these – we might term them information age forces[7] – the United States sets a standard in the exploitation of technology which, for reasons of cost, the United Kingdom and others aspire to but are unlikely fully to match. Surrounding this advanced epicentre is a mass of forces whose organisations and equipment owe more to the past than to the future. Such forces, which we might term industrial age forces, belong mostly but not exclusively to the nations of the developing world. Industrial age armies will often arm themselves with second-hand fighting systems no longer required by more advanced armies. These forces are likely to be larger than information age armies, if qualitatively inferior.[8] And enveloping all these are those groups whose war fighting is characterised by terrorism, insurgency and subversion. For convenience we shall call these groups 'minimalist'.

Information age, industrial age and minimalist forces exist in the 1990s; they will still be with us in 2025. For centuries minimalist forces have swarmed like jackals around regular forces, scavenging among the detritus of battle, picking off the weak and unnerving the strong. There is no evidence to suggest that such forces have had their day. Indeed the contrary is the case. There are powerful arguments to support the proposition that minimalist forces have a secure future. They are relatively cheap. Expensive organisations and bureaucracies are not required. Logistic and administrative arrangements can largely be handled on an individual or local basis. Weapons and ammunition can usually be obtained on an as-required basis at attractive rates; in any event, there will be little or no need for the advanced and complex fighting systems at the high-cost end of the market. Minimalist forces are especially difficult to combat, particularly for a democracy. For them there are no rules, no uniforms, no front line, no inhibitions or limitations, no territory to defend. So the minimalist can choose where and when to strike; he can appear and disappear, cloaking himself in the darkness of the underworld.

For those that oppose him, the difficulties are intense. These are not two boxers facing each other in the dark,[9] but rather two boxers one of whom is invisible. How can he be found if he cannot be seen? How can he be attacked if he cannot be found? The minimalist has all the advantages. The attractions of indulging in this form of violence are indeed overwhelming, particularly appealing to groups such as drug cartels, international crime syndicates, nationalist organisations operating outside the legitimate political arena, revolutionaries, as well as to the agents of those governments which choose to pursue their ends by terror. All these will have resort to minimalist forces and all of them, or something like them, will be with us indefinitely.

If the attractions of minimalist forces are so obvious, it may seem perverse to argue that industrial and information age armies have an equally bright future. In proclaiming the uselessness of the machinery of war, Martin van Creveld states: 'the plain fact is that conventional military organisations of the principal powers are hardly even relevant to the predominant form of contemporary war'.[10] If this is true, why do such armies continue to exist and why will they still be with us in 2025? It is tempting for some to find an answer in the imagined inertia of the military brain, in a determination to stick with what is familiar and in a desire to preserve the essential elements of an organisation that brings promotion and honour, and from which, through the image of the tank and the self-propelled howitzer, springs an appealing degree of machismo. As one recent work has put it: 'Changing any military's doctrine, however, is like trying to stop a tank armour by throwing marshmallows at it. The military, like any huge bureaucracy, resists innovation – especially if the change implies the downgrading of certain units and the need to learn new skills and to transcend service rivalries.'[11] But there is a more fundamental imperative at work. It is simply that so long as industrial and information age armies exist, and so long as there is no other practical way to counter them, no single nation will unilaterally abandon what it has, for fear that it will then be defenceless. Furthermore, until they can no longer sustain the financial burden of the ever-increasing cost of the machinery of warfighting, nations will continue to replace old systems with new so as to maintain their competitive, battle-winning edge. As Fuller put it: 'In all wars, and especially modern wars ... no army [equipped with weapons] of fifty years before any date selected would stand a "dog's chance" against the army existing at this date, not even if it was composed entirely of Winkelrieds and Marshal Neys.'[12] Thus, in the generic sense, there is an inevitability about the need to match the forces of others, like with like; if someone else has an armoured warfare capability, you have an absolute need for one as well.

So for the next 30 years or so it seems certain that examples of all three types of armed force will continue to be experienced around the world. If so, and if circumstances demand that conflict occurs, it seems equally certain that, whichever of the three types of force the protagonists possess, they will be used, simply by virtue of their existence.

The Future Battlefield: Minimalist

How then will war be fought? We must first examine the characteristics of the battlefield of the future. The argument so far indicates that there are likely to be two distinct types. The first type is in effect no battlefield at all, since it concerns the minimalist forces discussed above. This is not the place to rehearse in depth the strategies and tactics of insurgents, guerrillas and terrorists;[13] the results of their actions are too frequently paraded on our television screens for us to be unaware of what they are about. But in addition to the familiar toll of bombings, assassinations and subversive activity, we may confidently, if despairingly, look forward to the increasing use of weapons of mass murder and destruction. Nuclear, chemical and biological weapons have been, and will remain, the most feared of the controllable threats to human existence. If once they were exclusively in the hands of societies that could be expected to use them only *in extremis* and in practice not at all, now the expectation has became more of a forlorn hope. No great degree of sophistication or even organisation is needed to plan and execute a chemical or biological attack. March 1995 saw the sarin gas attack on the Tokyo subway system by the Aum Shinrikyo Sect. The Sect has shown to all what perhaps only a few knew before: lethal chemical agents can be easily obtained, easily transported and easily deployed. The same is true of biological weapons, only more so: only very small amounts of agent are needed to achieve a devastating effect. And in a post-Cold War world in which large stockpiles of nuclear weapons appear to be no longer under as strict control as once they were, it is possible that some of these may fall into minimalist hands.

Minimalists have yet another 'invisible' weapon on which to call. By attacking civilian and military computers they may be able to achieve their purposes by paralysing the electronic nervous system of information age societies. The US Defense Information Security Agency estimates that 88 per cent of US defence computer systems are vulnerable to some form of electronic intrusion,[14] leading to the theft or destruction of information and the possibility of catastrophic failure caused by electronic assault. Civilian systems will be equally vulnerable. Successful attacks on banks and stock exchanges, for example, could cause financial collapse to the extent that governments and societies might even start to disintegrate. The minimalist will find the bargaining power of such actions to be at least as significant as anything achieved by physical violence. What is more, the skills and equipment required to carry out electronic attacks on information systems are readily available, cheaply acquired and are likely therefore to be exploited.

As suggested earlier, for democracies, rightly determined to operate within the rule of law, the terrorist nut is an especially challenging one to crack. Hitherto terrorism has presented a hideous but manageable problem, in the sense that, taking due account of the human grief suffered, no modern Western democracy has come close to being toppled by the actions of minimalists. The awesome developments described above might threaten this record. Defences against terrorism must be as comprehensive as against any other form of attack. In parenthesis it should be observed that it is misleading to suppose that minimalist conflict implies low technology weapons and equipment; in some areas, particularly in electronics, this form of warfare is as highly technical as any other.

The Future Battlefield: Warfighting

The second battlefield is the one that naturally comes to mind when considering the word, namely the battlefield associated with warfighting, with armoured warfare, the clash of disciplined and recognised national armies. By studying the development of warfighting from the giant operations of manoeuvre on the Eastern Front in the Second World War, through the wars of national survival fought by the Israelis, to the destruction of Saddam Hussein's armies by a coalition in the Gulf War of 1991, one may detect indicators as to how this form of war will be fought in the first quarter of the next century – in the information age.

The Influence of Culture

The indicators are not as unequivocal as perhaps we might like. The chances of conflict occurring between forces that are more or less balanced in equipment and method seem quite remote. This lack of balance will be heightened by potential differences in attitudes to casualties, international law and public opinion: Western values cannot be attributed to all potential opponents. Of these differences, attitudes to casualties, whether inflicted or suffered, might be the most difficult with which to deal. 'Every minute, tens of thousands of men die. Even if they are Vietnamese that doesn't mean much.'[15] To note these words of General Vo Nguyen Giap is to question how possible it will be for armies with Western values to handle enemies characterised by such indifference. Those same Western values will demand an opposite effect: minimum casualties on both sides.

As to the law, the greater the minimalist characteristics of a conflict the less likely it is that the international laws of war will be observed by all parties. It is not even certain that it will be possible to trust industrial and information age armies to stay within the bounds of what is considered to be just and legal; one needs only to cite the name and deeds of Saddam Hussein to undermine any confidence in this regard.

And finally, there will be imbalance caused by the manner in which the news media report the conflict, and by the manner in which the opposing populations react to what they are told. The propaganda and deceit purveyed by puppet and compliant news organisations, a feature of dictatorships and police states, serve to solidify public support for the conflict or at least to suppress criticism of it. Meanwhile the Western media seek to portray events as they are, regardless (or perhaps all too well-aware) of the political and popular reactions that this will generate. So a population, already inclined to shy away from the inevitable consequences of war, will absorb images and words that will serve to undermine the nation's resolve, creating an imperative to bring potentially bloody encounters to an early conclusion.[16] Even before conflict erupts, differing public attitudes will play their part in how nations will construct their armies. For many, conscription ensures a fully manned force. For others, military service is still valued so highly that recruiting presents no difficulties. And there are those nations, the United Kingdom included, whose populations find it increasingly difficult to find the men and women needed to fill the ranks of its armed forces. For such nations, the manning issue becomes a powerful influence both on the force design process and on the way in which battle can be fought.

The Influence of Technology

Notwithstanding the above, it is clear that technology will be the ultimate arbiter of what can be done and how. As John Keegan puts it, referring to the superseding of copper and stone by bronze in the fashioning of weapons: 'Man bent to the almost universal rule that a superior technology obliterates an inferior one as fast as the necessary techniques and materials can be found.'[17] There will be improvements in the performance and capabilities of the weapon systems with which we are presently familiar. Missiles and gun-launched munitions will achieve longer ranges with greater precision. Mobility will improve both as regards speed and overcoming obstacles. Protection levels offered by a given weight of armour will improve; the ability to penetrate that armour will also increase. But all these improvements and developments will be achieved by a series of quantum (in the literal sense) steps, because we are reaching the limits of what is physically and practically achievable. Some commentators would find such a view to be unduly conservative.

Alvin Bernstein offers a more adventurous vision:

....what might be called 'fire-ant' warfare (fire-ants are small fiercely stinging, omnivorous ants). This innovation envisages a battlefield covered with millions of micro-chip sensors (small objects that give off signals), microbots (tiny robots), and mini-projectiles (extremely small munitions that do damage not because of their size but because of their speed), all linked together by a sophisticated command and control system made possible by miniaturisation (the science of making things smaller) and integrated software (sophisticated computer software designed to integrate and process information very quickly), capable of co-ordinating extraordinary amounts of information in a tiny fraction of a second.... Precise accuracy will force personnel out of vulnerable tanks, surface ships, and manned aircraft. Eventually, these large platforms will simply be outnumbered by systems of small but extraordinarily effective items all working in harmony toward a single lethal end.[18]

Even if these predictions, and others like them, do indeed represent Keegan's 'superior technology that obliterates an inferior one', it is surely stretching the credulity of even the most free-thinking soldier to suppose that these will materialise by 2025. This scepticism may remind the reader of General Sir Archibald Alison, who in 1886 expressed extreme resistance to the idea that the telephone might supersede the telegraph as a means of military communication, or of Brigadier Bernard Fergusson's 'Old Guard of very senior generals [who were, in 1936] mentally as well as literally horse-drawn'.[19] But the bets must be placed somewhere and it would be bold indeed to gamble with the nation's defences by putting money on these outsiders.

There are more fancied runners in the grand military technology stakes. Already parading in the paddock are several developments that seem certain to play an increasingly significant role in the land battle. We can expect to see the appearance of non-lethal weapons (NLW) such as incapacitants and immobilisers, and directed energy weapons (DEW), such as lasers but these will complement more conventional inventories; they will neither replace them nor fundamentally alter the principles by which war is fought. Stealth technology, already familiar in the air, will help to decrease the signatures of key equipments, but is unlikely to remove the continued need for high levels of physical protection and good fieldcraft.

It is only in digitisation that we may expect to see a change in the technology of warfighting so significant as to cause soldiers and their commanders to re-examine how they should fight their battles. Digitisation is the term generally used to describe the process in which all elements on the battlefield are bound together by an electronic web that permits the rapid transfer of data – to commanders so that they can make their decisions and issue orders, and to weapon platforms so that fire can be applied precisely where and when it is needed.

There has always been a requirement to pass information. The means to do so, initially primitive, have progressively set new standards in reliability and capability. In that sense there is nothing new in the idea of digitisation. What has caused the recent excitement in military circles is the opportunity afforded by new advances in the science of communications and data processing to make significant increases in the volume and extent of information that can be transmitted, thereby speeding up the command process. This introduces tempo[20] into the argument. The requirement is to achieve a higher rate of activity than the enemy, to make decisions and act faster than he can. As Fuller put it: 'Every principle of war becomes easy to apply if movement' [and, one might add, action] 'can be accelerated and accelerated at the expense of the opposing side.'[21] If this can be achieved the enemy will always be on the back foot, out-thought and out-manoeuvred; no matter how strong he might be in other respects, he will always be reacting. Never in control of events, he will lose the battle as surely as the bull in the *corrida*. Digitising the battlefield will provide everybody on it with a common picture of what is going on; more information about the ground, the enemy and own troops; the means to develop plans and pass orders far more quickly than is currently possible; automatically bring co-ordinated firepower to bear on key targets in the close and deep battles with speed and precision; and control and co-ordinate movement and logistic support much more efficiently.

But we must be cautious in basing predictions on such capabilities. It is easy to be deluded into an inflated view of what may be possible. The disciples of digitisation, in their more enthusiastic moments, give the promise of a wholly transparent battlefield on which one side knows everything and the other knows nothing which the first does not want him to know. The prospect of automated command and intelligence systems that will flatten command hierarchies and reduce decision and action cycles to immeasurably small dimensions is flaunted temptingly before our eyes. Many obstacles will intervene to make these prospects very much less than fully attainable. There is, for example, a serious question as to whether there will be sufficient bandwidth in the electromagnetic spectrum to carry all the data, however much it may be compressed, that everyone on the battlefield will demand to receive. The frustrations will be those of the committee member who has something to say but cannot catch the chairman's eye. Even with the most efficient of data management systems there can be no guarantee that the vital piece of information gets through while the less important waits its turn. Meanwhile the enemy will not be inactive. Not only will 'Intelligence, Surveillance, Target Acquisition, Reconnaissance' (ISTAR) systems be prime targets for destruction or neutralisation but so too will the command headquarters and the communications which link them. More mundanely, but equally threatening to the vision of a transparent battlefield, the cost of acquiring the means to achieve it will be high. The money spent on digitisation will not be available for weapons and vehicles; it seems more than probable that digitisation to the extent that technology might allow will not be affordable. For all these reasons the general's view of the battlefield will never be as comprehensive as a grand master's view of the chessboard; and even the chess-player cannot read his opponent's mind with the certainty that brings absolute confidence (and that, of course, is the whole point of the game and the whole risk of the battle). It is a curious paradox that, despite the obfuscation of artillery and musket smoke in 1815, and despite all the technological assistance available today, it is probable that Wellington knew far more about what was going on at Waterloo than any future general will know on his own battlefield. The fog of war may eddy and thin, but the general will still have to peer uncertainly through it.

The Joint Nature of Operations

With these remarks as a basis, it is possible to identify six characteristics of the future battlefield. First, battle will be fought jointly with naval and air forces, both national and, in the international context, in combined operations. So far this essay has referred exclusively to armies, but this has been misleading shorthand. Although inter-service rivalries seem often to deny it, modern war cannot be fought except in the joint context. Without air support, land and sea forces are fatally vulnerable to enemy air attack; without air support land and naval operations are unlikely to prosper. Air operations are valueless unless they are conducted in concert with land operations and achieve nothing unless they are consolidated by land forces. As in so much of what follows, there is nothing new about this.[22] These truths have been learned repeatedly from the first large-scale use of military aviation in the First World War to most recently in the 1991 Gulf War and the NATO intervention in Bosnia.[23]

The Pace of Battle

The second characteristic lies in the pace of battle. It will be fought non-stop until a result is achieved. Although extreme weather conditions will continue to impose insuperable restrictions on movement, it will not be possible to rely on the convenience of withdrawing to winter quarters to await in tranquillity the arrival of the next campaigning season. Nor can we rely on the pause at dusk; happy the times when fighting was a daytime business only. Technology has now provided the fighting man the opportunity to operate continuously and with the same facility by day and night, in fair weather or foul. The equipment may be equal to the task but for how long can the human frame cope with the stresses of continuous battle? The problem is increased by the expectation that future battle will be fought at an even more furious pace than before. This will be because things will happen very quickly, either in actual fact, because of the greater speed of land and air vehicles, enabling combatants to manoeuvre more rapidly; or in perception, because of a complex interaction between the volume of information that will be available, the speed at which it becomes available (through the medium of the digitised battlefield) and the inevitable circumstance in which a breakdown of communications, deception and surprise all become features. Either way there will be an increasing need for war fighters to absorb information rapidly and react rapidly. The consequences of not being able to do so are vividly described by Alistair Horne in his study of the fall of France in 1940.[24] In a haunting vignette he quotes an eyewitness to the reaction of General Alphonse Georges, commanding the North-East front, to the news that General Heinz Guderian's Panzer Corps had broken through the French defences on the Meuse. The eyewitness reports:

> The atmosphere is that of a family keeping vigil over a dead member. Georges rises ... he is terribly pale. 'Our front has been pushed in at Sedan. There have been some failures (*défaillances*)' he says. He falls into an armchair and a sob silences him. It was the first man that I had seen weep in this battle. I was to see many others, alas. It made a dreadful impression on me.

Here is the picture of a man who has had the initiative comprehensively removed from his grasp. This was in the comparatively slow-moving days of 1940. How much greater will be the pressures in the future!

The Scale of Battle

The third characteristic of the future battlefield will be its scale. On the one hand theatres of operations are likely to be extensive in their physical size. In this they will be no different to those that have been experienced in the past. In the case of general war (which one may assume is the least likely but the most dangerous eventuality) there will be no intrinsic geographic limits. In regional conflicts, by definition, there will be clearly understood boundaries within which hostilities will occur. The extent of economic and political interest, the reach of communications and the range of strategic and tactical transport will tend to expand these boundaries. In sharp contrast will be the size of the forces deployed within the theatre of operations. The ever-increasing cost of armed forces are certain to lead to armies which will be no larger than they are today and which may be even smaller. A return to the mass armies of the first half of this century is out of the question. Nations will simply be unable to afford to equip or man large forces: US Secretary of Defense, Richard B. Cheney, is quoted as saying that 'budget drives strategy, strategy doesn't drive budget'.[25] At the same time these smaller forces will deliver more fighting power, size for size, than has been possible in the past. Already a contemporary armoured brigade possesses the equivalent fighting power of a Second World War armoured division in terms of the volume and lethality of firepower that it can deliver. More significantly perhaps, the range of its surveillance and reconnaissance equipments, and of its direct and indirect fire weapons, allow it to dominate a far greater stretch of 'battle space'. Study of divisional deployments reveals an interesting trend. A First World War division could typically cover a frontage of about six miles. The equivalent figure for a Second World War division is ten miles; in the mid-1980s a divisional frontage might have been as much as 20 miles.[26]

Thus far there is no evidence of this trend being halted, far less reversed. So the future battlefield will be large in scale and on it increasingly small but powerful forces will manoeuvre with potentially greater freedom. This gives rise to the notion of the less dense battlefield in which there will be more room to move, and where the dividing lines between opposing forces will be much less clearly defined than they have appeared to be in the past. There will continue, of course, to be concentrations of force at places where a decision is sought; for those involved at the tip of the bayonet the battlefield will remain as it always has been – local, small-scale and chaotically crowded. The experience of the Battle of Britain is a useful analogy: vast expanses of empty sky in which concentrations of fighters and bombers suddenly clash for a period of hectic activity, before the skies abruptly empty while opposing forces regroup and manoeuvre for the next encounter.[27] Future land battles will resemble these battles in the air.

The Multi-Dimensional Battle

The fourth characteristic will be multi-dimensionality. British Army doctrine[28] has recognised that at brigade level and above there are three land battles to be fought: the deep, close and rear. The rear battle is protective in nature, ensuring a benign environment for logistic support and for the movement and deployment into action of the second echelons and reserves; the deep and close battles take the battle to the enemy. For best effect they should be fought simultaneously, so that the enemy is engaged throughout his depth, causing dislocation and disruption. To these three dimensions we may add, in the context of joint operations, a fourth, the battles in and from the air. And were we to be conducting littoral operations we might add two more: on- and below-water.

This six dimensional physical battlefield of the future will be overlaid by a seventh dimension, a super-destructive plasma, an invisible battlefield inhabited by chemical, biological and electronic agents. We have already seen how these may be used by minimalists. They are also options for the war-fighting commander. Priority will be given to electronic agents, operating in the electromagnetic spectrum and targeted against the enemy's command and control (C2) systems. Military activity in the electromagnetic spectrum has been increasing steadily. Armies' reliance on radio communications is already almost total. If the enemy's C2 systems can be neutralised there is a real possibility of achieving the near bloodless victories that will be demanded, for with no C2 brain the armoured fist will unclench and rattle into uselessness. Among the earliest Coalition targets in the Gulf War were Iraqi 'microwave relay towers, telephone exchanges, switching rooms, fibre optic nodes, and bridges that carried co-axial communications cables'.[29] By 2025 this will be a dominant feature of the land battle. Domination of the electro-magnetic spectrum will be at least as important as domination of the air and ground environments. The battles fought in it will have no visual impact for the spectator but their result will profoundly affect the outcome of the entire operation. This dimension of the battlefield, so often in the past left to the technical experts, will demand as much of the commander's attention as the land battles.

The invisible battlefield will also threaten human beings. Although many nations, the United Kingdom included, have forsworn their use, chemical weapons (CW) will be a major influence on the character of the future battlefield. Despite being susceptible to prevailing weather conditions and indiscriminate in their application, CW offer tempting military advantages to those not deterred by the moral and environmental implications of using them. Indeed, the threat itself may be sufficient to cause useful degradation of the enemy's fighting power, caused by the need to adopt cumbersome protective measures. Biological weapons (BW) represent an even more malign threat, but their insidious characteristics seem to have much more in common with the minimalist approach to conflict, being even more imprecise than CW in targeting terms. Rational judgements may tend to write down the significance of BW, but as delivery and propagation techniques improve it is perhaps unduly optimistic to suggest that BW will play only a relatively minor role on the future battlefield.

Nuclear weapons are wild cards that would intrude indiscriminately into all seven dimensions, overshadow the whole future battlefield, the ultimate Sword of Damocles. If used by one side only, they would bring a conflict to an abrupt end. If used by both sides they would so profoundly change the nature of the conflict that those still fighting would almost certainly have to extemporise; the destruction of a nuclear exchange would be so wholesale that attempts to forecast what may happen in its aftermath seem quite pointless.

It would be legitimate to protest that there is nothing novel in the proposition of multi-dimensionality, except perhaps in the terminology.

What may be new now and for the future is the recognition that all the dimensions of battle will be so inextricably interconnected that it will be essential to fight future battle as a single entity under a single commander, and not, as so often in the past, as a series of separate and imperfectly co-ordinated operations under dispersed and sometimes rival commands.[30]

Manoeuvre

The future battlefield will be in a state of constant flux. Situation maps (electronically displayed of course) will portray the progress of battles in which manoeuvre and counter-manoeuvre will be punctuated by fierce exchanges of direct and indirect fire, 'the skilful offensive use in combination of all available weapons, based on the principle of manoeuvre'.[31] Always the aim will be to unhinge the enemy's plan rather than, for its own sake, to destroy him. But Liddell Hart's 'perfection of strategy ... to produce a decision – the destruction of the enemy's armed forces through their unarming by surrender – without any fighting' will be achieved only in the rarest of circumstances; attritional engagements will be unavoidable.[32] Ground will continue to be fought for and held, usually in the context of how that ground can be used as an anchor for a further manoeuvre against the enemy rather than for its own intrinsic importance. Commanders and their troops will be spurred on by a spirit of restlessness, an attitude of mind, that will put them always on the front foot straining to break into the enemy's flank and rear. Set-piece battles, 'teed-up', Montgomery style, will be exceptional.

The Human Element

The final characteristic of the future battlefield which must be addressed is the most enduring of them all. We must not allow ourselves to believe that technology will somehow remove the realities of war from the field of battle. Whatever weaponry may be placed in the hands of tomorrow's soldiers, battle will ultimately involve the brutish business of closing with the enemy and engaging him in mortal combat face to face. This unpleasant business will be in the hands of men and, by 2025, women, who will be cold, tired, hungry and frightened. They will have to display the same degrees of courage and determination as their forbears; their commanders will require all the qualities of leadership that have been necessary in the past. In theory, it may be possible to fight wars remotely, unmanned systems engaging unmanned systems, destroying each other but causing no damage to the human beings whose battles, by proxy, they are fighting. But this automated form of ritualistic war by championship assumes that it can be fought in a vacuum, free of population, and that the human bystanders will accept the outcome of this clash of machines. Neither assumption stands the

THE NATURE OF THE FUTURE BATTLEFIELD 241

test of examination, least of all the human angle. If humans believe in a cause sufficiently to fight for it they will not concede victory until either they are killed or their mental resolve is destroyed; the destruction of their machines will not achieve this. Furthermore it is only the fear of death or injury that prevents war from becoming a game and there are no limits as to how often games (Clausewitz's 'war by algebra') may be played. 'The invention of gunpowder and the constant improvement of firearms are enough in themselves to show that the advance of civilisation has done nothing practical to alter or deflect the impulse to destroy the enemy, which is central to the very idea of war.'[33] Unmanned warfare may one day be possible, but it would have no point.

A Vision of Future War

From these descriptions of our two battlefields, the terrorist and the warfighting, we can derive a broad vision of future war. In describing them as separate entities, it is not suggested that a future war will necessarily be fought exclusively on one or the other. It is much more likely that elements of both will be closely intermingled during the course of conflicts that will defy tidy categorisation. As John Colvin puts it, in explaining General Giap's campaigns in Vietnam:

> Guerrilla warfare, in its wide expansion into the countryside, has been the political, then the military *fons et origo* of victory, sealing the mountains and plains to the enemy. But not for ever, or not uniquely. Methods changed with the situation, tactical or strategic. Politics was both the key and the objective. Giap's total war included guerrilla action, mobile warfare, uprising, main-force battle, political action at home and abroad through 'foreign friends', often concurrent and all under unremitting political, 'moral' and military direction.[34]

This may be a blueprint for some at least of the conflicts that are to come, which, at one extreme, may be fought between information age and industrial age opponents, at the other between minimalist forces, and with a range of combinations in between.

As if this was not difficult enough, we must recall that Britain's army, if current experience and trends continue, is likely to be increasingly called upon to fulfil missions that are not predominantly adversarial. These fall under the heading of what the British Army and other Western armies currently refer to, somewhat euphemistically, as peace support operations (PSO), encompassing peacekeeping, peace enforcement and humanitarian operations. Such operations are generally, although not exclusively, carried out under a flag of neutrality and impartiality, often symbolised by white painted vehicles. There is no shortage of danger in these missions and there is often a need to use, or to threaten to use, force. As the Yugoslavian Civil War has demonstrated, PSO may require a range of military responses from humanitarian-orientated logistic operations to a full-blown deployment, with offensive capability. The locations and circumstances of future PSO are if anything even more unpredictable than any other form of operational deployment because the options are not limited to those that might be judged to be in the national interest, themselves difficult enough to foresee. Altruism, a sense of international obligation and public pressures encouraged by reports by the news media will all serve to expand the number of PSO deployments.[35]

Designing The Forces of the Future

The uncertainty, the imbalance, of all this creates a substantial problem for those charged with the development of force structures for the future, and it is to these that we must now turn. The demands and opportunities of advancing military technology combined with the wide spectrum of conflict types[36] have to be accommodated if the Army is to have any utility in the next century. General Sir John Burnett-Stuart wrote in 1932 to Liddell Hart, 'We all know that our present old-fashioned divisions are suicide clubs; but it is not merely a question of reorganising them, but of remodelling the whole military machine and its responsibilities in peace so as to admit of the creation of modern war formations.'[37] In this he went further than we are able for present purposes. Questions relating to the role of reservists, the future of the Territorial Army, the prospects for the British regimental system and the integration of the three fighting services are among the many elements of the 'whole military machine' which will have to be answered before the 'war formations' of the future have been created. Here we shall restrict ourselves to matters of organisation and equipment.

The challenge is to design multi-purpose forces which may be best suited to one form of warfare or another but which may change relatively painlessly the emphasis of their capabilities as global geopolitics, and national intent, dictate. There are two trails to follow: the multi-purpose force and the fighting structure. There is no inherent obstacle to the idea that a force trained and equipped to conduct high-intensity armoured warfare cannot be retrained to engage in some form of minimalist conflict. The most valuable characteristic of a well-led and well-motivated soldier is that he is infinitely adaptable. Given the right training, for which there must be sufficient provision, he will be equally as proficient in the jungle on his feet as in the desert in the back of a fighting vehicle, as steady facing an urban terrorist as an armoured assault. In the same way, a whole army can adapt, although naturally the process takes a great deal longer than for a single soldier or indeed an individual unit. And for an army to be capable of adapting there is an additional consideration, associated with the conceptual component of fighting power.[38]

For a successful transition to be made from one form of conflict to another a standing army must preserve an understanding, a continuing expertise of each of the forms of conflict that it is likely to encounter. It may indeed be possible physically to re-equip and reorganise but if the expertise has gone, faded away with departed warriors, it will be vain to hope that it will be caused to reappear simply be issuing the relevant equipment and reading from some field manual drawn from the archives. This applies to all forms of conflict but most especially to armoured warfare. In so many ways, this represents the greatest challenge for the soldier and his commanders. However testing other conflicts may be, only in this environment is encountered the deeply demanding combination of extreme danger, rapidly changing circumstances in conditions of chaos and uncertainty, severe physical demands and a rate of activity that imposes severe strains on the mental robustness and agility of the participants. A proper comprehension of the consequences of this, a proper understanding of how all the many elements of a joint all-arms operation must be moulded together, these cannot be developed from a zero base. If hot water is required the tap is turned on; but if an armoured (or an anti-minimalist or PSO) capability is required, the tap must be left running all the time, although not necessarily at full flow. Whatever the current emphasis may be, an expertise across the spectrum must be maintained if an army is to demonstrate a credible multi-purpose capability. We may therefore expect an army to include both armoured and light forces among its regular, standing formations.

How will these armoured and light elements be equipped and structured? This is not the place to lay out an answer in fine detail, but from the preceding analysis it is possible to identify at least some of the ways in which future forces will differ from their current form. This is especially the case with armoured forces and it is on these that the rest of the essay will concentrate. The pointers for the future can be classified under the headings of firepower, mobility, command and control, logistics, manpower and training.

Firepower

The firepower of a force will be provided in the future (as it is now) chiefly by a combination of air support, artillery, and direct fire weapons such as anti-tank missiles, and naval support for littoral operations. But in the future the emphasis will shift. Long range engagements will grow in significance. The means to acquire and engage targets at greater ranges will be increasingly available; the force that fails to take advantage of this will find itself out-ranged by an opponent who can attack with all the advantages of the long-armed boxer. Furthermore, the greater the destruction and disruption that can be caused at long range, the less will be the requirement to engage in costly blood-letting in the close battle, thus satisfying the political and public demand to keep casualty lists as short as possible.

The current emphasis on unguided trajectory munitions will swing in favour of precision weapons. Precision will satisfy the demand that only military targets be engaged, although by no means completely; collateral damage in which civilians are killed and their property destroyed will be less and less acceptable. Equally importantly, precision reduces the logistic burden on a force, since fewer rounds must be transported and fired to achieve the same effect. A smaller logistic burden means that less need be spent on supporting a force and more on boosting its firepower. And a smaller logistic tail increases the force's mobility, a subject which will be considered in more detail shortly. It will become clear that greater damage will be done to the enemy by indirect artillery fire (smart munitions delivered by rocket, gun and missile) than by any other element of firepower. We should expect to see a greater proportion of artillery in the force of the future than has been seen in recent times. To create these additional gunners, given a fixed level of force as regards manpower, we can expect to see much smaller numbers of infantry than are presently found.[39] Field-Marshal Earl Wavell's 'Indispensable Infantry'[40] will have a vital but proportionally smaller role to play. There will be very little place on the battlefield of tomorrow for the infantryman who is not mounted on a machine offering the same mobility and protection as the tanks with which he is operating, or for the infantryman who has nothing more than a rifle for a weapon; in the environment that we have described this will have no use other than self-defence and will make no contribution whatsoever to the defeat of the enemy.

Mobility

A future force must be agile. It must be able to move quickly so as to apply its firepower before the enemy can. It will achieve its agility partly through the capabilities of its vehicles. No doubt marginal improvements will continue to be made in the speed and cross country performance of wheeled and tracked vehicles, but the real advantage will lie with the force that can fight its battles not on the ground but a few feet above it. The British Army will soon bring into service its first attack helicopters, representing the biggest single increase in its fighting capability since the introduction of the tank in the First World War. The speed with which they will be able to deliver a powerful weight of fire will be seen to be so valuable a feature that the demand for them will be insatiable. The land-bound element will

THE NATURE OF THE FUTURE BATTLEFIELD 245

continue to be essential, but to win its battles a future force will require a much greater proportion of attack helicopters and associated heliborne troops than has previously been imagined. By eliminating the friction of the ground, tempo will increase to a revolutionary degree. The pace of battle for evenly matched enemies will be ferocious; for the enemy still equipped for the industrial age, the contest will be brief and crushing.

Agility will also be increased organisationally. Modern armoured divisions and brigades are too big for the requirements of the future. This is not by any means to say that they pack too much punch, that overall there are too many tanks and guns. It is to say that there are too many of them in a single grouping. A modern armoured division has 20,000 to 30,000 troops and perhaps 8,000 vehicles. This mighty host will lumber like an elephant when it should be racing like a panther, whether in a strategic move or tactical manoeuvres on the battlefield. The German Panzer Lehr Division of 1944 provides a thought-provoking comparison. It had less than 1,000 vehicles and fewer than 15,000 men. Despite all the hazards of wartime movement, the Division demonstrated its strategic mobility by moving from Hungary to Chartres in France where it was ready for battle a mere ten days after receiving the original order to move. This agile force subsequently suffered grievously at the hands of Allied air power, but even so made a significant contribution to the German success in frustrating Montgomery's efforts to seize Caen in June/July 1944. Speculation is idle but how much more would Panzer Lehr have suffered if it had been the leviathan of the 1990s? A modern armoured brigade has so many vehicles that, if moving in a single column, it would take almost ten hours at regulation speed and spacing to pass a single point; the column would be 80 kilometres long. The figures for an equivalent group in the Panzer Lehr Division would have been three hours and 30 kilometres respectively. It seems superfluous to ask which of these would be more capable of keeping up with the pace of future battle. The requirement is for more but smaller all-arms formations that, as individual entities and as part of the co-ordinated whole, can act and react fluently and quickly.

Command and Control (C2)

It is in the area of command and control that the most profound changes will take place. The opportunities and problems associated with digitisation have been discussed above. But even the most pessimistic view of what may be achieved implies the need to examine the structure of the chain and method of command in battle. In future warfare the fundamental requirement will be for the command system to decide and act quickly so as to outmanoeuvre the enemy. We have noted the growing capability to gather, process and disseminate information and orders at speed. This suggests that the hierarchy of headquarters from corps or division down to platoon can and should be flattened so as to match technical speed with procedural speed. But herein lies a conundrum. The hierarchy of headquarters exists not only to formulate and disseminate orders but also to ensure that those orders are carried out in an appropriate way as the battle develops. This requires a multi-level hierarchy, because no matter how well motivated, troops will not respond to the demands of commanders with whom their only contact is the information on a plasma screen or the print-out of a coded burst data transmission. Once again the human element intrudes inconveniently onto the battlefield. It cannot be emphasised too strongly that future wars will not be directed by theorists engaged in arcade games. A solution to the conundrum is elusive but it seems likely that it will lie in a change of procedures and culture. So as not to slow down the dissemination process, subordinate commanders will merely note information and orders as they pass from top to bottom; their role as planners and decision makers in their own right will diminish. Instead they will concentrate their efforts on ensuring the success of an operation once it has begun by taking control of their particular sectors of the battle as the overall operation fragments into separate and widely dispersed engagements.

In this context digitisation will provide the means to move units and formations from one command to another with much greater freedom than has been possible in the past. It has always been understood that units and formations should be grouped according to the nature of the mission about to be undertaken. But in practice such grouping and subsequent regrouping has been done prior to an engagement or in pauses during it. Future battle will see changes of affiliation at all levels of command while a battle is in progress. If digitisation is required to make this possible, so too is a common, fully understood doctrine, encompassing principles, procedures and drills. Without such a doctrine it will be impossible to achieve the cohesion that will be needed to cope with the whirligig circumstances of future battle.

Finally, there will be increasing effort put into C2 warfare in which both offensive and defensive operations will be vigorously fought. Hitherto C2 warfare has been somewhat half-hearted with relatively few resources allocated to it. In the future this will change so as to give a capability in this area that will be of at least as much significance as the firepower of the force. We have already noted that firepower may have to be sacrificed if sufficient money and manpower is to be found to create the capability, indeed to carry out the whole process of digitisation. Establishing the relative values in fighting power as between digitisation and firepower is one of the more demanding problems that today's generals must answer on behalf of the generals of the future.

Logistics

Logistics represent one of the classic realities of war; without them all else fails. But as a discipline the subject has often been the poor relation of the military family, particularly when it comes to writing about it. Recent works[41] have done something to fill the vacuum. Great generals in the past have referred to the importance of good logistics: 'As Army Commander ... I first ensure that my administrative situation is such that I can carry out the operations envisaged; I tell my "Q" what I want to do, and ask them if it can be done.... The more I have seen of war the more I realise how it all depends on administration and transportation (what our American allies call logistics).'[42] Whatever the technology of war may be, fuel, ammunition, repair of battle damage, and the evacuation of casualties will always be required. But to match the requirements of future battle, logistics too will have to develop boldly in its methods and procedures. The supply of an army can benefit just as much from digitisation as the rest. Automatic asset tracking will permit a much more efficient distribution of stocks. This in turn will reduce the quantity of stocks that must be carried; the logistic tail, already shortened by smaller forces to support and precision weapons, will grow shorter still. The principle of over-insurance (itself leading to logistic tail inflation) will give way to the principle of just-in-time. Dumping and pre-positioning of large quantities of matériel will have no place on the future battlefield; the inertia that these impose will be wholly inappropriate. Formations will be self-sufficient logistically for longer periods of time. When resupply is required it will be carried out by high-capacity, high-mobility load carriers, with significant advantages accruing to those who have sufficient heavy lift helicopters to do this by air. Improving reliability will reduce the demand for battlefield repair and maintenance but when these are required better design and modular construction will permit increasingly easy and rapid field repairs. The overall demand for the repair element of the logistic tail will reduce accordingly. For casualties the probability is that tele-medicine (remote control treatment conducted by surgeons many miles from the casualty) will play a growing part. All these measures will be necessary if the logistic tail is to be docked sufficiently to match the demands of future battle. If tomorrow's generals have to ask 'if it can be done' it may be too late.

Manpower

We now return to the human element, the people who will engage in the 'brutish business'. The British soldier has the well-deserved reputation for courageous and steadfast resilience in the face of the worst that the enemy and geography can throw at him. He[43] has seen the nation through its most glorious and its most disastrous moments with a spirit that so many others have admired. His generals have usually been credited with the same degree of courage but have often attracted much anguished criticism for their alleged incompetence. The soldiers and generals of the future will require all the courage and resilience, mental and physical, displayed by their forbears. But in the past there was room, indeed a need, for large numbers of men doing what they were told *en masse*, the proverbial cannon fodder. Not so on the future battlefield, where every man on it will have an individual part to play, capable of making decisions and taking actions that, by virtue of the relatively small numbers of people involved and the degree of firepower that they will each control, will have a significant effect on the outcome of the battle. It follows that the fighting man will have to be a thinker as well as a doer, capable of assimilating complex situations and acting appropriately in highly stressful situations. When engaged in PSO he will have to display ever-increasing political and diplomatic skills under conditions in which any of his actions may be beamed instantly onto the television screens of the world. Future conflict will indeed be a test for the people involved; they will have to exhibit not just the skills demanded of them in the past but many more besides.

As for the generals, they will require all the traditional qualities of the leader and commander; regardless of the technology these are timeless. But the more complex and fast moving the battlefield, the more direct the pressure from government and news media, the greater will be the demands not only on skilful and rapid decision making but also on the commander's mental robustness. His skin will have to be as thick as rhinoceros hide. If it is not he will collapse like General Georges. Furthermore, he will have to be the absolute master of his business from the outset, for he, his men and the nation will not have a second chance if things go wrong. The splendid plumed figures of the first quarter of the present century, distinguished moustaches, impeccable manners, boundless dash and elan, but often lacking a perception of the requirements of contemporary war, will have given way by the millennium to tough, physically fit and highly trained men for whom *la vie militaire* is no longer a way of life but a skilled technical profession. The mutation is already almost complete.

Training

The final element in this section is related neither to organisation nor equipment but is nevertheless an essential feature of an army's existence. It is all too little understood by those who are not professional soldiers that an army equipped for warfighting has no value without the opportunity to train, to practice the complex interactions between all the constituent parts of a fighting formation. This requires resources, principally time, land, fuel and ammunition. Armoured warfare will occur at speed over very large areas, but pressures, largely environmental, to decrease the space available for manoeuvre are increasing. The future warfighting force will place growing reliance on simulation and on synthetic environments generated by computer. These will reduce the amount of time required to train in the field. But they cannot bring about a reduction so great that the need for training areas disappears. There can be no substitute for deployment into the field, the only place where the real friction of war may at least in part be experienced. Establishing a robust training regime that can be sustained financially and in the face of concerns for the environment provides yet another challenge for an army based on a small and crowded island.

The Buffalo Thorn

It has been suggested earlier in this essay that the turn of the century will witness one of those defining moments which change the character and form of warfare so profoundly that it will be neither appropriate nor sufficient to continue to prepare for battle as we have done in the latter decades of the twentieth century. There is so much that is apparently familiar in the picture of future conflict, despite the increased pace and complexity, that it is tempting to play down the significance of what is happening; it is certainly easier to do so because it removes the pressure to take difficult remedial action. But the impact of information technology on the way that an army will fight must not be underestimated. It will not merely be a question of absorbing new equipment into the inventory, nor indeed of making organisational change. The most important development will have to take place in the mind. Anyone who has anything to do with creating and delivering the fighting power of an army will need to examine every element in the light of the effect that information technology will have. That examination may call into question some treasured ideals or long-standing principles; it is these questions that institutions find it so difficult to address, but they cannot be shirked.

Our eyes strain as we stare across the years to 2025 – we see the zigzags of the Buffalo Thorn all too dimly. The thorns of opportunity urge us on. Some will point the way to success but some may play us false, setting us on the path to failure. The entangling thorns of the past restrain us. Some hold us back from the challenges that must be faced but some will be timely warning signals against misguided actions from which there could be no recovery. It is on identifying the appropriate thorns that an army's thinkers must concentrate their efforts, putting aside the natural human instinct to avoid change merely because of a desire to stay with what is familiar and with what has served well in the past. But as General Fuller put it in a lecture to the Royal United Service Institution in 1920: 'If we do not step forward today we shall be marking time, and if we mark time now ... believe me, we shall be marking time in our own graves.'[44] Nearly 80 years on, the step forward which must be taken by information age armies is at least as great as that advocated by Fuller. It is a step that must be taken.

NOTES

The ideas expressed in this essay are entirely the author's own and do not necessarily reflect official Ministry of Defence policy.

1. Alvin and Heidi Toffler, *War and Anti-War* (London: Warner 1994).
2. H.G. Wells, *War of the Worlds* [1898] (London: Everyman 1993).
3. B.H. Liddell Hart, *Paris, or The Future of War* (London: Kegan Paul 1925).
4. Martin van Creveld, *The Transformation of War* (NY: Free Press 1991).
5. Quoted in Brian Holden Reid, *J.F.C. Fuller: Military Thinker* (London: Macmillan 1987) p.82.
6. *Design for Operations: The British Military Doctrine* (Army Code 7145) (BMD). This is the capstone British Army doctrinal publication, revised and reissued in 1996.
7. The Tofflers (note 1) and others refer to these as 'Third Wave' forces.
8. See 'Defence Technology Survey', *The Economist*, 10 June 1995, which prints a table derived from figures supplied by the US Arms Control and Disarmament Agency and the Int. Inst. for Strategic Studies. This shows the top ten defence spenders in 1993 (by implication actual or candidate information age nations). These include the UK and the US. Of these only one (Saudi Arabia) features in the top ten list of highest defence spenders as a percentage of GDP. Only two (US and China) feature amongst the ten largest armed forces, and none appear amongst the top ten under the heading of Armed Forces per 1000 Population.
9. Liddell Hart's 'Man in the Dark' concept postulated two boxers facing each other in the dark; the requirement was to find the enemy by reconnoitre, to fix him in position, smash him with a decisive blow and then to exploit. See B.H. Liddell Hart,'The Essential Principles of War', *United Services Magazine* (April 1920) p.35.
10. Creveld (note 4) p.20.
11. Tofflers (note 1) p.62
12. Holden Reid (note 5) p.63.
13. I have chosen for simplicity's sake to refer to all these groups as terrorists.
14. 'Information Warfare Special Report', *Jane's Defence Weekly* 25/15 (April 1996).
15. John Colvin, *Volcano Under Snow* (London: Quartet 1996) p.102.
16. For a recent examination of this issue, see Barrie Dunsmore, *The Next War: Live?* (Harvard U.: Discussion Paper D-22, March 1996).
17. John Keegan, *A History of Warfare* (London: Pimlico 1994) p.134.
18. Alvin H. Bernstein, 'Conflict and Technology: The Next Generation'. A paper given at the Conference on 'British Security 2010' at Church House, London (Dec. 1995).
19. Bernard Fergusson, *Wavell: Portrait of a Soldier* (London: Collins 1961) p.37.
20. Tempo at the tactical level is defined as the rate of activity, relative to the enemy, within engagements. At the operational level it is the rate of activity, relative to the enemy, between engagements. For a fuller explanation see ADP-1 *Operations* (Army Code 71565 Pt 1, June 1994) p.3–19.
21. Quoted in Holden Reid (note 5) p.57.
22. E.g. J.F.C. Fuller: 'To think in separate terms of sea, land and air is, I feel, entirely wrong.' Quoted in Holden Reid (note 5) p.59.
23. See also Montgomery's principles relating to air power, articulated in 1943. Quoted in John Terraine, *Right of the Line: The Royal Air Force in the European War 1939–1945* (London:

THE NATURE OF THE FUTURE BATTLEFIELD

Sceptre 1988, orig. Hodder 1985) p.380. These remain highly appropriate.
24. Alistair Horne, *To Lose a Battle* [1969] (London: Papermac 1990) p.371.
25. Tofflers (note 1) p.240.
26. Put in another way, in 1815 battle was fought by as many as 1,000 men per sq km; in the late 1980s the average would have been about 30 men per sq km.
27. For two particularly good descriptions of this phenomenon, see Hugh Dundas, *Flying Start* (London: Penguin 1990) pp.61–2, and 'Johnnie' Johnson, *Wing Leader* (London: Chatto 1956) Ch.3.
28. ADP-1 *Operations*, pp.5–11 to 5–16.
29. Quoted in Tofflers (note 1) p.88 from *The Conduct of Persian Gulf War: Final Report to Congress* (Dept. of Defense April 1992) (COW Report).
30. The notorious disagreements between Montgomery and Air Marshal Sir Arthur Coningham during the Normandy operations are a dismal case in point. That Montgomery seemed unable to adhere to the principles he laid down in regard to air power merely demonstrates how difficult it can be to do what is recognised to be 'the right thing'.
31. Liddell Hart (note 9) p.35.
32. B.H. Liddell Hart, *Decisive Wars of History* (London: Bell 1929) pp.153–4. See also A.S.H. Irwin 'Liddell Hart and the Indirect Approach to Strategy', in B. Holden Reid (ed.) *The Science of War* (London: Routledge 1993) pp.63–81.
33. Carl von Clausewitz, *On War* (eds.) Michael Howard and Peter Paret (Princeton UP 1976) p.76.
34. Colvin (note 15) p.5.
35. Military Aid to the Civil Community (e.g. fulfilling essential services in times of strikes or natural disaster) profits from the organisational qualities of the forces and is possible simply because the troops are available. The requirement to be prepared to do this sort of work does not in any way influence decisions about force structures and is not considered further in this essay.
36. In the context of British security and defence policy, the extent of the requirement is expressed in terms of the three Defence Roles. See *Statement on Defence Estimates 1994* Cm 2550 pp.26/27.
37. Quoted in Harold R. Winton, *To Change an Army: General Sir John Burnett-Stuart and British Armored Doctrine, 1927–1938* (Lawrence KS: UP of Kansas 1988) p.vi.
38. See *Design for Operations* (note 6) for the Moral, Physical and Conceptual components of fighting power.
39. This is by no means a novel proposal for the British Army. In 1929 the CIGS, Field-Marshal Sir George Milne, instructed a study group to examine how four armoured brigades might be formed within three years. The group proposed the disbanding of four infantry battalions so as to provide the manpower necessary to create more tank battalions. The proposal received short shrift. See Winton (note 37) pp.114–5.
40. A.P. Wavell, *The Good Soldier* (London: Macmillan 1948) p.71. I make this point with a heavy heart. The Black Watch (Wavell's Regiment and my own) is itself an infantry regiment.
41. E.g. Martin van Creveld, *Supplying War* (Cambridge: CUP 1977) and Julian Thompson, *The Lifeblood of War* (London: Brassey's [UK] 1991).
42. Montgomery: 'TRIPOLI' Tactical Talks 15–17 Feb. 1943, Stephen Brooks (ed.), *Montgomery and the Eighth Army* (London: Army Records Society 1991) p.144.
43. I have here referred to 'men'. The place of women on the future battlefield is as difficult to predict as everything else. Even today it is widely debated. However much it may intrude on deep-seated instincts to protect women from danger, it is my own view that, by 2025, women will fight their nations' battles alongside the men. See also Richard Holmes, *Nuclear Warriors* (London: Jonathan Cape 1991) pp.219–26.
44. Quoted in Holden Reid (note 5) p.64.

About the Contributors

Brian Holden Reid is Senior Lecturer in War Studies, King's College, London, and since 1987 has been Resident Historian at the British Army Staff College, Camberley (of which he is a graduate). He is the first civilian to work on the Directing Staff for over 100 years and helped set up the Higher Command and Staff Course. From 1984 to 1987 Dr Holden Reid was Editor of the *RUSI Journal*. He is an elected member of the Councils of the Society for Army Historical Research and Army Records Society, and a member of the Awards Committee of the United States Society for Military History. His books include *J. F. C. Fuller: Military Thinker* (1987, 1990), and *The Origins of the American Civil War* (1996).

Ian M. Brown is a graduate of the University of Calgary and University of London. He currently resides in Pittsburgh, Pennsylvania. His most recent publication in the *Journal of Military History* examined operational doctrine in the Canadian Corps during 1917–18.

Joseph G. Dawson III is Director of the Military Studies Institute and Associate Professor of History at Texas A&M University, College Station, Texas, USA, where he has been on the faculty since 1985. Dawson earned his PhD in history from Louisiana State University and is the author or editor of several works, including *The Texas Military Experience* (1995) and *Commanders in Chief: Presidential Leadership in Modern Wars* (1993).

David French is Professor of History at University College London. His most recent book, *The Strategy of the Lloyd George Coalition, 1916–1918* was published by Clarendon Press in 1995. His is currently writing a book on the combat effectiveness of the British Army between 1939 and 1945.

Stephen Hart is currently a Senior Lecturer in the Department of War Studies, the Royal Military Academy, Sandhurst. Prior to this, he was a part-time assistant lecturer in the Department of War Studies, King's College London, and in the Department of Linguistics and International Studies, the University of Surrey.

Matthew Hughes is a Lecturer in Modern History at Nene College, Northampton. His doctoral thesis entitled 'General Allenby and the campaign of the Egyptian Expeditionary Force, June 1917–November 1919' will be published shortly. He has also published an article in the *Journal of the Australian War Memorial* on the fall of Damascus 1918 and has a forthcoming article in the *Imperial War Museum Review* on the Palestine campaign in the First World War.

Major-General **Alistair Irwin** CBE has held the appointments of Commander 39 Infantry Brigade in Northern Ireland and Director Land Warfare in Headquarters Doctrine and Development. Prior to these he spent three years closely associated with the British Army's Higher Command and Staff Course, a period that kindled his continuing interest in the development of warfighting doctrine and its application to the future. He is currently Commandant of the Royal College of Military Science, Shrivenham.

Major-General **John Kiszely** MC is currently commanding the 1st (United Kingdom) Armoured Division in Germany. He was formerly the Director of Studies and Deputy Commandant of the Army Staff College at Camberley.

Tim Moreman lectures in military history at the University of London and is the author of several articles and chapters on the British Army in India and colonial warfare during the nineteenth and early twentieth centuries. He is currently completing a book on the role of the British armed forces on the North-West Frontier between 1849–1947 and also a study of the professional military press in India.

Joseph Smith is Reader in American Diplomatic History at the University of Exeter where he has taught since 1971. He has also been Visiting

Professor at the College of William and Mary, Williamsburg (1976–77) and the University of Colorado at Denver (1990–91). Dr Smith has written several books on American diplomatic relations with Latin America including *Illusions of Conflict: Anglo-American Diplomacy toward Latin America, 1865–1896* (Pittsburgh UP 1979), *Unequal Giants: Diplomatic Relations Between the United States and Brazil, 1889–1930* (Ibid. 1991) and *The Spanish-American War: Conflict in the Caribbean and the Pacific, 1985–1902* (Longman 1994).

Colonel **J. J. A. Wallace** AM is a serving officer in the Australian Army. He is a graduate of the Royal Military College Duntroon and the British Army Staff College, where he has also instructed. His regimental service has mainly been with the Australian Special Air Service Regiment, which he commanded from 1988 to 1991.

Index

Note: Ranks and titles of individuals are the highest given in the text or the highest relevant.

Abbottabad, 14
Adam, Gen. Sir Ronald, 148
Adjutant General, 160
Advertiser (Newark, NJ), 28–9
advance force operations, 222
Afghanistan, 107, 113
'aid to the civil power', 110–11, 122, 124, 126
Ain es Sir, 76
'Air Land Battle', 192
Albert, 91
Aleppo, 59, 60, 81
Alexandretta, 67
Alger, Russell, 41, 47, 53, 56
Ali Muntar, 71
Alizai, 117
Allen, Maj. Gen. Harry T., 101
Allenby, General Sir Edmund (later Field-Marshal Viscount), 4-5, 60–2, 63, 64, 67, 68, 70, 71–2, 75, 78–9, 80, 82
Alison, General Sir Archibald, 234
Amanus Mountains, 67
American Civil War (1861–65), 3–4, 41, 45, 46
American Expeditionary Forces (AEF), 99
Amiens, 90, 91, 92, 93
Amman, 60, 73, 75, 76, 77, 79, 81
Amritsar Massacre (1919), 124, 126
Andover, 110
Anglesey, Marquess of, 60
ANZACs, 60, 75, 80–1, 99, 147
Angostura, Battle of (1847): see Buena Vista, Zachary Taylor
Arabs, 80, 107
Argyll and Sutherland Highlanders, 1st Battalion, 120, 166

Armoured arm, 185–7, *see also* British Army Divisions 1944–45, Royal Tank Regiment, tanks
Armoured Divsion in Battle (1952) 184, 186, 187, 199
Army infantry vehicles, 194
Ardennes, 146
Army in Burma, 123
Armistice (1918), 89, 95, 96, 99, 100, 102, 105
Armstrong, Lt. Bezabel, 19, 20
Army Quarterly, 105
Arras, Battle of (1917), 89
Arroyo Seco, 25
Artillery, 1815: 236; 1898: 42, 46-7, 50, 51; 1916–18: 64, 67, 68–9, 70–2, 73, 75, 76, 78, 80, 91; 1935: 120, *see also* attritional approach, British Army, Montgomery
Assistant Adjutant General 160
Assam Rifles, 120, 123
attack helicopters (AH), 244–5
attritional approach to war, 7, 133–34, 138–9, 149–50, 169–70, 179, 181, 182–3, 184, 187–8, 191, 192, 193, 201, 208, 208 (Fig. 1), 209, 213–14, 219, 220, 223
Aum Shinrikyo sect, 231
Australian Light Horse (ALH), 63, 65, 76, 77

Bagnall, Field-Marshal Sir Nigel, 7, 198–9
Baking, Arslan, 76
Balyamn, 117
Bannu, 119
Bapaume, 91
Barrow, Maj.-Gen. George, 63, 66
Bartholomew, Brig.-Gen. William, 64

256 MILITARY POWER: LAND WARFARE IN THEORY AND PRACTICE

Bates, Brig.-Gen. John C., 43
'battle exhaustion', 161–9, 170–1
Battle Notes (1981) by Lt.-Gen. Sir Nigel Bagnall, 199
Beersheba, 62, 64, 66, 67, 68, 72, 73, 75
Beirut, 60, 81, 218, 219, 220
Beisan, 78
Bent, Charles, 16, 18, 19, 24
Bent's Fort, 13
Berlin, 100, 101, 102
Bermuda, 106
Bey, Col Hussein Husni Amir, 69
Bible, 75
Bidwell, Brig. Shelford, 188
biological warfare (BW), 8, 231, 238, 239
Birkenhead, HM Troopship, 196
Blair, Francis P., Jr ('Frank'), 16
Blair, Montgomery, 16
Blanco, Gen Ramón, 40
Blitzkrieg, 149, 183
blockade, 46
Bosnia, 236
Boyd Cycle, 209, *see also* Lind, William; Manoeuvrist Approach; OODA Loop; principles of war
Bracknell, 108
Brazito, Battle of (1846), 21–4, 30
British Army Review, 190
Britain, Battle of (1946), 238
British Army,
 adaptability of its officers, 119, 243
 'Aldershot Type', 117
 approach to campaign planning, 7, 107–8, 109–23, 183–4, 187, 193–200, 202–3, 238
 attitudes to African troops, 112
 Bureau of Current Affairs, 162
 compared with US Army, 3, 200
 colonial warfare, and, 5–6, 105–27
 formations of: *Armies 1914–18*
 Fifth Army, 98, 91
 Fourth Army, 93, 94, 96
 Second Army, 6, 96, 97
 Third Army, 77, 90, 91
 Fifth Army, 77
 Corps 1914–18
  Desert Mounted Corps, 60, 73
  XX, 60, 64, 66, 70, 73
  XXI, 60, 63, 70, 73
 Divisions 1914–18
  Anzac Mounted, 75, 80
  53rd (Welch), 72
  54th (East Anglian), 71, 80
  60th (London) 66, 72, 76
  Yeomanry Mounted, 73

Brigades
 Camel Corps, 75, 111, 112
 2nd ALH, 76
 5th Brigade, 108
 NZMRB, 75, 76
Armies 1914–45
 see Second Army (British), Twenty-First (21st) Army Group and Canadian [1st] Army
Corps 1944–45
 I Corps, 137
 VIII Corps, 138, 141, 148, 160, 162, 163, 164, 165
 XII, 163
 XXX Corps, 137, 164, 166
Divisions 1944–45
 Guards Armoured, 138, 173 (table)
 3rd Infantry, 137, 170, 173 (table)
 6th Airborne, 166, 167, 173 (table)
 7th Armoured, 137–8, 156, 159, 166, 172 (table)
 15th (Scottish), 165, 173 (table)
 43rd (Wessex), 138, 165, 173 (table)
 49th (West Riding), 155, 156, 165, 173 (table)
 50th (Northumbrian), 144, 156, 158, 166, 170, 172 (table)
 51st (Highland), 137–8, 156, 172–3 (table)
 53rd (Welch), 173 (table)
 59th (Staffordshire), 168, 171, 173 (table)
Brigades 1944–45
 47th, 155
 56th, 165
 231st, 165
 future structures of, 8, 242–3
 historiographical neglect of, 7, 188
 India, units in, 112–13, 118–19, 126–7
 morale of (1944), 6, 134–41, 154–73
 mountain warfare skills of, 118
 performance in Second World War, 6
 'secondments' of, 117
 view of Spanish–American War, 37
 withering of administrative structures, 1918–19, 5, 98–101, 249 *see also* attritional approach; Bagnall; doctrine; Indian Army; logistics; manoeuvre warfare; principles of war; psychiatrists;
British Army of the Rhine (BAOR), 184, 193–5, 202
British Empire,
 'crisis' of, 105
 garrisoning of, 106, 112, 125
British Expeditionary Force (BEF, 1914–18), 89, 91, 98, 99–100

INDEX

Brooke, Gen. Sir Alan, 135, 144, 146–7
Browne, Maj. A. T. A., 160, 161
Brussels, 97
Buchanan, James, 15th US President, 18
Budenny, Marshal of the Soviet Union Semyon, 62
budgets, influence on strategy, 237
Buena Vista, Battle of (1847), 28
Buffalo Thorn (*Ziziplus mucroneta*), 227, 249
Buena Vista, Battle of (1847), 28
Bulfin, Lt.-Gen. Sir Edward, 63, 70
Bulmer, Brig. E., 171
Bureau of Insular Affairs, 18
Burma, 106, 121, 122, 126, 127
Burma Frontier Force, 123
Burma Military Police, 121, 122
Burma Rifles, 124
Burnett-Stuart, Gen. Sir John, 242

Caen, 147, 148, 245
Cairo, 77
Calais, 92
California, 12–13, 15, 17, 18, 20
Caldwell, Thomas, 22
Callwell, Maj.-Gen. C. E., 6, 109, 113, 126
Camberley, 108, 110
Cambrai, Battle of (1917), 89
Camino Real (Royal Highway), 45, 46, 51
Campos, Gen Assenio Martinez, 37–8
Canadian [1st] Army (1944–45), 137, 141, 143, 144, 148, 149, 154, 167
Canadian Corps (1917–18), 97–8, 99
Canal du Nord, 94
Cardwell System 106–7, 108, 194
Carpendale, Capt. W. St.J., 122
Carver, Field-Marshal Lord, 157, 186–7, 190, 196
casualty avoidance, 232, *see also* British Army, Montgomery,
Caucasus, 67–8, 81, 82
cavalry 1916–18: 60, 62–3, 64, 66–7, 73, 75, 77, 78, 80, 81, 107
Cervera, Admiral Pascual, 41, 54
Chadwick, Rear Admiral (USN) French Ensor, 55
Chateau Bronay, 157
Chauny, 91
Chauvel, Lt.-Gen. Sir Henry, 64, 66, 73, 77, 79
chemical warfare (CW), 231, 238, 239
Cheney, Richard B., 237
Chetwode, Lt.-Gen. Sir Philip, 64, 66, 68, 70, 72, 73
Chichanna, 117
Chihuahua, 19
Chihuahua City, 20, 24, 25, 28
Chillibagh, 117

Chin tribe, 121, 124
Churchill, Winston S., 144, 145
Cilicia, 62
Clark, Maj. Meriwether, L., 24–5, 26–7
Clarke, Lt.-Gen. Sir Travers, 95, 96
Clause F (section 34), of Armstice 1918, 100, *see also* Armistice
Clausewitz, Carl von, 2, 201
Clay, Henry, 10
Climo, Maj.-Gen S. H., 114
Cold War, 1
colonial warfare, 5, 111–25, 126–7
'colossal cracks', 6, 133–4, 140, 149, 150
Comet, HMS, 71
command, 180, 186, 192, 198–9, 203, 248; influence of automation on, 235, 248–9, 245–6
Commission Regulatrice, 102
computers, 231
Condé, General Pedro García, 25
conscription, 185–6, 233
'Constellation', Operation, 141
Corbin, Lt.-Gen. Henry, 41
Corps Exhaustion Centre, 162
counter-insurgency in Malaya, 193, 207, in Spanish–American War, 37–8; theory of, 211–12, 214–15, 217, 224
Counter-Revolutionary Warfare (CRW), 213, 214, 215, 216–17, 224
Courier (Charleston), 28
courts martial, 158, 160, 165
Cowans, Lt.-Gen. Sir John, 95
Crerar, Lt.-Gen. Henry, 137, 138
Creveld, Martin van, 213, 228, 230
Crocker, Lt.-Gen. John, 137
Cuba, 18; 41; guerrilla tactics in, 39–40 land battles in (1898), 4, 37–40, 54–5, 56 naval blockade of, 40
culture, influence on war, 232–33
Currie, Lt.-Gen. Sir Arthur, 94–5, 98
Cyprus, 106–10

Daily Picayune, 28
Daily Union (Washington), 29
Damascus, 60, 63, 76, 80, 81
Dau Traul Strategy, 213
Davis, Richard Harding, 52
De Courcy, Lt James, 26
Daiquirí, 42, 45, 46
Dawnay, Brig.-Gen. Guy, 71, 72
deception, 216, 221
Defense Reform Debate, The (1984), 192
Delta (New Orleans), 29
Democratic Party, 29
Dempsey, Lt.-Gen. Sir Miles, 148, 161
demobilisation, 98–101, 106

demography, 8
Deputy Director Medical Services (DDMS), 163, 165
Derajat Column, 113
'Desert 1', 223
desertion, 158, 159, 170, 171
Design for Military Operations: The British Military Doctrine (1989), 228
Devonshire Regiment, 2nd Battalion, 158
Dewey, Commodore George, 55
Dhoda, 117
digitization of combat, 234–5, 236–7, 245–6
Dill, Field-Marshal Sir John, 111
direct energy weapons (DEW), 234
Director of Army Psychiatry, 169
Dobell, Lt Gen Sir Charles, 72
doctrine, British Army,
  'ad hoc' approach to, 126-27, 202
  in continental warfare, 6, 135–6, 140, 141, 184–85, 191, 193–95, 199, 238, 246
  in small wars, 5, 105–10, 113–14, 120, 122, 125, 207
  limitations of, 185, 210,
  see also British Army, Montgomery, manoeuvrist approach
Doniphan, Colonel Alexander W., 3
  battles of, 21–9
  character of, 10–11, 20, 29
  crossing of Santa Fe Trail, 13
  expansionist outlook, 10, 13, 16, 19, 30
  legal skills of, 3, 11
  Military Governor of New Mexico, 15–18, 29–30
  oratory of, 23
  regimental duties of, 19–21
  relations with Indians, 16, 18–19
  elations with Kearny, 12
  role in formulating Kearny Code, 17, 19
  tactical arrangements, 22–3, 26–8
  Xenophon, likened to, 29
Duffield, Brig Gen Henry, 42, 50
Durham Light Infantry, 8th Battalion, 167, 10th Bn, 156
Duke of Cornwall's Light Infantry, 5th Battalion, 165
Duke of Wellington's Regiment (DWR), 6th Battalion, 155, 156–7
Duties in Aid of the Civil Power (1934), 110–11

'Eagle Claw', Operation (1980), 219, 223
East Yorkshire Regiment, 2nd Battalion, 170
Eastern Front (1941–45), 140, 232
economy of effort, 133, 138, 224
ecology, 8
Edwards, Frank, 27

Edwards, Marcellus, 23
Egypt, 59, 67, 105, 106, 110
Egyptian Expeditionary Force (EEF), 59, 60, 62, 63, 66, 69, 72, 73, 75, 78, 80, 82
Eisenhower, Gen. Dwight D., 133, 139, 145
El Alamein, Second Battle of (1942), 183
El Caney, 47, 50–1, 53, 55, 56
El Paso, 20, 21
El Paso del Norte (modern Ciudad Juarez), 19, 24, 30
El Pozo, 51, 56
electronic warfare (EW), 8, 209, 216, 231, 234, 238–9, 240
Eliot, George, 228
Elliott, Lt Richard, 12
Enquirer (Cincinnati), 28
Entebbe, raid on (1976), 219, 223
environmental pressures, 198, 249
'Epsom', Operation (1944), 140, 143, 147, 163
Es Salt, 75, 77, 78

Falaise, 147, 148
Falkenhayn, Gen. Erich, 189
Falls, Capt. Cyril, 62, 69
Feisal, Emir, 63, 80
Fergusson, Brig. Bernard, 234
Field Service Regulations (1920), 108–9, 112, 113, 114; (1924), 115
financial collapse, 231
First World War (1914–18), 5, 59–88, 89–102
Florida, 15
Floridian (Tallahassee), 28
FM 100-20, 211
Foch, Marshal Ferdinand, 94, 101
Foco Theory, 213
Fort Aguadores, 50
Fort Leavenworth, KS, 4, 11, 12, 192, 199
forward defence, strategy of, 184
Foundations of the Science of War, The (1926) by Maj.-Gen. J.F.C. Fuller, 228
Free Trader, 28
Frémont, Capt. John C., 29
Freud, Sigmund, 162
Freyberg, Lt.-Gen. Sir Bernard, 146–7
Frontier Warfare (Army and Royal Air Force) 1930, 120
Fuller, Maj.-Gen. J.F.C., 2, 6, 182–3, 188, 191, 212, 221, 228, 230, 235, 249–50
future battlefield,
  automation of, 234–6, 240, 246–7
  command on, 240, 245-45
  divisional frontages, compared with past and present, 238
  human element on, 247–8

INDEX

influence of media on, 232–3
joint nature of, 236-41, 243
mobility on, 244–5
six characteristics of, 236–41
size of armies on, 237–8
training for, 248–9
weapons deployed on, 233–5, 239–40, 243
women on, 240
Gallipoli Campaign (1915–16), 59, 196
Garca, Calixto, 42
Garsia, Col Clive, 70, 72
Gatling guns, 42, 52
Gaza, Third Battle of (Oct.–Dec. 1917), 5, 59, 60, 62, 63–73, 65 (map), 77
  case for concentration at, 64-7, 70, 71-2
General Defence Plan (GDP), 184, 194
German Army *see Wehrmacht*
Georges, General Alphonse, 237, 248
Giap, General, 232, 241
Gibraltar, 106
Gilpin, Maj. Willian, 12, 26, 27
Gómez Máximo (Cuban guerrilla leader), 38, 40
'Goodwood', Operation (1944), 143, 148, 163
Gordon, Maj.-Gen. Charles, 196
'Grenade', Operation (1945), 149
Grenada intervention (1983), 219, 220
Grigg, Sir James, 134
Grimes, Capt. George, 51
ground, in war, 240
Guadalupe Hidalgo, Treaty of (1848), 18
Guam, 18
Guantanamo Bay, 42, 46
Guderian, Col. Gen. Heinz, 237
guerrilla warfare, 38–40, 181, 212–13, 241,
  see also 'small wars'
Gulf War (1991), 2, 236, 239
Gullett, Henry, 66, 70, 72, 77, 78
Gurkhas, 121, 122,
Gwynne, Maj.-Gen. Charles, 6, 111, 125

Haig, Field-Marshal Sir Douglas, 5, 63, 99
Haldane, Lord, 194
Hall, Private Willard P., 16–17
Ham, 91
Hannibal, 201
Harding, Maj.-Gen John, 144
Hargest, Brig. James, 155
Havana, 38, 40, 41, 54
Haycock, R., 113
Hayes, Col Rutherford B., 19th US President, 20
Hazebrouck, 90, 92
Hart, Senator Gary, 190

helicopters, 216, 244–5
Henniker, Gen. José A., 25
Higher Command and Staff Course (HCSC), 199
Hill, Alex, 73
holding force, 216, 224
Hong Kong, 106
Howard-Vyse, Brig. R.G.H., 79
Husni, Col Hussein, 70, 73
Hussein, Saddam, 232
Hutcheon, Lt.-Col E., 164
Imperial Camel Corps, 75
Imperial Defence Conference (1909), 113
imperial policing, 105, 109, 110, 125–6
Imperial Policing (1934) by Maj.-Gen. Sir Charles Gwynn, 111
India, 105, 106, 107, 112-13, 134
Indian Army, 59, 60, 77, 79, 80, 99, 112, 113, 114, 117, 118, 121, 126
  Divisions 1914–18
    4th Indian Cavalry, 63, 80
    5th Indian Cavalry, 80, 81
    7th Indian Infantry, 81
Indiana State Sentinel, 28
Indians, 12, 15, 16
Industrial Age armies, 229, 230, 232, 241, 245
intelligence, 180, 209, 212, 216, 217, 219, 221
infantry, 106, 114, 171, 186, 244–5
Information Age Warfare, 228, 229, 230, 232, 241, 250
information technology (IT), 8, 249
inter-arm co-operation, 60–3, 67, 70, 77, 80, 83, 180–81, 186, 202–3
international law, 232
intervention operations, 218–23, 224
'invisible' battlefield, 8, 45, 238–40
Iraq, 105
Ireland, 105
Isandhlwana, Battle of (1879), 196
Israeli Army, 190
Islington Daily Gazette, 62
Istanbul, 67
ISTAR systems, 235

Jackson, Andrew, 7th US President, 15
Jaffa, 67, 79
Jerusalem, 60, 62, 67, 71, 73, 79
Jisr ed Damieh, 77
Joint Note 12, 79
Jomini, Lt. Gen. Baron, 2, 8
Jordan, River, 63, 73, 75, 76, 77, 78
Journal of the Royal Artillery, 120
Journal of the Royal United Services Institute, 7

Journal of the United Service Institute of India, 115, 118, 122
Judge Advocate General's Department, 158, 160, 166
Junction Station, 67
jungle warfare, 45–6, 121–4, 127

Kachin tribe, 122, 124
Karm, 66
Kearny Code, 3, 17, 19, see also Doniphan; Mexican War
Kearny, Brigadier General Stephen W., 3, 11, 12–13, 15–16, 18, 19, 29
Keegan, John, 195, 233–4
Kennelly, Capt. D.M., 120
Kent, Brig.-Gen. J. Ford, 42, 53
Kentucky, 16–17
Kettle Hill, 47, 51, 53
Khartoum, 111
Khilifat Movement, 124
Khwaja Kizar, 117
King's African Rifles (KAR), 111, 112
King's College, London, 107
King's Own Yorkshire Light Infantry, 1/4th Battalion, 160
Kirkpatrick, Col C., 115
Kohar District, 117
Kolwezi intervention (1978), 219, 223
Kressenstein, Gen. Kress von, 66, 68, 69, 70
Kuki tribe, 121
Kurdistan, 107
Kut-al-Amara, Siege of (1915–16), 59

Lancashire Fusiliers, 2/5th Battalion, 160
Larcher, Comdt M., 71
Las Gusimas, 45, 50, 56
Lashkars, 114
Lawrence, Col T.E., 63, 82–3
Lawton, Brig.-Gen. Henry W., 42, 45, 50, 55
'layer cake', NATO formation, 184
Le Parc de Boislande, 155, 156
Leavenworth Series of Tactical Manuals (1891), 4
Lebanon, 67
Lenin, V.I., 213
Leon, Col Antonio Parce de, 21
Leonhard, Robert, 7
less dense battlefield, 238
Liddell Hart, Sir Basil, 2, 6, 7, 62, 181–2, 187–8, 191, 200, 213, 215, 228, 240, 242 *see also* Strategy of the Indirect Approach
Lille, 97
Linares: see Pomba, Gen. Arsenio Linares
Lincoln, Abraham, 16th US President, 10
Lind, William, 7, 180, 192, 209, 222
Lloyd George, David, 72, 79, 82, 99, 100, 102
logistics, 5, 47, 67, 75, 81, 92, 93–4, 96–8, 100, 229, 238, 243, 244, 247: *see also* sea supply
Louisiana, 17
Ludendorff Offensives (March–July 1918), 60, 77, 79–80, 89–92
Lushai tribe, 121
Luttwak, Edward N, 7
Lyne, Maj.-Gen. L.O., 168
Lys, River, 92

MacNamara, Robert S., 189
McKinley, William, 25th US President, 41
Maceo, Antonia, 38
Machine Gun Corps, 98
Macmillan, Maj.-Gen. Gordon, 165
Madrid, 54
Magoon, Charles, 18, 29
Magoon's Reports, 18
'Maginot mentality', 190
Malabar, 122
Malaria, 81, 167
manoeuvre, 7–8, 181, 240, 244–45
manoeuvrist approach
 adoption of, 179–80, 183, 184, 199–200, 207, 208 (Fig. 1)
 centre of gravity, 201, 213, 214, 216
 commander, role of, 181, 214, 220–2
 decisive points, 201
 disadvantages of, 200–1
 German interpretation of, 188, 191, 196, 197, 207
 lack of agreed military vocabulary, 197
 'main effort',222
 'mission orders', 207, 209, 222, 224
 opposition to, 183–4, 185, 186, 195–7
 prerequisites of, 180–1, 201–2, 188, 208–10, 212, 215, 218
 psychological surprise and, 216
 'reconnaissance pulled', 207, 209, 216, 217, 221–22
 relationship to attrition, 179, 181, 188, 208, 219–23
 relationship to strategy of indirect approach, 181-83, 208
 Revolutionary Warfare and, 212, 214
 risks of, 201, 207, 217–18, 223
 role of firepower in, 179, 185, 191, 192, 194, 201, 213, 214, 221, 224, 235
 simultaneity and, 213, 219, 220, 222, 223, 224
 Soviet view of, 190, 191, 207
 Special Air Service (SAS), and, 193, 209
 Vietnam War, influence on, 189–90,
 see also: attritional approach, *Blitzkrieg*,

INDEX

Fuller, Liddell Hart, Montgomery *Maneuver, The Art of* (1990) by Robert Leonhard, 200
Maneuver Warfare (1985) by William Lind, 192
Maneuver Warfare: An Anthology (1993), edited by Richard Hooker, 200
'Manifest Destiny', 10
Manual of Operations on the North West Frontier (1925), 115, 116, 120
Manzanillo, 47
Mafid Jozelle, 77, 78
'Market Garden', Operation (1944), 138, 145
Marcy, William L. (US Sec. of War), 10, 12–13, 15, 19, 29
Mariel, 41
Marshall, Gen. George C., 139
Maryland, 16
Martel, Lt.-Gen. Sir Giffard, 184
Matamoros, 15
martial law, 15
Marx, Karl, 213
Mayaguez intervention (1975), 219, 220, 223
media, 8, 217–19, 232, 242, 248, *see also* television
Medina, 67, 81
Megiddo, Battle of (Sept.–Oct. 1918), 5, 60, 62, 79, 80–2
Melvin, Col, 165
Mesopotamia, 67
Mexican War (1846–8), 3, 14 (map)
 handsome appearance of Mexican troops, 21–22
 US participation in, 10–30
 weakness of US forces in, 19
Mexico City, 15
Michigan, 41
Middlesex Regiment, 8th Battalion, 161
Miksche, F.O., 184
Miley, John D., 52
minimalist forces, 229–32, 238, 239, 241, 242
minutarisation, 233
military government, 3, 10, 15–18
military history, study of, 2, 187–89
minor tactics, 107, 109, 111, 112, 126
Mitchell, Lt-Col David, 26, 27
Mitchell, Brig. Gen. William (Billy), 1
Missouri, 16, 17, 23, 28, 29, 30
Moab plateau, 76
Mogadishu, 223
Mohmand operations (1935), 120
Monclova, 20
Montdidier, 91
Montgomery, Field-Marshal Sir Bernard (later Viscount)
 casualty avoidance and, 6, 132–3, 140–9, 150
 deliberate preparation of, 6, 139–40, 157, 186–7
 legacy of, 6, 7, 183–4, 186, 195, 203, 240
 'master plan' of, 6, 134, 183, 245
 morale, concern with, 132, 134–9, 149, 150
 political dimension, understanding of, 142, 143–6
 reputation of, 132–3, 139
 See also attritional approach; manoeuvrist approach
Montgomery-Massingberd, Field-Marshal Sir Archibald, 107
Moplah Rebellion (1921–22), 122–4
Morale, 60, 62, 134–41, 149, 154–79 *passim*
Mountain Warfare, School of, 114; tactics of, 113–20
Morgan, Lt.-Gen. Sir Frederick, 118
Murray, Lt.-Gen. Sir Archibald, 62, 63, 72
Muslims, Sunni, 80
Muslimie Junction, 60

Nablus, 78
Naga tribe, 121
Natchez, 28
National Era, 28
Navajo Indians, 16, 18–19
Nesle, 91
New Mexico, 12, 13, 15, 16, 17, 18, 19, 24, 25, 30
New Orleans, 15, 28
New Zealand Mounted Rifle Brigade (NZMRB), 75, 76
Ney, Marshal, 230
Non-cooperation Movement, 24
non-lethal weapons (NLW), 234
Normandy Campaign (1944), 6, 135–6, 137, 140, 147, 149, 156, 157, 158, 166–7, 171
North Atlantic Squadron (USN), 41
North Atlantic Treaty Organization (NATO), 1, 8, 184, 189–90, 191, 192–3, 198, 236
North-East Frontier, 120, 122–3, 127
North-West Frontier, 108, 112–120, 124, 126
North-West Frontier Province (NWFP), 114
Northern Arab Army (NAA), 63, 80, 81
Northern Ireland, 193, 214, 217
Northamptonshire Yeomanry, 2nd, 161
Notes on Imperial Policing (1934), 110, 111
nuclear war, 8, 187, 231, 239

O'Brien, Richard, 143
O'Connor, Lt.-Gen. Sir Richard, 138, 165, 166
Okeechobee, Battle of (1837), 23

'OODA loop' (Observe, Orient, Decide and Act), 180, *see also* Lind
operational level of war, 2, 133, 140–1, 146, 147, 149, 150, 191–2, 199, 201, 211, 212, 214, 216, 217, 224
Operations Other Than War, 7–8, 207–25
Oriente, province of, 38, 40, 54
Orre, River, 148
Ottoman Empire, 59, 67–8, 71, 77, 79, 80, 82
Ouistrehem, 157
'Overlord', Operation: see Normandy Campaign (1944)

Palestine Campaign (1917–18), 4–5, 59, 60, 62, 63, 67–8, 69, 76, 77, 79, 81, 82–3, 102, 110, 111, 126
Panama intervention (1989), 219, 220, 224
Panzer Lehr Division, 155, 245
Papen, Col Franz von, 68–9, 71, 79
Parker, Lt. John, 52
Pardoe, Maj., 71–2
Parras, 20
Pasha, Djemal, 68
Pasha, Gen. Refet, 69
'Passchendaele', Battle of (1917): see Ypres, Third Battle of,
'Passchendaele, Basic Truths of', 188
Passing It On: Short Talks on Tribal Fighting on the North West Frontier of India by Gen. Sir Andrew Skeen, 119
Pathans, 113, 114, 115, 117, 119, 120
Patton, Lt.-Gen. George S. Jr, 149–50
'Peace For Galilee', Operation (1982), 214
peacekeeping, 210–11, 241–2
peacemaking, 218
Péronne, 91
Phillips, Brig. E., 165
Phillippines, 18
Plain Dealer (Cleveland), 28
political decisions, influence on campaigns, 72, 79, 82, 215, 216, 218–19, 221, 233; factor, in OOTW, 211–12, 215, 216, 217, 218–21, 222, 223, 224–5
Polk, James K., 10th US President, 11
Polish Armoured Division, 137, 138
Pamba, Gen. Arserio Linares, 46–7, 50, 54, 55
Preston, R.M.P., 66
Price, Col Sterling, 19, 25
principles of war, 8, 108, 109, 110, 114, 115, 126, 200
propaganda, 214, 217, 232
psychiatrists, 6, 162–3, 164, 166, 167–8
public opinion, and war, 8, 213, 214, 218–19, 233
Puerto Rico, 18

Punjab Frontier Force, 113

Q Branch, 95
Quartermaster General (QMG), 99
Quitman, Brig. Gen. John A., 15

Rabin, Gen. Yitzhak, 190
Race to the Swift (1985) by Brig. R. Simpkin, 192–3
railways, Belgian, 96–8; French, 99, 102; Turkish 67, 75, 76, 77, 80
Rangoon, 122
Rarotongan islanders, 67
Rayak, 67
Razmak, 119
Reagan, Ronald, 40th US President, 1
Reconnaissance Regiment, 43rd, 157
Regimental Medical Officers (RMOs), 163, 164, 165
regimental system, 159, 170
Regulations of the King's African Rifles (1925), 111
Reid, John, 23, 26
Reports of the Law of Government in Territory (etc), see *Magoon's Reports*
Report of the War Office Committee of Enquiry into 'Shell Shock' (1922), 161, 168
Republican (Savannah), 28
Rhineland, occupation of, 96, 98, 100, 102
Richard I, 62
Richardson, Lt-Col Frank, 165
Richardson, William, 27
Rifle Brigade, 1st Battalion, 159
Rio Grande River, 16, 19, 20, 21, 24, 30
Ripley, Maj. Roswell S., 23
Robertson, Gen. (later Field-Marshal) Sir William, 70, 79, 82, 100–2
Roebeck, Vice-Admiral John de, 196
Roer Valley, 149
Roosevelt, Col Theodore, 26th US President, 45, 55
'Rough Riders', 45; see also Volunteer Cavalry, Theodore Roosevelt
Royal Air Force, 120
Royal Armoured Corps, 184
Royal Scots Fusiliers, 11th Battalion, 160, 170
Royal Tank Regiment, 192
1st Battalion, 159
Royal Navy, 106, 200
Royal United Service(s) Institution (Institute since 1971), 108, 187, 188, 190, 250
Royal West African Frontier Force (WAFF), 111
Roye, 91

INDEX

Ruff, Lt-Col Charles, 12
Ruhr, 146
rules of engagement (ROE), 217, 223
rules for opening fire (RFOF), 217
Russian Revolution, 67
Ryne, Brig.-Gen. Granville, 66, 76

Sacramento, Battle of (1847), 3
Saladin, 62
Sampson, Rear Admiral William T., 41, 42, 46, 50
Sanders, Marshal Liman von, 68, 77–8
San Juan Hill, 47, 50, 51–4, 55, 56
San Juan River, 52
Santiago Campaign maps, 44, 48
Santiago de Cuba, 41–2, 45, 46, 51, 52, 53, 54, 55, 56
Santa Fe, 12, 13, 15, 18, 19, 21, 24, 25, 28, 30
Santa Fe Trail, 13
School of Advanced Military Studies (SAMS), 192, 199
Scott, Brevet Lt. Gen. Winfield S., 28, 29
sea supply, 47, 67
Second Army (British, 1944), 6, 141, 147, 154, 155, 157, 158, 160, 161, 162, 163, 164, 166, 167, 168–9, 171
Second Seminole War, 23
Second World War, 1, 132–78, 213, 238
self-inflicted wounds, 160
Sevilla, 45, 46, 47
Shafter, Maj. Gen. William A.; appraisal of 55–6, differences with USN, 46, 55; strategy of, 4, 37, 41, 42–5, 47, 50–1, 52, 54
Shanghai, 102
Shea, Maj.-Gen. John, 78, 79
Shinware, 117
Shunet Nim, 75, 78
Siab, 117
Siborey, 42, 45, 46, 50
Sikh Gurdwara Movement, 124
Simonds, Lt.-Gen. Guy, 137
Simpkin, Brig. Richard, 7, 192–3, 208
Sinai Peninsula, 59
Singapore, 106
Skeen, General Sir Andrew, 6, 119
Slim, Field-Marshal Viscount, 114, 202
'small wars', 3, 4, 8, 109–10, 111, 113, 125, 207
Small Wars: Their Principles and Practice (1896), by C.E. Callwell, 110, 126
Smuts, Field-Marshal J.C., 79, 144
Somme, Battle of (1916), 71, 91
Son Tay raid (1970), 219, 223
Soviet First Cavalry Army, 62

Soviet Union, 107
Spanish–American War (1898), 3, 17–18, 37, 54, 55–6
See William A. Shafter, Spanish Army, United States Army, Volunteer Soldiers
Spanish Army, 37–40
defensive strategy of, 39, 40, 42, 46–7, 54–5
disease, effect on, 40
poor morale of, 39, 54, 56
resolution of, 50–1, 52, 55, 56
surrender of, 54
Sparrow, Lt-Col J.H., 154
special forces (SF), 209, 217, 220, 221, 222
Staff College, The, 110, 111, 183–4, 192, 195, 197, 199
Staffordshire Regiment, 2/6th Battalion, 171
Stanhope, Henry, 194
Statesman (Columbia), 28
Stephens, Alexander H., 10
Storrs, Col Sir Ronald, 71
Strategic Defense Initiative (SDI), 1
Strategy of the Indirect Approach, 7, 8, 181–83, 187–88, 200, 208, 221, 240, *see also* Liddell Hart; manoeuvrist approach
Strong, Maj.-Gen. Kenneth, 145
Sudan Defence Force, 111
Suez Canal, 59, 106
Sun Tzu, 182, 212, 213
Supply, *see* logistics
Supreme War Council (1918), 79
Suweilah, 76
Syria, 59

tactical air power, 81–2, 92, 133, 140, 146
tactical nuclear weapons, 187
Tafilah, Battle of (1918), 80
Tampa, Florida, 41, 42
tanks, 116, 120, 194 *see also* Armoured arm
Taos Revolt, 19, 24, 25
Targul-Frumos, Battle of (1944), 140
Taurus Mountains, 67
Taylor, A.J.P., 79
Taylor, Capt. A.W., 121
Taylor, Lt-Col George, 165
Taylor, Maj. Gen. Zachary, 12th US President, 20, 28, 29
technology and war, 8, 9, 227–8, 233–6, 240, 242
television, influnce on war, 213, 221, *see also* media
tempo, 180, 209–10, 212, 215, 216, 219, 220–1, 222, 223, 224, 235, 236–7, 245, 248, *see also* manoeuvrist aproach; operational level of war
Ten Years' War (1868–78), 38

Terraine, John, 188
terrorism, 229, 231–2
Tet Offensive, 213
Texas, annexation of, 10
Third Afghan War (1919), 113
Thompson, Capt. Philip, 19–20, 22, 27
Thompson, Sir Robert, 214
Tientsin, 106
time, military, 180, 222, 248
Tolstoy, Leo, *War and Peace*, 8
Toral, Gen. José, 54
total people's war, 213
'Totalize', Operation (1944), 137
training, 108–111, 113, 114, 115–20, 135, 126–7, 134, 185, 220; training exercises without troops (TEWTs), 124, 187, 198, 120
Training Regulations (1934), 107
Trans-Jordan Raids (March-May 1918), 5, 60, 73–80, 111
Turkish Army
 priority allocated to Caucasus front, 67–8
 effect of disease on, 68, 81
 fighting spirit of, 71, 76–7, 81
 formations of,
  Army of Islam, 67
  Fourth Army, 78
  Seventh Army, 81–2
  Eighth Army, 81–2
  XX Corps, 70
  XXII Corps, 69
  3rd Division, 69, 70
  3rd Cavalry Division, 78
  7th Division, 69, 70
  24th Infantry Division, 78
  53rd Division, 69
  54th Division, 69, 70
Tuker, Lt.-Gen. Sir Francis, 195, 196
Turner, Lt-Col A.J.D. 155, 156
Twenty-First (21st) Army Group, 132, 134, 136–8, 140–1, 142–3, 144, 146, 147, 149, 158, 159, 169,
see also British Army, Montgomery, Normandy Campaign, Second Army

United Nations (UN), 218
United States Army, see also: AEF
 campaign planning of, 190–2, 219–20
 compared with British Army, 3, 4, 200
 disease, effect on, 40
 inexperience of, 51
 influence of Civil War on, 4, 45, 46
 influence of technology on, 229
 size of, 4, 40
 volunteer soldiers in, 3, 10
 formations of, Army of the West, 12, 19, 29
  1st Dragoons, 11, 13, 19, 27
  2nd Dragoons, 20
  Leclede Rangers, 12
  1st Missouri Volunteers, 12, 13, 21, 22, 25, 29
  2nd Missouri Volunteers, 19, 26
  5th [Army] Corps, 41, 42, 54, 55
  1st Infantry Division, 42, 50, 51, 52, 53
  2nd Infantry Division, 42, 45, 50
  Cavalry Division, 42, 50, 53
  Independent Brigade, 42
  71st New York Volunteers, 52
  First Army, 94
 see also Doniphan; Mexican War; volunteer soldiers
United States Defense Information Security Agency, 231
United States Marine Corps, 192, 219
United States Military Academy, West Point, 12, 29, 192, 200
Utah Indians, 18
utility, of military power, 1–2

Valenciennes, 98
Varro, 201
Vera Cruz, 15, 20, 28
Verdun, Battle of (1916), 179
'Veritable' Operation (1945), 138, 141, 149
Verney, Maj.-Gen. G.L., 138
Versailles, Treaty of (1919), 5, 100–2
Vickery, Col C.E., 105
Victorian values, 196–7
victory, notion of, 212, 222
Vietnam War, 189–90, 213–14, 241
Vigil, Donaciano, 16
Villers-Bocage, Battle of (1944), 140
Villers-Bretonneux, 91
volunteer soldiers
 discipline of, 23
 reputation of, 29
 training of, 12
 Michigan Volunteers, 42, 50
 Missouri Volunteers, 12, 13, 19 (2nd), 21, 22, 25, 26, 29
 71st New York Volunteers, 52
 Volunteer Cavalry, 45

Wadi Arseniyat, 78
'Wah Wah' tribe, 108
Waldo, Capt. David, 16
Wana, 119
War and Peace, by Leo Tolstoy, 8
War with Mexico (1849) by Maj. Roswell S. Ripley, 23
Warsaw Pact, 1, 8, 184, 194
Washington, Gen. George, 1st US President, 38

INDEX

Waterloo, Battle of (1815), 236
Watson, Maj. D.J., 166
water, need for, 59, 64–6, 73, 81, 113, 140
Waterson, Maj. J., 157
Wavell, Brig. A.P. (later Field-Marshal Earl), 69, 76, 78, 108, 244
Waziristan, 113, 114, 115, 119–20
  Field Force, 114
  Military District of, 117
weather, effect on military operations, 40, 41, 75, 76, 98, 113, 140, 236
Weeks, Lt.-Gen. Sir Ronald, 142
Wehrmacht, 133, 135, 138, 140, 149, 150
Weightman, Capt. Richard, 26
Wellington, Field-Marshal Duke of, 236
Wells, H.G., 228
Westmoreland, Gen. William C., 189, 213
West Point, see United States Military Academy

Weyler, Gen. Valeriano, 38, 39, 40
Wheeler, Maj.-Gen. Joseph, 42, 45, 46, 50
Whig and Advertiser (Richmond), 28
Whig Party, 10, 18, 28, 29
Williams, T. Harry, 3, 20
Wilson, Field-Marshal Sir Henry, 80, 100–1
Winkelried, 230
Wiltshire Regiment, 5th Battalion, 160
Wintringham, Tom, 184
Wool, Brig.-Gen. John E., 20
Wooster, Charles, 19, 20, 22, 27

Yilderim, 68, 70
Young, Capt. J.W., 122
Ypres, Third Battle of (1917), 89, 92, 142, 143
Yugoslavian Civil War, 242

Zulus, 227
Zuni Indians, 18